Praise for

THE
FRAGRANCE
of TEARS

'Sheds light on the human side of a courageous
politician who could not escape her dynastic destiny.'

Victor Mallet, *Financial Times*

'Gives a vivid sense of a courageous leader,
and of Pakistan's wild charms... a moving insider's account
of the first woman to become prime minister
of a modern Muslim state.'

Isambard Wilkinson, *Spectator*

'The story of a remarkable woman,
but not as history has already written it. This intimate
account, which brings unique insights into the life and
times of Benazir Bhutto, could only have been written
by someone like Victoria Schofield.'

Lyse Doucet, BBC Chief International Correspondent

'A beautifully written and deeply moving
account... In the true style of memoir, Schofield captures
the person – dutiful daughter, erstwhile matchmaker,
loyal friend and, above all, courageous woman.'

Peter Galbraith, US Diplomat and Foreign Policy Adviser

THE FRAGRANCE
of TEARS

My friendship with
Benazir Bhutto

VICTORIA SCHOFIELD

An Apollo Book

This is an Apollo Book, first published in the UK in 2020
by Head of Zeus Ltd
This paperback edition first published in the UK in 2021
by Head of Zeus Ltd

9 7 5 3 1 2 4 6 8

A catalogue record for this book is available
from the British Library.

ISBN (PB): 9781789544466
ISBN (E): 9781789544473

Typeset by Adrian McLaughlin
Map by Jamie Whyte

Printed and bound in Great Britain by
CPI Group (UK) Ltd, Croydon CR0 4YY

MIX
Paper from
responsible sources
FSC® C020471

Head of Zeus Ltd
First Floor East
5–8 Hardwick Street
London EC1R 4RG

WWW.HEADOFZEUS.COM

*To Benazir's children, Bilawal, Bakhtawar, Aseefa,
and mine, Alexandra, Anthony, Olivia.*

Contents

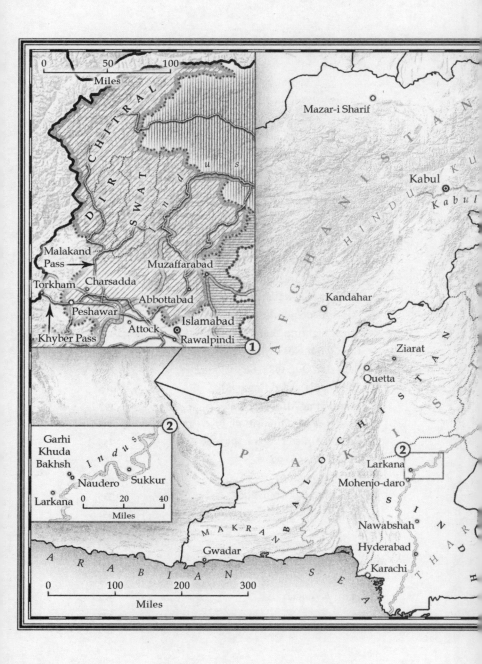

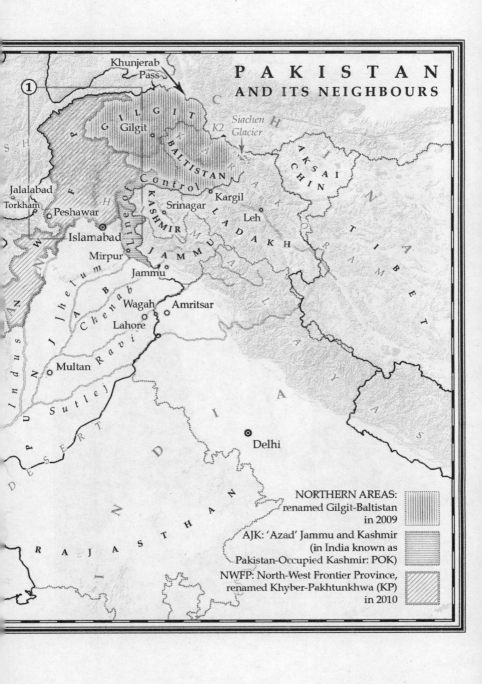

PAKISTAN
AND ITS NEIGHBOURS

Khunjerab Pass

① ────

GILGIT

Gilgit

K2

Siachen Glacier

AKSAI CHIN

TIBET

BALTISTAN

N.W.F.P.

Jalalabad
Torkham
Peshawar

Control

KASHMIR

Srinagar

Kargil

Leh

LADAKH

Islamabad

Line

JAMMU

Mirpur

Jammu

Jhelum

Chenab

Wagah

Amritsar

Lahore

Ravi

Multan

PUNJAB

Sutlej

DESERT

INDIA

Delhi

RAJASTHAN

HIMALAYAS

Indus

K2

KARAKORAM

NORTHERN AREAS:
renamed Gilgit-Baltistan
in 2009

AJK: 'Azad' Jammu and Kashmir
(in India known as
Pakistan-Occupied Kashmir: POK)

NWFP: North-West Frontier Province,
renamed Khyber-Pakhtunkhwa (KP)
in 2010

Dearest
Vides,
So glad you
were with us
on the day we
won the vote —
again!
Benazir
4 November
1988.

Foreword

This memoir is not a biography. The narrative does not intend, as would that of a biography, to examine the life of an individual from a detached distance, interrogating the good and the bad, the failures and successes. It is above all the story of a friendship between two women of different cultures which began in the sociable environment of Oxford University but which, when transported into the real world, was marked by tragedy. Most of the events described took place against the backdrop of a turbulent country which alternated between elected civilian government and military rule; a country whose liberal values changed to conservative so that more and more women felt obliged to cover their heads in public, where blasphemy and adultery became punishable by death; a country which, defying the odds, attained nuclear capability, whose strategic location meant that it became a frontline state in the 'war on terror' and yet was nearly classified as a terrorist state itself; where kidnappings and suicide bombings were a daily occurrence; where a minority enjoy extreme affluence, while millions live in poverty; whose population, now estimated at over 200 million, over a third of whom is illiterate, is outstripping the country's resources.

That country is the Islamic Republic of Pakistan and my friend was Benazir Bhutto. When I first arrived in Rawalpindi in the summer of 1978 she was the only person I knew in Pakistan and she was under house arrest. Her father, the former prime minister, had recently been overthrown in a military coup, and was in prison, condemned to death for conspiracy to murder; but, thanks to her, in the decades to come, I made countless friends and came to regard Pakistan as a second home and to admire its people for their resilience as well as being grateful for their hospitality.

Both during Benazir's lifetime and since her assassination numerous books have been written about her and the influence of the Bhutto family on the politics of Pakistan. Many have praised Benazir, who served twice as prime minister in the late 1980s and 1990s, for her liberal progressive mindset, her vision and charisma, while others have criticised her failure to meet expectations. My motivation has been to share my personal experience of an exceptional woman who, despite operating in a complex and highly challenging environment, showed a wonderful gift for friendship, kindness and generosity of spirit. This is my tribute to a friend, who was killed in her prime; it is my testament to her bravery and courage.

THE FRAGRANCE OF TEARS

Prelude: 27 December 2007

I was on a train. The low-volume buzz of other people's conversations filled the compartment, the voices of young and old discussing the best (and worst) part of having spent Christmas with their families. I too had been with my extended family of in-laws in Lincolnshire, and was returning alone to London to spend a couple of days with my sister. I was then planning to rejoin my husband and children for the new year: the sort of humdrum arrangements anyone might make during the holiday period.

Unexpectedly my mobile phone went, a shrill sound intruding on the muted chatter around me.

'Hello,' I said, thinking maybe it was one of my children calling. But instead it was Rita Payne, Asia Editor at BBC World Television.

'Have you heard the news?' she asked expectantly.

'No,' I responded, sudden tension gripping my voice. 'I'm on a train. What's happened?'

'There's been an explosion in Rawalpindi where Benazir was addressing an election rally; initial reports are that she's unharmed. But we're waiting to hear more. I'll let you know.'

I hung up, an uneasy sensation saturating my thoughts. Benazir Bhutto, my close friend since our days together as students at Oxford University in the 1970s, was standing in Pakistan's forthcoming general elections. If her party, the Pakistan Peoples Party

(PPP), won, she would become prime minister of Pakistan for the third time, having made history in 1988 as the first female prime minister of a Muslim nation aged just thirty-five. The stakes were high. Regardless of the mood of change sweeping the country, the president, General Pervez Musharraf, was hoping he could retain supreme authority, having just lifted a state of emergency. But after eight years of military government people were tiring of men in uniform in high places. Instead they wanted a return to civilian government. Opposing Benazir and the PPP was Nawaz Sharif, leader of the Pakistan Muslim League (Nawaz faction). He too was hoping he'd become prime minister for a third time, having been ousted by Musharraf in a bloodless coup in 1999. Finally, the former cricketer, Imran Khan, leader of the Pakistan Tehrik-i-Insaaf (PTI or Justice Party), had also thrown his hat into the ring, and was making news by tarring all his opponents with the same brush of corruption and nepotism. For Benazir the physical dangers were great. In October, on her return to Pakistan after eight years in exile, she had already been targeted by a suicide bomb, which killed over 150 people, although miraculously she had survived.

My phone rang again. This time it was Colin Freeman from the *Sunday Telegraph*.

'Hello Victoria,' he said, the tone of his voice deathly. 'I hope I am not the bearer of bad news.' Before I had time to say anything, he continued: 'I'm sorry to say that Benazir has been killed in a suicide bomb attack.'

No, no, I internally screamed. That's not right. Rita said she was unharmed. 'Are you sure that's true?' I asked feebly, in a desperate attempt to give Colin the chance to tell me that he'd made a mistake and that she was all right.

'I'm afraid so. She was rushed to the hospital but was pronounced dead.' He gave me a few more details and then hung up, saying that he knew the *Telegraph* would want me to write something for the paper and would be in touch. Another call was already coming through. It was Rita again.

'I know, Rita,' I said, before she had time to repeat Colin's dreadful words, my voice breaking in the prelude to tears.

'We'll want you to come into the studio as soon as you reach London, if that's OK?'

I agreed. Somehow, if I couldn't instantly transport myself to Pakistan, being in a BBC studio, where I'd gone so often as a commentator on South Asia, was the next best thing. My first priority was telephoning Benazir's sister, Sanam – known as Sunny to her family and friends – who lived in London. By the time I got through to her, I'd arrived at King's Cross and so I found myself sobbing and, at the same time, shouting to make myself heard above the noise of the station. Sunny was crying too.

'You see what they've done. They've gone and killed her.'

'I'm so sorry,' I replied, barely able to comprehend the overwhelming heartbreak of a woman who had already lost her two brothers and father violently and had now lost her sister. 'I'm leaving for Karachi,' she continued, her voice a little calmer. 'The funeral's tomorrow. The children and Asif have already left from Dubai.'

When I got to the BBC studio in White City, the news of Benazir's assassination was running almost continuously as the lead story. I sat watching the coverage in disbelief as large industrial-size hoses washed down the scene of the crime.

'Why are they washing the streets?' I thought. 'Surely they want to preserve as much evidence as possible?'

And then there was a flashback to Benazir proudly addressing the rally at Liaquat Bagh in Rawalpindi shortly before her death. She had a large garland of red and white flowers around her neck and looked her usual defiant self, standing on a podium as she spoke to the crowds gathered in front of her. The camera cut to a still of her face with the dates '1953–2007'. It seemed so shocking to see the date of her death joined to her date of birth, indicating the finality of her life. When, at last, I made my contribution to the news programme, I paid my respects to the woman whose personal and political highs and lows I had witnessed as a journalist, commentator and, most importantly as a friend, for thirty-three years. Eventually I went home. I still felt stunned. I simply could not believe that she was dead. It seemed like the most horrible nightmare. I got into bed exhausted, hoping that the next morning I would wake up and find it was all a dream.

1
Our Salad Days: 1974–77

My salad days, when I was green in judgment,
cold in blood.[1]

The Oxford Union bar was particularly crowded that October day in 1974. It was Freshers week and the doors of this venerable debating society were open to all first-year students for a tour of the buildings to attract new members. One person was pushing at my elbow, another had trodden on my foot. Sweet sherry was being offered on trays. As I moved forward into the throng, I caught sight of someone I'd met the day before, but whose name I'd forgotten.

'Hello, again,' he said, 'I think you said you were at Lady Margaret Hall. You must meet Benazir Bhutto; you know, she's at LMH too.'

'Oh, yes,' I responded, breaking into a smile as I noticed a tall woman, who was also smiling. She had long black hair and was wearing jeans.

'Hello,' she said, her foreign accent mildly overlaid by an American intonation acquired during the four years she'd already spent at Harvard. 'That's great you're in my college. You must come and have tea.'

Before we could talk more, she'd been swept away in another direction by a surge of potential new members. As the crowd intermingled, the purpose for which I had come was uppermost in my mind. Should I join the Oxford Union, the main benefit of which was the opportunity to listen to the weekly debates, modelled, so I understood, on our British parliamentary debates. Being a member of the Union also provided the opportunity to stand for election to the various student committees, with the goal of becoming president, following in the footsteps of well-known twentieth-century politicians such as Edward Heath, Michael Foot and Michael Heseltine. After viewing the busts of past prime ministers in the debating chamber, and visiting the beautiful Old Library, the former debating chamber built in 1857 with its famous murals painted by William Morris and Dante Gabriel Rossetti, I decided to make inroads into my student grant (no loans in those days) and join for life.

Not long after that first meeting in the Oxford Union bar, a message came from Benazir that she was having some friends around to her room and would I like to come. Predictably, with its sparse student furniture, by the time I arrived, people were already sitting on the bed and the floor and perched on the desk, drinking tepid cups of tea. Benazir was chatting energetically. In the summer her father, Zulfikar Ali Bhutto, the prime minister of Pakistan,* had been on a goodwill visit to Moscow and she was describing how, during the state dinner, she'd exchanged 'pleasantries' with the formidable Soviet premier, Alexei Kosygin.

'What subject are you reading?' someone suddenly asked in my direction.

'Modern History,' I replied.

---

* Zulfikar Ali Bhutto (1928–1979) was president of Pakistan 1971–73 and prime minister of Pakistan 1973–77.

'I'm reading PPE – well Philosophy, Politics and Economics – same as Pinkie,' came the response, my interlocutor calling Benazir by her childhood family name.

Having gone to Harvard in 1969 aged just sixteen, when Benazir arrived in Oxford four years later, in 1973, she was one of the 'older' students, aged twenty. Ringing in her ears were the words of her father, who had studied law at Christ Church in the early 1950s:

I feel a strange sensation in imagining you walking on the footprints I left behind over twenty-two years ago. I was happy by your presence at Radcliffe,* but, since I was not at Harvard, I could not picture you there through the same camera. Here I see your presence like mine in flesh and blood, over every cobble of the streets of Oxford, over every step you take on the frozen stone ladders, through every portal of learning you enter. Your being at Oxford is a dream come true. We pray and hope that this dream turned into reality will grow into a magnificent career in the service of your people.

He'd also given her a picture of ancient Rome which had hung in his room at Christ Church. 'Before you went to Oxford this print could not have had any meaning for you. Now I am sending it to you in case you want to keep it in your room.'

She hung it in her room, 'warming to the sense of continuity that now stretched from the dust of Pakistan to the clean-swept streets of Oxford'.[2]

'The four years in which she was to be at the university were to see it move from the era of armchair Che Guevaras, with long hair

---

* In her first two years Benazir lived at Radcliffe (the campus of the former all female coordinate college).

and scruffy clothes constantly demonstrating, to the beginnings of the yuppie era,' observed a contemporary who met her in 1973. Her first term had seen the occupation of the Examination Schools (where lectures and exams were held) by students demanding a Central Students Union in preference to the elite and largely male and public-school-dominated Oxford Union. Then, on 4 March 1974 – coincidentally the day Edward Heath resigned as prime minister having failed to obtain a working majority at the general election the previous week – the unthinkable happened: a demonstration by 'moderate' students protesting against the continued disruption of university life by 'left wing' agitation, indicating the beginnings of a change of national mood.

From what I was told, Benazir stayed aloof from both sides. Being foreign, she did not fit into other students' perceptions of what constituted left or right wing. Although she joined the Labour Club and wanted to champion issues relating to the 'third world', she came from an old Sindhi landowning family and mixed easily with students from varying backgrounds. 'She was unlike anything anyone had met, with her combination of American brashness and charming naivety and generosity,' continued her 1973 contemporary.[3] She was also unusual in that she had a car: a present from her parents for having graduated from Harvard. It was a yellow MG sports car which gained a certain notoriety, being instantly recognisable in and around Oxford and the recipient of numerous parking tickets as well as messages from friends wanting to get in touch.

During her first year at Oxford she'd missed her life at Harvard and so she had frequented the company of some Harvard friends who had come to Oxford, among them the son of the well-known economist J. K. Galbraith, Peter,* who was studying for a second

---

* J.K. Galbraith, OC (1908–2006) and Peter Galbraith (b.1950).

BA in Politics and Economics, as well as E. J. Dionne and Lief Rosenblatt, both Rhodes scholars. There was also Freya Darvall, who'd been an English Speaking Union scholar in New York during her gap year and who'd met Benazir through a Pakistani friend; when they re-met at Oxford it was 'as old friends'.[4] By her second year, when we met, she'd settled into Oxford, and, in time, she came to love it as much as she had Harvard.

Although the medieval traditions of terms called Michaelmas, Hilary and Trinity (according to the Christian calendar, corresponding with the more familiar names of winter, spring and summer) must have seemed old-fashioned, like other undergraduates she had adapted, both to the terminology and the routine, having her meals in Hall, attending tutorials and lectures, and picking up her letters from her designated pigeon hole in the Lodge, where the porter kept an attentive eye on the comings and goings of the undergraduates. In those days there was no need for security for 'celebrity' students and she wandered about the college like anyone else. On occasion she could be heard at the end of a particular corridor where there was a telephone, having assembled enough coins for a long-distance call to her parents in Pakistan.

When it came to the choice of room, there was a prescribed order of seniority: at the end of one year the oldest students could select the room of their choice first; the following year the order would be reversed and the youngest students would choose their rooms first. In her second year, Benazir was at the top of the list and was occupying a comfortable room with en suite bathroom in one of the modern blocks, Sutherland, named after an esteemed LMH former principal, Dame Lucy Sutherland.* When the order was reversed the following year, she was at the bottom of the list

---

* Dame Lucy Stuart Sutherland, DBE, FBA, FRSA (1903–80).

and was allocated a small room on the ground floor underneath the library, near the clock tower – the clock chimed noisily – with a shared bathroom along the corridor. But she didn't complain.

Since Benazir and I weren't reading the same subject and were in different years, our academic careers took different paths. I never shared a tutorial with her and we rarely discussed our respective subjects. But we often saw each other in college and in the Oxford Union. Given her political background – and to please her father – as I realised from our first meeting, Benazir was already a member of the Union. To date, since women had only been allowed to stand for election in the 1960s, there were only two past female presidents (Geraldine Jones in 1968 and Susan Richards in 1971). But that was about to change. As a Pakistani, by being active in the Union, Benazir was following in the footsteps of Tariq Ali, president of the Union in 1965, who had since made a name for himself as a political activist vociferously opposing the Vietnam War. A Pakistani contemporary was Imran Khan, who had gone up to Keble College in 1972; since his main interest then was cricket, he and Benazir moved in different circles.* Only later did they become political rivals.[5]

Before standing for election for the various committees of the Union, an obligatory formality was to make two short speeches from the floor of the debating chamber after the main debate. Generally, as the evening wore on, only a few people remained in the draughty chamber. Benazir had lost no time in making her first 'floor' speech in the second week of Michaelmas 1973, opposing the motion: 'That American society is in an advanced state of decay'. A week later she made another speech, which meant

---

* Tariq Ali (b.1943) is a political activist, writer and filmmaker; Imran Khan (b.1952) became prime minister of Pakistan in 2018. The first Indian president of the Union was D. F. Karaka (1911–74), Trinity term 1934.

she could stand for election to the treasurer's committee, the first stepping stone in the Union hierarchy (followed by library and then standing committee). When the results were announced, she came top. At the beginning of her second term – Hilary 1974 – the president, Simon Walker,* gave her the opportunity to make her maiden speech during the debate in first week – the custom being for four to six undergraduates to make a short 'paper' speech before the invited guests. The motion could not have been more topical: 'This House would impeach President Nixon' (the impeachment process against the US president beginning two weeks later, on 6 February).† Benazir was asked to speak in favour.

'It is ironic that a man who ran for the presidency on the issue of law and order did his best to break the law and cause disorder in the length and breadth of the country,' she began, criticising him for 'taking crime off the streets and putting it in the White House'. After outlining the charges of impeachable offences against Nixon, including his violation in Vietnam of the war-making powers of Congress and the secret bombings of Cambodia – all serious charges – she concluded: 'Today Nixon is not only hated, but he has lost all credibility. By losing credibility with his people, Nixon has lost his moral authority to lead the American nation. This is the tragedy of Nixon and America.' The motion was overwhelmingly carried by 345 votes to 72. For Benazir, there was a personal aspect to what she said. Only four months previously her family had been received by the Nixons at the White House when her father was on an official visit to the United States.[6]

*

---

* Simon Walker, CBE (b.1953) was communications secretary to The Queen 2000–02; director general of the Institute of Directors (IOD) 2011–17.

† President Richard Nixon (1913–94) was the 37th US president 1969–74.

By the time I joined the Union in Michaelmas 1974, Benazir had just been elected to standing committee.* In the third week she spoke, opposing the motion 'That the censorship of violence is not a denial of artistic freedom'. 'Beyond dispute, violence is an inextricable element of human life,' she argued. 'To tear violence from human existence would be to convey a truncated view of human society, for we must not forget that violence is a state of human interaction in which rational responses have collapsed and reality has been suppressed. If the artist wishes to reflect human nature, if the artist wishes to reflect society, if the artist wants to portray a nuclear holocaust, we cannot take away his freedom and dump it into the trash bin.' The motion was successfully defeated, Benazir's energetic manner of speaking recorded in the minutes by the secretary, Victor van Amerongen: 'Miss Bhutto, Lady Margaret Hall, spoke fourth with her usual powerful delivery. Indeed if God had meant Miss Bhutto to speak at the Oxford Union, he would surely have provided a volume control'![7]

With the terms lasting only eight weeks, student activity was intense. Our only real concern was the weekly – or possibly twice-weekly – essay which had to be produced; this invariably triggered an 'essay crisis' since, whatever the subject, essay writing was likely to be left until the last minute. Whenever anyone was absent from the Union for a couple of days, it generally meant he or she had an essay crisis. Once over, the person so afflicted would re-emerge, immediately resuming the focused discussions around who was to be given a 'paper' speech and, as the term passed, who might win the next election. Looking back, it's amazing to think of the energy we expended on the Union elections, deliberating who would vote for whom, which college members might vote *en bloc*,

* At the end of Hilary term 1974, Benazir stood for library committee and again came top.

both Magdalen and University College having the reputation of operating a 'machine' which could make or break an election, although canvassing was strictly prohibited. There were no manifestos and the election for president was supposed to be decided on how amusing or witty the prospective candidate was when speaking in the presidential debate in seventh week. The election took place the following day, with the outgoing president's farewell debate taking place in eighth week.

A welcome distraction during Trinity term in the summer was punting on the Cherwell while enjoying strawberries and cream, one of Benazir's favourite non-Union, non-study activities. And since the summer of 1975 was gloriously hot (only outdone by the summer of 1976 when there was a record heat-wave), the outdoors could be enjoyed to the full. In terms of lunchtime meeting places, Benazir liked Colonel Bogey's in the Covered Market – a complex of shops, stalls and restaurants* – because it was one of the few places which served hamburgers, a favourite food from her days in the United States. She also loved peppermint-stick Baskin Robbins ice cream, then only available on periodic visits to London.

'I used to love whizzing from Oxford to London in 50 minutes,' Benazir admitted. 'I would drive to London just for an ice cream.'[8]

And we all loved 'Anna Belinda', the dress shop, whose distinctive fashion garments were dresses with covered buttons and piping, a particular favourite being the velvet pinafore with a William Morris design bodice. (Only later did we discover that the premises were used for drug smuggling!) There were also parties galore. At weekends, it was not uncommon to have a handful (literally) of invitations and to work our way around the

---

* The Covered Market, opened in 1774 to rid Oxford's streets of the profusion of stalls on the main streets, is on a quadrangle of land accessible from the High Street, Cornmarket and Market Street.

various colleges, making an appearance at five or six parties on one night. In the summer of 1975, having decided to try my hand at acting, I'd secured parts in *The Merchant of Venice*, performed in St John's Gardens, and the musical *Salad Days* at the Oxford Playhouse. Such indeed were our 'salad days'.

For us Union 'hacks' – as we were called by those who shunned the Union for its reputed elitism – the Oxford Union remained our main social activity. Despite Benazir's speedy ascent to standing committee, she had failed to get any further. At the end of Hilary term in 1976, instead of standing again for treasurer or secretary, as she had done previously, she decided to make a bold leap by standing for president. But she and another woman, Vivien Dinham, who also stood, did not have a chance against the popular cox of the Oxford rowing team, the Hon. Colin Moynihan at University College, who was also a bantamweight boxer, later becoming a 'double blue'.* And so she remained on standing committee.

By this time I too had been elected to standing committee and that's when our friendship really began. There were still relatively few women involved in Union politics and we used to make a point of sitting next to each other during meetings, passing notes if we felt bored, and using nicknames to describe those we might mention, a habit we continued in later life. Another bond was that both Benazir and I were a little older than our contemporaries, she because she had gone to Harvard first, and I because I had worked in London and Paris before going up to Oxford.

In the summer of 1976 Benazir had to take her final exams and, like so many others, she entered that 'pressure cooker' phase when she disappeared from view to study. Once again her father wrote a letter of encouragement: 'Please do not feel nervous. Attend to

---

* The Rt Hon. the Lord Moynihan (b.1955) was MP for Lewisham East 1983–92 and minister for sport 1987–90.

all your papers with supreme equanimity. Think clearly and write clearly. Do not get hustled. Having been through Oxford, I can well imagine the strain. Insh'allah [God willing], I am sure you will do very well. Please telephone me after you have finished. I do not have to tell you that I am praying for your great success.' In hindsight she believed that the Oxford exam system helped her to get through the crises which lay ahead, which included her home in Pakistan being raided by the military. 'My mind would immediately sort out priorities: burn the papers in this room – immediately send the servants with messages before the house is cordoned off – collect my medicines for prison. I would trace the invaluable lesson of learning to cope efficiently under extreme pressure back to Oxford.'[9]

When finals were over she re-emerged, her twenty-third birthday on 21 June providing the opportunity for yet another party. But after finals came decisions, her father having already warned her not to succumb to the 'siren song' of the West by staying in Britain. 'The raw and ruthless life outside the gates of University awaits you. It is both pleasant and unpleasant, colourful and colourless, exciting and dull.... You are about to step into the lecture hall of life.'[10]

Even so, when the Union elections were held, she stood again for treasurer, and on this attempt she was successful. It meant that the president – the Hon. Richard Norton (later Lord Grantley) – had three female officers, since Vivien Dinham had won as librarian and I had won as secretary. Since Benazir's election victory would enable her to try again for president the following term, with her father's approval she remained in Oxford for another year. As she was no longer an undergraduate, she moved from LMH to St Catherine's College, familiarly known as St Catz, having enrolled on a one-year Foreign Service programme at Queen Elizabeth House, in St Giles, to study international law, economics and diplomacy.

Despite the semblance of feminist solidarity among the Union officers, there was a rupture. Vivien had already been elected as president for Michaelmas 1975 (after defeating Benazir as treasurer at the end of Hilary 1975). But her election had controversially been quashed by an election tribunal on the grounds that she had broken the rules by 'canvassing' for votes by holding a party at University College Boathouse after nominations had already opened. Vivien's supporters were outraged at the tribunal's ruling, and friendships in the Union were subsequently divided between those who had supported the 'Dinham tribunal' – of which, as a member of standing committee at the time, Benazir was one – and those who had opposed it. Throughout the Michaelmas term the relationship between librarian and treasurer was, at best, polite, as they sat during debates on the raised podium in the chamber, the president in between, with me as secretary sitting at a desk a level below.

In seventh week Benazir and Vivien took to the despatch boxes to make their speeches in the presidential debate, addressing the motion 'That the pen is mightier than the sword.' Benazir recollected:

Unhappily, I had been assigned to speak for the opposition. In reality I believed that the intellectual pen of ideas was mightier than all the swords of the generals. But I was not permitted to argue for the pen. I justified my opposing position to myself by thinking of the curved sword my father had chosen as the symbol of the Pakistan Peoples Party. The symbolic sword, drawn from my father's name, Zulfikar Ali, which means 'the sword of Ali', was not meant to be the sword of force, but the sword which was to cut away poverty and backwardness. And so I prepared my argument:

'We, on this side of the house, are not the modern day

descendants of Genghis Khan. We are no Caesars intent on seeking glory through the use of force. We do not extol militarism. But it is our reluctant but realistic conclusion that the Pen is not mightier than the Sword... the might of the pen does not exist in a vacuum. It exists within a framework. The framework within which democracy functions here is the framework of the state in Great Britain. The state, Mr President, is backed with institutionalised force, and it is this institutionalised force which enables the pen to be so strong. Let there be no mistake. If the society were to crumble, if law and order were to break down, if anarchy were to prevail, the pen would be lost in the debris of the dead democracy.'

I did not know, as I concluded my remarks, how prophetic my argument would be for my own country.[11]

The motion was carried by only two votes 184 to 182.

Voting for the presidency took place the following day. 'In an election, one side has to win and the other has to lose,' Benazir's father had wisely told her. 'You have to do your best but the result must be accepted in good grace.' When the votes were counted Benazir had won by 329 votes to 265, a tribunal rejecting allegations of 'malpractice' because Benazir had received 'undue publicity' through articles in the *Daily Telegraph* and *Private Eye*. While Vivien was of course dismayed at her defeat, Benazir was thrilled. The news instantly reached the Pakistani press and her father, who sent a telegram: 'Overjoyed at your election as President of the Oxford Union. You have done splendidly. Our heart warming congratulations on your great success, Papa.'[12]

One of her first invitations as the new president of the Oxford Union was to meet former prime minister and chancellor of the University of Oxford, Harold Macmillan, who had memorably addressed Union members in Michaelmas 1975 in support of a fundraising appeal. Benazir invited me and a couple of others to accompany her to the Vice Chancellor's lodgings where the meeting was to take place. To us on the threshold of life, Macmillan was an old man. His premiership – twenty years earlier – seemed a lifetime away but the allure of meeting 'Supermac', who, in 1960, had predicted the 'wind of change' sweeping over Africa, in anticipation of Britain's decolonisation of the continent, was high and we were not disappointed.*

A few days later Benazir went to speak at a debate at Marlborough College in Wiltshire. Again I and a few other friends accompanied her. The motion she was asked to propose was 'That no face can launch a thousand ships'. 'Oh, it is all very noble and romantic to say that for a beautiful face, or for love, one would do anything,' she proffered. 'But let's face it. In this day and age, there are a plethora of pretty faces. If we were to fight over every one of them, what would distinguish us from animals? Are the opposers of the motion trying to tell us that our desires should rule every action?' I have no idea what the Sixth Form boys made of this glamorous twenty-three-year-old addressing them, but some thirty years later, I met the alumni master, Martin Evans, who told me that the event had become part of the school's folklore.[13]

During the Christmas vacation Benazir set about revitalising what was still regarded as a rather moribund male enclave. One of her first initiatives was to paint the president's office powder-blue, a rather harder task than she imagined because of the many bookshelves which lined the walls and the books, which had to be removed; even the army of friends she'd drafted in became weary of the enterprise. A priority was preparing her term card, deciding both the topics of the eight debates and the identity of the

---

* Harold Macmillan, 1st Earl of Stockton, OM, PC, FRS (1894–1986) was prime minister of the UK 1957–63.

speakers. One of the first people she invited was her father, but, as prime minister of Pakistan about to go into an election campaign, he refused. She also invited the new leader of the Conservative Party, Margaret Thatcher, but she too declined. Mrs Thatcher did, however, invite Benazir to tea at the House of Commons, and Benazir asked me (as the new librarian), as well as Damian Green and Andrew Turner, who were both on standing committee, to accompany her. Also present were some members of the Shadow Cabinet including Sir Keith Joseph, who had already served in the Cabinet of three prime ministers (Harold Macmillan, Sir Alec Douglas-Home and Edward Heath).* Sitting in Thatcher's wood-panelled office, we discussed Benazir's term ahead, ate chocolate cake and reminisced about Thatcher's visit to Pakistan, when she had been hosted by Benazir's parents in 1976.

In addition to painting the president's office blue, Benazir broke with tradition by starting her first week debate – 'That capitalism will triumph' – with music: 'Part of the Union' by the Strawbs blasted through the debating chamber and took everyone by surprise. In the hope of attracting new members she had opened the debate to all members of the University and the chamber was packed. One of the guest speakers was former president of the Union, Tariq Ali, who opposed the motion while the prospective Conservative candidate for Oxford, John Patten (now Lord Patten and a member of the Privy Council) proposed it.† I remember Tariq Ali's delivery being compelling and the motion was defeated. Afterwards he and I squashed into Benazir's two-seater car to go back to her room for more chat and tea. This first week debate set

---

* Baroness Thatcher, LG, OM, DStJ, PC, FRS, HonFRSC (1925–2013) was prime minister of the UK 1979–90; Rt Hon. Damian Green, MP (b.1956) succeeded me as president of the Oxford Union; Sir Keith Joseph, CH, PC, QC (1918–94).
† Baron Patten of Wincanton, PC (b.1945) stood as a member of parliament for Oxford in 1979 and transferred to Oxford West and Abingdon in 1983.

the tone for how Benazir's presidency would be: high profile and animated. Even her term card – printed in green ink against a white background, the colours of the Pakistani flag – showed her individuality.

Messages travelled frequently between Oxford and Pakistan: 'The Prime Minister of Pakistan wishes the President of the Oxford Union to call him.' Her younger brother, Mir,* was now at Christ Church, having, like Benazir, gone first to Harvard, and he too addressed his sister with due deference, beginning his notes: 'Dear Ms President...'¹⁴

Eager to achieve something concrete during her term as president, Benazir had also embarked on some administrative reforms, making it clear that the Union needed to modernise. Apart from the debates held in the debating chamber, among the Union's key assets were the two libraries – the Old Library and the New Library. In order to ensure that they met the requirements of the students, Benazir decided to send out a questionnaire to all members to determine usage of the books and periodicals. Key among the questions was which of the many journals, for which the library had a subscription, were actually read. Since the Union was perpetually short of money she decided that, if, in response to the questionnaire, it was revealed that a particular journal was hardly ever read, then the subscription should be cancelled. As librarian, I was in charge of sending out the questionnaire and collating the answers. Predictably it was discovered that there was a range of journals which no one ever read and books which hadn't been looked at for years and so a suitable cull was made.

At the same time, under the direction of Dr John Renton, an older Union member and now lecturer in the Department of Engineering, the restoration of the William Morris murals was

---

* Mir Ghulam Murtaza Bhutto (1954–96).

under way.* Having viewed the murals from afar I now took more interest in them, understanding that it was Tennyson's *Morte d'Arthur* which had inspired Morris and Rossetti to choose the legend of King Arthur with which to illustrate the various panels. By restoring the murals, it was hoped that with some cleaning and proper lighting they would be preserved for posterity and made more visible to tourists. When the task was finished the murals were photographed and souvenir postcards printed. As thanks for our assistance, Dr Renton presented both Benazir and me with large symmetrical photographs. While mine was of the murals showing King Arthur receiving his sword, Excalibur, from the lake, against the backdrop of the Old Library's domed ceiling, Benazir's photograph showed Excalibur being thrown back into the lake after King Arthur's death. I still have mine but I think Benazir's was lost in the turmoil of her later life.[15]

Another of Benazir's unusual debates was her fifth week 'funny debate' – 'That this house would rather rock than roll'. A note on the term card warned that 'mystery musicians will perform'. Among her guests were Clive Anderson, former president of Cambridge's theatrical club, *Footlights*, and Peter Bazalgette, a former president of the Cambridge Union. I was seated next door to Peter at dinner and I remember being dazzled by all the celebrity guests he had invited during his term of office; one of them was Esther Rantzen who later took him on as a researcher

---

* Work on the murals began in 1857 after Rossetti was invited to tour the new building by its architect, Benjamin Woodward. Admirers of both Rossetti and Woodward, former Oxford undergraduates William Morris and Edward Burne-Jones soon joined the project. They also enlisted Valentine Prinsep, John Hungerford Pollen, Arthur Hughes and John Rodham Spencer Stanhope. For various reasons, the murals were left unfinished by the original artists and the Union employed William and Briton Rivière to complete them two years later. The floral ceiling design is also by William Morris.

for her programme *That's Life*, launching him into what was to become a successful television career (including introducing 'Big Brother' to our television screens).* As the debate drew to a close, the two mystery musicians – two friends, David Profumo and Michael Parker, both at Magdalen – began to perform. As recorded by David's future wife, Helen Fraser (with whom I'd acted in *Salad Days*):

> David was dressed up à la David Bowie in a tight-fitting red jump suit, ill-concealed under an overcoat. He pretended to get very cross with Michael, leapt to his feet and threw a jug of water over him before storming out of the debating chamber. Michael then started to undress, stripping down to his underpants before putting on white jeans and a shirt, picking up a microphone and starting to sing. David then burst back in (his overcoat removed to reveal his red jump suit) and together they sang a duet to a song from *Jesus Christ Superstar* with words by David about Union corruption. The whole thing ended with David and Michael carrying Benazir out of the debating chamber. This was the first time the president had been carried out of the debating chamber during one of her own debates and it was headline news in the *Cherwell* the next day![16]

More serious in tone was her fourth-week debate: 'That terrorists should be hanged', the motion defeated by 229 votes to 170.[17] To speak in her sixth-week debate, 'That industrial democracy is incompatible with trade unionism', she'd invited the trade union leader Arthur Scargill, president of the National Union of

---

* Sir Peter Bazalgette (b.1953) is now non-executive chairman of ITV.

Mineworkers. A former coalminer, he had become a household name during the coal strikes of 1972 and 1974. I was deputed to look after him in the Union bar while the other guests assembled. Mildly intimidated by this formidable trade union official, I fell back on observing how beautiful the Yorkshire countryside was.

'Oh, which part did you visit?' he asked, a flicker of interest in his eyes.

'Ripon,' I proffered. 'The father of one of my friends is head-master of the cathedral choir school there.'

Any further interest he might have had in conversing with me was swiftly extinguished. 'Tory country', was his only response.

During this desultory conversation, Benazir was receiving her other guests, among them, Moss Evans, national organiser of the Transport and General Workers' Union and, at the opposite end of the political spectrum, the Conservative member of parliament Ronald Bell, QC. Before the debate, the traditional termly standing committee photograph was taken, all members of the committee assembling to be photographed with the guest speakers and officers of the Union. The photograph encapsulates our diversity: the trade union officials wore suits, while Ronald Bell was in black tie. Seated in the middle of the front row was Benazir in a beautiful green sari. I was standing behind her in an 'Anna Belinda' dress, flanked by the male officers, who, as custom dictated, were in white tie while the other members of standing committee were in black tie. When, after the debate, the votes were counted, the motion passed, 256 votes in favour and 193 against.

In addition to organising debates, another commitment was speaking at the Cambridge Union, the tradition being that the president of the 'other' Union would be asked to speak and vice versa. The current president of the Cambridge Union was an Indian, Karan Thapar, later to become a respected journalist and commentator.* Long before either he or Benazir played an influential role in their respective countries, that an Indian and Pakistani were both president of the Union at the same time was not lost on interested commentators and they remained friends for life.

When it came to seventh week, having decided to stand for president, it was my turn to speak in the presidential debate. Also standing for president were the other two officers, the treasurer, Bernard Longley (now Roman Catholic Archbishop of Birmingham) and the secretary, Phillip Bergson, who had a passion for cinema and founded the Oxford International Film Festival, as well as a member of standing committee, Andrew Turner. The motion, which I proposed, was: 'That the individual still has the power to shape the course of history'.

'Madam President,' I began, addressing Benazir. 'I stand here tonight, not as a shapeless number, not as a computer index card, and not as a machine.' Citing the influence of Jesus Christ, Joan of Arc, Karl Marx and Winston Churchill, I described the choice as one 'between optimism on this side of the house and negativism on that side, between retaining faith in the individual on this side, and abdication of faith over there, between rising invigorated to individual challenge or wallowing before we start in self-defeat'.[18]

Before the debate I had received a circular card around the edges of which was written: 'Dear Victoria, the very best of luck tonight and tomorrow, from an anonymous voter.' I knew the card was from Benazir, since her handwriting was easily recognisable and she was using her favourite turquoise ink. When, the following day, after the election had taken place and she had heard that I had

---

* Karan Thapar (b.1955) received the International Press Institute-India Award for excellence in the field of journalism in 2013.

won, she wrote congratulating me on my 'terrific' victory. To me, her enthusiasm for my success demonstrated her generosity of spirit. Anyone else might have preferred to retain the distinction of being the 'last' woman to hold the office for a bit longer. But she was overjoyed. 'Dear Blonde Bombshell,' she wrote in another note. 'Have promised *Daily Express* reporter that you will give her an interview at 6.00 p.m. in the Union bar this evening. Hope it wasn't presumptuous of me but I thought the publicity would be good for the Union... love B.'[19]

Yet despite the excitement of my electoral win, another election was troubling her. Soon after the Union elections, a general election was held in Pakistan. Although her father's party, the Pakistan Peoples Party (PPP), won, the result was immediately contested by the opposition parties, who had combined together to form the Pakistan National Alliance (PNA) and were alleging widespread rigging; thousands of people had come out onto the streets to protest. One day we were having tea in Oxford's Randolph Hotel with Alan Jones, an Australian graduate student at Worcester, who was to make a career as a 'shock jock' radio broadcaster.* After discussing my recent election, we had fallen into discussing politics in the real sense. Benazir looked more anxious than I had ever seen her. Although our student lives still had one more term to run, I think that, throughout the remainder of her time at Oxford, Benazir's heart and mind were already beginning to transport themselves back to Pakistan. The motion for her farewell debate – headlined as 'B.B.'s Bye-Bye' – was 'That this house likes dominating women', which we all regarded as an amusing double entendre, the secretary, Phillip, colourfully describing her as 'the Rainbow of Rawalpindi' in the minutes. At

---

* Alan Jones, AO (b.1941) also worked as a school teacher, rugby coach and speech writer to Prime Minister Malcolm Fraser.

that point, none of us could imagine how dominant Benazir's personality as a woman would be in the political life of Pakistan nor how she, as a woman, would be dominated by the traditional society in which she was to operate.

At the end of Hilary 1977 Benazir had decided to stay in Oxford. I also wanted to remain for a few days, mainly to study for my finals, but also to prepare my term card for the Union debates. Since I'd already had to move out of my room at LMH, Benazir suggested I could bunk down on her floor in her room at St Catz, which she had retained. It was cold and my nights were spent wrapped in her warm Afghan coat, which was the height of fashion. We talked long into the night, reminiscing about our different adolescences – hers in Karachi, mine in the Thames Valley – and playing records on her old gramophone, a favourite being the Andrew Lloyd Webber/Tim Rice song, 'Don't cry for me, Argentina'.*

As I was soon to find, being president of the Oxford Union meant that you could write to anyone in the world, including the president of the United States, which I duly did, President Jimmy Carter being the recipient of my letter.† If you felt so inclined you could also write to Her Majesty the Queen, who had memorably visited the Union in 1968. It was not that it was expected that such VVIP guests would come, but because, within the portfolio of responses, there would be some significant souvenir signatures. Unfortunately, when the next president started to prepare his (or her) term card, there was very little record of who had previously been approached because the outgoing president wanted to keep the file. In our internet age, where everything is backed up and retrievable, it is hard to imagine how handwritten our lives were forty years ago. Given her background, with her father

---

* Recorded in 1976 by Julie Covington for the album *Evita*.
† Jimmy Carter (b.1924) was the 39th US president, 1977–81.

habitually meeting heads of state, Benazir did not attach the same importance to celebrity signatures. When she vacated the still powder-blue president's office, she had gladly handed over her file of correspondence to me.

Benazir and me after I'd won president of the Union [*Daily Express*, 10 March 1977]. *When, the following day, after the election had taken place and Benazir had heard that I had won, she wrote congratulating me on my 'terrific' victory.*

My term as president had none of Benazir's glamour – no packed house with Tariq Ali, no rock music reverberating around the debating chamber – but it was summer with all its pleasures. My first-week debate was 'That the integrity of British public life is a myth'; one of those to whom I gave a paper speech was a third-year geography undergraduate and future prime minister, Theresa Brasier, who proposed the motion, while future BBC and ITN journalist, Michael Crick, opposed.* Benazir came less

---

* As Theresa May (b.1956), she was prime minister of the UK 2016–19; her husband, Sir Philip May (b.1957), was president of the Union in Trinity term

frequently to the Union during my term as president, telling me that she didn't want me to feel overshadowed by an ex-president hanging around (as some of our predecessors occasionally did). But we often met up: the Nosebag restaurant, which advertised its 'healthy home-cooked food' opposite the Union in St Michael's Street was a favourite place for lunch as well as Brown's at the top of St Giles and Pippins in Ship Street; and there remained the usual round of parties. As the weeks passed, and it was time for me to take my finals, Benazir asked me the date of my last exam so that she could meet me afterwards. When the day came, sure enough, there she was standing on the pavement in the High Street, outside Examination Schools, with a bottle of champagne to give me in celebration.

The last major event on our 1977 summer social calendar was her twenty-fourth birthday party on 21 June, held at Queen Elizabeth House, to which all her guests received an invitation edged in gold: '...... darling, what would the party be without you?'

'Am getting a bit nervous,' she wrote shortly before the party. 'What if no one turns up, what if all the people don't get on. Horrors, horrors!'[20] Of course her fears were unfounded. As she later admitted, she had invited 'the entire contents of her Oxford address book, and, judging from the crowd of people, everybody came'.[21] Mindful that soon we were to go our separate ways, there were lots of goodbyes, especially to Benazir who would soon be returning to Pakistan.

Shortly before the end of term a journalist from a London daily had come to interview her about her future. The headline of the article was 'No politics for the premier's daughter who became

---

1979; she frequently acknowledged the fact that Benazir introduced her to Philip; Michael Crick (b.1958) was president of the Union in Michaelmas term 1979.

president', since, as Benazir explained, she was not intending to become a politician but would be joining Pakistan's Foreign Service. I wasn't surprised by her decision. With her outgoing personality and charm, I thought that, in time, she would make a superb ambassador or high commissioner, who knows, perhaps even returning to London!?[22]

Thanks to Benazir, I was going to spend two months in the United States in the autumn.

'Here, Vicks,' she had said one day, as she handed me a letter which was addressed to her. 'This is the application for the English Speaking Union Debate tour of the States. I can't apply for it. But you can. It would be a great opportunity.'

I had duly applied and been selected to be one of a two-person team on the ESU Debate tour, which meant debating at universities throughout the eastern and central United States over an eight-week period from mid-September to mid-November. As I hadn't yet got a job, my summer was relatively free and Benazir had invited me and another of our LMH friends, Claire Wilmer, who had read History a year ahead of me and had already gone down, to come to Pakistan for a few weeks in the summer before I went to the United States. By accepting her invitation we would be following in the footsteps of six other friends who'd stayed with her the previous summer* – her letter describing how she was having 'to mother' them making me laugh.[23] So when I went to her room in St Catz at the end of June, it was not to say goodbye but *au revoir*.

'Will you take care of George?' she suddenly asked.

'Of course,' I replied, as I took possession of a beautiful gardenia.

George, alas, did not re-flower after the first year, but since then,

---

* The six friends were Patricia Yates, Roshan Dedhar, Antonia Alafouzou, David Soskin, Keith Gregory and Victor van Amerongen.

whenever I've had a gardenia, I've called it George.

*

On 5 July 1977 I woke to the news that Benazir's father had been overthrown in a military coup and that martial law had been declared in Pakistan. All the political leaders, including her father, had been arrested. Not long afterwards Benazir wrote to me saying that, although I might not feel comfortable in the atmosphere of 'politicking', I was still welcome; but I decided that I should postpone my visit to Pakistan. Initially I thought the situation would calm down within a few months.[24]

When launching his 'Operation Fair Play', Pakistan's chief of army staff General Mohammed Zia-ul-Haq had declared: 'My sole aim is to organise free and fair elections which would be held in October this year. Soon after the polls, power will be transferred to the elected representatives of the people. I give a solemn assurance that I will not deviate from this schedule.' In the meantime he had set himself up as chief martial law administrator, or CMLA for short, which, in time, came to stand for 'Cancel My Last Announcement'.*

---

* General Mohammed Zia-ul-Haq (1924–88) was army chief of staff 1976–88 and president of Pakistan 1978–88.

2

'Bhutto to hang': 1977–78

Unlike Oxford's, the stakes here are
life and death.[1]

After the military takeover in July 1977, news on Pakistan appeared intermittently in newspaper articles as well as on the radio and television. Having been held in protective custody at a rest house in the hill station of Murree, north of Islamabad, Zulfikar Ali Bhutto was released on 28 July, huge crowds coming to greet him on his arrival in Karachi. But on 3 September the military came again to the Bhutto home to arrest him. This time the charge was conspiracy to murder 'a political opponent'. I wrote immediately to send Benazir moral support.

'Thank you very much for your letter,' she responded. 'It always makes me happy to hear from England. Actually it's like being President of the Union again. I get tons of mail from party workers but eagerly flip through them to see if there is a familiar handwriting.' The circumstances she described seemed bizarrely Byzantine or, as she put it, 'life is like a B-grade spy movie. There is the bad guy (Zia) out to destroy the country. He has his hood-lums (commandos) who burst into rooms at night armed with submachine guns throwing things about, breaking telephones into three pieces – although the line has already been cut from outside. They take the good guy away on false charges but the character assassination is of such a magnitude that it is hysterically funny and the people do not desert the good guy.' The incident she was describing was the 3 September raid, when the family was woken in the middle of the night, the house raided, and her father taken into custody. At this stage, their circumstances didn't seem as serious as they were to become and she was pinning all her hopes on the October elections.

'The PPP is confident of winning a landslide. Punjab and rural Sindh are solidly with the PPP and that is where the bulk of the National Assembly seats lie,' Benazir continued. She then apologised for her letter being 'all politics, but then that is what my life has become at the moment. Unlike Oxford's, the stakes here are life and death... you should see the places I go to. All my time is spent on meeting party workers and addressing party workers in different localities. In Rawalpindi the Martial Law served me a warning of violating one of its Regulations punishable by ten lashes (you faint after the second and are revived by cold water. The back is a completely open wound) and one year's rigorous imprisonment... Take care do write and don't worry about me, Love, Benazir.'[2]

Mindful that she had invited me to stay for the summer, she added a postscript: 'Just as well you weren't here this summer because the commando raid was quite a traumatic experience.'[3]

But then, having been briefly released on bail, Bhutto was again arrested and in late September the elections were cancelled. Benazir was visiting her father's party workers in the Punjab and was briefly detained in a house designated a 'sub-jail', signifying her first period of 'house arrest'. On 24 October her father's trial began. From the haven of my home in the Thames valley, the details of the case, relating to a shooting which had happened in 1974 at a roundabout in Lahore, were unclear. A former member of the

PPP, Ahmed Raza Kasuri, was the alleged target, but his elderly father was killed instead.* The only person to link the former prime minister to the murder was the former director-general of the Federal Security Force, Masood Mahmud, who had become an 'approver' or, as we would say, had turned State's evidence. In his testimony he alleged that the prime minister had given him instructions 'on the telephone' to get rid of Kasuri; four 'confessing co-accused', who, like Mahmud, had been held in custody since the coup, had carried out the deed. Since the incident had taken place in Lahore, the trial was being held in the Lahore High Court.

'At least I was free to continue working with my mother on my father's behalf. I had been released from my detention shortly after the elections were cancelled,' Benazir later recalled. But in December she was detained again. 'Am confined to house as some people think I am a danger to "human life and property"!' she wrote cheerfully on a postcard which she sent to wish me Happy New Year.[4] Soon afterwards I received a thick envelope from her, containing a letter and another envelope. 'Am terribly busy meeting families of people and arranging lawyers as there have been wide-scale and arbitrary arrests. 90% of our organisation is behind bars,' she wrote. 'Please do me this great favour. My father wrote this letter which is enclosed to Mir three to four weeks ago. The censors grab anything with the name Bhutto. I am asking a friend to post this letter to you from a post-office in a different locality... please see that Mir gets it. Thank you very much.'[5] Later Mir released excerpts to the press. 'The important thing is that time will pass,' Zulfikar Ali Bhutto had written, 'the most important thing is that I must pass through it with honour. Whatever this end, it must be faced bravely.'[6]

---

* Ahmed Raza Kasuri (b.1940) is son of Nawab Mohammad Kasuri (1922-74), a magistrate.

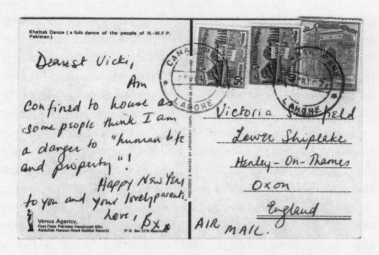

Benazir's New Year postcard. *Am confined to house as some people think
I am a danger to "human life and property"!, December 1977.*

*

On 18 March 1978 I was horrified to see 'Bhutto to hang' displayed
on the news-stands in London. 'That's my friend's father,' I said to
my shocked American friend, Ann Grossman, when we were out
on a day's sightseeing at the Tower of London. From then onwards
I realised that the situation in this faraway land was much more
serious than I, in my Western ignorance, had assumed.

After being released in January, Benazir had again been detained.
Her mother was also under arrest but in a house in Lahore,
because the trial had been held in the Lahore High Court. Meanwhile her father had been shifted to a jail in Rawalpindi, close
to the federal capital, Islamabad, because his appeal against the
death sentence was going to be heard in the Supreme Court of
Pakistan. There was never any question of being allowed out on bail.
Zia had already shown an alarming severity in his pronounce-
ments, which were increasingly being made in the name of Islam.

Without knowing if a letter would reach her, on 15 April I wrote to Benazir.

The reason I am writing this is just to 'talk' with you a little bit. I know you must be very depressed and even though I can by no means comprehend the agonizing days you must spend, I try to share your anguish in my thoughts and conversations with other people... I wish that we had turned our minds more to the real world when we were together at Oxford rather than the various problems of Oxford life, important tho' they seemed at the time. There was so much more we could have discussed – a particularly memorable time was when we went to dinner together at La Sorbonne* and we did turn to discussing Pakistan and the Muslim faith – do you remember and also the hours we spent talking early into the morning when I stayed with you in St Catz.[7]

In May I received a letter which changed my life. It had taken nearly three weeks to reach me. 'I do not know what your plans are for the summer,' Benazir began. 'I don't even know what your parents would think of your visiting a country ruled by bayonets in the heat of the summer. However if, in these circumstances, you are able to come, please do.' Her tone was deadly serious. As I later understood, her father's trial had been held 'in camera' in Lahore under the jurisdiction of a judge, Maulvi Mushtaq Hussain, who had a personal dislike of Bhutto – the judge's prejudice evident from several hostile altercations during the court proceedings. So disenchanted had Bhutto been with the whole process that he had boycotted the trial and no defence witnesses were called.

---

* La Sorbonne was a restaurant which was tucked down a passage off the High Street; for a while the chef Raymond Blanc worked there.

Benazir was thinking that if the international media knew what she termed a 'miscarriage of justice' was being committed through Pakistan's courts, whose practice was derived from British criminal law, then world leaders and opinion-makers would take note and ensure that the appeal was fair. And if his appeal were fairly heard, then her father would be acquitted. 'It will be even better if you can get some newspapers or magazines to give you a journalist pass so that you can enter as press and watch the circus known as the Supreme Court of Pakistan,' she continued.

Having addressed the letter to me and Claire, Benazir thought perhaps other Oxford friends might come as well, especially those who had studied law. 'We can have them stay with friends but because of the fanatical atmosphere pertaining within, we will have to pretend they are acquaintances.' Saying that she was sending the letter through a friendly police guard, she had added a postscript: 'Flogging and hanging are the rule of the day. Jails are jam-packed with political prisoners. People have been terrorised into silence. It does not seem like a state in the 20th century. Islam, a merciful religion, is wrongly invoked for acts of brutality.'[8]

And so I decided to go to Pakistan, with my parents surprisingly perhaps, under the circumstances, giving me their full support. Mindful that accredited stringers and correspondents who covered the region for the major British newspapers were already in Islamabad, I realised that, if I wanted to write some articles, I would have to find an appropriate outlet. Shortly before my departure, a chance meeting with the deputy editor of the *Spectator* at a friend's twenty-first birthday party in Oxford gave me accreditation to this respected journal. No funds, simply, 'yes, you can write the odd article for us' and even more valuable, a letter from the editor, Alexander Chancellor,* which confirmed that I would be

---

* Alexander Chancellor, CBE (1940–2017) was editor of the *Spectator* 1975–84.

in Pakistan on behalf of the *Spectator* and requesting me to be given 'every assistance'.[9] I planned to be away for about six weeks because that was how long it was assumed the appeal would take. I was convinced that Bhutto would be acquitted. Benazir would then join her country's Foreign Service and the family's life would resume as normal. Mir, who was in his second year at Oxford, could continue his studies without worrying about his father; their younger sister, twenty-year-old Sanam (Sunny) could complete her degree at Harvard, where she was currently studying, while Shahnawaz – the youngest of the four children – could finish his education at school in Switzerland.*

Spectator

56 Doughty Street London WC1N 2LL Telephone 01-405 1706 Telegrams Spectator London Telex 27124

24 May 1978

TO WHOM IT MAY CONCERN

Miss Victoria Schofield is a journalist visiting Pakistan on behalf of the Spectator. I would be grateful if you could afford her every assistance.

Alexander Chancellor

Alexander Chancellor
Editor

Letter from the *Spectator* asking for me to be given 'every assistance' in Pakistan.

---

* Sanam Bhutto (b.1957) and Shahnawaz Bhutto (1958–85).

Since Bhutto's appeal against the death sentence had already started in the Supreme Court, I felt I must get there as soon as possible, which meant cancelling my holiday with my parents and sister in the South of France. Instead of travelling directly to Karachi, where Benazir was under house arrest, Mir had suggested I go immediately to Rawalpindi. I booked my flight and set aside a few hundred pounds to take with me. There were no rupees to be purchased prior to departure and no ATM machines on arrival, no credit cards either. If I needed more money, I would have to ask my parents to wire it to me. I also had some essential things to do: quit my researcher's job at the International Coffee Organisation in London, inform my French housemate that I was going away for a few weeks, and have the necessary injections for typhoid, tetanus and cholera. Because I realised it would already be hot in Pakistan, I selected several short-sleeved shirts, some dresses and a few skirts to take as my wardrobe. Also in my suitcase was the unfinished manuscript of a short educational book I'd been contracted to write on 'The United Nations' and which I'd been working on in my free time and hoped to find time to complete.*

As I was going to a country where literally the only friend I had was in detention, my father thought it prudent to write to the British Ambassador in Islamabad, informing him of my arrival in Pakistan in the hope that, if I got into difficulties, the British Embassy would look after me. No visa was required and so there were no other formalities. I also had to recognise that I was heading east to a region about which, historically, I remained almost entirely uninformed. Although I was a History graduate from Oxford, as I had often told my parents when they asked me a question about a particular event, I hadn't studied 'that bit'. My immediate reading material was the recently published

---

* Later published as *The United Nations* (Wayland Press, 1979).

Freedom at Midnight by Larry Collins and Dominique Lapierre, an account of the events of 1947 when India and Pakistan achieved their independence amid the trauma of partition. Since I knew very little about the subject, I could not judge the accuracy of their narrative but it was the most accessible introduction to Pakistan's recent history then available.

Shortly before my departure Mir telephoned, assuring me that some friends – two brothers – would meet me at the airport. 'It'll be fine,' he said encouragingly, because I still had no idea where I was going to stay. 'They've said you can stay with them.'

Almost unawares, I was stepping into the unknown, without any of the systems of support we now take for granted. In today's world of mobile phones, emails, WhatsApp and the internet, it is extraordinary how easily geographical separation can be circumvented, but in the 1970s communication at long distance was still mainly carried out by letter. If I wanted to telephone my parents, I would have to book a call, which would be expensive. Computers did exist but only in laboratories. If I wanted to write an article, I would have to do it by hand or find a typewriter. I would then have to send it by telex, the long-departed system of transmitting information by a system of dots and dashes on a thin strip of paper which somehow could be interpreted as printed text the other end. It was faster than putting a letter in the post but utterly antiquated if we fast-forward to the world wide web. So, armed with a camera and a notebook, I set out for Pakistan, hoping that, at some point, I would be able to see Benazir.

As I emerged from the plane at Rawalpindi airport, a blast of hot air assailed me. I expected Pakistan to be hot, but not that hot. Out of the throng of people crowding around the exit, two young men emerged.

'Are you Victoria?' one of them asked, my foreign appearance singling me out amongst the hundreds of Pakistanis.

'Yes,' I replied, as one of them took charge of my suitcase. Introducing themselves as Nadeem and Pervez Yousuf, they transported me to their home in Rawalpindi. After offering me tea and introducing me to their wives, they started asking me questions. They seemed to think that Bhutto's appeal must be headline news in the British press. I kept trying to remember what, if anything, I had seen in the newspapers since the death sentence had been announced. Once their questions came to an end, they showed me to a room so I could rest. Suddenly I felt very strange, my foreignness accentuated by being in a Pakistani home. My skirt felt too short and I wished I'd brought a long-sleeved shirt. I was of course in complete culture shock. In those days there were fewer concerns about travelling to Muslim countries and less focus on understanding cultural differences. Instead it was assumed that whatever we wore in the West was fine in the East as well.

I tried to sleep; a large fan was fixed to the ceiling above the bed, its whirring blades creating a gentle breeze. My eyes closed because I was very tired but I found myself irrationally worrying about the fan falling off the ceiling and its propeller blades slicing me in half. Having decided to turn it off, I went to sleep but woke up sweating. Soon afterwards one of the wives came into the room.

'Oh,' she said, 'so hot, is the fan not working?'

I was too embarrassed to explain why I had turned it off. She turned it on again, and the breeze sent me to sleep. When I woke, the fan had not fallen off the ceiling and I had not been sliced in half by its propeller blades. My first task was to write to Benazir to tell her that I'd arrived, 'because', as I explained in my first letter to my parents, 'via a communication of loyal servants, correspondence is possible'. In this instance Pervez was going to Lahore and would give my letter to a servant who was travelling to Karachi.[10]

The next day the brothers took me to the Supreme Court, a white colonial building which, before 1971 and the secession of East Pakistan, had been East Pakistan House. 'Ask to see Mr Bhutto's lawyers,' Nadeem said. 'Tell them you are Benazir's friend. They'll be pleased to see you.' I was unsure of the lawyers' names, which were so unfamiliar to my Western ear, but I assumed I would find out who they were. The court was already in session but before I could enter the courtroom I had to get my pass from the registrar whose office was in a small room along the corridor. After I produced my letter from the *Spectator*, a pink cardboard pass permitting me entry on 'all days' was duly issued.

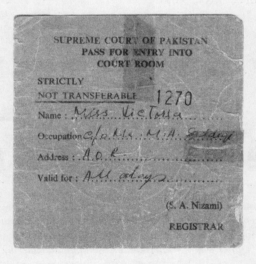

My Supreme Court pass so that I could attend Zulfikar
Ali Bhutto's appeal against the death sentence.

I had never been inside a courtroom. Having taken a place on the wooden benches at the back, I took in my surroundings. At the front a tall distinguished-looking man with black hair was making a speech at a podium directly facing a row of judges. I deduced the man must be Yahya Bakhtiar, former attorney-general under Bhutto and now his chief defence lawyer.* He was speaking in English but I was so unfamiliar with the court proceedings that I could not follow what he was saying. I got out my notebook and tried to take notes.

'The Supreme Court has long benches and wood panelling,' I began. 'There are nine judges and they look like they have not seen the sun for a long time because their faces are pallid. They are not wearing wigs and because it's summer they are also not wearing robes.'

(a) My sketches of the nine judges 1978. *Top left to right: Anwar ul Haq, Dr Naseem Hassan Shah, Dorab Patel, Karam Elahi Chauhan, Malik Mohammad Akram; bottom row: Ghulam Safdar Shah, Qaiser Khan, Waheeduddin, Mohammad Haleem.*

Sitting beside Bakhtiar at a table to his right were several other men, who were taking notes and looking at law books.

---

* Yahya Bakhtiar (1921–2013) was attorney-general under Zulfikar Ali Bhutto and again during Benazir Bhutto's first administration in 1988.

Occasionally, one of the lawyers handed Bakhtiar a large book to read from, citing some point of law. To the left, three more lawyers were seated, whom I assumed to be the lawyers for the prosecution. I hadn't studied law and so I had no idea how an appeal worked. A visual diversion was provided by some men dressed in white, with a gold sash across their chests and wearing turbans, with a piece of pleated stiff material sticking up like a feather. These I later discovered were called 'pugarees', and the men themselves 'peons'. 'When the justices get up to leave for the recess, the peons stand behind their chairs to pull them out. Two judges, one tall, one short, clasp hands and walk out together.'*

(b) A peon in the Supreme Court of Pakistan – they were in regular attendance when the judges arrived and left.

---

* The nine judges were Anwar ul Haq (1917–95), 9th chief justice of Pakistan 1977–81; Malik Mohammad Akram; Dr Naseem Hassan Shah (1929–2015), 12th chief justice of Pakistan 1993–94; Karam Elahi Chauhan; Ghulam Safdar Shah (1922–86); Dorab Patel (1924–97); Mohammad Haleem (1925–2006), 10th chief justice of Pakistan (1981–89); Qaiser Khan, who retired at the end of July 1978; Waheeduddin Ahmed, who fell ill in November 1978 and was not permitted to return to the bench.

As soon as the court recessed, I made my way to the front where the lawyers were standing. Yahya Bakhtiar was sipping water and he looked tired, his eyes slightly watering.

'Hello,' I said falteringly, 'I am Victoria, Benazir's friend. I have come from London to attend the appeal.'

'Hello, Victoria, that is very good that you have come. We are going for our recess and so you can take tea with us,' he said, guiding me towards a room where tea with hot milk and sandwiches on metal trays was being brought in by waiters dressed in white; as I entered the room there was an acrid smell of cigarette smoke. Beckoning me to sit down at a table, Bakhtiar introduced me to the other lawyers present: Dost Mohammed (known as D. M.) Awan and Ghulam Ali Memon, whom I recognised as the lawyer who kept handing law books to Bakhtiar during his submissions. Two other lawyers working on Bhutto's defence were seated near by: Hafeez Lakho and Mohammed Sharif. If they were surprised at my presence they didn't show it.

'You are most welcome to be here,' one of them said. There was a buzz of conversation among the few other people who were in the tea room, but I felt so new that I had nothing to contribute. If challenged, I would say that I was Benazir's friend from Oxford and that I would be writing an article for the *Spectator*. I still had no idea where I would find a typewriter.

When the court proceedings were over, I returned home to Nadeem and Pervez's house. They greeted me with curiosity after my day at the Supreme Court but also with some bad news. 'We are sorry, but the police know we are friends of the Bhuttos and so we are watched. They have heard that you are living in our house. To intimidate us, they have used their agents to break down the wall to our garden, and so tomorrow morning we will take you to a hotel owned by a friend of ours.'

I was slightly thrown by this sudden turn of events but, since

I knew no one else in Rawalpindi, the following day I packed my bags and went with them to Gatmells Motel, a white bungalow-style building with the sinister address of 'Jail Road'. The first thing which greeted me when I put the light on in the bathroom was a huge cockroach, its feathery tentacles waving territorially where it had taken up position before it then darted into a crack. I had never seen a cockroach before, its brittle body surprisingly intimidating. Having accustomed myself to my new surroundings, I set off again to go to the Supreme Court, once more taking tea with the lawyers and learning more about the case. I was also finding their accented English easier to understand.

'The appeal will review all the evidence of the forty-one prosecution witnesses, all of whom have testified that the director-general of the Federal Security Force was responsible for killing Kasuri's father together with the four confessing co-accused,' explained Awan. As Bhutto's defence lawyer for the trial, he was the only lawyer working on Bhutto's appeal who had been present throughout. 'The appeal started in May and Yahya Bakhtiar is already on witness no. 3's testimony,' I noted in my diary. 'The main thrust of their argument is that the case is politically motivated in order to eliminate Bhutto physically.'

The following evening a young man called Athar, who had come from the Bhutto home in Karachi and was helping with some administrative work, came to see me at Gatmells. 'Miss Benazir is sending you a ticket,' he said. 'She wants you to come to Karachi. Her habeas corpus petition against her detention is being heard in court. Soon she may be set free.' He also handed me a letter from her: 'My dearest Vicks, What a *pleasant* surprise,' she wrote. 'Your letter has reached me by special messenger just before I am taken to Rawalpindi after almost 2 weeks under heavy police escort to see my father. Somehow I thought they would have freed me by now, but they have not. I am to appear in Sindh High Court on

June 5th.' I was so happy as I read her letter. 'Do come on June 4th,' she continued. 'At least we will be able to see each other on the 5th and talk for a few minutes. I have also written to the provincial home secretary to allow you to visit & stay with me.'

Indeed she had, because the reverse side of her letter was a copy of what she had written in her most engaging style.

I have just learnt that a very dear and close friend of mine has arrived in Pakistan to visit me... the solace of a friend at this time can be very comforting. I do hope that you will allow Victoria permission to come and stay with me in Karachi... Miss Schofield is the closest friend I had in Oxford. We shared many times together and she succeeded me as President of the Oxford Union. When she has spent so much on coming here, I hope you will not disappoint her because if she is refused permission to see me, she will carry back a bad impression of our country.

'Please write on the same lines to them,' she continued in her letter to me. 'Omit you are a journalist or have a journalist pass, otherwise they will never let you near me. Say you only came to see me.'[11] Before leaving for Karachi, I wrote a letter which the lawyers said they would take to Benazir's father: 'I am both proud and privileged to be able to call myself a close friend of Benazir. I have come to Pakistan not so much because I believe I can be of much use but because of my friendship with her.' My letter was returned with a handwritten note from Zulfikar Ali Bhutto at the top: 'Very kind and thoughtful of you. I am indeed touched.'[12]

On 4 June, as I packed my suitcase, I took one last look at my room at Gatmells. I had learnt to sleep with the light on because the cockroaches were less likely to emerge and at least, if I got up in the middle of the night, I would be able to see them. The thought of treading on a cockroach in the dark was best uncontemplated. My flight to Karachi was in the evening. As I waited in the departure lounge, a stranger offered me tea and asked me what I was doing in Pakistan.

'I'm going to Karachi to see a friend,' I responded. I had no idea who he was and whether he would be happy to know that I was Benazir's friend. Not wanting to get drawn further into conversation, I politely refused the offer of tea.

The flight was delayed and by the time I arrived in Karachi it was 3 a.m. I was met by Benazir's two school friends, Samiya and Salma Waheed, who had been waiting for me at the airport in order to take me to their home. Both had been to college in the United States and I felt less awkward talking to them than with Nadeem and Pervez's wives. 'Tomorrow we'll go to the court together,' said Samiya, just before my head hit the pillow. 'And then you will see Benazir.'

The Sindh High Court had more windows than the Supreme Court in Rawalpindi and therefore seemed more spacious. I walked in with Samiya and Salma. Luckily the court was briefly in recess. Suddenly I caught sight of Benazir sitting on the bench talking to some other people. Aware of new arrivals, she turned around to see me and her face lit up. I suddenly felt shy. I had known her so well at Oxford. But in this new environment, everything seemed so different. Her hair was longer, and, dressed in *shalwar kameez* – the attractive long shirt over baggy trousers which was the traditional attire for both men and women – with a long scarf or *dupatta* on her shoulders, she looked more oriental.

'Hello Benazir,' I said timidly. 'I bring you lots of love from everyone at home.' Before the court resumed I was able to describe a little of what I'd absorbed about the Supreme Court proceedings from her father's lawyers. Once the court recessed for the day, Benazir told me to go to the home secretary of Sindh province to hand in my letter, which I'd prepared along the lines she'd suggested. 'If they find out about the journalist part, say that is incidental,' she'd warned. 'Promise them not to "interview" me etc. But only if they find out.' In the event of a refusal, I was to 'shout and scream and cry about how *cruel* they are being not allowing you to see your friend when she needs comfort most'.[13]

Since I had no idea where to go, another friend, Najeeb Zafar Khan, who had also been in the courtroom, accompanied me. He seemed to know someone who knew someone because, in no time, I was ushered into a room where the home secretary was sitting behind a desk piled with papers. I waited patiently as he sat reading my letter and the letter he had received from Benazir, slightly curling the top edges in his fingers as he got to the bottom of each page. Finally he looked up.

'Yes,' he said. 'Permission will be granted.' I hoped he couldn't hear me breathe a sigh of relief. There'd been no mention of journalism or writing any articles. After waiting a little longer a clerk arrived with another sheet of paper confirming that I had the right to stay with Miss Benazir Bhutto d/o Zulfikar Ali Bhutto at 70, Clifton, Karachi.

Although Najeeb couldn't go inside, he accompanied me to Benazir's home, a large mansion behind white walls in one of Karachi's more affluent areas. On the gate-post I noticed a brass plaque: 'Zulfikar Ali Bhutto, Barrister-at-Law' – a reminder that, before he had entered politics, Benazir's father had qualified as a lawyer. Like so many Pakistanis before and after him, he had been a member of that hallowed institution, Lincoln's Inn, where the founder of Pakistan, Mohammed Ali Jinnah – revered as Quaid-e-Azam ('great leader') – was called to the bar. My immediate thought, as a servant ushered me through the front door, was how lonely it must be for Benazir living here without the rest of the family she had grown up with.

A huge smile greeted me. 'Oh, they let you come!' she exclaimed in delight. Her bedroom was at the top of the stairs. Opposite was Sunny's room, where, since her sister was abroad, Benazir said I could stay. She also kindly gave me two *shalwar kameez* to wear instead of my Western clothes, which made me feel much less like a foreigner who'd just arrived in Pakistan.

To my Western eye, the house appeared as I imagined a home to be in the Arabian Nights, full of exotic objects collected during a lifetime of travelling – vases, carpets, wall hangings and pictures. One impressive work was a portrait of Zulfikar Ali Bhutto depicted in blue and white *lapis lazuli* mosaic by the renowned artist, Gulgee. During the 1970s the self-taught artist had made a name for himself by creating life-size representations of prominent individuals. As a skilled naturalist painter, he developed the medium of making large abstract calligraphic works inspired by verses from the Holy Qur'an. His son also became a well-known artist and sculptor.*

During our wanderings through her house, Benazir showed me her father's pride and joy, a fine library which housed numerous rare books, including a substantial collection of volumes relating to Napoleon, one of the historical figures whom Bhutto admired. 'If you need to, you can work here,' she said thoughtfully, knowing that I had brought the manuscript of my book on the United Nations with me.

Benazir's main occupation was revising a book called *Foreign Policy in Perspective*, which she'd written at the end of the previous year when she was under detention. A slim volume, it had over fifty sections, some of which Benazir wanted to redraft – which meant retyping the relevant section. I now realised that there was something practical I could do to help her, since I had

---

* Ismail Gulgee (1926–2007) and Amin Gulgee (b.1965).

already learnt to 'touch' type, a skill I'd acquired at a relatively young age at home (inspired by my father who, having retired from the Royal Navy, now wrote books on naval history). And so we started working on the revisions of the book together. Some of the sections were brief essays, others no more than a paragraph: for example, focusing on personalities such as the Egyptian President, Anwar Sadat (the chapter entitled 'Sadat's Sand Prints'), or on themes like 'The Struggle between Rich and Poor' or 'Fighting Colonialism'. Halfway through the book was a 'Note' explaining why her father was first referred to as president, and then, following the signing of the 1973 Constitution, as prime minister. When the book was published Benazir gave me a copy, inscribing it with a quotation from the great Sindhi poet, Shah Abdul Latif Bhittai:*

> O Lord, into this camel's head
> Put something that in sense doth share,
> O, save him, Lord of Mercy, save:
> Such is Latif the poet's prayer.[14]

'We could not take you to the poet's mausoleum in Bhit Shah in Sindh,' she wrote in her dedication, 'but I think you will agree with his words which surely have a universal ring.'[15]

We also worked on retyping articles from the international press for reprinting in the local newspapers so that Pakistani readers could read a more balanced commentary on what was happening in Pakistan. In the cool of the evenings we sometimes walked in the walled garden. One evening we sat upstairs where

---

* She gave me the book on 28 November 1978 when yet again she was under detention. Shah Abdul Latif Bhittai (1689–1752) is considered to be the greatest Sindhi poet. His mausoleum at Bhit Shah is north of Hyderabad.

the bookshelves were full of photograph albums of her father's state trips abroad. As Benazir excitedly turned the pages, I saw Zulfikar Ali Bhutto in a well-tailored suit standing beside the American president Richard Nixon; in another he was meeting the Chinese leader, Zhou Enlai. There were also photographs of her parents with the Kennedys. As we finished looking through one album and then started on another, Benazir's face was alight with joy, reliving the past and temporarily forgetting the present.

Along with everything else that was new and different came mangoes. In 1970s Britain we ate our way around the seasons with strawberries in summer and apples in winter and mangoes were a luxury I had barely seen, let alone eaten. In Pakistan June and July were the mango months and, if we liked, we could eat them for breakfast, lunch and dinner. The first time I tried eating a mango I was slightly baffled at how to separate the delicious flesh from the long cuttlefish-like kernel in the middle. Benazir looked at me in amusement as I made a messy attempt to cut it open, ending up with my fingers dripping with juice and mushy fruit. Taking another mango from the bowl she gave me my first lesson in the art of eating a mango, deftly slicing first one side and then the other lengthways close to the kernel, before peeling the protective skin off what remained. With a knife she then made a criss-cross pattern on the oval shapes which she opened outwards to reveal several easily accessible fleshy cubes. It was a lesson I never forgot.

We had just settled into a comfortable routine when, a week after my arrival at 70, Clifton, a policeman crossed the lawn holding a piece of paper which he handed to Benazir.

'Oh no,' she said, looking downcast, 'your permission to stay with me has expired. They are now asking you to leave.'

Rather than remaining in Karachi, she suggested that I return to Rawalpindi to continue attending the appeal. 'With luck,' she said, 'when the hearing of my habeas corpus petition is finished, I will be released and then I will come up to Pindi.' I took my leave despondently; despite the drastically different circumstances, we had resumed the pattern of our old familiar friendship, and I hoped that my presence had at least broken some of the monotony of her solitude.

Back in Rawalpindi, I did not return to Gatmells. Instead Benazir had arranged that I should stay at Flashman's Hotel, where the lawyers were based, conveniently located along the Mall a short drive from the Supreme Court. Founded in the late nineteenth century by a British property owner, Charles Thomas Flashman, and sharing the name of the hero in the popular novels by George Macdonald Fraser, the hotel was built in bungalow style and each room had a verandah facing the courtyard. Hidden behind some trees was a small swimming pool, but I was beginning to realise that the culture of swimming in Pakistan was very different from ours and only if I was sure there was no one else around did I make use of the pool.

The lawyers had taken up residence in a series of rooms along one side of the hotel. Another room had become an office from which the more junior lawyers worked, law books piled high and typewriters occupying the tables. In addition to those I had already met, another young lawyer, Saleem Zulfiqar Khan, had joined the team. Also helping the lawyers was Amna Piracha, a staunch supporter of Zulfikar Ali Bhutto and the PPP who had briefly worked in Begum Bhutto's office in Rawalpindi during the 1977 election campaign. In time Amna and Saleem would marry, but that was in the future.*

On arrival I wrote again to Benazir's father:

---

* Amna Piracha married Saleem Zulfiqar Khan (d.2010) in June 1980.

I have just returned from Karachi where I have been staying with Benazir (until I was issued with an order to leave). It was wonderful to be able to see her and also be present at the Sindh High Court for her petition against her sentence of detention... We have spent many hours talking and I have also been reading extracts from your speeches and writings. I enclose a letter from her and have also brought Nixon's memoirs for you which Mr Bakhtiar will give you from Benazir. I know she is awaiting impatiently her next visit and is trying to get the proper rights to visit you once a week. She was well and courageous.

My letter came back with another note: 'How can I thank you enough. Only in such conditions it is possible to appreciate the goodness of the few.'[16]

One of the first of the many foreign journalists who came to observe the appeal was Simon Henderson. He had come to Islamabad as a 'stringer' for the BBC and *The Financial Times* – this meant he only got paid for what he submitted. If nothing much was happening he would, apparently, starve. But, as he told me later, he had made so much money out of all the stories he wrote when the military coup took place that he was able to buy a car, which he called his 'Zulfikar Ali Bhutto memorial car'. In the weeks that followed we often met, exchanging news, his interest being the morale of the 'Bhutto camp'.

Another journalist who appeared at the Supreme Court was Simon Winchester, whose name was very familiar, although I couldn't bring to mind anything he'd written. He was en route home from somewhere exciting – Hong Kong, I think. Since I was the only other 'foreigner' in the Supreme Court that day, he engaged me in conversation, asking what I was doing. I gave him the professional reason for my presence, that I had the opportunity to write some articles for the *Spectator*.

'Ah,' he said, 'I write for the *Spectator*, but I normally do so under a pseudonym.'

In my so far non-existent journalistic career – two articles published when I was at University – I couldn't imagine how anyone could have published so many articles that some of them had to be written under a pseudonym. When I confessed that I was Benazir's friend and had recently come down from Oxford, and that I hadn't yet written anything for the *Spectator*, he said he would help me.

'It is a funny thing,' he admitted, 'but if you were a man I probably wouldn't bother.'

'Oh,' I responded, entirely unconcerned by what today might be classified as a sexist remark, 'thank you very much.'

Most importantly, he said he had a typewriter which I could use. Since I was writing an article for a prestigious journal with which he had some association, he felt duty bound to give me some instructions on how to write the requisite 1,000 words.

'What you have to think of is a parabola – your article will have an introduction to set the scene, then the main part which will come to a crescendo, then the conclusion,' he said, drawing an arc at the top of the newspaper where there was a blank space. 'You don't want it to be a series of disjointed paragraphs.'

Responding with another 'Oh', I began to write my article on his typewriter. It was late by the time I had finished and so I could not send it until the following morning.

The telex machine was in a small building whose location everyone knew because, unless you were of sufficient stature to be requested to read the article 'down the line' on the telephone to a 'copytaker' who would type it out, it was impossible to send an article to a newspaper without going to the telex operator. When there was some piece of breaking news, there would be a massive queue. But since the news from Pakistan was quiet, when

I arrived I was the only person there. I handed my carefully crafted article over to the telex operator and he keyed it in. All of this procedure, which a more seasoned journalist would take in his or her stride, was an entirely novel experience. But I was absolutely at the beginning of my writing career. So important was the telex machine in the life of a journalist that the AFP correspondent, Jean-François Le Mounier, had called his dog Télex – his arrival heralded by his accented English shouting 'Télex, Télex' as he came into view, the dog following on behind. When the *Spectator* published my article they gave it the headline 'The trial of Bhutto'.[17]

On 15 June Benazir was released from house arrest. 'Benazir's freedom was fantastic,' I enthused in a letter home. 'We are all so excited.'[18] She came at once to Rawalpindi from Karachi. Almost immediately the Court was adjourned for two weeks because the chief justice, Anwar ul Haq, was going to attend a Jurists' Conference in Jakarta. And so we returned to Karachi. On 21 June Benazir celebrated her twenty-fifth birthday. But she did not enjoy the day at home. Instead she flew back to Rawalpindi to see her father, the jail authorities having given special permission for both Benazir and her mother to visit at the same time. To mark the occasion, her father had written her a long letter: 'My dearest daughter,' he began, 'How does a condemned prisoner write a letter of birthday greetings to a brilliant and beautiful daughter fighting for the life of her father, being in bondage herself?... You are in the springtime of your years but living in a world of gloomy winter.' Running to several pages, with observations on world history and his own period in office, as with the letters he had written to her at Oxford, the letter sought to advise and encourage, thus beginning that period of tutelage which continued in earnest for nine months. 'I am fifty years old,' he concluded. 'And you are exactly half my age. By the time you reach my age, you must accomplish twice as much as I have achieved for the people.'[19]

The adjournment and Benazir's release provided a much-needed opportunity for her to have a minor operation on her ear, which had been troubling her. Before she went into hospital, because of the tremendous heat she had thoughtfully arranged for me to go swimming at the Sind Club where her father was a member, as was Naseem Islam, the husband of his sister Munnawar, always known as Aunty Manna. The oldest club in Karachi, founded in 1871, it was a relic of the city's colonial past with beautifully manicured lawns, flowerbeds, wood panelling and portraits of past members. Since no immediate family member could accompany me, I went with Uncle Naseem, who sat at a discreet distance while I enjoyed my swim.

Once Benazir was well enough to receive visitors, together with her schoolfriend Samiya I went to sit with her in hospital. Much to the media's interest, Benazir's mother, who was still under house arrest in Lahore, was allowed to come to Karachi, arriving at the hospital with a huge police guard. 'This meant everyone who possibly could flocked to the hospital and the place has been crawling with policemen and CID [Criminal Investigation Department] agents,' I told my parents. It was the first time I had met Benazir's elegant mother, whom force of circumstances had turned into a political activist.* 'She has the dignity and maturity of age and experience which a young person lacks.'[20]

Ten days after Benazir's release, General Zia made a speech, broadcast on state television, again promising elections. But, he said, certain preparations were necessary. The process of accountability had to be concluded. Electoral rolls to separate out Muslims and non-Muslims also needed to be drawn up.

---

* Begum Nusrat Bhutto (1929–2011) married Zulfikar Ali Bhutto in 1951.

Increasingly, the need for 'Islamisation' was being mentioned in the press. Zia also announced that the government was going to produce a White Paper to tell the people about the 'misdeeds' of the previous government. Volume 1 was to be on the conduct of the general elections in March 1977; Volume 2 was to be on Bhutto's alleged misuse of the media. As Benazir said, it was all part of the process of character assassination designed to poison public opinion against her father while his appeal against the death sentence was being heard.

After the recess, we returned to Flashman's Hotel, where, to keep each other company and save money, we shared a room. It was by now even hotter than when I had arrived and the rudimentary air conditioning was so noisy that we slept in our narrow beds with our heads under the pillow to try to block out the sound. Benazir's presence meant that a vital energy was injected into the legal effort and her father's defence. With publication of the White Papers imminent, she wanted to write a pamphlet called 'Rumour and Reality' which would rebut the allegations circulating in the press against her father and his government. So that we could work on it and also help with the legal work, she dispatched someone to the market to buy two Olympia typewriters; henceforward we sat noisily typing in our room together. Benazir had never learnt to type properly and, after a few days, she had to put band-aids on all her fingers because they kept getting stuck between the keys and had started bleeding. But she continued undaunted. With the appearance of the White Papers, the need to work on 'Rumour and Reality' was more pressing and we worked late into the night. The structure of the book was as follows:

Rumour: Zulfikar Ali Bhutto is perhaps [sic] the only head
    of a Government to have been convicted of conspiracy to
    murder...

Reality: Zulfikar Ali Bhutto is the victim of a two-layered
conspiracy hatched and carried out against him because he
refused to compromise on his country's vital interests...

And so it continued, detailing numerous 'rumours' countered
by the same number of 'realities'. Also included were articles
reprinted from the international press, as well as the statements of
'Monarchs, Presidents, Prime Ministers, Parliaments' following
the 18 March Lahore High Court verdict. Among the messages
of support was one emphasising that more than 150 members of
the British parliament belonging to all the political parties had
expressed 'their deep concern about the death sentence on former
Premier Bhutto. They have asked Her Majesty's Government to
urge the Government of Pakistan not to carry out the sentence.'
Although the publication was basic (the first four pages were
accidentally printed upside down), Benazir believed that the refuta-
tions were useful for visiting journalists who would inevitably be
targeted with government propaganda against her father and the
PPP, without much opportunity to hear opposing viewpoints.[21]

The fifth of July 1978 signified the first anniversary of the military
coup. Instead of being in power for ninety days, which Zia had
originally stated, he had been CMLA for 365. Since all the main
leaders of the PPP were still under detention, Benazir was now
the effective spokesperson for the party. 'Poor Benazir is weighted
down with the virtual sole responsibility of carrying on their
political party,' I informed my parents. 'The administration has
made every possible effort to eliminate it altogether.'[22] And so, in
addition to typing, she had started meeting countless people who
came to see her at Flashman's, including journalists and party
workers. Sometimes I sat with her during her interviews, listening

to what she said, as my understanding of the political dynamic in Pakistan grew. Combined with the heat, for Benazir especially each day was exhausting. 'On some days I had to force myself to get up in the morning,' she later wrote. 'Quickly. Get up. Get dressed. Face the day. More charges to refute. Meet with the few party workers not in jail. Give interviews to the press gathering in Rawalpindi.'[23]

Her routine also included visiting her father in jail every week. Emotionally involved as I had become in the struggle to save Bhutto's life, I could not imagine what it must have been like for Benazir to see her father in such abject circumstances. Although I did not realise it at the time, these meetings were helping to forge her political character, both in terms of her resilience in adversity and her understanding of her father's political vision.

After 'Rumour and Reality' we started work on another 'top secret' document. Instead of writing his memoirs in jail, which was technically illegal since he was not permitted to work on anything other than court material, Bhutto had decided to respond more fully in his own voice to the allegations against him in the White Papers in a document called the 'rejoinder'. But instead of giving a simple answer, he intended to write extensive replies where he felt appropriate, which would include talking about his achievements, matters of state and his vision for the world. Another friend, Nighat (Niggy) Shafi, came to the hotel to help. First we typed from Bhutto's handwritten original on foolscap sheets of paper. Then the lawyers took the typewritten sheets back to him for checking; we then retyped what we had already typed with his amendments. On one of his notes he told me to send 'only that material for checking which you consider to be essential, that is mainly on the political issues. No point in sending me material on the legal or economic issues. The security here is very stiff. Leakage would be a disaster.' Zulfikar Ali Bhutto also told me that 'work of poor quality and done in haste is more damaging than doing nothing' and so, although the time factor is important 'we do not have to go crazy'. On another note he asked how, with two ex-presidents of the Oxford Union helping him, could he fail?[24]

Since the typewriter could produce only about three copies by using carbon paper, if we wanted more copies we had to go to the market where there was a photocopier. This was riskier than might appear. Also helping the lawyers with administrative work was a young man, Peter Jilani. One day I asked him to go to the market to do some photocopying. But he never returned. We then heard that he had been arrested. A year later he contacted me care of the BBC World Service, where I was working, describing his arrest, release, re-arrest, his eventual release and move to Germany, where he was granted asylum. 'Last I saw you was in Pindi: I was in the police van, handcuffed of course, you passed me by... I wanted to shout but then I couldn't do because of my circumstances.'[25]

While the appeal was being heard, several foreign lawyers came to attend the Supreme Court, their presence, we hoped, a reminder to the judiciary and the authorities that the rest of the world was keeping an eye on the proceedings. The first to come was Etienne Jaudel, general secretary of the International Federation for Human Rights, who arrived soon after the appeal began. Another was former US attorney-general Ramsey Clark, who also had a meeting with General Zia.* Although Zia received him politely, permission to see Bhutto was refused, despite his having been 'in prisons on five continents and on Death Row in five continents'.[26] I was pleased to meet this genial American, who, during his time as attorney-general, had vigorously opposed the death penalty and championed civil rights. Another opponent of the death penalty

---

* Etienne Jaudel (1931–2011); Ramsey Clark (b.1927) was US attorney-general 1967–69.

who visited Rawalpindi was the French lawyer Robert Badinter, accompanied by his wife Elisabeth.* They too sat in court listening to the proceedings. Since both Amna and I spoke French, Benazir asked us to look after them during their stay. Badinter's comment – 'History will judge the judges' – stayed with me.[27]

In late July, with the court again in recess, Benazir and I went to the Bhutto ancestral home in Larkana. 'We have a swimming pool and you can pick oranges from the tree while you are in the pool,' Benazir enthused. 'You'll love it.' Larkana is a dusty town established in the early eighteenth century, and it was from here in 1843 that Major General Sir Charles Napier's troops had set off to fight against the Talpur rulers of Sindh; their victory led to Napier's annexation of Sindh, which gave rise to the apocryphal story of his despatching a punning message to his superiors consisting of a single word in Latin – *Peccavi* (I have sinned).[†28]

When we arrived at Al Murtaza – the house named after Benazir's great-grandfather, Ghulam Murtaza Bhutto – there was a sense of its feudal antiquity, the walls in the hall adorned with portraits of her ancestors, with crystal chandeliers and beautiful carpets. Ghulam Murtaza Khan's son – Benazir's grandfather, Sir Shah Nawaz Bhutto – had been knighted by the British in 1940 for having 'effectively exercised influence in support of the Government'. He had also made a contribution to altering the map of South Asia. During the 1930s while attending the Round Table Conference in London, he had campaigned for Sindh to be

---

* Robert Badinter (b.1928), in 1981, as minister of justice, enacted the abolition of the death penalty; Elisabeth Badinter (b.1944).
† General Sir Charles Napier, GCB (1782–1853). The real author of 'Peccavi' was Catherine Winkworth, who sent it to the magazine *Punch*.

separated administratively from the Bombay presidency (which covered large tracts of the western and north-western parts of British India). This meant that, when discussions took place over partition, as a separate Muslim majority province, Sindh would become part of Pakistan, making the new country viable.

In 1947 Sir Shah Nawaz had become Dewan or prime minister of Junagadh, situated in the coastal region of what is now Gujarat and one of the 565 princely states in India over which the British had retained paramountcy. Once more his role was pivotal. Although ruled by the Muslim nawab, Sir Muhammad Mahabat Khan III, the population was mainly Hindu. At partition, as instructed by Jinnah, Sir Shah Nawaz had prevailed upon the nawab to accede to the new dominion of Pakistan, even though there was no geographical contiguity other than by sea. But, with its Hindu majority population, the new dominion of India was not prepared to accept Junagadh's accession to Pakistan and instituted a blockade, cutting off supplies, and severing air and postal links. By November, realising that the state's accession to Pakistan could not be sustained, Sir Shah Nawaz was obliged to request the government of India to assume authority.* Subsequently a plebiscite was held confirming its accession to India.[29]

Soon after our arrival we set out to visit 'the lands' owned by the Bhuttos since they first migrated from Rajasthan in the early eighteenth century. It was date-harvesting time and Benazir insisted on stopping by the roadside to greet the men who were picking

---

* At partition in 1947 the rulers of the princely states had to decide which new dominion to join. For most the decision was dictated by location and religious affiliation. In Hyderabad the ruler was a Muslim but the majority of his population were Hindu; while the reverse was true in Jammu and Kashmir. Some sources say there were 584 princely states, but 565 is the number normally given. Two principalities owing allegiance to Junagadh had also acceded to India.

them. 'Here,' she said, 'try some,' as she thrust a few yellow dates
into my hand. Freshly picked, their succulence bore no resemblance to the dates I'd tasted in England. As we continued on our
way we stopped at several houses, the people all greeting her as
the daughter of Bhutto, while I was introduced as her friend from
England. As the jeep in which we were travelling rumbled onwards,
the children ran excitedly alongside, shouting *Jeeay* Bhutto!' ('Long
live Bhutto!') while Benazir waved at them, smiling.

When I was seventeen, I was entranced when I first saw the
great Mississippi river in the Midwest of the United States; now
I was seeing the mighty Indus, the vast river originating in Tibet
and flowing southwards, watering the plains of the Punjab and
irrigating large areas of Sindh. As we drove along beside it, the
water looked resplendent in the hot sunlight, swirling onwards
to its mouth east of Karachi. At one place we saw how, without
the resources to build a bridge, the local people had constructed
a bridge of boats, numerous fishing vessels tied one to the other
across the breadth of the river. For me, the experience of going
into the interior of Sindh was unforgettable. It may not have had
the romance of travelling in the North-West Frontier (now known
as Khyber Pakhtunkhwa) and along the Grand Trunk Road,
immortalised by Rudyard Kipling in *Kim* and his other writings,
but there was a sense of being in the land of ancient history, close
to the route followed by Alexander the Great in the fourth century
BC. Having travelled through Afghanistan, he encountered King
Ambhi of Taxila with his elephants 'appearing like castles between
his troops' before entering the Indus Valley, where he continued
to advance, until his men became too weary and refused to march
further east. Instead of making the long and arduous journey
back across Central Asia, Alexander sailed down the Indus to
the ocean, where he divided his forces. While Alexander and half
his forces crossed the Gedrosian desert – today's Makran – in

Balochistan, the remainder of his army took passage west from Karachi in a fleet of several hundred ships.

As I'd already realised, in addition to being a valuable method of transport, the Indus had (and still has) a political significance. At partition one of the major issues was sharing its valuable waters between the two new dominions. After a decade of negotiation and with the assistance of the World Bank, in 1960 the Indus Waters Treaty was agreed. While India would receive the waters of its three major tributaries in the east, the Ravi, Chenab and Beas, Pakistan would benefit from the Indus itself as well as its other major tributaries, the Jhelum and the Sutlej. Punjab's partition meant that both countries had retained an area that took its name from the Indus's five tributaries ('Punjab' deriving from the Persian *panj* meaning 'five', and *āb* meaning 'water'). The creation of the Mangla dam, built on the Jhelum river, requiring an area of the land to be flooded in the area to the north near Mirpur, led to a number of Mirpuris choosing to spend their compensation by coming to Britain, signifying the beginnings of what has become a thriving British Pakistani community.

During our stay we went to Garhi Khuda Bakhsh, the cemetery where the Bhutto ancestors were buried, in the village established by the ancestral head of the clan, Khuda Bakhsh Khan Bhutto. I noticed the clean marble grave of Benazir's grandfather, Sir Shah Nawaz, who had died in 1957, when she was only four years old.* Several small graves of children who had died in infancy were visible near by. It was a beautiful, tranquil spot and, for a while,

---

* Khuda Bakhsh Khan Bhutto was the father of Ghulam Murtaza Bhutto (1862–1940) whose son was Sir Shah Nawaz Khan Bhutto, CIE, OBE (1888–1957); Sir Shah Nawaz's first wife was a cousin, Amir Bano, by whom he had four sons and three daughters. His second wife, Khursheed, was Zulfikar Ali Bhutto's mother.

Benazir stood and murmured prayers, the palms of her hands facing the skies. I stood quietly beside her.

On another day Benazir arranged for me to visit the ancient ruins of the Indus Valley civilisation at Mohenjo-daro. Meaning 'mound of the dead', and dating from at least 2500 BC, Mohenjo-daro had been excavated in the 1920s by the British director-general of the archaeological survey of India, Sir John Marshall, and his Indian colleagues. I observed the drains and an observatory which indicated the level of sophistication reached by the inhabitants of this ancient city, who also had their own writing system. Not having seen any other ruins in South Asia, I was reminded of Pompeii, albeit centuries later.

As promised, Benazir had arranged for the swimming pool to be filled and, just as she described, it was possible to pick an orange from the tree while in the pool. But she did not come swimming with me. 'Pakistani women of a certain age no longer swim,' she said. 'But I am so happy that you are enjoying the water.'

A particularly attractive feature of the décor at Al Murtaza was the design of the tablecloths and table mats made from the Sindhi ajrak, a long piece of fabric, block-printed with a particular red and blue pattern (or red, black and white). Ajrak shawls made of pure cotton are worn by both men and women when the warmth of wool is not required. Another hallmark of Sindhi culture is the embroidered Sindhi cap or *topi*, often with decorative mirror-work, which is circular in shape and flat on the top, a V-shaped opening in the front exposing the forehead. Some people in southern Punjab wear a similar cap, which is in stark contrast to the elaborate turbans worn by men from the North-West Frontier (Khyber Pakhtunkhwa).

Our visit to Al Murtaza had enabled me to understand the prestige of the Bhutto family. Their pedigree as landlords in Sindh meant that they were owed fealty by all who worked for them in much the same way as was Britain's landed aristocracy in days gone by. Social equality had not come to Sindh and the subservience of those who worked for the Bhuttos and other big landowners in Pakistan was part of the ingrained fabric of society. But for all their wealth and privilege the Bhutto family had not been spared early death. Zulfikar Ali Bhutto's only surviving sister was Aunty Manna; another elder sister, Mumtaz, had died in 1974, while his younger sister, Benazir (after whom Benazir was named) had died of meningitis as a young girl. His half brothers had also pre-deceased him.[*][30]

As we prepared to leave, I hoped the days we had spent in Larkana had given Benazir some respite, enabling her to draw strength from her roots. She reminded me of Scarlett O'Hara returning to her home, Tara, in Gone with the Wind.

Back in Karachi we continued to type. 'We sit and work together,' I told my parents, 'until it is time for a break or a meal.'[31] My current task was to type several long letters from her father to all the presidents and prime ministers he had known during his five years in office. One was to Giscard d'Estaing, president of France since 1974.[†] The tone was both intellectual and humble, as the former prime minister, who was now classified as a 'common criminal', apologised for writing to men with whom he had once been on the same level. 'If I live, we shall undoubtedly share the honour of contributing to the enlightened thrusts of humanity for a more equitable dispensation. If I die, I bid you au revoir, with the prayer that better men may come to accomplish the unfinished task of combatting the appalling poverty and misery of my people.'[32]

*

---

[*] Mumtaz (1926–74) and Munnawar (1927–94); Benazir (?c.1930–45) is buried in Pune, India.

[†] President Valéry Giscard d'Estaing (b.1926), president of France 1974–81.

In early August we returned to Rawalpindi. Ramadan, the Muslims' holy month of fasting, had begun on 5 August which – given that it was summer – profoundly altered our routine, the lawyers rising early for breakfast before sunrise and abstaining from food and drink for fourteen hours until they could break their fast at sunset. Benazir said, being non-Muslim, I did not need to fast but I felt embarrassed having lunch when no one else was and so, on some days, I also fasted.

From our room in Flashman's we resumed our work on the rejoinder, which we'd codenamed 'Reggie'. Niggy had left, and so while I typed Benazir was free to do the checking. Since typing the rejoinder, I'd begun to experience the strange sensation of working for a mystery figure with whom I communicated but had never met. The more words I typed, the easier Bhutto's handwriting was to read, and the more I learnt about his personality and sense of humour. At one point he criticised the production of the White Papers, which were being translated into numerous languages including Arabic. 'How does the subject matter of elections concern the Arab States?' he asked. 'The system of government in Arab countries is of monarchy or the one party state.' In another passage he described how one-sided the investigation into the alleged rigging of the elections was since the PNA's conduct was not being investigated. 'The omission of PNA's commissions is conspicuous in the White Paper. It is so one-sided as to close even the other eye of Lord Nelson. Double standards have been applied by this regime in double dosage.'[33]

When the draft was finished, Bhutto sent us another note: 'I feel a great relief. Thank you and Benazir for all your troubles. Now it is in your hands. Take it to a high level of excellence. I am sure you will. From time to time I might send guidelines. I will welcome any clarification you might want. Thank you again.'[34]

The rejoinder, running to over 300 typed pages, was an immense work which had kept Bhutto busy in jail and us both in Flashman's. When eventually the document was submitted in court, it did not generate much interest among the judges, the chief justice merely accepting it and putting it on record. But that was not the end of it. In addition to the document submitted in court, we had made several photocopies, the intention being that it should be released to the international media. Writing in the *Guardian*, Martin Woollacott's article was entitled: 'The life hanging by 80,000 words'. Acknowledging the difficult conditions under which Bhutto had written the document in jail, Woollacott concluded: 'It is far from a masterpiece, but it is full of perception, wit and interesting, often convincing, analysis.'[35]

One passage which caught the attention of the Western press was Bhutto's claim that he had enabled Pakistan to obtain nuclear capability, as quoted by David Housego in *The Financial Times*: 'We were on the threshold of full nuclear capability when I left the Government to come to this death cell. We know that Israel and South Africa have full nuclear capability. The Christian, Jewish and Hindu civilisations have this capability. The Communist powers also possess it. Only the Islamic civilisation was without it, but that position was about to change.'[36] When, in 1998, Pakistan demonstrated its nuclear capability by carrying out six nuclear tests, the paper trail led back to Bhutto's tenure of office: following Pakistan's defeat in the 1971 Indo-Pakistan war, research had begun in earnest for the development of a nuclear weapons programme.[37] Among other initiatives, Bhutto had patronised the Pakistan Institute of Nuclear Science and Technology (PINSTECH), as well as reviving the Pakistan Atomic Energy Commission (PAEC), under the direction of the nuclear engineer and physicist Dr Munir Ahmad Khan.*

---

* Dr Munir Ahmad Khan (1926–99).

In 1979 Vikas publishers in New Delhi published the document as a book with an introduction by the Indian journalist, Pran Chopra. The title given to the book was a quotation from Bhutto's narrative: 'If I am assassinated…'[38]

3

'Within four walls': 1978

They call her daughter of the People and
daughter of Pakistan.[1]

In September General Zia lifted the ban on political rallies 'within four walls' and so Benazir's father suggested that she undertake a political tour of Pakistan's North-West Frontier Province, known as the NWFP. First we returned to Larkana to celebrate Eid al-Fitr, signifying the end of Ramadan. 'Larkana is so beautiful and peaceful,' I told my parents. 'I swam a lot even at night under the stars. We had to visit various relations and also the graves of the ancestors. B. had thousands of people to meet, but she held up magnificently. They call her daughter of the People and daughter of Pakistan.'[2]

After our return to Rawalpindi, we prepared for our journey to the NWFP – or Sarhad, as Benazir called the province, meaning 'Frontier'. Since the houses had very big courtyards, they could accommodate large crowds within the stipulated 'four walls'. General Naseerullah Babar, a former governor of the NWFP under Bhutto, made the arrangements and we set off together in his silver Mercedes.* The terrain was very different from what I had seen in the more fertile region of the Punjab and Sindh. At Attock, which marks the boundary between the Punjab and the Frontier, the Indus river joins with the Kabul river, its bluer water contrasting dramatically with the Kabul river's brown murkiness.

At the time, I had little understanding of the politics of the region or of its people, whom we British had called Pathans but who are more correctly known as 'Pashtuns' in the south or, with a more guttural pronunciation, 'Pakhtuns' in the north.[3] Having prized their independence throughout history, they had frequently clashed with the British, becoming renowned as fierce and redoubtable fighters. As the British political officers had learnt, their lives were governed by a strict code of behaviour – Pashtunwali – whose tenets included *melmastia* (hospitality), *izzat* (honour) and *badal* (revenge). With their rugged faces and distinctive turbans, they bore little resemblance to the Punjabis or Sindhis with whose physiognomy I had become familiar. As yet there was no sign here of the escalating turbulence in neighbouring Afghanistan following the Soviet-backed overthrow of the government of President Mohammed Daoud Khan in April. In what was known as the Saur revolution, all the royal family were summarily killed, foreshadowing the civil war to come.

Our first stop was Charsadda to visit the grave of Hayat Sherpao, who had worked with Bhutto to found the PPP in 1967, becoming governor of the NWFP in the early 1970s. In 1975 he was assassinated in a bomb blast on the campus of the University of Peshawar, the province's capital. When later we went to Peshawar, I enjoyed the opportunity of seeing this celebrated town, with its

---

* General Naseerullah Babar (1928–2011) was governor of NWFP 1975–77. He threw his Hilal-i Jurat (with bar) and other army medals at the presiding officer of a military tribunal after Bhutto was hanged in 1979.

street of the storytellers – the famous 'Qissa Khwani' bazaar – all the shops brimful of fabulous objects including carpets, rugs, copper pots and *lapis lazuli*, quantities of which are mined in northern Afghanistan. Also for sale was 'Gardner' porcelain, made in the factory founded by the Englishman Francis Gardner in 1766, which was favoured by the Russian Imperial court. As I later learnt, what was on display and in constant use at the *chai khanas* – the tea houses – may have included items from the dessert services commissioned by the Empress Catherine the Great, many of which found their way into the bazaars of central Asia after the Russian Revolution.

Benazir's tour was rapid and the heat intense, although brightly coloured *shamianas* (large marquees) erected at each location we visited provided some shade. It was the first time that I became aware of the push and pull of a huge crowd. Having got out of the car, I quickly learnt to keep just behind Benazir within the cordon of arms linked around her to protect her, because otherwise it was easy to get left behind or crushed by the hundreds of people who surged forward to be near her.

It was amazing watching Benazir as she made her speeches, using the same mannerisms I'd seen in the Oxford Union but with the language, subject matter and location so very different. She had not yet adopted the tradition of covering her head with a *dupatta* and, with her hair cut short, she presented a different image from the one which, in later years, became so familiar internationally. Since she had mostly spoken English at home, and had spent eight years abroad, her Urdu was not yet fluent; each evening she practised her speeches, which were written out for her in Urdu, spelled in the Roman alphabet, in order to learn them by heart. (Later, with assiduous practice her reading of the Arabic script became perfect, while her encouragement of my own attempts to learn Urdu was always enthusiastic.) The message of her speeches to the Pakthuns was direct: 'I am the daughter of Bhutto,' and then, pointing to the cap which she had brought with her, similar to that worn by Chairman Mao and which her father used to wear at his political rallies, she would shout *'Meri topi meray baap ki hai'* ('My hat is my father's hat'). The crowds roared in appreciation that she had come to see them, even though, as General Babar told me, since their language was Pashtu, they were unlikely to have understood everything she said.

After she finished speaking, we would be ushered towards trestle tables on which vast platters of food were laid out, including piles of pilau rice, delicious pistachio-filled naan and freshly barbecued chicken, a speciality of the region. Regardless of the time of day or our appetites, Benazir told me we must sample what had been prepared, otherwise it would appear rude to those providing hospitality.

'At Abbottabad, a semi-hill station, quite high up, the crowd had already gathered – tons of people,' I informed my parents.

And as soon as the car door opened we were all swept along to the marquee and [the] stand prepared for Benazir [from where she would speak]. It was impossible to see where we were going – we just had to keep up with the pace – the men formed a circle around us to prevent pushing and shoving but even so it was inevitable, and was sometimes more rough than others; only the sight of the brightly coloured shamiana and hundreds of PPP flags strung up like streamers, showed us that we were near our destination – and all the time people were shouting *'Jeeay* Bhutto!' ('Long live Bhutto!') as well as other slogans. Speeches from a number of PPP officials and local politicians were followed by Benazir's; as soon as it ended people virtually hurled themselves towards her once more. We escaped into the women's quarters, where she gave an impromptu speech, and then had lunch – a stupendous feast, the table groaning with food... We left in a hurry to be punctual for our next meeting.[4]

After Abbottabad we travelled onwards to Malakand, northernmost of the agencies during British rule, which included the former princely states of Chitral, Dir and Swat. After their status as princely states was dissolved in 1969, the following year the agency became known as the Malakand Division and was divided into separate districts.

The scenery as we drove through the Malakand Pass was quite breath-taking [I recorded], a narrow road winding round and round the green and brown hills and mountains, up and up until finally we reached the hill station. At the boundary people were waiting to welcome Benazir with garlands. We also drove along the side of the Swat river; coming off the mountains it was icy cold as it has melted from a glacier. It is fishing territory; also being well watered it is ideal for rice growing and we could actually smell the rice... needless to say all methods of transport were primitive – ox and plough to plough the fields, donkeys overladen with bricks, hay or other produce – skin and bone horses drawing crowded tongas. The graveyards changed as we moved northwards; as opposed to being mounds of earth, or just covered with large rounded pebbles, they were marked by large slabs of slate; wherever there was shade there was a graveyard. In one place people were drying their clothes on the flat surface the graves provide.[5]

As we journeyed onwards, Benazir wanted me to see Churchill's picket, the spot where the future prime minister had set up post as a young man while serving with the Malakand Field Force during what was known as the 'Malakand uprising' in 1897. 'But,' as I observed in my diary, without knowing exactly why Churchill had set up a picket, 'the British presence [is] now a distant memory from the present day.'[6]

After being on the road for five days, we headed home, General Babar informing me that we had driven more than 1,500 miles. Instead of returning to Flashman's Hotel, we went to stay with the family of Dr Zafar Niazi, whose house was in Islamabad, the city built as the federal capital in the 1960s along a series of grids identified by letters of the alphabet. The Niazis' house was in F/6 – the area known poetically as Shalimar. Dr Niazi was dentist to most of the expatriate community, as well as being Bhutto's dentist. As such he had been one of the few people who was permitted to see the former prime minister in jail. Having bravely spoken out about the unhygienic conditions in which Bhutto was kept, in May he had been arrested on the spurious charge of having a bottle of whisky in his house and was currently in jail in Jhelum, about 100 miles from Islamabad.

On arrival his wife, Shaukat, greeted us warmly and, throughout my years of friendship with the family, I have never forgotten her kindness. It was wonderful to be in the comfort of a home rather than a hotel. Instead of sharing a room, even though they had to accommodate their own four girls and a boy, they had made space for us to have separate rooms. I had already met Yasmin, the oldest daughter, who was just nineteen and had spent Eid with us in Larkana as well as accompanying us on Benazir's Frontier tour; her sister Samiya, who was eighteen, was engaged to a Pashtun, Tariq Akbar. Then there was Samina (who later followed in her father's footsteps and became a dentist) and finally, twins Mona and Sultan, who were nine years old. Dr Niazi's mother also lived in the house and often sat outside on the verandah, crying because her son was in jail.* Needless to say the change of location did not mean that the team of intelligence CID (Criminal Investigation Department) men, who had been following Benazir since her arrival in Rawalpindi, stopped their surveillance. Instead of being parked outside Flashman's, they took up a position along the road leading to the Niazis' house. Whenever Benazir moved, they followed.

The day of our return from the Frontier, Benazir told me that we had been invited out to lunch at the Holiday Inn (now the Marriott Hotel) in Islamabad by Peter Galbraith's mother, Catherine Galbraith, who had known Benazir since her Harvard days, when she and Peter were contemporaries.† 'My father specifically asked my mother to go to Pakistan with two goals in mind – to let Benazir (Pinkie as they still thought of her) and Nusrat know that they were not forgotten by their American friends and to signal to the Pakistani military that there was prominent American interest in ZAB,' recalled Peter decades later. Amna Piracha, who was still working with the lawyers, came with us. It was a welcome distraction from reality to see someone seemingly from another world who was genuinely concerned at what might happen to Benazir's father. 'I remember my mother's report on meeting you all,' continued Peter. 'It was so sad as it seemed nothing could stop the juggernaut to the hanging and both you and Benazir seemed so alone.'[7]

On the same day – 15 September – we received the unsettling news that Zia had made himself the sixth president of Pakistan, enabling him to act with even less accountability than if he were just chief martial law administrator. More ominously, his self-promotion meant that if the time came for a mercy petition to

---

* Dr Zafar Niazi (1930–2002) and Shaukat Niazi (1931–2017).
† Catherine Galbraith (1913–2008).

be made to save Bhutto's life, Zia had the authority to accept or reject it. 'I hope the struggle will be over soon and all will be well,' I wrote in my diary the following day. 'But somehow I fear there is worse to come. And, in a way, I have been so much part of it, I have forgotten what it is like to be without it.'[8]

In early October Benazir began making preparations for another political tour, this time in the Punjab. Yasmin, who had taken on the role of her personal assistant, helping to keep note of her interviews and appointments, accompanied her while I stayed in Islamabad to attend the appeal in Rawalpindi. Within days, Benazir was arrested in Multan. Her mother had already been moved from Lahore to Islamabad where, in order to be closer to visit her husband, she was staying in a house – designated a sub-jail – placed at her disposal for the duration by Ehsan Piracha, Amna's brother. Benazir was taken directly from the airport to join her mother, who mistakenly believed that she'd come for an unscheduled visit. It seemed ironic that her tours to address people 'within four walls' had now confined her, yet again, within four walls. 'It is terrible the way they arrested B.,' I told my parents, 'dragged her on the runway and her feet are all injured. Later tonight Yasmin and I are taking her things around and maybe I shall get a glimpse of her.'[9]

In the days ahead, having brought one of our Olympia type-writers with us, I continued to type whatever Benazir asked me. Often in the evening while in my room at the Niazis', I would hear the roar of a motorcycle followed by the ring of the doorbell, indicating the arrival of one of the servants, Ibrahim. From the folds of his *shalwar kameez*, or sometimes from under his helmet, he would produce sheets of paper in Zulfikar Ali Bhutto's familiar handwriting. There was always an urgency and so, regardless of what else I was doing, I would begin to type, sometimes two or three hours into the night. The following morning Ibrahim would return to pick up the typewritten sheets together with the originals. Since the servants delivered food to Benazir in her sub-jail, I was able to write to her virtually every day, my letters carefully concealed, as were her responses to me. On one occasion, when D. M. Awan was going to visit her, Yasmin and I thought we would ride in the car with him so we might catch sight of her, our previous attempt having failed. 'There was a great hue and cry,' I informed my parents, 'because the policeman said that Yasmin and I would have to get out, if the car were to proceed. All we wanted to do was wave and say hello.'

Eventually in the distance we saw her figure on the balcony and we waved. 'It was quite sad,' I continued in my letter home. 'It is a strange feeling knowing that she is in the house locked up.' 'Cannot believe how very mean they are not to even let you come to the gate,' Benazir later wrote to me. 'What dire secrets did they think we would exchange or what devious plots hatch that they could not let you near?'[10]

With Benazir back in detention, it was as though things had gone full circle to when I had arrived in Pakistan five months earlier. But, from knowing no one, my friends in Islamabad now included the Niazi family, the lawyers and the journalists – who were regularly in attendance in the Supreme Court, not only from Britain but numerous other countries worldwide. Simon Henderson had gone home and his replacement as the stringer for *The Financial Times* and BBC was Chris Sherwell. Then there was Peter Niesewand, who had arrived in Pakistan as the *Guardian's* correspondent. He had already made a name for himself, having spent six months in prison under Ian Smith's regime in Rhodesia (now Zimbabwe): his 'crime', as I discovered, was that he had written three reports on Rhodesian security forces' operations against guerrillas and, when challenged by the authorities, had refused to divulge his sources. He had also worked in Beirut during the worst days of the Lebanese civil war and so Pakistan was still regarded as a comparatively soft posting.* Another journalist who regularly attended the Supreme Court was Bruce Loudon, correspondent for the *Daily Telegraph*. My encounters with the resident Reuters correspondent, Trevor Wood, were more unsettling because he kept telling me that I had got too emotionally involved and, with Benazir under house arrest, I ought to go home.†

Although Benazir was no longer living at the Niazis' house, the family kindly agreed for me to continue to stay; but the intelligence agencies had not forsaken their position along the road, and two cars and a motorbike had started following me wherever I went. 'They are so stupid they do not merit consideration,' I had reassured my parents. 'They are just a nuisance.'[11] But their presence did have some effect since being followed by Pakistan's CID had the potential to isolate me from the diplomatic community, whose members I wanted to keep informed about Zulfikar Ali Bhutto's appeal, as well as hearing what they had to say. On one occasion, I had been invited to a reception to celebrate the Chinese New Year, where I had met a diplomat from the Austrian Embassy. He invited me to dinner at his residence, but once he realised I was under surveillance, the invitation was not repeated. When I encountered him again, he said half-apologetically that, although it was nice to have a 'new face' at a dinner party, he could not risk having his address noted down by the intelligence agencies. Luckily others didn't care.

'Things here do not look very hopeful,' I wrote home in early November. 'I have met a number of diplomats – they are all saying that Zia is not only intending but preparing to hang Mr Bhutto.'

---

* Chris Sherwell (b.1947); Peter Niesewand (1944–83).
† Bruce Loudon now writes for the *Australian*. He came to Karachi in 2007 and still writes on Pakistan; Trevor Wood (1939/40–2016).

But, I continued in another letter, 'Of course what one hopes is that it will not reach the military and the judiciary will free him.'[12]

While continuing to attend the Supreme Court, I was trying to get permission to visit Benazir, which meant filing an application to the Punjab home secretary in Lahore and following it up with a series of phone calls. 'Hello,' I would say. 'I hope you have received my application to visit Miss Benazir Bhutto?' I would then hear a distinct shuffling of papers at the other end. 'Madam. Sorry Mr Home Secretary is not here. Please call back.'

Finally – nearly six weeks after she'd been detained – permission came through. 'They said two hours but I was allowed to stay for 3 and a half hours and lunch,' I told my parents. But the attentive ear of a policewoman sitting near by meant that our conversation was more stilted than it might have been. As I got up to leave, Benazir encouraged me to make another application straight away because 'now that they have let you come once, they should do so again'. Soon after my visit, Begum Bhutto was freed. Fortunately she was allowed to stay in the house where Benazir was confined and so at least there was some coming and going to mitigate the loneliness of her continuing detention.

Meanwhile the appeal in the Supreme Court was taking its inexorable course. 'Things are beginning to move,' I informed my parents. 'The prosecution has finished arguing.'[13] In late November the veteran BBC journalist, Mark Tully, arrived from Delhi to report on the progress of Bhutto's appeal. Given the length of time he had spent in South Asia including his childhood (and working for the BBC since 1965), he had a particular way of getting himself established; the story I heard was as follows: in order to find the same driver he had used on previous visits to Rawalpindi, he used to go to the taxi stand and shout, in a very loud voice: 'Saleem'. After a few minutes a rather scruffy but very competent driver would appear either from inside or under his car and drive him about town for the duration of his stay. On arrival Mark took up residence at Flashman's, his proximity giving him easy access to Bhutto's team of lawyers. In view of his stature and the reputation of the BBC, it was inevitable that what he broadcast would reach a wide audience, and, while he was reporting from Rawalpindi, we hung on his every word.*

At the same time as the arrival of 'Tully Sahib', there was some good news: Dr Niazi had been released on bail and, for the first time, I met this quiet but courageous man who had not been afraid to speak out. It was lovely to see the family reunited and his mother no longer sat on the verandah and wept. Although I was still doing some typing for Benazir, in my spare time (having finished the short educational book I'd written on the UN and sent it to the publishers), I'd decided to write a book on what I'd witnessed in Pakistan. Still hoping that the appeal would be upheld, I thought I had nothing to lose by documenting what I had learnt about the trial and appeal. 'Finally put my fingers to the typewriter to begin to write,' I noted in my diary on 26 November.[14] Instead of making it 'my' story and writing in the first person, I chose to record events as they had unfolded in the third person. When I told Benazir she was delighted. 'If it is half as good as your article for the *Spectator*, it *will* be published.'[15]

'Meantime, books are being read with a voracious appetite,' she continued in another letter.

Aside from the seven new Mills and Boons sent by Yasmin – hors deauvres (wrong spelling) – have finished William Buckley's rather disturbing but quite devastating novel, 'The Stained Glass'. Buckley may be to capitalism what Karl Marx

---

* Sir Mark Tully, KBE (b.1935) was BBC correspondent and bureau chief in Delhi until 1994.

was to Communism, but he is truly a man of tremendous depth and intelligence and talent – all this in such an arch reactionary? America provides the stimulus for creative thinking and development of talents in a manner quite unlike any other country... perhaps if I have some time, I will take a summer course at Harvard just to revive my brain cells. Don't laugh, I'm quite serious.[16]

What was remarkable about Benazir during these days was her strength of character, and, with all she had to worry about, her concern for me. 'I know you did not come for a holiday, but it cannot be too pleasant in a foreign country not knowing many people and being hounded by the CID and with the person you are visiting locked up,' she wrote in late November. The stress she was under was immense. In the same letter she again referred to the night the military came to take her father away from their home. 'You see the army invaded our house on September 3 in such a brutal and barbaric manner that I still suffer from it. It has scarred me psychologically. If I hear the slightest sound, I think it is the Army commandoes breaking into the house with their submachine guns.'[17]

Given the harsh reality of Benazir and her family's situation, I marvelled how, on occasion, her old sense of humour shone through. In another letter she told me that Yasmin had made a sponge cake which she'd been enjoying. 'There go all my wonderful plans of dieting.' She ended her letter with news of a visit to the dentist (not, alas, Dr Niazi), who, she said, in addition to doing some fillings, had slightly straightened her front teeth so she felt she looked 'less like a rabbit', although neither of her parents had noticed! As usual I tried to send her some small items with my letters. 'Thanks for the mars bars and the smarties,' she continued. 'Now that my cavities have been filled up I can begin anew on the process of having them eroded through the pleasurable process of sweets. If you could find some black magic chocolates that would be even nicer.' She ended her letter with news about her typing. 'I have been quite a busy little beaver with the typewriter but somehow my typewriting does not improve and to boot, my handwriting has deteriorated. Now I will not be able to tease you about your handwriting. Nonetheless, now I understand why people who type rarely write letters in their hand. It just feels uncomfortable to hold a pen and more laborious when the fingers get used to tip tapping. Love, B xxxxx.'[18]

'All Pakistan is for Bhutto apart from the people at the top,' I informed my parents at the beginning of December, describing how, when I was out shopping with a friend, the shopkeeper had said: 'So you are Miss Victoria? I can tell you all our community is for Mr Bhutto, but our mouths are sealed.'[19]

As the heat of the Pakistani summer was replaced by beautiful crisp sunny days and cold nights, there was bad news, along with some more good news: the bad news was that one of the judges, Justice Waheeduddin Ahmed, had fallen ill and been hospitalised. On being discharged from hospital, he sent a letter to the court confirming his intention to return. 'But he was stopped from returning to the bench by design,' recalled Amna Piracha, 'as the military had come to know that Justice Waheeduddin had decided to concur with the opinion of Justice Safdar Shah who was evidently going to uphold Mr Bhutto's appeal.'

This meant that instead of the original nine judges who had begun hearing the appeal, only seven remained; another judge, Justice Qaiser Khan, had retired at the end of July. In this instance, the established procedure was not followed. 'The practice is that where the retirement date of a judge falls during the pendency of a case it is unprecedented to ask him to proceed with retirement.' Since both these judges had been resolutely questioning the prosecution's case, from having believed that there was the chance of a majority 5–4 vote in favour of upholding the appeal, it now appeared that the vote could be 3–4 against. Although this was speculation, Waheeduddin's departure cast a dark shadow over our spirits.[20]

The good news was that Yahya Bakhtiar's request for Zulfikar Ali Bhutto to be allowed to appear in court to present his defence had been granted on the grounds that, owing to what the defence lawyers had argued was the bias of the Lahore High Court, he had boycotted proceedings and no defence witnesses had been called. Despite rumours of Zia's intent, the fact that permission had been granted seemed positive. My immediate priority was securing a new pass, since all our old passes were cancelled. Others, whose passes were not renewed, were disappointed, as was Benazir, who was not allowed out of house arrest to see her father's appearance in court. 'It is so unfair – here I have been illegally detained and cannot go to see my Father's historic appearance to address the Court. My blood is really boiling.'[21]

On the appointed day – 18 December – Peter Niesewand and I arrived early at the entrance to the Supreme Court where crowds were already beginning to gather, hopeful of gaining entry. We secured a good position in the courtroom almost directly in front of the podium where Bhutto would stand so that we could see him from the front rather than the back. As he entered the courtroom, there was sudden silence before, almost simultaneously, everyone got up from their seats to salute him. Dressed in a suit which seemed a little too large, he began to speak. It was like a spell had been broken. While working on the rejoinder, I had written numerous notes to him but this was the first time I was seeing the former prime minister in the flesh. He began slowly, as though it had been a long time (which it had) since he had spoken in front of people.

'Not only my life but according to my objective appreciation, far more is at stake,' he said. 'My reputation, my political career, the honour and future of my family and above all the future of Pakistan itself are involved. This is my view. It might be a mistaken view but it is an honest and sincere view and I am not trying to dramatize or exaggerate it.'[22] On that first morning, after he had finished speaking, he turned towards Yahya Bakhtiar and said something. Suddenly he leant over the side of the podium and stretched out his hand to me. I heard Bakhtiar saying, 'Yes, that is Victoria.' Instantly I shook his outstretched hand but then suddenly the handshake was broken by security officers surrounding him. Later Bakhtiar told me that he had wanted to thank me for all the work I had done. 'It was just all I ever wanted by way of gratitude,' I noted in my diary.[23]

The following day when Peter and I tried to get the same places, we saw that oversized security officers were already occupying them. I found a seat where at least I could see Bhutto's profile so I could do some sketches, having already drawn most of the judges and some of the lawyers. When the local journalists saw what I was doing they offered to buy my sketch of Bhutto but I refused, saying it was for Benazir. Thinking back, my amateur sketch was the last pictorial representation anyone made of him. Zulfikar Ali Bhutto's appearance lasted four days. Each day he went from strength to strength, as he refuted the accusations against him. Having dealt with the charge of conspiracy to murder, he addressed the more personal aspects of what he termed his maltreatment and the bias of the Lahore High Court which had tried him. 'I want to be under the law but not underground the law.' His concluding comments mirrored those of the defence. 'There was no agreement. It is all a fantasy to involve me. There was no motive, no conspiracy.' He finished by thanking the judges again for allowing him to speak. 'When talking about taking the life of an innocent man, at least hear him.'[24] And then he was gone. I never saw him again nor did anyone else other than his family members, the lawyers and prison guards. After his appearance I wrote another article for the *Spectator*. I also wrote up his appearance for my book which I sent with some draft chapters to Benazir. I was gratified by her response. 'The chapters I have seen are so well written and they completely capture attention. The one on Appearance made the whole scene at the Supreme Court reappear before my eyes.'[25]

(c) Zulfikar Ali Bhutto during his appearance in the Supreme Court of Pakistan, December 1978. *I found a seat where at least I could see Bhutto's profile so I could do some sketches, having already drawn most of the judges and some of the lawyers.*

With the excitement of Bhutto's appearance over, and the court about to adjourn, I had decided to go home for Christmas. All the arguments had been presented and judgment was not due until sometime in January or even February. When I told Benazir, she had responded by saying that she wished she too could 'hop over to England' to see her brothers and sister. 'It's simply ages since we have all met. In fact, I do not think we have ever been apart for as long a period ever before.'[26] She also recognised that my parents must be missing me. 'And I am glad for myself that you are coming back.' Despite everything on her mind, she had managed to get me a Christmas present to open when I got home as well as a present for my mother. 'The green present is for your Mummy and the blue one for you. It is very difficult shopping thru' staff. In your present's case, I had the whole shop brought here before deciding – which took a week.' It was a simple gold bangle which I have treasured.[27]

My flight was booked for Christmas Eve. I was still wearing a cotton *shalwar kameez* when I arrived at Heathrow late at night during what was to be one of the coldest winters on record. My parents had not received the telegram I had sent telling them that I was coming home, and so there was no one to meet me. Having found a telephone box, but with no English money, I put in a 'reverse charges' telephone call. By the time I got through to speak to my mother, I had started crying out of the sheer emotion of being back in England. I had been away for seven months but I felt as though I had come from a different planet. On Christmas Day we went to drinks with some of my parents' friends. No one knew anything about Pakistan and they had no idea about Zulfikar Ali Bhutto's appeal against the death sentence. I felt as awkward and lacking in conversation as a teenager.

4

'Martyrs do not die': 1979

*Even if they go so far as to hang my father, they can't
take away his genius or his place in history.* [1]

It snowed heavily at New Year all over England and, so I was told,
remained extremely cold for four months. Before returning to
Pakistan I'd decided to write to the prime minister, the Rt Hon.
James Callaghan, drawing his attention to the conclusion of
Bhutto's appeal and the impending judgment.* 'In spite of the appeal
people are still afraid that the death sentence might be upheld
and clemency might not be shown,' I informed him. A response
came from his political assistant: 'The Prime Minister has asked
me to reply to your letter concerning Mr Bhutto. He was interested to read your comments and will certainly bear your views in
mind': non-committal but at least I had made my views known. [2]

I'd also written to Margaret Thatcher, reminding her of our
meeting after Benazir was elected president of the Union (not forgetting her visit to Pakistan in 1976 when she had been received
by Benazir's father as prime minister):

---

* Baron Callaghan of Cardiff, KG, PC (1912–2005) was prime minister of the
UK 1976–79.

Although the appeal was conducted in a fair manner, it is still possible for political considerations to be taken into account when determining the judgment. I fully realise that interfering in the internal affairs of Pakistan is not possible for any politician, but I do believe that his case is still a matter for Britain's concern, especially bearing in mind the number of Pakistanis we have here. I therefore felt it my duty to write to you. Benazir has good memories of our tea together in the House of Commons, which to her seems a lifetime ago.

'Your letter was read with interest here and a careful note has been made of what you say,' responded Matthew Parris, from the 'Private Office of the Leader of the Opposition'.[3]

While I was in England, I went to London to see Mir. It felt strange seeing Benazir's brother again after the seven months I had spent in Pakistan: I was no longer the naïve English friend of his sister he had last seen, but a well-informed commentator. Or at least that was how I felt. In the meantime he and Shahnawaz had been busy trying to impress upon the international community that the due process of law in Pakistan could easily be subverted under Zia's military dictatorship. While we spent time discussing positively what might still be done, our goodbye was non-committal, neither of us knowing what would happen before we met again. Before taking the train home to my parents, I went to Oxford Street to buy some blank videos which Benazir had asked me to get for the Niazis, as well as some jeans which they'd asked for. After all their kindness it was the least I could do.

On 10 January I flew to Islamabad. Two weeks in the comfort of my home had made me realise how much I had missed my secure environment. At the same time I felt I must go back for Benazir's sake. My book was half-written – and if I didn't return, how would I ever write the ending? Such was the pent-up emotion that I found myself crying the whole way back to Islamabad; my neighbour on the plane, a Canadian, offered to get me a drink, perhaps in the hope of finding out why I was crying. I found it impossible to explain that I was crying because my friend's father was languishing in a death cell and could well be hanged.

On arrival my bags were searched. The blank videos were confiscated, but I was allowed to keep the jeans. I went immediately to the Niazis. Their security had been doubled and, since the intelligence agencies had detected my arrival and were once more trailing me, we decided that I had better stay somewhere else. Given my few friends and the surveillance I was under, my options were limited. Before Christmas I had met Gustavo Toro, who worked for the United Nations Development Programme (UNDP) in Islamabad. At the time he'd had another house guest, Jamil Dehlavi, a film director who'd recently made a film called the 'Blood of Hussain'. I was hoping that he might have space for me so long as he did not mind taking in an Englishwoman who was writing a book on the trial (and possibly execution) of the former prime minister. He agreed, I think, partly because, being from Chile, he had lived through the assassination of Allende in 1973 and had no sympathy for military dictatorships and surveillance tactics. I was grateful for the safe haven he provided and the Chilean background music which I listened to all the time. Most importantly he lent me a typewriter.

My first priority was to get a note to Benazir and tell her about my visit home and give her first-hand news of her family. In addition to some cosmetics and magazines, I'd brought back a novel to give to Benazir by Celia Thomson, another LMH Oxford friend, who'd written it as a challenge to see if she could write a romantic novel in the style of Mills and Boon. Having read it, Benazir returned it to me with a note: 'If Celia can write a novel like this, why can't we?!'! She concluded her letter with a sentence which again revealed her bravery: '... love as always, keep your chin up, no matter how bad the times we must pass it with courage and dignity... B xxxxxx'.[4]

The court had not yet assembled. One by one the journalists began to reappear after a welcome break from the mounting tension. Chris Sherwell was following a story about Pakistan's nuclear programme which it appeared was not solely for 'peaceful purposes'. Apart from the possibility that plutonium might be extracted from the country's existing nuclear facility, the suggestion was that the government had a clandestine programme to enrich uranium. The key man was a nuclear physicist, Abdul Qadeer (A. Q.) Khan; his activities were part of the larger nuclear programme instigated by Zulfikar Ali Bhutto in the early 1970s, alluded to by Bhutto in the rejoinder, when he had emphasised his own contribution. Once General Zia took over, Khan was given a more prominent position, with the research centre at Kahuta (named the Khan Research Laboratories) coming under direct military control.[5] It was an extraordinary story which was to have its denouement twenty-five years later when Khan admitted (and was later pardoned for) his role in nuclear proliferation.* At the time, these events were a relative sideshow to our focal point of interest: the outcome of Bhutto's appeal. After talking to Chris and other journalists, I realised that the euphoria following Bhutto's Supreme Court appearance seemed to have evaporated and people were now fearing the worst.

International media interest had dramatically increased. On

---

* Dr A. Q. Khan, NI, HI, FPAS (b.1936). In July 1979 while trying to locate Khan's house in Islamabad, Sherwell was beaten up and held in custody; freed after several hours, he had to leave Pakistan as a result. Khan was pardoned in 2009 but forbidden to leave the country.

31 January I received a phone call from the ITN TV presenter Sandy Gall, who'd arrived in Islamabad with his television crew. Having invited me out to lunch at the Holiday Inn, he asked what the mood was like among Bhutto's supporters, as we awaited the verdict. 'Not very hopeful,' I found myself saying. In the days to come, other senior journalists flocked in, among them Brian Barron from BBC News;* Mark Tully also returned from Delhi. Often Peter Niesewand and Bruce Loudon asked me to join them for lunch 'poolside' at the Holiday Inn where they were more or less in permanent residence. The hotel had a good bookstore and was one of the best locations to find books for Benazir. She especially liked biographies.

Meanwhile I continued to work on my book. Having written the later chapters on the period I had experienced, one of the challenges I faced was filling in the period before I had arrived in Pakistan. I gained inspiration from the book Peter had written after his time in prison in Rhodesia. What he had done very effectively was to recreate the dialogue of his trial by using the court transcripts, and so, having borrowed the transcripts from the lawyers, this was the technique I now used to capture the atmosphere of Yahya Bakhtiar's opening remarks at the beginning of May:

> *Bakhtiar*: I will briefly state the main points. The defence case,
>   as is apparent, of Mr Zulfikar Ali Bhutto is based on three
>   main grounds.
> *Chief Justice*: Yes.
> *Bakhtiar*: It is a false, fabricated and politically motivated case –
>   a case of the international conspiracy of which Mr Zulfikar
>   Ali Bhutto is a victim. He was removed from power as

---

* Sandy Gall, CMG, CBE (b.1927) was ITN reporter and news reader from 1963 to 1991; Brian Barron, MBE (1940–2009).

elected Prime Minister of the country forcibly, with a view
to eliminating him politically and physically.

Chief Justice: Politically and physically?

Bakhtiar: So that he is politically and physically eliminated.

Another judge: Politically eliminated.

Bakhtiar: Yes, my Lord, and physically. My second ground of
attack is that he was tried by a thoroughly hostile and biased
Bench.

Another judge: Pardon?[6]

And so the dialogue proceeded.

I also had to learn about the trial. A key element, as Awan
explained, was the *malafides* of the Lahore High Court bench,
which Bhutto maintained was prejudiced against him (and which
explained why he was so intent on making his defence in the
Supreme Court). As I went through the relevant court documents,
my narrative took shape. Having acquired an old briefcase, I
carried my manuscript around with me wherever I went, mindful
that if I lost the chapters then I would have lost the book (no time
machine or cloud in those days on which to save my chapters).
When the early chapters were drafted I sent them to my parents
in England through several friendly couriers. Especially helpful
were other journalists or those working for the UN because their
suitcases would not be searched. My conversation with a target
courier invariably began: 'I am writing this book, but I don't trust
the post. Would you mind posting this envelope when you get
to England?' My letters to my parents always included a request
to send more British stamps so that I could more easily request
someone to post a letter at home. I also kept up my correspondence
with Benazir, filling her in on everything which was happening
and what I was doing.

So preoccupied were we with Bhutto's appeal that events in

neighbouring Afghanistan seemed less important. But it was already apparent that Pakistan was not going to be immune. Ever since the Soviet-backed coup in April 1978, hundreds of Afghan refugees had been entering the NWFP across the porous Durand Line, established by the British in 1893 to mark the frontier between British India and Afghanistan following an agreement between the foreign secretary, Sir Mortimer Durand, and the Amir of Afghanistan, Abdur Rehman.* While most refugees found a new home in the refugee camps which were established throughout the province, others made their way to Islamabad in search of work. My UNDP friend, Gustavo Toro, had taken pity on one of them and hired him as a gardener even though his house did not have much of a garden. One day I came into the house and found him listening to the portable radio. He looked embarrassed because he was in a part of the house into which he was not supposed to venture. But when I realised that he was listening to the BBC World Service for news of Afghanistan, I let him finish. A few weeks later, he disappeared and took the radio with him.

Subsequently I met the Afghan experts Louis and Nancy Dupree, who had a specialist knowledge of the country's cultural heritage.† Being American, they were regarded with suspicion by the Afghan authorities and had recently been asked to leave, which explained their presence in Islamabad. Their descriptions were of a beautiful country, locked in time, which they had been visiting since the 1960s, but which was now being devastated by a civil war. As they explained, the inhabitants of this land-locked territory, which did not have a single railway, were very conservative and the

---

* Sir Mortimer Durand, GCMG, KCSI, KCIE, PC (1850–1924) was foreign secretary of India 1884–94; Abdur Rehman Khan (1840/44–1901) was Amir of Afghanistan 1880–1901.
† Louis Dupree (1925–89) and Nancy Dupree (1927–2017).

new regime, with its socialist ideology, had not been well received in the rural areas.

Yet there was another side to the argument. Much as we were concerned about the communist influence in Afghanistan, people also realised that backing the conservative element in Afghan society might not be the solution to the country's problems either. 'You see these bearded fundamentalists who are opposed to the new government?' an American (almost certainly CIA) said on another occasion when Afghanistan came up again in conversation: 'We are bound to support them against any government backed by the Soviet Union. But have you any idea how conservative they are? For example, has anyone thought about how they treat their women?' In some respects he was right. At the time we had no idea of the extent of their conservatism, and nor had many of their backers.[7]

Neighbouring Iran was also in the throes of revolution. Once again, only a few seemed to understand the gravity of the situation. When I met the Iranian ambassador at a reception before Christmas, he had wrongly assured me that the Shah of Iran, Reza Pahlavi, whose father had founded the dynasty, would never be forced out of Iran by what he termed 'the religious fanatics'. But on 16 January the Shah went into exile. On 1 February the Shia religious leader, Ayatollah Khomeini, received a rapturous welcome when he returned to Iran after nearly fifteen years in exile. A year later the impact of the Iranian revolution was brought home to us when, in May 1980, one of our Oxford friends, Bahram Dehqani-Tafti, a gifted musician, was murdered, while his father, the Anglican bishop of Iran, Hassan Dehqani-Tafti survived an assassination attempt.*

---

* Mohammed Reza Pahlavi (1919–80) was Shah of Iran 1941–79; Sayyid Ruhollah Musavi Khomeini (1902–89) was supreme leader of Iran (Ayatollah

In Islamabad many were feeling suffocated under the political ban. Elections were promised for 1979 and so people wanted to campaign, but the date had not been announced and it was clear that no elections would be held until Bhutto's fate was decided. No one quite knew what was happening and so fantastic rumours were circulating: that Bhutto had made, was making or would make a deal with Zia; that Zia had visited Bhutto in jail – which we all knew was nonsense. Censorship was widely in evidence, newspapers appearing with long blank columns. The propaganda campaign against Bhutto in the press and on television had not abated, one programme called *Story of Atrocities* giving vignettes of the alleged 'tyranny' of the Bhutto government. Various people were interviewed on state-run television, relating their own 'tales of woe'. Not content with the TV programmes, more White Papers were published, excerpts of which were given pride of place in the newspapers. For PPP political supporters it was very depressing; for the family it was devastating. 'I am afraid people are expecting the worst, which is too terrible for words,' I told my parents. 'There have been a number of arrests. We are all just waiting.'[8]

On 6 February the seven justices of the Supreme Court re-assembled to give their judgment. I hadn't realised that we all needed new passes and so I was not allowed into the courtroom. 'You are not a journalist,' I was informed, 'but a friend of Benazir Bhutto. Sorry there is nothing we can do.'[9] The gates to the Supreme Court were locked and for the duration I sat glumly on the roadside at the entrance. Suddenly people started running from the courtroom. One of the first to exit in great haste was the BBC's Brian Barron. Then Peter Niesewand came out. 'The appeal

Khomeini) 1979–89; Bahram Dehqani-Tafti (1955–80); Bishop Hassan Dehqani-Tafti (1920–2008).

has been rejected,' he said, confirming what I had already begun to suspect. We started walking along the road together to Flashman's to see the lawyers. What was staggering was that three out of the seven judges had upheld his appeal, while four rejected it, making it a split verdict. According to Anwar ul Haq's judgment: 'Any omissions, errors or irregularities, or even illegalities, that have crept in, were not of such a nature as did not [sic] vitiate the trial.' The three judges who upheld the appeal were the ones who, throughout the proceedings, were most vocal in their questioning: Dorab Patel, Mohammad Haleem and Ghulam Safdar Shah, whose judgment stated that he did not have 'the slightest doubt in my mind that the prosecution has totally failed to prove its case against Mr Bhutto'.[10] Our thoughts turned immediately to the fact that two judges had been retired while the appeal was being heard. Had they remained, would the verdict have gone the other way? When Peter and I reached Flashman's the expression on all the lawyers' faces showed how utterly deflated they were. Their last resort was to draft a petition to review the judgment.

'I expected acquittal. The Punjab judges have pronounced the death sentence on Pakistan,' Benazir wrote to me, highlighting the fact that the four judges who had upheld the judgment were all from the Punjab whereas those who had upheld the appeal were from the other provinces. 'The political implications of it will tear the country apart. If a hair on my Father's body is touched, I shall file an FIR [First Investigation Report] naming Zia, the Lahore High Court judges and the four Supreme Court Judges along with Kasuri for murder. They accuse us of conspiring and using police officers as assassins. How ironical. They have conspired to murder and their assassins are the judges.'[11]

I immediately sat down to write another article for the *Spectator*. 'Judgment in Zulfikar Ali Bhutto's appeal against the death sentence came swiftly,' I began. 'It took only a few minutes for the

Chief Justice of the Supreme Court of Pakistan to state that, by a majority decision, the appeal of the former prime minister was dismissed.' I found it hard to be optimistic. 'Those who had previously been unable to conceive of the judgment being upheld are now more sceptical,' I continued. 'General Zia-ul-Haq, Pakistan's military ruler, had previously announced that if the Supreme Court upheld the verdict, he would send Mr Bhutto to the gallows.'[12]

Once more my priority was to request another visit to see Benazir (her mother once more with her under house arrest). Soon afterwards a typewritten letter on a scruffy piece of paper arrived, granting me permission to see 'detainee Benazir Bhutto'. The print was faint and I thought I must have missed something as there was no date for my visit. So I phoned up the home secretary's office in Lahore to tell him that I had been given permission to see Benazir but I didn't know when. When finally I got through to his office I was informed that the permission had elapsed and that I must apply again. It was so upsetting that my simple request could be so mired in obfuscation. When, on my behalf, Benazir wrote what she described as 'a stinking letter' about my visit (or lack of it), the response was that I should 'have contacted the Jail Superintendent for the purpose', as if I should have known.[13]

'Yet again I write to you requesting permission to visit my friend Miss Benazir Bhutto. Unfortunately due to a misunderstanding the permission which you kindly granted to me did not reach me until after the specified date and time,' I wrote again to the home secretary, Punjab government.[14]

On 11 February I received another note from Benazir. She had begun it on the 9th but said that no one had come to the house to enable her to send it sooner. Although she didn't have any particular news, she had wanted to thank me for my 'solidarity and for helping out when everything is in such turmoil'. Once again I marvelled at her strength; my situation was as nothing compared to hers and yet she had chosen to thank me. The news she now gave me was disturbing.

'I think they want to ensure that Mummy or I do not run away. They are taking us away to an isolated rest house in Sihala called the PIDC [Pakistan Industrial Development Corporation] rest house, which means that our contact with the outside world will be perforce less.' She then continued with a request: 'dearest Vicks please could you go to the Am. and Brit. libraries and photostat all material on Pakistan since the judgment. It is awful not having any foreign press clippings to see the world reaction.'[15] When I asked the lawyers what was the significance of the move they looked at me despairingly.

'This is a bad sign,' Awan said, 'because it means if the worst happens the crowds will have more difficulty in gathering outside the house.'

On 12 February I received a telephone call telling me that I was allowed to see Benazir the next day. Later I received a confirmatory carbon letter which said: 'Miss Victoria Schofield is hereby' – the 'hereby' was crossed out – 'allowed to see Miss Benazir Bhutto for two hours on 13-2-1979.' It took about an hour to drive to the heavily guarded rest house on the outskirts of Rawalpindi. When I arrived a policewoman was at the gate to search me. I hadn't brought anything and so there was nothing to search. 'We sat out in the gardens until it was too cold and too dark,' I told my parents. 'In her optimism B. managed to say "it must have been really lovely here [when the property was maintained], it's a bit like Murree".' Now the garden was neglected and the house had been turned into office buildings which smelt and were in bad repair.[16]

However, I felt that my company had not been very distracting and so after my visit I wrote to apologise for being boring. She responded:

> If you think you were being boring, think of the complex you will give me because I see no one so I'm the one who'll become boring... To see you was so good and somehow refreshing. It's a strange word to describe a meeting such as ours but when you live in such cramped and stultifying circumstances, cut off and isolated, what other words but refreshing can one use to describe a meeting with an English rose (... oh dear, I can see I am getting into practice for the Mills and Boons that I aim to write...) Love, B.[17]

How we both longed to turn the clock back and be back in Oxford talking freely like we used to and, most importantly, laughing! One comment which Benazir had made during my visit was prescient: 'Even if they go so far as to hang my father, they can't take away his genius, or his place in history.'[18]

As if there wasn't enough to worry about, a contempt of court notice had been issued against several journalists for the articles they'd written after the judgment. The papers and agencies against whom the contempt notice was issued were the *Guardian*, the *Daily Telegraph*, *Reuters*, *Newsweek*, the BBC and the *Spectator* – that is, the articles and reports written by Peter, Bruce, Trevor Wood, an American journalist, Mark Tully and me. The complainant, Mr Wahabul Khairy, an advocate in Rawalpindi, was objecting to the fact that we had all emphasised that the four judges who had rejected the appeal were from the Punjab, while those who had upheld it were from the 'minority' provinces, and alleging that we were inciting provincialism. Benazir saw it as 'a heaven sent opportunity for the foreign press to play up the total alignment of the Judiciary with the Executive'.[19] When I asked Awan for his opinion, he said that the case would be dropped, which eventually it was. But given how insecure my position was, with my tenuous connection to the *Spectator*, for a few days I was worried.

In the short time allowed them after the rejection of Bhutto's appeal, the lawyers had been working on the review petition. I went regularly to see them, helping out with typing if they needed me. For some months I had been doing all the lawyers' accounts with Flashman's which Begum Bhutto had requested me to do. Although the lawyers were all working *pro bono*, their accommodation and meals had to be paid for and the bills needed reconciling. The weather was cold and wet. 'The rain makes me think of fireplaces and roasted marshmallows,' Benazir was writing on 4 March. 'But at the moment they must remain thoughts. I pass the time by listening to the TV or radio and reading what the Harvard Class of 73 is up to, having just received my only mail so far in the many months of detention – a book on the class of 73. Sounds like a movie title!'[20]

Fridays were normally days of rest, equivalent to our Sundays, and Friday 9 March appeared to be like any other. Yahya Bakhtiar had told me not to come into Rawalpindi because they did not need me. I was relieved because I was tired and glad to have a day to myself. Around lunchtime Bakhtiar's driver, Iqbal, noted for his military posture and handlebar moustache, arrived at the kitchen door. He only spoke Punjabi and so our conversation was always monosyllabic. 'Bakhtiar Sahib,' he gestured in the direction of Rawalpindi. My heart sank.

'Are you sure?' I asked him.

He repeated again affirmatively: 'Bakhtiar Sahib.'

Since I didn't want to spend forty-five minutes going to Rawalpindi unnecessarily, I motioned to Iqbal to wait while I spoke to Bakhtiar on the phone to make sure that he did need me.

'Victoria, hello, no, it's fine you take rest... no, wait, Mr Memon is saying something to me, hold on.'

Memon then came on the line. 'Ah Victoria, I know you are tired, the position is that we are all tired but, yes, I would like you to come.'

I set aside my own fatigue and got in the car to go to Rawalpindi. When I arrived Memon was sitting with Saleem.

'So you are tired?' he said to me again. I nodded. 'Yes, I understand but I am glad that you have come.'

Since Memon knew all the legal aspects of the case, he was the most competent person to write the final 'epitaph' to what would be Yahya Bakhtiar's concluding remarks and it was this document he wanted me to type while he dictated. I sat down at the typewriter. Saleem sat near Memon, ready to hand him any reference books he required. After half an hour the sentences he was dictating came more slowly and I looked up, my fingers poised over the keys waiting. Memon's face had the most awful expression and he was struggling to speak. Suddenly he cried out:

'Allah o Akbar – God is Great' and fell sideways on the sofa, where he'd been sitting.

Both Saleem and I were horrified. While he immediately picked up the telephone to call a doctor, I rushed to the next door room to alert Bakhtiar. Despite the seriousness of the situation, I remember being frightened that Bakhtiar might be annoyed at being disturbed during his afternoon rest.

'Mr Bakhtiar,' I called, knocking furiously. 'Come quickly, it's Mr Memon.'

Bakhtiar immediately followed me out of his room. In my brief absence, Memon's face had become contorted and he was groaning what, it transpired, was his last breath. He had had a massive heart attack. I had never seen anyone die before and the shock was appalling. I could not imagine what Benazir would feel at losing such an important member of her father's legal team at this critical time, when her father's life was perilously close to being taken from him. Yet again my first thought was to get a note to her so that she was forewarned when the news came on the BBC. Since Memon was from Karachi his body had to be flown immediately to his home town; the lawyers would accompany it and so I found myself booking air tickets for several lawyers and a coffin.[21]

The following morning the courtyard of Flashman's was full of people coming to pay their respects, including the lawyers for the prosecution. It seemed strange suddenly to see this intermingling of the legal fraternity who, for so many months, had kept their distance in the court room. Ghulam Ali Memon's body was lying in the coffin with his face exposed, according to Muslim custom. In the afternoon the funeral party, including Yahya Bakhtiar and D. M. Awan, left to go to Karachi for the funeral and I returned to Islamabad. Soon afterwards I received a note from Benazir. 'I could simply not believe it. I am too upset to write anything but I am so glad you wrote to us. I was relieved to know he was not on his own when it happened. His poor family; he had hardly been with them all year. I kept hoping I had heard wrong, that there was a mistake, that it was not true. Too tragic.'[22]

Memon's death meant that Anwar ul Haq was obliged to allow a short recess. When the court reassembled, the chief justice looked sympathetically towards Yahya Bakhtiar. Having expressed his admiration for Ghulam Ali Memon, he continued: 'Yes, as life has to go on, yes, Mr Bakhtiar, let's start.'

When Bakhtiar spoke, he was visibly unnerved. 'I feel like an airplane whose engine has failed and I am just waiting to fall down. I relied so heavily upon him, I just cannot believe he has gone.' Most of what he had to say was taken from Memon's 'epitaph' on the judgment, highlighting the important contradictions in the majority judgment. He concluded by giving the reasons for a lesser penalty: there was no motive to kill the man who died; the appellant was not present at the occurrence, the conviction was based on the testimony of one man who had turned 'approver', three of the seven judges of the Supreme Court had acquitted him. 'With these submission I conclude my case,' he said and sat down.[23] It was 17 March – a long year had passed since the sentence of death was passed on 18 March 1978.

Once more, we had to wait.

In the interval I spent time typing a long document which Bhutto had written, and which, in our usual fashion, Benazir arranged to have delivered to me by one of the servants. Bhutto's intention was to counter an article captioned 'Before the President fell', written by former civil servant and journalist Altaf Gauhar, and published in the *Guardian*. Gauhar, who was now co-editor of the *Guardian Third World Review*, was a federal secretary in the information ministry during Ayub Khan's military rule (1953–69) and had known Bhutto since Bhutto's appointment as foreign minister in 1963. The article was a scathing attack, accusing the former prime minister of running the country 'like his private estate'. Whatever Gauhar's animosity, at this critical juncture, when it was clear that Bhutto had so little time to live, his article seemed both inopportune and cruel.[24] By way of rebuttal Bhutto wrote a lengthy document, titled 'The growth of bureaucracy', validating his actions both as foreign minister under Ayub and as president and prime minister from 1972 to 1977. He also related what he considered were some 'home truths' about Gauhar. Unlike the rejoinder, since this was not a court document Benazir asked me to put it in the third person. As I sat once more looking at Bhutto's handwriting, with which I had become so familiar, it seemed unbelievable to think that this might be one of the last things he wrote. Running to nearly thirty typed pages, it became known as 'Bhutto's Testament'.*

On Benazir's suggestion, I wrote again to the home secretary to request regular visits to see her. She said that I should also complain about being constantly followed. 'Dear Mr Home Secretary,' I began.

> As a foreigner, albeit friend of Miss Benazir Bhutto, I see no reason why my every action should be subject to scrutiny by between two and four men (at times it has been six travelling in a jeep, a car and a motorbike). Not only is it an invasion of my privacy but it is making my life in Pakistan quite unpleasant. In addition, the fact that I am surveyed so minutely makes my own presence in Pakistan appear to be far more controversial than it is; it is making me into an important personality, which is not the case at all.

An added complaint was that the men had begun to peer into the windows of the house which was 'a further intrusion into my privacy unless I choose to sit all day with the curtains drawn'.[25]

---

* Zulfikar Ali Bhutto, 'The growth of bureaucracy', ('Bhutto's Testament'), typed manuscript. In an article published in the *New Statesman* on 23 October 1981 Tariq Ali cited passages from Bhutto's Testament which became the subject of a court case against the journal, alleging defamation. Part of the case rested on the fact that the article was not by Bhutto but contained information only Bhutto could have known and that it had handwritten amendments which were not in Bhutto's writing. I was asked to provide an affidavit, affirming that I had typed it, that the handwriting was Benazir's (there was no time to retype it and she had made some grammatical corrections) and that she had told me to put it in the third person. The case was settled out of court in 1983, the *New Statesman* paying damages of £10,000: Stephen Cook, 'New Statesman pays for libels on journalist', *Guardian*, 4 November 1983.

On 21 March I received permission to see Benazir. I had not seen her for over a month. Her face lit up when I arrived. She had a towel around her head after washing her hair.

'I didn't know you were coming,' she explained, and went on to describe how the ritual of washing her hair was something she planned and looked forward to because it filled in the day. In a way my impromptu visit was disrupting, and, by not warning her, she did not have the enjoyment of looking forward to it. Even so she was happy to let her hair dry, as we sat together outside for two hours. 'The sun was shining and it all looked more cheerful than my last visit,' I wrote home. 'I was able to tell B. about the death of Mr Memon which she wanted to hear about.'[26]

The following day I received a letter from her, apologising for writing on 'scrappy' paper (a chunk was torn off the side). 'It was truly lovely to see you yesterday and so good to hear from you today,' she began. 'Please do keep sending me news. For instance, I did not know about President Giscard's appeal and what was in the letter until you told me.' As was all too clear, the wheels already seemed to be in motion for what lay ahead, as appeals flooded in, not just from the French president but from heads of state worldwide, urging General Zia to grant clemency.

'I do not know why the lawyers panic every time we ask them a simple question,' Benazir continued. 'Last night I heard on BBC that if the Review Petition is dismissed any time after Thursday, the sentence can be carried out. I was under the impression that when the Review Petition is dismissed, and if it is dismissed, the family has one week in which to make a mercy plea and to have a last meeting.' She then described how she had written to the lawyers to ask them the 'correct legal and technical position'. But they had started to panic and did not answer her question, telling her that they were feeding wrong information to the BBC to keep the momentum(!). 'Well frankly, I am not outside so I do not

wish to comment on their strategy, but I would like to know what
the position is. Do you think you could calm the lawyers down
sufficiently to find out for me? They must be in a state of extreme
nervousness that they cannot answer a straight question like that.'[27]
I wrote back saying of course I would do as she requested, not
wanting to confess that I too was in a state of extreme nervousness.

With the situation looking so dire, Benazir's cousin Tariq –
Aunty Manna and Uncle Naseem's son – had arrived from London.
It seemed neither Mir, Shahnawaz nor Sunny could come, lest the
military authorities fabricate some cases against them and put
them in jail. Tariq had come on their behalf to see his uncle and, I
feared, to say goodbye. After his visit to jail, we had lunch together
but our conversation was desultory. Neither of us had anything
hopeful to say to each other and we picked at our food with little
appetite.

Friday 23 March was 'Pakistan Day', the day when members
of the All India Muslim League had passed what became known
as the Lahore Resolution, affirming their objective of creating
separate 'sovereign states' for the Muslims of the subcontinent, to
be called 'Pakistan'. Although, as I subsequently learnt, the creation
of Pakistan was more complicated and bloody than envisaged in
that one proclamation in 1940, since then the date had always
been celebrated as a national holiday. Thanks to my UNDP friend,
Gustavo Toro, I had a ticket to go to the parade at Rawalpindi race
course. It was the first (and only) time that I saw General Zia in the
flesh. Dressed in his military uniform with medals on his chest,
he rode in a glittering coach, lined with blue velvet, pulled by a
team of horses and accompanied by other senior generals. Later he
stood on a red dais and made a speech announcing that elections
would be held in November. To a Martian, the scene might have
looked like a perfectly normal celebration; but behind the smile,
who knew what General Zia was thinking?

The following day I went to the Supreme Court (having managed to get my pass renewed). In a voice that had become all too familiar, Anwar ul Haq announced that the review petition was dismissed. It was all over in a matter of seconds. Even though three of the judges had upheld the appeal, all seven judges rejected the review petition. The sense of depression in the Bhutto camp was indescribable. I sent another article to the *Spectator*, which was given the title: 'Bhutto prepares to die'.[28] For the family the dismissal of the review petition was desperate news. 'My head has been in a whirl since Saturday,' Benazir wrote, 'and the tension has given me migraines... but your notes have been *comforting*. Thank you so much.'[29]

On 29 March I was given permission to visit. My heart was very heavy as I travelled again to Sihala. Benazir looked thin and strained. Again we sat outside although it was cold. As we talked, she took a coffee cup and started to mix the coffee, sugar and milk to make it frothy before adding the hot water. This took some time and, as she was stirring, I tried to give her as much news as I had gleaned from what the journalists were writing and thinking. We talked about all eventualities but the worst scenario seemed unreal. 'If they go ahead it's clearly murder,' she said. We then reverted back to our favourite topic of conversation – Oxford friends – but we both had less enthusiasm to discuss the past when the present was so black. After sitting for an hour, the policewoman told me that my visit was over. I hugged Benazir and she hugged me back. 'Take good care of yourself, Vicks,' she said. And I said the same. It seemed unthinkable that after all the struggle, she was going to lose her father.[30] As I left Sihala I turned back to wave her goodbye. I never imagined that I would not see her again for nearly five years.

Returning to Islamabad the sadness I felt was immeasurable. The next couple of days passed in suspense. It was no longer a question of 'if' but 'when'. 'What justice is there? What mercy?'

I wrote in my diary, with the righteous indignation of an English-woman caught up in a South Asian tragedy. 'How will I ever be the same again after what I have seen and heard?'[31]

Benazir had been issued with another detention order 'under clause (a) paragraph 2 Martial Law order No, 12 vide order No. 20/88/2/DMLA'. The lawyers gave me a copy and it was hyper-bolic in its allegations that Benazir was 'a [sic] irresponsible and dangerous speaker, and thereby you have delivered highly inflam-matory speeches in the public in flagrant violation of the ban imposed on political activities, which proved prejudicial to the public safety, good order and deterimental [sic] to the security in general'. Ominously the order detained her for another fifteen days.

Although Bhutto was adamant that he would not ask for mercy and had told his relatives to refrain from doing so, his half-sister by his father's first marriage, Begum Shaharbano Imtiaz, insisted on writing a letter. Since the original was too faint to photocopy Benazir asked me to type it five times. I had tears in my eyes as I read her urgent plea. In my Western mindset I simply could not comprehend how clemency could not be shown. But I was too trusting to understand the arrogance of a military dictatorship, whose intentions were clear to many from the start. Countless world leaders had asked for clemency to be shown to the former prime minister but their requests were also disregarded.[32]

During these last frantic days Bhutto's relatives continued to arrive from Sindh to say goodbye. Soon Benazir's turn would come. I knew that she was feeling unwell with an upset stomach. 'They came and wanted to take Mummy and me together to jail today,' she wrote to me.

As I was not well, Mummy said she would go alone *unless* it was the last meeting following the dismissal of the Mercy Petition filed by millions. In that case I would go with her no matter how ill I felt. They *refused* to confirm or deny that it was the last meeting. Instead they said that they would send a doctor today and we would *both* be taken 'sometime' tomorrow. So it looks like Zia is to commit murder. But like us you must be brave and control your emotions. If the worst happens a great man is being executed for a cause he relentlessly pursued and refused to abandon his principles.[33]

On 3 April Benazir and her mother were taken to the jail. Yasmin and Amna went to stand outside so they could glimpse them when they came out. Later Yasmin told me that they knew by the expression on their faces that it was the last visit. All the collective hours Benazir had spent visiting her father and all his political instruction was at an end. Soon his political mantle would fall onto her shoulders. She was still only twenty-five years old.

In the afternoon I'd been phoned by the *Spectator* asking me to write an article because they had heard on the BBC that Bhutto's hanging would probably take place 'the following morning'. I still could not believe it would happen so soon after the rejection of the review petition and was slightly surprised at their forward planning. At the same time, there was nothing to indicate that General Zia would have a change of heart at this stage and grant clemency. Because I had no idea how I would be feeling once I knew the execution had taken place, in the evening after dinner, I sat down to write. I decided to think myself into the following day, although for the short space of time before dawn, when I knew that Bhutto was still alive. This is how I began:

As Zulfikar Ali Bhutto left his prison cell for the last time no one could know what last thoughts occupied an undoubtedly great mind which for so long had been crammed full of the affairs of state: the economy, industry, poverty and international politics. Nor could anyone be sure how he bore himself but, in keeping with the forbearance he had shown throughout his year and a half in solitary confinement, it was undoubtedly with courage, conviction and a clear conscience.[34]

As usual my article had to be about one thousand words. I continued:

For the last few days of his life it poured with rain. It was not the drizzling rain to which Europeans are accustomed but the torrential rain of countries which have hot climates. People in Pakistan were sombre, silent and depressed. They felt helpless in the face of martial law which arrested anyone on the spot who tried to organise a procession of protest. The uncertainty was agonising – any day they might wake up to find that the former prime minister was already dead. Only in the imagination was it possible to conjure up the vision of the solitary figure – once sturdy and robust – waiting in a cold concrete cell with an unwanted beard growing on his pale face, since the use of a razor was no longer permitted.[35]

Then, with the knowledge I'd acquired over the past year, I went back in time:

For those who wish to give Bhutto a place in history, he deserves this for having restored the morale and prestige of a country of 70 million people which was discredited and demoralised after the war of 1971 when East Pakistan seceded to become independent Bangladesh. After the instability of civilian governments and military dictatorships, Bhutto's people's government was the first in the history of Pakistan to have a populist ring. Bhutto started off on a good footing.

He had all the advantages and opportunities of a rich family background and a good education combined with his own talents and ambitions to reach the top. He was only forty-three years of age when he became President and then Prime Minister of Pakistan after the 1971 war. Undoubtedly throughout his tenure of power Bhutto made enemies – people who envied his success, abhorred the policies of socialism he felt it was necessary to implement, and those who believed his Western style of life was un-Islamic. Bhutto himself admitted the conflict of a man who was an aristocrat and yet who fervently believed in helping Pakistan's poor. His supporters give him credit for awakening the political consciousness of the people and for giving them dignity and self-respect. He took trouble to campaign in the poor areas of the country and they were heartened by his promises of a better life.[36]

I proceeded to outline the circumstances of his dismissal from power after the elections in March 1977, his trial, the sentence of death and the rejection of his appeal. I concluded with some of my own analysis: 'His condemnation without the grant of mercy was clear proof that those now in power were determined to be rid of Bhutto in any circumstances. Angry and disheartened, his supporters pointed to the substantial grounds for mercy…'[37] I stopped typing. It was late at night. I dared not think what was happening in Rawalpindi District Jail.

The following day I woke, with the feeling of having hardly slept. It was not raining any more but the sky was dull and overcast and it was still cold. As usual, the surveillance men were outside the house standing by their cars. When they saw me open the front door, instead of immediately rushing to get into their cars as they normally did, they walked towards me. I hadn't yet had the heart to turn on the radio, but there was a stillness about

Islamabad and I knew that Bhutto was dead. As the security men approached, I asked them where Benazir and her mother were. 'Gone' they gestured to the air 'with the body to Larkana.' In fact this information was wrong because, as I later heard, they were not allowed to accompany the coffin. Only Bhutto's first wife and cousin, Shireen Ameer Begum,* was permitted to see him before he was laid to rest in the family graveyard at Garhi Khuda Bakhsh. He was fifty-one years old.

I read through my article and then went to the telex machine. The telex operator had been busy all morning and I offered to type my article into the machine myself so that he could have a break. Ever suspicious of maladroit censorship, it meant I knew that nothing of what I had written would be left out. As news of Bhutto's execution spread, there were street protests. People's anger was fuelled by rumours which began to circulate about how he had died. Some said that he had been beaten and tortured and was already half-dead when he reached the gallows. His last words were reported to be: 'Lord help me I am innocent.'

In protest at Bhutto's execution, a big rally was organised in Rawalpindi, to be led by Bhutto's cousin, Mumtaz Ali Bhutto, and Hafeez Pirzada, his former minister for education and law who, after being released from detention, had been taken on to Bhutto's legal team. Shaukat Niazi, with her three daughters, Yasmin, Samiya and Samina, as well as Amna, her sister and students from the Islamabad College for Girls all joined in, a crowd of thousands filling Liaquat Bagh where they had arranged to assemble. 'When Mumtaz Ali Bhutto and Hafeez Pirzada appeared there was a tremendous cheer and the crowd started moving towards the

---

* Shireen Ameer Begum (c.1918–2003); Bhutto was married to her when he was a young teenager, the custom being for Bhutto women to marry their cousins so as to keep the property within the family.

road,' recalled Yasmin. 'But suddenly the two men disappeared and so the crowd dissipated because there was no one to lead us.' With the military standing by, the arrests began; all the Niazi women were first taken to a police station and then to Attock jail. 'We slept on straw mats and were locked up in cave-like cells like animals,' continued Yasmin.[38] When, after their disappearance, Peter Niesewand and Bruce Loudon had gone in search of Mumtaz Ali Bhutto and Pirzada, they had found them having lunch, their desertion of the crowd unexplained.*

The only shred of comforting news was that Benazir's school friend, Samiya, had been given permission to come from Karachi to stay with her for a couple of days in Sihala. Begum Bhutto's niece, Fakhri Ahmed Khan, had also been allowed to stay. On the morning of 6 April they were all taken by Pakistan Air Force plane to Garhi Khudha Bakhsh. Recollecting the visit, Samiya described the heart-breaking scene as Benazir threw herself on her father's grave, piled high with rose petals, weeping.[39]

As the events leading to Bhutto's execution were taking their un-natural course in Pakistan, a group of eminent jurists and British members of parliament were gathering in London. Not realising exactly when the death sentence would be carried out, Bhutto's sons, Mir and Shahnawaz, had organised a two-day 'Convention of International Jurists' to discuss the trial, hoping perhaps that the outcome of their deliberations would be sufficient testimony to the world to save their father's life.

By the time the Convention met on 6 and 7 April, the motiva-tion had shifted from trying to save his life to acknowledging his achievements after his death, as well as stating their positions on

---

* Mumtaz Ali Bhutto (b.1933); Abdul Hafeez Pirzada (1935–2015).

the trial and appeal. Among those present on those sombre April days was former US attorney-general Ramsey Clark, who had travelled to Pakistan the previous summer to attend Bhutto's appeal against the death sentence in the Supreme Court of Pakistan. In his remarks he described how he had 'pleaded' with General Zia to be allowed to meet Bhutto, but to no avail. The prosecution of Zulfikar Ali Bhutto, he continued, exposed 'the enormous perils of freedom and dignity, the power of the state to lie and murder, to confuse and divide, to use the hope for justice, through law, to have its way'. He told the audience how 'stunned' he was (as were we) when, having started with a bench of nine judges, one had been retired and the other removed because he was alleged to be ill. 'Ordinarily, if a judge begins a case, a judge also finishes a case unless something finishes the judge in the interim.' As we now knew, this critical change to the composition of the bench altered the balance since the two judges who were retired may well have upheld Bhutto's appeal.[40]

Also present at the Convention was John Matthew, QC, who had attended the trial in the Lahore High Court in 1978, ominously concluding 'that the trappings were a facade behind which one could readily see the stark realities of the political trial, the outcome of which was a foregone conclusion whichever way and whichever course the trial took'. Stan Newens, MP, emphasised that 'from the left of the Labour Party to the right wing of the Conservative Party, right across the spectrum, there was a deep sense of revulsion at this trial, at the verdicts… and now, at the so-called sentence being carried out'.* In the lawyers' opinion, Bhutto's trial failed to meet the minimum accepted standards of justice, not only because the trial court was biased but because an accurate record had not been kept and Bhutto had not been able to

---

* John Matthew, QC (1927–2020); Stanley Newens (b.1930).

present his defence properly. Their conclusions were then sent to the secretary-general of the UN, Kurt Waldheim: although it was too late to save Bhutto, at least there was a record of what independent jurists thought about the trial.[41]

After Bhutto's execution I felt numb. I desperately wanted to see Benazir to condole with her. Having again sent a letter to the home secretary to request permission for a visit, I continued to work on my book, writing up the last chapter which, like my article for the *Spectator*, I called: 'The final act'. The lawyers had all gone home. The rooms in Flashman's Hotel, which they had occupied for so many months, were now empty. There were no more bills for me to pay, no more accounts to do.

Spectator cover, 'Bhutto: the final act', 7 April 1979.

'I can still hardly believe it,' I wrote to my parents. 'Most people seem to be in a vacuum.'[42] A week after the execution I received the copy of a note signed by the Section Officer directed to the Superintendent, District Jail, Rawalpindi. No.3-16-H-SPL-1/77 Part-III. The subject matter was: 'Permission to Interview with Benazir Bhutto'. It read: 'I am directed to inform you that Miss Victoria Schofield is hereby allowed to see Miss Benazir Bhutto for a day for two hours.' I read it again. My eyes halted on the last few words: 'for a day for two hours'. But when? Yet again, there was no date. I immediately telephoned to ask on what day I was given 'permission for interview with Benazir Bhutto'. But I never managed to get through, having sometimes spent an hour on the telephone. The date, I was eventually told, had expired. I must apply again.

I went often to sit with the Niazis, but we were all too sad for conversation. In addition to their grief at Bhutto's death, Shaukat and the girls were still recovering from the weeks they had spent in Attock jail. Only Samina, because she was under age, had been released after a few days. By the end of the month I had heard nothing more in response to my request to visit Benazir and my telephone calls were in vain. Through our continuing correspondence, Benazir knew that I had tried to see her but understood that the main reason for my presence in Pakistan – to give her moral support during her father's appeal and write some articles – was at an end and that I must go home. 'It is going to be agony leaving whenever I go,' I told my parents.[43]

'It is simply perverse of the Junta not to let you visit,' Benazir wrote in a goodbye note. She went on to tell me that she had been assailed 'with a feeling of weakness/lack of energy', describing how the authorities kept playing 'a cat and mouse game' with them. 'They keep saying they are taking us to Karachi and then changing their minds.' She was especially distressed that, on the order they wrote regarding her continuing detention, they had so immediately adjusted to the new situation, addressing her as 'daughter of late Zulfikar Ali Bhutto'. 'I was so furious. Martyrs do not die. They live forever.' I was very upset that I had to leave without seeing her. I felt a terrible void, wondering when I would see her again. But, as she wrote: 'We'll meet again, I am sure, and have a good long talk.'[44]

The night before my departure to London, Dr Zafar and Shaukat Niazi came to say goodbye.

'Go,' they said tearfully. 'Go back to your parents and your home.'

I hugged them both. They had been my family, my home from home. I had lived in Pakistan for nearly a year. Most of my time was spent in Rawalpindi and Islamabad, with a fleeting visit to Lahore, longer stays in Karachi and Larkana as well as Benazir's tour to the Frontier. During that time the revolution in Iran had gained momentum. The Soviets had tightened their hold on Afghanistan and thousands more Afghan refugees had crossed into Pakistan. I had no idea about other world news because I had been so preoccupied with events in Pakistan. I barely knew what was going on in India, except that Indira Gandhi was still out of power and Moraji Desai was prime minister. Apart from the news I had managed to glean in order to share it with Benazir, I didn't know which of our friends had married or had a baby, or who had got what job. I didn't know what film was popular in Britain or what music, although I had bought a cassette of Bonnie Tyler to listen to as a change from Chilean music. I had no idea what was going on politically in Britain, although a general election was shortly due to be held and it looked like Margaret Thatcher was going to become the first female prime minister of the United Kingdom. Almost the only letters I wrote were to my parents. But I had typed thousands and thousands of words.

As I headed down the main road from Islamabad towards the airport, I passed for the last time the plaque which stated expectantly 'Supreme Court of Pakistan', indicating where the new Supreme Court was still to be built in Islamabad, to replace the old building in which I had spent so many hours sitting on the hard benches, taking notes, trying to comprehend the charge of conspiracy to murder, the intricacies of which were initially so alien to me, but then became so familiar that I could recite the names of the forty-one prosecution witnesses by heart. I took one last look at the Margalla Hills, slightly purple in the morning mist. Throughout the drama I had witnessed, they were a constant pleasure to behold, beckoning me onwards, alluringly, to the white-capped ranges of the Karakoram and Himalayan mountains, although I had never had time to visit.

I had no idea if the surveillance men who had followed me for so many months knew that I was leaving or what they thought when I took the turning in Rawalpindi towards the airport. I had hardly ever spoken to them and I never knew any of their names. Apart from the intrusion into my privacy, their presence made me stilted in my actions. I would never let a friend kiss me on the cheek or embrace me because any familiarity might get noted and misrepresented to the authorities and cause embarrassment to Benazir. Even after I returned to England, I used to recoil at the approach of a social embrace until the memory receded.

When I reached the airport, before being allowed to board the plane, I was taken into a separate room so that my suitcase could be searched. All my possessions were pulled out so that I had difficulty fitting everything back in again. The searching agents were attracted by the draft of my short United Nations book, which mentioned the word 'Kashmir' (in relation to the UN Military Observer Group in India and Pakistan (UNMOGIP) stationed on both sides of the Line of Control, dividing the two regions of Jammu and Kashmir). They started looking at some of my notebooks in which I had written in a form of rudimentary shorthand I'd taught myself long ago; they paused in their searching to ask me to transcribe what I had written but after a few minutes they realised that this was a pointless exercise. I told them to take the draft of the UN book because I had no need of it. I had no idea if they were looking for my manuscript on Bhutto but they did not find it, since each chapter had already been sent with friends, who had agreed to take responsibility for the one small chunk of history which I had entrusted to them.

As I boarded the plane, I felt wrenched from a country and a cause which I had adopted as my own. Since Benazir was detained at the beginning of October, I had written to her nearly every day, telling her what was happening in the outside world and trying to keep her spirits up, ever hopeful that her father's life would be saved. With his death, there was nothing more I could say.

5

Street Fighting Years: 1979–81

Sometimes it is hard to realise this is the same woman who
debated in the Oxford Union, loved Anna Belinda dresses
and drove a yellow MGB sports car.[1]

For weeks after returning from Pakistan I felt restless. What previously had been familiar was now strange, what had initially been so strange felt like home. Soon after my arrival, I went to see Mir and Shahnawaz. Sunny had finished at Harvard and was with them. They were a sad trio, sharing a rented flat in London, the horror of having had to live through their father's death *in absentia* still palpable. Our conversation lacked any of the usual lustre, manifest when friends are meeting again after an interval. Too much grief still hung in the air.

In late May Benazir and her mother were released from house arrest. Begum Bhutto would not appear in public until *iddat* – the prescribed period of mourning, lasting four months and ten days – ended in mid-August. After her release Benazir went immediately to Larkana; since she was not allowed to travel by air, she made the long journey into the heart of Sindh by train. Sitting in the garden at Al Murtaza she gave the most moving interview to David Lomax, broadcast on the *Tonight* programme, in which she described her last meeting with her father.* 'At the end of the meeting I said I'd like to hug my father goodbye. He had been the President, the Prime Minister, he'd brought the prisoners back from the camps of India. They wouldn't even open the cell door to let me kiss him goodbye,' she said tearfully. 'And then we just went back and started the countdown until death.' Hearing Benazir's voice was heart-breaking, as she relived all that had happened just over two months earlier.[2]

'The crowds that came to see her were from all over the country and went into several thousand a day,' Samiya Waheed told me. 'On the one hand they come for condolence, and on the other hand they come to show how happy they are that we have been freed,' Benazir said in her interview. 'I just meet them for a few seconds. All they want to do is catch a glimpse of me. I'm quite frightened of the responsibility.' And so she must have been. Turning twenty-six on 21 June, the direction of her life had irrevocably changed. Years later she made a memorable statement: 'I didn't choose this life. It chose me.'[3] And that was how it was to be. Quite apart from having to deal with the agony of her father's death – or, as she described it, his 'judicial murder' – almost overnight she had become a political leader.

Officially Begum Bhutto was chairman of the PPP, while Benazir acted as her deputy.† When asked by David Lomax whether she saw herself inheriting her father's political position in the party she had responded: 'I don't think political power in Pakistan is heredi-tary. And I don't see myself inheriting it as such, but I think that the people have faith in me, and I'm very proud of the faith and trust that they have lodged in me. And it's because of the sacrifices

---

* David Lomax (1938–2014) was a television reporter and interviewer.
† Benazir became co-chairman of the PPP when Begum Bhutto went abroad for medical treatment in November 1982.

we've rendered.' For the remaining thirty years of her life, this belief became her mission statement and the reason why she felt she must complete her father's work and leave a legacy. 'I did everything for my father,' she continued. 'All my education, everything I did was for his approval. And now I feel that whatever I am doing is for his people, the people for whom he sacrificed his life and they are the oppressed masses of the four provinces of Pakistan'.[4]

When Benazir returned to Karachi, more people flocked to see her. 'It seems as though the seat of government is here in Karachi,' Samiya continued in her letter to me.[5] With General Zia still in supreme authority, and unable to return to Pakistan, Mir and Shahnawaz had decided on a more radical approach. In the summer of 1979 they founded a 'revolutionary and militant' organisation called the Pakistan Liberation Organisation. Modelled along the lines of the Palestine Liberation Organisation, one of their mentors was Yasser Arafat, whom their father had invited to attend the Islamic Summit conference held in Lahore in 1974; another was Colonel Muammar Qadaffi of Libya.* I remember sitting in their flat one day as they excitedly described their strategy: their objective was to obtain some weapons and make targeted attacks on military installations in order to highlight to the world the injustices of Pakistan's military dictatorship. They considered themselves 'freedom fighters', but such an enterprise was obviously impossible from Britain and so they decided to move to Kabul, Afghanistan, the director of Afghanistan's state intelligence agency, KHAD, Dr Mohammad Najibullah,† promising logistical assistance.[6]

'I would like to have had an opportunity to talk to you before I

---

* Yasser Arafat (1929–2004) was chairman of the Palestine Liberation Organisation 1969–2004; Colonel Muammar Qadaffi (1942–2011) ruled Libya 1969–2011.

† Dr Mohammad Najibullah Ahmadzai (1947–96) was president of Afghanistan 1987–92.

left London,' Mir wrote to me in August, telling me that the Martyr Bhutto Memorial Trust, which they'd set up, had elected to give me a medal for the help I'd given. Lest his letter fall into the wrong hands, he concluded by saying that he didn't want to give any more details of his activities.[7] For the rest of his life, Mir (or Murtaza, as he became known, using his other name) justified his stance by quoting a popular aphorism attributed to Thomas Jefferson: 'when injustice becomes law, resistance becomes duty'.* Mir put this in his own way: 'I resisted tyranny and I obeyed God. When the military closed all avenues of peaceful protest, resistance became legitimate.'[8] His move to Kabul set him and Shahnawaz along a different path from the political one Benazir had taken.

Sunny had returned to Karachi, celebrating her twenty-second birthday in August. In another life, after Harvard, like Benazir, she might have gone to Oxford, as her father had hoped, but with his death the pattern of her existence had also changed.

My first priority was to finish my book, which – since Bhutto's death sentence had been upheld – Cassell & Co. had agreed to publish. In my absence my mother had retyped the manuscript from the pages which she had received in the post from so many strangers. Ideally I would have liked more time to review the immediacy of my account. But, from the publisher's viewpoint, topicality was key, so publication was scheduled for November 1979.

My other priority was to get a job. The only place I wanted to

---

* Thomas Jefferson (1743–1826) was 3rd US president 1801–09. In 1787 he said: 'The spirit of resistance to government is so valuable on certain occasions, that I wish it to be always kept alive. It will often be exercised when wrong, but better so than not to be exercised at all. I like a little rebellion now and then. It is like a storm in the atmosphere.' The shortened quotation is derived from this comment.

work was the BBC World Service in Bush House, whose broadcasts, over the past year, had been an aural lifeline. Having met, by chance, the head of the Urdu service, David Page, in Rawalpindi in late 1978, I wanted to work in the Eastern Service which broadcast in many languages to the countries of South Asia, including India, Pakistan, Bangladesh and Burma (Myanmar). When it came to my interview for an advertised position, my strength proved to be my weakness. While my CV demonstrated the advantage of having been 'out in the field', my friendship with Benazir was considered to have the potential to tarnish the BBC's reputation for impartiality in its broadcasts. Despite initial disappointment at not getting the job, I realised that, even if I couldn't work in the Eastern Service, there were other departments which would give me invaluable experience as a journalist. So I readily accepted an opportunity to report on more general stories as an 'Outside Contributor' (OC) in the BBC World Service's Talks and Features Department. All interviews had to be recorded on heavy reel to reel Uher tape recorders which, in today's digital world, would appear like museum artefacts but were highly valued for their broadcast quality.

I also worked one or two days a week in Central Current Affairs Talks or 'CCAT'. Roland Challis, the BBC's South East Asia correspondent in the 1960s, who had covered President Sukarno's downfall in Indonesia, was the head of CCAT, and Leslie Stone, who had a deep understanding of American politics was deputy, later taking over from Roland as head. Both were veteran journalists with distinguished careers, but I was too inexperienced to appreciate the events they had covered or their specialist knowledge.* My job in CCAT, which Roland had given me on the

---

* Roland Challis (1929–2020); Leslie Stone (1934–2001) died of motor neurone disease aged 67.

strength of my *Spectator* articles, was either to write 'talks' which were broadcast in different languages on specific subjects or to 'copy-taste' the enormous amounts of 'copy' which came in from the various agencies including Reuters, United Press International (UPI) and Associated Press (AP). Having made a selection of the most important stories, the team of writers in CCAT would write the talks. On Mondays the task was particularly onerous because, after the weekend, treble the amount of copy was piled in huge cardboard boxes.

In both positions in the BBC my proximity to world news meant that I could follow what was going on in Pakistan, my copy-tasting job giving me immediate access to the latest events by the hour. In the absence of any internet search engines like Google or Wikipedia, another valuable resource was 'NewsInf' ('news information'), the BBC's press-cutting department, where information from the national and regional press on a given subject could be accessed. There was also a sound archive department, where excerpts from speeches were retained on long-playing records and, in my free time, I went to listen to the recordings of Zulfikar Ali Bhutto's speeches. At lunch (if I wasn't in the sound archive department), I would gravitate to the BBC canteen in the basement and sit with members of the Eastern Service from whom yet more information could be gleaned.

For a few weeks, until I found somewhere to live in London, I stayed on the sofa in a flat which our friend Claire Wilmer was sharing with another LMH friend, Gianetta Rands. Since Benazir was now free, Claire – or 'Clara' as we often called her – was making plans to take up her invitation to visit, which Benazir had given us both in 1977. Her departure was now fixed for the end of July. I was happy that she could pick up where I had left off: an Oxford friend providing Benazir with emotional support.

*

Elections in Pakistan were still scheduled for 17 November 1979 and the PPP was a key contestant. To me these were Benazir's 'street fighting years': while Begum Bhutto was dignified and poised in her statements, Benazir was feisty, seemingly ready to take on the military regime of Zia-ul-Haq single-handedly if need be, regardless of the consequences. It was this steely determination which transmitted itself through the newsreels and copy which found its way into the BBC and onto my desk. I used to marvel at the intensity of her statements berating General Zia. 'She really is incredibly brave and quite fearless,' Claire was writing from Karachi soon after her arrival. 'Many of us fear that she will be arrested soon because of the fiery speeches she is making.' Her inspiration remained her father. 'My father is ever-present. I can feel his presence all the time,' said Benazir in an interview with BBC reporter David Lay, who went to Karachi in September to interview her and several others (including Dr Niazi, Amna and Claire) for a profile to be broadcast on BBC Radio 4. 'In fact I do not think I could have survived if I didn't feel he was around me and protecting me. All the time I just feel it.'[9]

Meanwhile my book had gone into 'production' which required regular visits to Cassell's offices in Red Lion Square, near Holborn, to discuss the copyediting in my lunch hour. An added requirement was for the manuscript to be read by a lawyer for libel. Cassell was still reeling from the after-effects of a 1970 lawsuit, which had resulted in having to pay damages of £40,000.* None of this

---

* The lawsuit was filed by Captain John (Jackie) E. Broome, DSC, RN (1901–85), the escort group commander of the ill-fated convoy PQ17, travelling to the Soviet Union in 1942. In a book published by Cassell, David Irving had alleged that Broome's withdrawal of the destroyers was the main reason for the decimation of the convoy by the Germans. The book was withdrawn and later republished with corrections. The award of £40,000 damages to Broome

had anything to do with me, but, when it came to narrating the story of a trial and appeal for conspiracy to murder, the publishers wanted to be sure that they would not be facing another lawsuit. The whole procedure added further anxiety to what was anyway a stressful process. I was already worrying how, despite her initial encouragement, Benazir would feel when she saw the story of her father's trial and execution in stark black and white, at a time when the events I was describing were still so recent, the hurt of her father's loss so raw.

While continuing to work for the BBC, most of my spare evenings were spent in an office off Commercial Road in London's East End, writing short articles for the London edition of *Daily Musawaat*, a PPP newspaper, which continued to criticise the Zia regime. Among the Urdu-language writers was Bashir Riaz, or 'Bash' as we all called him, one of the large number of Pakistanis who continued to follow politics in Pakistan with a passionate intensity although he was now living in London. When the proofs of my book were ready, with Bash's help I found a reliable courier who could take them to Benazir so that she could go through them. Looking back it might seem absurd how challenging this was, but, under military dictatorship, a package with potentially controversial literature could easily not reach its destination.

Having ensured that Benazir had indeed received the proofs, we arranged to speak on the phone to go through the aspects which she thought needed clarification or amendment. As I have long since learnt in my writing career, a turn of phrase, inadvertent comment or factual mistake can be upsetting and I could tell by her voice how difficult reading my manuscript had been. Out of necessity, embedded in the text, were the arguments used by the

---

(which he gave to charity) was the largest until Jeffrey Archer's case against the *Daily Star* when he was awarded £500,000 damages.

▲ 1. Benazir when, as president of the Oxford Union, she was invited to speak at the Cambridge Union. She is wearing 'an Anna Belinda' dress. *We all loved 'Anna Belinda', the dress shop, whose hallmark fashion garments were dresses with covered buttons and piping.*

► 2. Benazir's term card as president of the Oxford Union, Hilary 1977. *Even her term card – printed in green ink against a white background, the colours of the Pakistani flag – showed her individuality.*

OXFORD UNION SOCIETY

HILARY TERM, 1977

President: Benazir Bhutto

▲ 3. Begum Nusrat Bhutto (right) arriving to visit Benazir in hospital with her niece, Fakhri Ahmed Khan, Samiya Waheed and me behind, Karachi, June 1978. *It was the first time I had met Benazir's elegant mother, whom force of circumstances had turned into a political activist.*

◄ 4. Benazir and me, July 1978, outside the Supreme Court tea room. Also present are party supporters and Yahya Bakhtiar (right), former attorney general and Zulfikar Ali Bhutto's chief defence lawyer. *Benazir's presence meant that a vital energy was injected into the legal effort and her father's defence.*

5. Benazir campaigning for her father's life on tour in the North-West Frontier, September 1978. *It was amazing watching Benazir as she made her speeches, using the same mannerisms I'd seen in the Oxford Union but with the language, subject matter and location so dramatically different.*

6. Mir Murtaza Bhutto and Shahnawaz Bhutto, London, 6 April 1979. *Bhutto's brothers, Mir and Shahnawaz, had organised a two-day 'Convention of International Jurists' to discuss the trial.*

7. Anne Fadiman and me at Benazir's wedding, December 1987. *We Westerners felt dull in comparison – or, as Anne Fadiman said, 'like drab little caterpillars surrounded by butterflies'.*

8. Benazir with her family at the Mehndi ceremony. *Benazir looked stunning, dressed in red… surrounded and supported by her family and her close friends.*

9. Benazir at the Nikah ceremony. *A special 'wedding dais' with a canopy decorated with red and white flowers was prepared in the garden.*

10. Benazir and Asif at the Nikah ceremony. '*I found joy and fulfilment in marriage despite difficult circumstances,' said Benazir.*

◂ 11. Benazir with Amna Piracha campaigning for the 1988 elections. *This photograph by Roger Hutchings won the First Prize, National Union of Journalists competition 1988.*

▴ 12. Benazir as prime minister with Rajiv Gandhi, Prime Minister of India, December 1988. *'I am sure each of us will give our best and I hope the time would come when historians would point to your time in India and my time in Pakistan for heralding the dawn of a new era,' Benazir proclaimed.*

▾ 13. Benazir taking part in BBC's 'It's Your World' after her first 100 days in office 1989. *'I do consider myself as a role model,' Benazir responded to one of the questions.*

14. Benazir and me, 10 July 1989, leaving the Oxford Union debating chamber. On my right is Diana Gerald, president of the Union, Michaelmas 1989.

15. Benazir's waxwork at Madame Tussauds with Sanam and her daughter, Azadeh, unveiled on 27 November 1989. *"You" are being unveiled at Madame Tussauds, I informed Benazir. Dressed in the same green shalwar kameez which she'd worn at her swearing-in ceremony, the impression was so realistic that, seeing the photograph of her sister, Sunny, standing next door to her, waxwork 'Benazir' almost seemed real.*

16. Benazir's waxwork at Madame Tussauds with me.

prosecution lawyers in favour of upholding the sentence of death for conspiracy to murder. As we went through each point, she was particularly sensitive about the description of her father's confinement in jail (which she had witnessed and I hadn't); for example, she wanted to point out the fact that it wasn't just one sparrow that came into her father's cell but that there was a nest of sparrows, illustrating the unhygienic conditions he had to endure. While I was able to make some amendments, the publishers were not willing to change other points, like the sparrow's nest. One omission, which was difficult to rectify at a distance, was not sourcing my quotations from the legal documents I had consulted. Not for the first time I wondered why I had attempted such a hugely difficult task. I wasn't a lawyer. Nor was I an experienced writer. 'It will take time,' Bash counselled. 'What you have produced is a record. Without that record no one will know what happened. Your book will stand the test of time.'[10]

By the time my book, *Bhutto: Trial and Execution*, was published, elections had again been cancelled and political parties banned. Benazir and her mother were once more under house arrest in Al Murtaza. All communication was cut, the house designated a sub-jail. 'House arrest normally means that you are arrested in your house; you can't go out but the rest of the world can come in; thus, although you are confined, you are not really cut off from social interaction or from information in the world. But General Zia didn't just confine us in our house; he declared it a sub-jail,' Benazir later said. It was her seventh political detention since the coup two years previously.[11]

For a few weeks after the cancellation of the elections, Pakistan stayed in the news and a number of national newspaper and journals reviewed my book, most pointing out my inherent bias because of my friendship with Benazir. Ann Callender, writing in the *Daily Telegraph*, categorised the book as 'pure hagiography'.

Describing me as a 'chum' of Benazir, Tariq Ali was direct: 'her book makes no attempt at objectivity and is written as a defence of Bhutto's record'. Christopher Dobson in *Now!* magazine had a more nuanced viewpoint: 'She is biased, of course, but no more so than the judges who tried him.'[12]

In neighbouring Afghanistan events were shaping a different narrative, far removed from any concern there might be about continuing military dictatorship in Pakistan. As I had already witnessed in Pakistan, since the April 1978 coup the communist government, led first by Nur Muhammad Taraki and then by Hafizullah Amin, had been under attack from rural Afghans who had adopted a guerrilla style of warfare against the Afghan army and security forces.* The conservative elements of society were also troubled by what appeared to be an abnegation of Islam, the colour green having been removed from the Afghan flag, as well as the growing influence of the 'godless' Soviet Union. Having competed with the Soviet Union for many years, the United States was like the proverbial cat on a hot tin roof, dancing about diplomatically lest their Cold War adversaries gain a strategic regional advantage. Tensions trebled when, on 24 December 1979, in order 'to protect their southern border', as Leonid Brezhnev put it, the Soviets sent troops into Afghanistan, commandos seizing strategic installations in Kabul, while armoured columns crossed into Afghanistan by road.

On 27 December Soviet forces killed Amin; his successor was another committed communist, Babrak Kamal.† Two days later, thousands more troops entered Afghanistan, hundreds of

---

* Nur Muhammad Taraki (1917–79) was chairman of the Presidium of the Revolutionary Council 1978–79; Hafizullah Amin (1929–79) was chairman of the Presidium of the Revolutionary Council 1979.

† Babrak Kamal (1929–96) was chairman of the Presidium of the Revolutionary Council 1979–86.

tanks rumbling southwards towards Kabul.[13] The United States' reaction was immediate, President Jimmy Carter saying that the implications of the Soviet invasion of Afghanistan 'could pose the most serious threat to the peace since World War Two'.[14] Analysts interpreted the invasion as the next stage in the Soviet Union's long-standing ambition to gain control of a warm water port and the oil fields of the Gulf – the latest development of the Cold War, or, as some liked to say, the new Great Game. The Soviet invasion also gave General Zia a new lease of life; having been kept at a distance following his refusal to show clemency to Bhutto eight months previously, he now became a necessary Western ally, returning Pakistan to the global limelight.

In view of the perceived threat to the established world order, Western countries, especially the United States and the United Kingdom, focused their attention on providing assistance to the Afghan rebels fighting the Soviets. In the post-Vietnam War world, and mindful of the 55,000-plus body bags taken back to the United States from Vietnam, there was no stomach for putting 'boots on the ground' which could escalate the conflict. Henceforward a new word entered our vocabulary: *mujahideen* (which in print journalism became the subject of debate: since it was a foreign word, should it be written in italics or with inverted commas?). The translation meant 'soldiers of the holy war', which seemed apt because the Muslim Afghans were fighting against communist Soviet soldiers. There was, however, a deeper significance: the jihad, the holy war, which Muslims have traditionally fought against the 'infidel', could be against any non-believer, a fact which seemed to be overlooked by the United States in the early stages of the war. Following the invasion, millions more refugees began to pour across the border into the North-West Frontier, which became the staging post for mujahideen returning to Afghanistan to fight.

*

While Afghanistan was being torn apart, Benazir and her mother remained under house arrest in Al Murtaza, leaving Sunny at 70 Clifton with Claire, who had stayed on in Pakistan. After six months, in April 1980, they were released. 'Dearest Benazir,' I wrote at once,

> I have not written to you whilst you were in detention because it seemed that letters would not get through and would only be censored. Now someone is travelling to Pakistan and so I thought I would accept this opportunity to send you a few words. My last letter was written before your arrest in October, but my thoughts have been with you since the long months of arrest. The press reports say you kept well by eating fruit and doing exercise… everyone asks after you continually… I shall not begin to comment on the world situation or the changed situation in the last six months. Suffice it to say that I wish you well… my thoughts were particularly with you on April 4th.[15]

Having been asked to write a short entry on Benazir for the 1980 *Encyclopaedia Britannica Book of the Year*, covering the events of 1979, there was only one way I could begin: 'For Benazir Bhutto, the elder daughter of the former Prime Minister of Pakistan, 1979 was a year of tragedy.' Part of my modest 'fee' was to receive a complimentary copy; when I said that I wanted to send a copy to Benazir, the editor agreed to send me two copies. When the books duly arrived, before repackaging one to send to Benazir, I put rose petals in the place of her entry and that of her father, which came in the section 'Obituaries'.[16]

After spending a year in Pakistan, Claire was preparing to come home. She too had become caught up in the political drama, describing how the response, whenever Benazir and her mother went shopping, 'merely shows the depth of their support and sympathy. Whenever elections are held, be it in three months or three years, I think they will win,' she wrote shortly before leaving. On the day of her arrival in London, Bashir Riaz and I went to meet her at Heathrow airport. As she excitedly greeted us, she produced out of her suitcase one of Benazir's 'Anna Belinda' dresses, which Benazir knew I loved and had lent me on a few occasions: another gesture, another kindness. Claire also told me that Benazir wanted to have my book on her father translated into Sindhi; I interpreted this as meaning that a fraction of her pain had healed.[17]

From what Benazir had said in a recent interview with Peter Niesewand, who was still the *Guardian* correspondent based in Delhi, covering Pakistan, it was clear that a protest movement against the military dictatorship was being planned, with 'signs of an alliance [being formed] between the PPP and other political parties, with the aim of ousting General Zia'.[18] 'I recently read your comments in the Peter Niesewand interview in the *Guardian*,' I told Benazir in early October, always pleased when someone I knew had met her. 'My work at BBC continues and I am very busy. The war in Iraq/Iran occupies people's attention the most... I've made some nice friends and have been going out more and enjoying life a good deal more recently. As you know I found it hard to settle into London for quite some time.'[19] When using the regular post, I was necessarily guarded in my comments, and for good reason. 'By the time your letter reached us it was completely mutilated by censors, the card was intact though,' Dr Niazi informed me on receipt of a letter I had written to the family.[20]

Despite her recent period of house arrest, Benazir was continuing to make strong statements, accusing General Zia of pursuing a vendetta against her family, following reports that a secret military trial of twenty-four students, including Murtaza *in absentia*, had begun 'on charges of subversion, sabotage and attempting to wage war against Pakistan'. Her objection was to the establishment of a military court, which, she said, showed that the allegations were 'weak and false'.[21] I'd had very little contact with Murtaza since he'd moved to Kabul but Bashir Riaz kept in regular touch, including travelling to Kabul to see him. He told me that the organisation was now functioning under the name 'Al Zulfikar'.

Of particular interest to those of us present in Rawalpindi during Bhutto's appeal was the fate of one of the Supreme Court judges who had upheld Bhutto's appeal against the death sentence, Ghulam Safdar Shah. In October 1980 he left Pakistan, trekking 'for three days, on mule back and foot, across the line of battle in an area of fighting between Afghan rebels [i.e. the Afghan mujahideen] and Government troops'. While in Kabul he gave an interview, which Peter picked up and used to write a front page article: 'Bhutto judge says trial was unfair'.[22]

Once Safdar Shah reached London in late November, a mutual contact put us in touch. It was fascinating to meet this earnest man, who for months I had observed in the Supreme Court but to whom I'd never spoken. He now wanted to write an article, which I helped him submit to the *Observer*. Under the headline 'Why I fled Zia's justice', he described the pressures he'd experienced both throughout and after Bhutto's appeal. 'In Pakistan today, there is no rule of law, and, as one who has spent the best part of his life in the service of his people for the rule of law, I must speak out now against some of the injustices I have witnessed,' he began. '... for it seems to me, that the only reason I fell from favour, so to speak, and frivolous charges were brought against me, was because, as a "dissenting" judge of the Supreme Court which heard Mr Bhutto's appeal, I declared that he was innocent.' His article was yet more testimony to support our belief that Bhutto's appeal was manipulated by the military authorities.[23]

'It's been very interesting to meet the judge, and discuss with him the things we all knew anyway, but are now confirmed by him,' I told Benazir. As usual, I kept her in touch with our Oxford friends, informing her that I hadn't seen Claire recently. 'The last time I did she was well and happy... she is wanting to move out of London. She's still teaching... Jane Brooks married to Nick St A[ubyn] is very pregnant with the baby due in the Spring. I went to a party they had before Christmas and there were lots of familiar faces... they always ask after you.'[24]

In early 1981 I decided to go to India. Although I was happy working on other stories, I knew that if I wanted to become an 'expert' on South Asia, I had to understand more about the region, rather than being content with my one-sided focus on Pakistan. My plan was to record some interviews for a variety of feature programmes, one of which was a profile of Indira Gandhi, who had won the 1980 election and was once more prime minister. 'If you are going to India,' BBC producer Justin Rowley said, 'it would be great if you could get me some first hand interviews with anyone close to her you come across.'*

Before leaving I had written to Benazir; on this occasion I had a reliable courier, another BBC colleague, Keith Parsons, who was travelling to Pakistan specifically to record an interview with her for the BBC World Service's programme 'Assignment'. 'How nice to know that you will be in the region by the end of the month,' she responded. 'I do hope that you will drop by here for a few days to say hello. They are still not letting me out of the country under some vague idea that I would form a government-in-exile.' After describing how numerous PPP workers were being arrested, she

---

* Indira Gandhi (1917–84) was prime minister of India 1966–77 and 1980–84.

continued: 'Last New Year was the first one I spent, since my return from Oxford, without detention. The suppression here continues; censorship makes everything frustrating. The Generals are making money, houses and buying plots [of land]. The poor are continuing in a state of numbness. Nevertheless, all this will change for time waits for no-one... Love to you and to your parents and to any of our mutual friends you may meet, B xxx.'[25]

It was wonderful hearing her voice again when Keith's programme was broadcast, but, as always, depressing realising the continual harassment she faced. 'The intelligence men are always outside our gates; and they tend to harass the people who visit us... and it's really a terrible feeling, that each step you take is matched by another step behind you... Because we believe in a democratic concept we are being harassed.'[26]

As described by Peter Niesewand in his September 1980 article, the PPP was working to form an alliance with other political parties. On 6 February 1981, from the drawing room of 70, Clifton, the Movement for the Restoration of Democracy was launched. Known as the MRD, its objective was self-evident: to restore parliamentary democracy in Pakistan. Benazir and her mother had had to accept that, if they were to defeat Zia, they needed a coalition, even if it meant going into an alliance with those who had worked to destabilise the PPP government in 1977. Included among its members were former rivals, the ANP (the Awami National Party, led by the Pashtun nationalist, Abdul Wali Khan),* the Jamiat Ulema-e-Islam, the Tehriq-i-Istiqlal and a faction of the Muslim League. But making an alliance with former political

---

* Abdul Wali Khan (1917–2006) was president of the National Awami Party (NAP), renamed Awami National Party (ANP) in 1986. He was the son of Abdul Ghaffar Khan (1890–1988), known as the 'Frontier Gandhi' because of his espousal of non-violence and his support of the independence movement against the British.

opponents did not mean having any dealings with General Zia. When Keith Parsons had asked her whether the PPP would ever contemplate 'some sort of accommodation' between the PPP and the army, Benazir's comments were true to form: 'We are against a military regime. We do not believe that the solution to Pakistan's problems lies in military dictatorship. So if your question means arriving at an accommodation with a view to perpetuating military dictatorship – No. But if it means trying to find a transition or a way to bring in civilian rule, that can be considered, minus General Zia.'[27]

I landed in Delhi on 24 February 1981. In those days visas were still not required to enter either India or Pakistan and so there was no question of seeking permission. Almost as soon as I arrived, I booked a telephone call to speak to Benazir to tell her that I was planning on coming to see her the following week. But I never managed to get through. Instead I spoke to Samiya on a very bad line to tell her of my impending arrival, although I wasn't sure by which flight I would travel.

My first two nights in Delhi were spent at the YMCA but I then gratefully moved to stay with Suzanne Green, the UPI correspondent in Delhi. From the comfort of her home in Sundar Nagar, not far from the tomb of Humayun, the second Mughal emperor, I began to contact the few people I knew. Although it wasn't part of my BBC brief, since I would be interviewing people for the profile on Indira Gandhi, I thought I would try to secure a meeting with the prime minister herself, without of course treading on Mark Tully's toes as the BBC's correspondent in Delhi. As often happens, one contact led to another, and before long I found myself in touch with an influential member of India's civil service, J. N. Dixit (later to become foreign secretary),* who

---

* J. N. Dixit (1936–2005) was Indian foreign secretary 1991–94.

agreed to put my name forward to meet the prime minister. First I had to send a formal written request. I went immediately to the Oberoi Hotel, where a friend of a friend, who owned a carpet shop, had a typewriter. 'Sat crossed legged on the floor typing my letter,' I recorded in my diary. 'Some American tourists wondered what on earth I was doing!' Again the difference between then and now was vast. There was no business centre providing all facilities and communication was basic. Having delivered my letter by hand to the prime minister's residence at 1, Safdarjung Road, I did not have long to wait for a response. My meeting was fixed for 12.30 on 11 March.[28]

One of my main contacts, who had introduced me to the carpet shop owner, was a young Kashmiri, Bashir Butt, whom I'd met in London the previous year. Like many Kashmiris, his family owned houseboats in the valley of Kashmir – a favourite haunt of the British in colonial days – as well as a business selling the beautiful embroidered shawls and carpets for which Kashmir is renowned.* Although it was early in the season, because I wanted to record a feature on Kashmiri handicrafts, and knowing that I planned to go to Pakistan the following weekend, Bashir and his wife, Zahida, insisted I fit in a visit to Kashmir first. Travelling over-night by train to Jammu – the state's winter capital – I then made the long journey by bus to the summer capital, Srinagar. Snow was still on the ground and it was very cold, with the Kashmiris enveloped in their pherans – thick long coats – with their kangris – heated fire-pots – clasped under them. I too gratefully wore a

---

* Bashir Butt (b.1948), whose father, Gulam Mohammad Butt – was known as 'Haji' because he had gone on pilgrimage to Mecca; before independence in 1947, he was left ownership of the houseboats on upper Dal Lake by a British businessman. Haji Butt was an embroiderer and while two of his sons con-tinued in the handicraft business, the other two took over the houseboats, the extended family of cousins also becoming involved.

pheran and warmed my hands on a kangri. The valley of Kashmir was the most beautiful place I had ever seen and I have never forgotten my first sight of Dal Lake, looking clear as crystal, against the backdrop of the snow-capped Himalayan mountains.

There had, however, been some disturbing news from Pakistan. On 2 March, a Pakistan International Airlines (PIA) plane with over 130 passengers en route from Peshawar to Karachi was hijacked and diverted to Kabul. The hijackers were demanding that over fifty political prisoners be released. Since the prisoners were mostly PPP supporters and from other left-wing parties in the MRD coalition, it was assumed that Al Zulfikar, whose aim was 'to avenge' Zulfikar Ali Bhutto's hanging by Zia, was behind the hijacking, a supposition that was given credence when Murtaza arrived on the tarmac at Kabul airport to talk to the hijackers. Although he denied any personal involvement in the planning (instead stating that some members of Al Zulfikar, Karachi division, had hijacked the plane 'on their own initiative'), the hijacking provided yet another reason for Zia to order a clampdown on all political activity in Pakistan, especially in relation to the PPP.[29]

With news of the hijacking, I cut short my stay in Kashmir. 'There's trouble and civil unrest which will surely mean BB will be arrested soon. Plus the hijacking of a plane from Karachi to Peshawar diverted to Afghanistan,' I noted in my diary.[30] Travelling from Srinagar to Amritsar, it seemed quickest to cross the border at Wagah and then fly from Lahore to Karachi. Since I wanted the authorities to think I was on a personal visit and I would not be working as a journalist, I had deliberately given Bashir my camera and my BBC Sony professional tape-recorder (an upgrade from the Uher and definitely lighter to carry) to take back with him to Delhi. When I mentioned this to a friend of Mark Tully's I'd met in Amritsar, he said that, because of the strict controls of importing electrical equipment into India and the fact that I'd entered the country with a camera and a tape-recorder, which had been marked on my passport, I wouldn't be able to exit without them (unimaginable in today's world!). So I had to retrace my steps to Delhi to pick up the camera and tape-recorder, which meant that, more than twenty-four hours later than planned – on 5 March – I flew directly from Delhi to Karachi.

My flight was in the evening and, as I stood in line to check in, I found myself dwarfed by a woman and a man in front of me pushing trolleys with a large amount of luggage which looked like bales of material and which I later understood they had brought from China. The next minute, they were engaged in an animated discussion with an airline official behind the counter.

'Sorry Madam, too much luggage, you will have to pay a big surcharge.'

The woman, who was speaking in German to her colleague, protested and the passengers behind fidgeted. On the spur of the moment, I interjected.

'I am just going to Karachi for the weekend. I don't have any luggage to check. Could this lady not have my allowance?' Today such a suggestion would never be countenanced. But the Indian Airlines official looked up at me and said:

'Well, yes, that would be fine,' whereupon the woman turned around and thanked me; her luggage was duly dispatched along the conveyor belt and everyone seemed happy. As we walked towards the plane together, I discovered that the recipient of my baggage allowance was not German, as I had initially thought, but an Austrian business woman who imported textiles from China. I explained that I was working in India for a few weeks and that I was going to see a friend in Karachi for the weekend.

On arrival in Pakistan, as I approached the immigration desk, I handed my passport to the official, my hand poised to receive it back after he had stamped it. But instead, after looking at my photograph, with my passport still in his hand, I heard him call to another official: 'Victoria Schofield is back.'

Two men then came to me on the other side of the immigration barrier and asked me to 'come this way', directing me into a room, which was bare except for a chair. As they closed the door behind them, I noticed a policewoman sitting outside. There was no explanation, no cup of tea, no glass of water. So I sat on the chair and waited, literally not knowing whether I was coming or going: coming into Pakistan or going back to India. It was well past midnight and I was beginning to feel embarrassed at the prospect of turning up at 70, Clifton so late.

After waiting a little longer, I opened the door and found that the policewoman who had been sitting outside was no longer there. I could hear some people speaking and so I went in the direction of the voices. On seeing a man seated with a telephone at each ear, flanked by several men on either side, I went into the room. Suddenly aware of my presence, he looked up, continuing to talk rather more excitedly into the telephone.

'What do you mean, she is on the plane?' There was a pause, as he scrutinised my face. 'She is standing here in front of me!'

There was another pause, as he put one telephone down and started talking into the other one. I did not instantly realise what had happened but, as it transpired, the authorities had somehow forgotten that they had left me confined in the room; instead they thought that I had meekly boarded the Indian Airlines plane I had arrived on, and so they had given clearance for it to return to Delhi.

Faintly amused at this apparent incompetence, I was thinking that my chances of being allowed to stay for even twenty-four hours were increasing with no plane available to take me back to Delhi. But in the next breath, I heard the same man giving instructions for the plane, which was still in Pakistani air-space, to be summoned back. With a plane returning especially to pick me up, I reluctantly had to come to terms with the fact that no amount of pleading was going to enable me to stay.

I still wanted to know upon whose authority I was being refused entry into Pakistan. When I demanded to see some documentation, a huge lever-arch file was produced and placed on a table at which I was invited to sit. An official leafed through the pages rapidly and then, about halfway through, came to a halt, pointing triumphantly to my name at the top of a sheet of paper. There, with my own eyes, I saw that an order had been passed in May 1979, shortly after I had left Islamabad, forbidding me entry into the country 'by land, sea or air'. I was dumbfounded. There was an additional note which said that I was claiming to be a student but that I was a journalist (they might as well have written 'spy' for all the mistrust implicit in the description). Of course the explanation was that in the days when all passports had a line stating 'profession', mine was still entered as 'student', which, after all, when I first went to Pakistan in 1978 I so recently had been. After I had absorbed the implications of my situation, I was left to wait. Another half-hour elapsed. I desperately wanted to get a message to Benazir to tell her what had happened to me, but I dared not ask to use the telephone. Eventually I was informed that the plane had returned and I was to board it.

Feeling tired and light-headed from the strain of the last few hours, I walked slowly towards the aircraft. As I reached the gang-way, one of the officials stopped me abruptly and told me to open my bag. This seemed too much and I protested that, since I had not entered the country, I could hardly be considered to be exiting, and therefore they had no right to search my bag. The officials were in no mood to listen. My bag was duly opened: the pots of English honey I had brought to give to Benazir rolled onto the tarmac. When they started rifling through my cosmetics bag, I shouted again.

'This is a lady's bag, you should have a lady to search it,' but to no avail. Once the officials had finished rummaging through my possessions – a look of disapproval on their faces as they came upon the tape-recorder labelled 'property of the BBC' – I was left to scramble my things together and put them back into the bag, including the tape-recorder which miraculously they did not confiscate. As I was directed to board the plane, I saw my passport being handed over to an Indian Airlines official who was informed that I was a 'deportee'. I understood that it was not to be returned to me until I had paid my return airfare. The British High Commission in Delhi would be informed that if I turned up on their doorstep and told them that I had lost my passport, they must not issue me with another one because I was in default of paying an airfare.[31]

As I boarded the plane I averted my eyes from looking at the other passengers, who must have been furious at having to return to Pakistan, with the result that none of us would get to bed until the early hours of the morning. I tried to sleep, refusing a second round of dinner. On arrival at Delhi airport, an authoritative Sikh in Indian Airlines uniform came towards me. Once again I caught sight of my passport in his hand.

'Are you the deportee?' he asked in a more friendly manner than one might have expected. When I replied in the affirmative, he looked bemused.

'What!' he exclaimed. 'This little girl is such a threat to General Zia that my plane and my passengers had to be so inconvenienced?' I smiled feebly and accompanied him to the ticket counter where I purchased – in arrears since I'd already arrived – a return ticket from Karachi to Delhi. He handed me back my passport and left me to make my way back to Delhi in the middle of the night.

As usual there were plenty of taxi drivers on hand to offer me the best price. 'You want Old Delhi, you want New Delhi?' I was helpfully asked.

Truth to tell, I had no idea. Suzanne, with whom I was still staying, was well and truly tucked up in bed, safe in the knowledge that I had gone away for at least two days and I simply did not dare arrive at her home at past four in the morning to tell her that I was back forty-eight hours early. I was reluctant to check into a hotel for a quarter of a night which would further diminish my already depleted funds and I could not face the YMCA.

Suddenly a voice out of the crowd said:

'You've had a long night, would you like a lift into Delhi?' I was amazed. Who did I know at Delhi airport who knew where I had been? I looked at the man, who was another Indian Airlines official.

'Oh,' I said, 'yes, I have, as a matter of fact.' I did not say what was in my mind ('how on earth would you know?'), but he read my thoughts.

'I checked you in to the Karachi flight a few hours ago.' The penny dropped. 'You helped that lady with her luggage allowance on the way out,' the official was saying. 'I am off duty now and can take you into Delhi, where would you like to go?' He then added hastily that his method of transport was a motor cycle, 'if that is all right'. Considering that a ride with an Indian Airlines official on a motor cycle whom I had met once was better than any one of the numerous strange taxi drivers offering their services in the middle of the night, I accepted. On the instant, since I still did not have a destination in mind, I said that he could drop me at the Ashok Hotel, where I knew there was an all-night coffee shop and where I could sit. This he duly did and I spent the remainder of the night writing a letter to my parents as well as to Benazir and Samiya to tell them what had happened to me.

Later in the day I went to see Mark Tully who was intrigued

that the Pakistani authorities were so anxious to get rid of me that they had called back an Indian Airlines plane, a competitive tit-for-tat always bedevilling their relations even when they weren't overtly at war.

'Would you mind,' Mark asked, 'if I write a story on your deportation?'

'No,' I said, rather amazed that my deportation was of sufficient interest for the legendary Mark Tully.[32]

It was now Saturday and my meeting with Prime Minister Indira Gandhi was the following Tuesday. I spent the intervening time worrying that, because of the 'international incident', the interview would be cancelled. On the appointed day, in the absence of any instruction to the contrary, I made my way to the Indian parliament, the Lok Sabha. As I was ushered into the prime minister's office, she was standing at her desk with the huge map of India behind her, the map looking larger and she smaller than when I had seen the same image on television. She beckoned me towards a seat in front of her desk.

'So they did not allow you into Pakistan?' she began, without requiring an answer. 'Never mind, you are welcome here in India.'[33] I smiled and so did she.

Even before I could begin asking the questions I'd prepared, I found myself at the receiving end of the prime minister's enquiries. 'Did I know how Begum Nusrat Bhutto was? And how was Benazir?' Explaining how difficult communication was, I told her what I knew about the current political unrest and the crackdown on political activity in the wake of the hijacking. After a few more solicitous enquiries, including about Bhutto's death, our roles reversed and I began to go through my list, beginning with the different challenges she faced in her second tenure as prime minister, to which she replied that in government there are always problems: 'today it is oil, before it was famine'. In response to my question about India's relationship with the Soviet Union which, for us in the West was always a matter of concern, she was brief: 'India is not pro-Soviet; India is pro-Indian'; their relationship, she said, was dictated by geography.

With my recent experience of visiting the valley of Kashmir and my friendship with the Butts, I felt emboldened to ask her when it might be possible to resolve the contentious situation relating to the former princely state of Jammu and Kashmir, which, since partition and the first Indo-Pakistani war 1947–49, was left de facto divided along the ceasefire line (and which she and Bhutto had renamed the 'Line of Control' in the 1972 Shimla agreement concluding the Bangladesh war). Once again, her reply was forthright. There was, she said, no 'situation' to be resolved. In other words, since, in October 1947, the maharaja of Jammu and Kashmir had acceded to India – albeit under duress, because his state was being invaded by tribesmen from Pakistan's North-West Frontier Province – the whole state was legally part of India. Anyway, she continued, the Kashmiris were much better off under Indian governance and, at the time, I was compelled to agree that, since Bhutto's death, the Muslim Kashmiris I'd met didn't seem that anxious to join Pakistan under General Zia. What also emerged from our conversation was her dislike of General Zia's dictatorship. Events in Afghanistan, she said, were helping him to stay in power. Soon my allotted half an hour was over and I got up to leave. Mrs Gandhi stood up too, her small figure again framed by the map of India. She shook my hand graciously and bid me farewell. 'So now I have met my first Prime Minister in office,' I recorded in my diary, 'apart from Mrs Thatcher in opposition, Harold Macmillan, when retired and, of course, Mr Bhutto when under sentence of death.'[34]

Some days later, I went to the prime minister's residence where traditionally every day she emerged after breakfast to greet whosoever might choose to wait in the gardens. 'Security was very tight,' I noted in my diary, 'but even so it was amazing that so many people came to see her.' Progressing through the crowd, she paused, exchanging a word or two with one person and then another, shaking hands, and moving on. Having so recently met her, I held back. For a brief moment, she looked at me, a smile of recognition on her face, before she passed by.[35] Three years later Indira Gandhi was assassinated by her Sikh bodyguards near where I had last seen her.*

Throughout my *aller-retour* to Pakistan, the PIA plane had remained grounded at Kabul airport and negotiations were taking place with the Pakistani government. The drama had intensified when, on 7 March, a passenger, Major Tariq Rahim, was shot by one of the hijackers, Salamullah Tipu. Controversy remains as to whether he was the intended victim or whether it was a case of mistaken identity and Tipu had shot Rahim, Bhutto's former ADC, in the belief that he was the son of General Rahimuddin Khan, the II Corps Commander in Multan. This created the grounds for another supposition (also denied)† that Murtaza had ordered his shooting because he believed Rahim had let down his father.[36]

Benazir had immediately condemned the hijacking and any links with the PPP. Within days of my deportation, both she and her mother were detained, as were thousands of others throughout the country. As Benazir later recorded: 'Amnesty International, whose figures were always conservative, estimated that over six thousand people were arrested in March 1981 alone... Everybody

---

* Indira Gandhi was assassinated in 1984 following Operation Blue Star, the storming of the Golden Temple in Amritsar to capture Sikh insurgents.

† Fatima Bhutto denies her father's involvement: see *Songs of Blood and Sword: A Daughter's Memoir* (Jonathan Cape, 2010), p.223. Salamullah Tipu was executed in Kabul in 1984 for having killed an Afghan.

with the slightest connection with the MRD or the PPP was being imprisoned.'[37]

When the police went to arrest our friend Amna Piracha, they realised she was heavily pregnant and so they took her husband Saleem instead; both were well known for their PPP sympathies since working together on Bhutto's appeal. Dr Niazi, who had been put in jail again in 1980 for distributing 'objectionable literature', was warned that he might once more be arrested; he had therefore decided to leave the country overland, travelling via Kabul. Unfortunately, en route, he had a heart attack and arrived in London badly in need of medical attention. The authorities did not spare his wife, Shaukat Niazi, who had stayed behind, and she was once more arrested. Such wide-scale arrests put the MRD on hold, just when, as Benazir said, Zia was 'on the threshold of being forced out of office by popular uprising'.[38]

Meanwhile, having left Major Rahim's body on the tarmac in Kabul, the plane had been flown to Syria, landing in Damascus. On 14 March the hijacking was resolved with Zia's agreement to release fifty-four political prisoners in return for the lives of the passengers and crew. Among the men released was one woman, PPP political activist Farkhanda Bokhari from Lahore, whose experiences were illustrative of how intent the military were on linking Benazir and Begum Bhutto to acts of 'terrorism' even prior to the hijacking.* 'On 5 January, at about 2 am, we

---

* Farkhanda Bokhari (b.1938) was deported without travel documents and had to seek political asylum; she remained in Britain until 1989. Her three children joined her in September 1981. While in exile she was sentenced to 14 years' hard labour and confiscation of their home. Her husband, Professor Shohrat Bokhari (1925–2001), a distinguished Urdu poet and educationalist, was sacked from his job and banned from all appearances on state-controlled media TV and Radio Pakistan. The family remained loyal to the Bhutto family throughout.

were woken by armed soldiers, holding guns in our bedroom,' recalled her daughter, Maqsooma. 'My mother was handcuffed and blindfolded and put into an army van.' For over two months she was kept in solitary confinement in Lahore Fort, where, in an attempt to make her 'confess' that, on Begum Bhutto's instructions, she had gone to Libya for armed training, 'her hands were burned with cigarettes, she received cuts on her arms, and was abused by female constables'. Having been released at the end of the hijacking, she and the other political prisoners were unable to return to their homes. 'We had no idea,' said her daughter, 'that she was being deported until Zia made an announcement on PTV [Pakistan Television] in the evening that he has thrown out 54 bad eggs and exchanged them for the PIA passengers. That's when we knew. We had no idea! I was ten years old! A lot of trauma for us all. We then saw a picture of her in the English paper *Observer* where she is climbing the plane's stairs handcuffed and the pain on her face told the tale.'[39]

The hijacking had serious repercussions not only for Benazir and Begum Bhutto, but also for Murtaza and Shahnawaz. Quite apart from the acts of sabotage Al Zulfikar had undertaken in Pakistan, the hijacking and the murder of Tariq Rahim sealed their reputation as 'terrorists'. As with the Soviet invasion of Afghanistan, General Zia was able to make political capital out of the sequence of events. 'Pakistan reaction to hijacking shows Zia's strength', reported Frank Prial in the *New York Times*. '"Before the hijacking," a senior Pakistani official said the other day, "every Westerner stepped off the plane here and asked: 'Will the regime fall this week or next?' I think that's all over now."'[40]

Benazir's arrest and my deportation from Pakistan meant I had no idea when we would meet again.

6

Living But Not Living: 1981–83

*Time relentless, monotonous. To keep my brain
stimulated, I recorded everything that was
happening to me in a thin little notebook.*[1]

While the PIA hijacking was reaching its climax, I had stayed on in India, recording interviews for the BBC including the profile on Indira Gandhi. Most importantly, although I did not realise it at the time, having moved from Suzanne's to stay with the Butts in Delhi, I had laid the groundwork for my long-standing interest in the 'Jammu-Kashmir' issue.

By early April, armed with my numerous tape-recorded interviews, I was back in London, once more reading the news about Pakistan which came over the wire at the BBC. As usual I searched for any news about Benazir. It emerged that when she was first arrested she was taken to Karachi Central Jail rest house, while for the first time her mother was detained in Karachi Central Jail in a C-class cell for 'ordinary' prisoners. A few days later Benazir was moved to Sukkur Jail in central Sindh, also in a C-class cell.*

---

* According to the Pakistan Prison Rules 1978, A and B class was for 'better class' prisoners, as defined by character, social status, education and lifestyle

'For the first time I felt afraid,' Benazir later wrote. 'I had heard rumours that the jail authorities sometimes took controversial prisoners into the desert at night and simply killed them.'[2]

With a virtual news blackout on her situation, it was hard to comprehend the trauma of being in solitary confinement. Only later did I understand how appalling the conditions were under which she was being kept in the height of summer. 'The skin gets parched and because it gets dry, it gets pulled and cracked; that means it starts bleeding. But because of the heat, you sweat, and the acidity cuts into your wounds and makes them worse. Then the dust storms come and the dust gets imbedded.' Remarkably, looking back, her humour was intact. 'I remember, when we were children, we used to hear that the desert heat is so strong that, when the British were here, instead of cooking eggs on the fire, they kept them out in the sun to cook. Of course, by the time I was in jail, there were no eggs to practise with to see if it was really true or not!'[3]

After nearly five unbearably hot months in Sukkur, she was moved to Karachi Central Jail. Begum Bhutto had been released from jail 'after vomiting blood' and being diagnosed by the jail doctors as having an ulcer; Benazir was put in her mother's old cell. In late August, hoping that she might be released when her six-month detention order expired on 13 September, I attempted to get a letter through to her. 'Dearest B, I am writing you a letter in anticipation that there is the vague hope that you might be released soon – maybe at the end of the 6 months they have kept you in. I cannot believe their cruelty and inhumanity.'[4]

But she was not released and I have no idea if she received my letter, nor the birthday telegram Claire and I had sent to her on

----

(entitling them to books, newspapers, personal bedding and food); C class was for ordinary prisoners who had none of these benefits.

21 June; at least, as we later heard, while she was still in Sukkur, she had been allowed a visit from Sunny, who had given her the good news that she had accepted a proposal of marriage. Her future husband was Nasir Hussain, whose grandfather, like Sir Shah Nawaz, was a former prime minister of Junagadh. The newspaper headlines stated: 'Grandchildren of two former prime ministers of Junagadh state to marry.'

Sunny's wedding took place in Karachi in September. For a few precious days Benazir was allowed out of jail for the wedding, another headline reading: 'Sister attends sister's wedding'. But as soon as the festivities were over she was taken back and her detention order renewed for another three months. 'The familiar sound of the jailer's keys opening padlock after padlock greeted me at Karachi Central [Jail],' Benazir later wrote.[5] And so it continued. Until she renounced politics, she was told that she would remain in prison.

Meanwhile Zia continued as president and chief martial law administrator. Despite the hiatus in any political freedoms and the wide-scale arrests, his regime was continuing to be supported by the US administration and its allies to help fight the war in Afghanistan. In October 1981, having become prime minister after the 1979 general election, Margaret Thatcher arrived on a brief visit to Pakistan. She was the first Western leader to visit Pakistan since Bhutto's execution and I remember feeling particularly dismayed to see her standing beside General Zia, who accompanied her to the North-West Frontier where she met Afghan refugees and looked out at Afghanistan from the border town of Torkham. At an official banquet she said that her stopover demonstrated Britain's 'support of Pakistan in the wake of the Soviet invasion of Afghanistan' with apparently no overt pressure on General Zia to restore democratic government.[6]

At the end of 1981 Benazir was moved from jail to Al Murtaza in Larkana. But being at home on her own was an emotional challenge. 'Even in jail prisoners see each other and they can interact. But when I was under detention, there was simply no interaction. It was a situation where one was living and yet one was not living. It was as if I did not exist, I did not have a voice, I could not communicate, I could not inter-relate. It was like being paralysed.'[7] As time passed it seemed so harsh that she was spending her youth in detention, while we were getting on with our lives, finding life partners and marrying, as did I when, in March 1982, I married Stephen Willis. As a graduate from Cambridge he had never met Benazir, although he already realised her importance in my life.

Even Benazir's brothers, who had not been able to come from Kabul to Pakistan for Sunny's wedding, had married. Their wives were two Afghan sisters, Fauzia and Rehana Fasihuddin, whose father was an Afghan diplomat. In May 1982 Murtaza's wife, Fauzia, gave birth to Fatima, while Shahnawaz's wife, Rehana, had given birth to Sassi.* At this stage, as recalled by Elizabeth Colton, a producer for ABC News TV and Radio covering the war in Lebanon,† who'd met Murtaza soon after he'd moved from Kabul to live in Damascus in the summer of 1982, he did not express any misgivings about his sister being the 'chosen one' to become their father's political heir. 'He described it more as a fact and as an explanation how she, though a girl, was a natural and trained leader. He always spoke admiringly of her.' Sadly, in the years to come the gap between them was to widen.[8]

Filtering through to London was the alarming news that Begum Bhutto was unwell with suspected lung cancer. Although no longer in jail, she was not permitted to travel abroad for medical treatment. In order to highlight their continuing detention a group of

---

* Fatima Bhutto (b.1982), Sassi Bhutto (b.1982).
† Elizabeth (Liz) Colton (b.1945).

concerned individuals, called 'Save the Bhutto Ladies', was set up. Claire and I were asked to join and we introduced another Oxford friend, Colin Clifford, who was working as a journalist for the *Sunday Times*. One of the leading lights was Lord Avebury, the British Liberal politician and human rights activist, and we held our first meeting in his home in Pimlico on 14 October. Other key members were Begum Bhutto's sister, Behjat Hariri, Dr Niazi, Connie Seifert, whose son, Michael, was a human rights lawyer, and Syeda Mubashar (Bashan) Rafique, whose family was involved in the All Pakistan Women's Association, founded in Pakistan by prime minister Liaquat Khan's wife, Begum Ra'ana, in 1949. 'At this time we had lost Zulfikar Ali Bhutto and Nusrat and Benazir were vulnerable and we needed to bring this out in the Western world,' recalled Bashan.[9] Our first goal was to lobby for Begum Bhutto to be allowed to leave Pakistan, to which end an Early Day Motion in the House of Commons was sponsored by Jonathan Aitken, MP, and Joan Lestor, MP.* To our surprise, this objective was achieved sooner than we expected. On 12 November we heard that Begum Bhutto had been given permission to go to Germany for medical treatment. We now redoubled our efforts in relation to Benazir.

We also heard news of promising initiatives by Benazir's friend, Peter Galbraith, who, after Harvard and Oxford, was working as a staff member on the US Senate Committee on Foreign Relations, chaired by Senator Charles Percy, of which Senator Clairborne Pell was the minority leader.† 'Our efforts included the Pell

---

* Jonathan Aitken (b.1942); Joan Lestor, Baroness Lestor of Eccles (1931–98); Michael Seifert (1942–2017). The Seiferts introduced Benazir to the formidable human rights lawyer, Baroness Helena Kennedy of the Shaws, QC, FRSA, Hon FRSE (b. 1950).

† Senator Charles Percy (1919–2011), chairman, Senate Foreign Relations Committee 1981–85; Senator Clairborne Pell (1918–2009), chairman, Senate Foreign Relations Committee 1987–95.

Amendment (1981) linking US assistance to Pakistan to respect for civil liberties and the restoration of representative government; we also had repeated meetings with the foreign minister, Sahabzada Yaqub Khan,* and the Pakistani ambassador to argue for her release.' Peter had already gone to Pakistan the previous August armed with a letter from Pell 'requesting the regime to permit me to visit Benazir. I made a big pitch to the Pakistani Foreign Ministry, as well as to the US Embassy, which at that time was quite hostile to the Bhuttos. The regime didn't even respond to Senator Pell's request, nor to mine.'[10]

Another opportunity for Peter to speak out on Benazir's behalf came in December 1982 when General Zia made his first official visit to the United States (a visit which we cynically believed might have accounted for Begum Bhutto's sudden release in November). This 'included a lunch at the Senate Foreign Relations Committee with Zia where he promised that friends could visit Benazir', continued Peter. 'We immediately followed up by demanding that I be able to see her since, of course, I was indisputably a friend. The Pakistanis dragged their feet on this for a year and it became increasingly embarrassing for Yaqub Khan who was there when Zia made his statement.'[11] Peter had started to lobby for her release in 1981, but it would be three years before his efforts came to fruition.

I was still working at the BBC World Service on general stories as well as continuing to relish my proximity to the news, which I monitored in my copy-tasting job in the Central Current Affairs Talks department. I'd also begun to write another book, having been approached by an editor I'd met at a book launch – Toby

---

* Sahabzada Yaqub Khan (1920–2016) was a former general and diplomat. Born into a princely family, he served with the Indian army in World War II and was foreign minister of Pakistan 1982–91 and 1996–97.

Buchan, the grandson of the famous author, John Buchan, who'd been at Cassell when I was working on *Bhutto: Trial and Execution*.

'Are you still interested in writing on South Asia?' he asked.

'Oh yes,' I replied. 'In early 1981 I was in India.'

'Fine,' he continued. 'I've set up my own publishing company. With all the interest in Afghanistan I'd like to publish a book like Charles Allen's *Plain Tales from the Raj* but focusing on the North-West Frontier – say, "Plain Tales of the Frontier". There must be so many stories of the British who served on the Frontier and in Afghanistan – you know Lady Sale's diary? Think about it and send me a proposal.' It was as simple as that: not much of an advance, but a commission to write a book which kept me focused on the region.

In addition to making contact with former Indian Civil Service and Indian Political Service officers now living in picturesque houses in the English countryside, many of whose families had served for generations in India, I wanted to understand more about the Frontier from the locals. One of the first people I went to see was Dr Niazi, whose tribe, the Niazis, came from Mianwali in the Punjab, bordering the North-West Frontier. He was only too happy to spend an afternoon telling me about the customs and traditions of the Frontier. As he was talking it seemed that he was transported back to his homeland, the difficulties of living abroad and being separated from his family temporarily forgotten. One comment which interested me was about the effect of the hippies in the 1960s. 'Before their arrival all we had known was the very proper British memsahib. But suddenly across the horizon from Afghanistan came all these young men and women, shabbily dressed, taking drugs. It didn't matter whether they were German or Danish or Swedish, they were Western and that is what altered the stereotype of Western women.' It was clear that the image it created of their behaviour was not favourable, contributing to a cautionary approach in terms of what 'progress' and 'liberalisation' might mean in a traditional society.[12]

Christmas 1982 passed and Benazir remained under detention in Al Murtaza. In the six years since we'd left Oxford she'd only been free for one New Year's Eve celebration and that was two years earlier.

On 4 February 1983 I awoke to the news on the radio that Peter Niesewand had died of leukemia aged only thirty-eight. I had last seen him in Delhi in 1981 when he told me that he was writing a fictitious account of Bhutto's trial and execution, to be called 'The Word of a Gentleman', describing all the things we couldn't say, mainly relating to the immense pressure the judges were under. In terms of the journalists who had followed Bhutto's trial and execution, he and Bruce had been the most steadfast, maintaining their journalistic integrity yet obviously retaining their sympathy and admiration for the Bhuttos. We were all deeply saddened by Peter's death. Although we did not know his family, Yasmin (who'd joined her father in London) and I went to his funeral.

Unexpectedly, in late March 1983 Benazir reappeared in the news. Throughout this period General Zia was using the war against the Soviets in Afghanistan as a pretext to crack down on all communist and left-wing sympathisers in Pakistan. In pursuit of this objective a series of investigations had identified certain individuals who were accused of plotting to overthrow the regime and replace it with a socialist system. One of those who was being tried was the Sindhi communist leader, Jam Saqi.* Together with five others, he was accused of sedition and allegedly acting against

---

* Jam Saqi (1944–2018) was founder president in 1968 of the Sindh National Students Federation – a student wing of the Communist Party. He supported the socialist manifesto of the PPP. He joined the Communist Party of Pakistan (CPP) in 1964, becoming general secretary 1990/91.

'the ideology of Pakistan' and Benazir had been called as a defence witness. 'For Miss Bhutto's appearance there were unprecedented security measures, clearly suggesting that she's still seen as the greatest potential threat to Pakistan's military rulers,' reported BBC reporter Ian Hoare. 'Road blocks were set up on the main routes leading to the sports complex where the court is situated and all the entrances were locked with police guards posted at them.' Journalists were forbidden entry into the courtroom but when some photographers were given permission, Ian Hoare managed to get in with them. His report continued: 'Miss Bhutto, dressed in traditional Pakistani clothes, appeared composed and in good health and proceeded to demonstrate that she had lost none of her eloquence during her two years of enforced silence as a political prisoner. As she took the oath, she was asked what caste she belonged to, she replied "I thought there are no castes in Islam, and so I have no caste".'[13]

Benazir as a defence witness in the Jam Saqi trial, 1983.

It was heartening to read her bold words as Jam Saqi questioned her in his defence. When asked about the significance of the Iranian revolution for the region, as Ian Hoare reported, she said revolution was not the 'monopoly' of Iran.

Revolutions occurred when all the organs of state in a given territorial unit are identified with a status quo that is repugnant to such a wide spectrum of people that they feel they have nothing to lose if they show courage and take for themselves what is rightfully theirs. In a revolution, Miss Bhutto said, the people bring down the corrupt and degenerate organs of the existing order and replace it with those they choose. She said that a system that does not provide society with a means of resolving conflict inevitably collapses. Dissent, Miss Bhutto went on, was as old as civilisation. Individuals were entitled to their views and should not be persecuted for them, particularly when the ruling authority has no popular mandate.[14]

According to Ian's report, she continued giving evidence for several hours but after an hour he was ordered to leave the court and was therefore reliant on what one of the lawyers told him for much of what she subsequently said. In answer to a question relating to the charge against the defendants that they had worked against the ideology of Pakistan, she replied that the basic ideas behind the creation of Pakistan were contained in the first five articles of the 1973 Constitution and anyone opposed to these articles would be guilty of working against Pakistan's ideology. But, she continued, although one article stated that the state religion was Islam, this did not mean that everyone living in Pakistan would be a Muslim. She went on to argue that there was no scope in Islam for martial law, that Islam was submission to God, whereas martial law was submission to a military commander. From the lawyer's report which Ian then transmitted, Benazir argued 'against all the reasons given by the country's present leadership for promulgating martial law in 1977 and maintaining it ever since. She said one reason put forward was the situation in Afghanistan, but, she said, the military government in Pakistan was demanding rights for the Afghan people, such as the right to self-determination, that it denied to its own countrymen.'[15] Since this was the first statement she had made in ages, I eagerly devoured the news coverage, even if the report was only second and then third hand.

In the hope that Benazir would know we were thinking of her on her thirtieth birthday on Tuesday 21 June 1983, I arranged for a minute's silence at the Oxford Union before the debate the previous Thursday. Later David Johnson, ex-president of the Cambridge Union, who had since entered the Church, wrote to tell me that, having been in the debating chamber for the minute's silence, he had organised for prayers to be said for Benazir at all public services the following Sunday in St Paul's Cathedral and Westminster Abbey.[16]

I also contacted various newspapers with the result that Polly Toynbee of the *Guardian* wrote an article, based on the reminiscences of a number of Oxford friends I'd invited to come to my London flat, including Claire, Freya and Helen (now married to David Profumo). The caption beside a photograph of Benazir looking defiant said it all: 'The glittering socialite was transformed into a formidable political operator. Now she is in solitary confinement in one room at the other end of the world.' 'Her life could not have changed more since those spoilt, frivolous Oxford days,' Polly concluded. 'None of her friends then expected her to become a political force – nor would they have guessed she could resist such catastrophe and oppression, alone and friendless for so long.'[17]

Benazir was back in the news again in August when various news agencies reported that the Indian publisher Vikas, who had published *If I Am Assassinated*, was about to publish a book by Benazir entitled *Pakistan: The Gathering Storm*, which was a scathing attack on Zia and 'fake' Islamisation. Before the book was published, Benazir issued a denial through her lawyer, saying that she was 'astonished' over the book's planned publication and that she had not written it. Narendra Kumar, Vikas's managing director, however, said the sources were 'unimpeachable' and publication went ahead. I had no immediate contact with Benazir and so had no idea what had happened but since Benazir was adamant that she had not written it, Vikas then had to withdraw the published book from circulation.*

Despite the arrests and political repression throughout Pakistan, two years after the founding of the Movement for the Restoration of Democracy its spirit was still alive, adherents hailing the sixth anniversary of the military coup on 5 July as a 'black day.' Although political rallies were banned, the MRD organised a protest march in Karachi. The lawyers showed their sympathy by flying black flags on their office buildings. Remarkably, General Zia seemed impervious to the mounting disaffection. When interviewed by BBC correspondent Jeff Cox for a programme to be broadcast in mid-August to coincide with Pakistan's 36th independence day, he described the conditions in the country as being 'stable' enough for him to consider holding elections on a non-party basis to the provincial and national assemblies 'in about eighteen months from now'.[18]

But Zia's announcement was not greeted with the enthusiasm he might have expected. Instead, on independence day, 14 August, a civil disobedience movement was launched, modelled on the non-violent movement orchestrated by Mahatma Gandhi against the British in colonial days. It was the first serious challenge to Zia's dictatorship since the coup in 1977. 'The MRD campaign of

---

* *Pakistan: The Gathering Storm* under Benazir Bhutto's name is still available on numerous websites. Both Bashir Riaz and Shahnawaz denied that Benazir had written it, as did she, when I interviewed her in New York, 22 April 1985.

courting arrests, a tactic used widely in the subcontinent's struggle for independence from Britain, continued despite heavy monsoon rains with two arrests in Karachi, three in Lahore and 17 in Sindh,' wrote Reuters correspondent, Tom Heneghan, on 22 August.[19] As the protests gathered momentum, particularly in Sindh, with widespread attacks on government buildings and communication systems, the army moved in. From London I was reading the news reports: 'several dozen people were wounded in violent clashes... five agitators killed... fifteen demonstrators killed... General Zia warned that he would treat the leaders of the movement with "an iron hand" during a tour of Sindh province.' And so he did, the 'worst' incident taking place at the end of September when seventeen were killed and forty-eight injured after the army fired into a crowd in the village of Chandio in Nawabshah district. By October, as the movement became localised, the protests abated.[20]

Compared with previous years, my correspondence with Benazir was minimal. But whenever the opportunity arose in the form of a trusted friend travelling, I would write a letter. Although she was still under house arrest in Al Murtaza, the authorities had to allow visits from her lawyers. Since Saleem Khan was now Benazir's lawyer, he was an ideal courier, provided I could get a letter to him. 'Please would you ask Saleem if he would mind taking the enclosed letter to Benazir the next time he might have a chance to see her,' I wrote to Yasmin in early November. 'As [Saleem is] one of the few people who has a chance to see her it seemed such a pity not to take the opportunity to write.' One of my reasons for wanting to do so now was to thank her for some presents she had managed to send me and Claire, as well as sending a small pair of earrings in return. 'It's so hard to think of things to send which are small enough to pass by without attracting attention,' I continued in my letter to Yasmin. 'In the end I settled on the earrings, which are very simple, and I hope she'll like.'[21]

'It is one of those autumnal evenings when the sky has just gone pink before going dark,' I began my letter to Benazir. 'It has been so difficult to write because of the fear of the letter being seized, etc. but I did want to say thank you so very much for the scent and the little charm of the Qur'an. With all that you have on your mind both C[laire] and I were really touched that you went to the trouble to get something for us. I've been thinking of you often these past months (and years) wondering how you are keeping, and trying to see what can be done about keeping the publicity going.' Yet again I regaled her with the activities of our friends, some of whom were now members of parliament following the 1983 general election. 'I have been in touch with Colin Moynihan re. the human rights situ. in Pakistan and he seemed willing to help... They always want to know how you are and have bits of news about you.' Finally I wanted to tell her that I was moving to the United States because my husband Stephen, who worked for Citibank, had been transferred to New York. 'I shall keep in touch with Dr Niazi while I'm away and hopefully have news of you as well as see what can be done in the USA. Sorry, this letter is a bit short and disjointed. Somehow it's a bit difficult to write about the silly day-to-day things which go on here; and then it's too difficult also to write about politics.'[22]

At the end of 1983 the Pakistani political landscape was still bleak. In December Begum Bhutto, who was recovering after medical treatment in Munich, issued a statement saying that 15,000 political prisoners 'without the least judicial protection, were suffering torture and privations'. Unsurprisingly Benazir spent another New Year's Eve in detention.[23]

7

Benazir's Out: 1984–86

*Exile? Why should I go into exile? I am only
in England for medical treatment. I was born in
Pakistan and I'm going to die in Pakistan.*[1]

After spending Christmas and New Year 1984 in Britain, sharing our time between Stephen's parents in Lincolnshire and mine in Henley-on-Thames, I was planning on returning to New York. Stephen had already gone back and I intended to follow him after a few more days with my parents. On 12 January I went to London for some last-minute meetings. As I returned home on the train, I was surprised to see my mother waiting on the platform to greet me. Our house was only a short walk from the station and it was cold and wintry. She looked excited.

'What is it?' I asked.

'Benazir's out.'

'What!' I shrieked. I couldn't believe it. After all these years. She'd been flown to Geneva and was due to arrive in London on the 14th. I knew I couldn't go back to New York without seeing her and so I telephoned Stephen to tell him I'd be postponing my return.

Arriving at Heathrow on 14 January there was no doubt that

something unusual was happening. The airport was exceptionally full of people, pushing and shoving, wanting to get as close as they could to 'Arrivals'. I immediately saw the familiar faces of Pakistanis who I knew were Bhutto supporters, among them Bashir Riaz, with whom I'd worked at *Musawaat*. Yasmin was there as well as Claire, Freya and another Oxford friend, Keith Gregory, who'd visited Benazir in Pakistan in the summer of 1976. Damian Green – my successor as president of the Oxford Union – who was now working for Channel 4 News, had come as part of the large press contingent who were waiting expectantly. Suddenly I caught sight of Helen. She'd come to the airport with her young son, James, in a pushchair. With no experience of the enthusiasm with which a Pakistani crowd could surge forward, she soon realised that her baby, in his exposed position at ankle level, might easily be overwhelmed by the throng. While we were waiting, I rehearsed in my mind what I would say:

'Hello, Benazir, it is wonderful that you are out.' No, that sounded too clichéd.

'Hello, Benazir, I am just so glad that you are safe.' Well, she knows that.

I was still thinking of what I would say when suddenly the crowd was on the move and we were carried with it. And there Benazir was walking out of 'Arrivals', accompanied by Sunny who had flown to Geneva to be with her. The crowd was ecstatic, chanting the familiar slogan '*Jeeay* Bhutto!' Amazingly from out of the mass of people, she saw me.

'Hi, Vicks,' she said with a smile.

I just managed to respond 'Hello, Benazir.' With her supporters continuing to shout enthusiastically, even if I had decided what else to say, I don't think she would have heard me.

Arrangements had been made for her to give a press conference at the airport and we were swept along into a nearby room where there were photographers and newsmen and flash bulbs lightening and darkening, like lights on a Christmas tree. As Benazir began to speak there was a deathly hush. For a few brief seconds no words came. And then she began, at first haltingly and then in a rush. She apologised for the speed with which she was talking and said that she was not used to being surrounded by so many people all at one time.

'When you are in solitary confinement,' she said, 'you are used to being alone.'

'Have you come into exile?' one member of the press asked. For those who might have thought that her years of solitary confinement might have broken her spirit, her response told them otherwise.

'Exile? Why should I go into exile? I am only in England for medical treatment. I was born in Pakistan and I'm going to die in Pakistan. My grandfather is buried there. My father is buried there. I will never leave my country.'[2]

Once the press conference was over, we went to her aunt Behjat's flat in Pont Street near Sloane Square. While she recorded an interview for *Newsnight*, Sunny, Claire and I hovered in the background. The following day we all met up again, joined by one of Benazir's earliest friends at Oxford, Patricia Yates, another of those who'd visited her in the summer of 1976. Still shy at being out in public – and not wanting to be recognised – Benazir was dressed in a long coat and a woolly hat – the first Western clothes she'd worn in seven years since she'd returned to Pakistan in 1977. 'After all the years of living alone behind prison walls, even the crowded streets in London seemed threatening,' she later wrote.[3]

The following day I returned to New York. I was still in a daze myself that she had at last been released from house arrest – undoubtedly due to the continuing pressure exerted by the US senators – and that we had met again after nearly five years. 'Your arrival in London seems almost unreal to me now that I'm back in the USA!', I wrote in early February. 'It's something I'd dreamed of for so many years, and it's wonderful to think that you are still there – free... it's somehow hard to know where to begin in a letter which I know definitely will reach you.'[4]

Benazir's first priority was to get admitted to University Hospital to have surgery on her ear. Ever since her operation in Karachi in 1978 she'd been troubled by an infection in her middle ear and mastoid, which was exacerbated during her detention. Although her operation was successful, she was warned that she might need another operation in about nine months' time. So she decided, in London's benign environment, to spend her time raising awareness in the West about the large numbers of political prisoners in Pakistan's jails. 'Perhaps then the democratic countries would use their leverage to help stop Zia from making arbitrary arrests and holding political prisoners for years without charge or hearings, and sentencing more and more innocent men to death just for their political opposition.'[5]

'Guess who is coming to stay?' I asked my husband when he returned home from work on 19 March. He couldn't guess and so I put him out of his misery.

'Benazir!' he repeated in amazement. He had never met this important figure in my life, whose presence he had had to accept sight unseen when we'd married two years earlier.

'Yes,' I said. 'She and Yasmin are in Washington and are coming to New York for the weekend and they want to come and stay. We do have room, don't we?' A rhetorical question. Of course there was going to be room for Benazir.

A decade since her last visit to the United States, and seemingly a lifetime ago, Benazir had now come to meet members of Congress;

she'd also been invited to speak at the Carnegie Endowment for International Peace in Washington, DC. 'I urged her to come to DC to thank the senators who had been key to her freedom and, of course, to make her case,' recalled Peter Galbraith, who was still a staff member on the Senate Foreign Relations Committee. 'She was totally charming. She did very well in her public speeches and TV appearances, once she was persuaded to talk more slowly and to stick to a couple of key points.'[6]

While in DC, in addition to meeting all the influential Congress members, Peter introduced her to one of his friends, Mark Siegel, president of Public Strategies Washington, a boutique public relations firm;* as Mark later related, he was 'intrigued' when Peter had suggested he meet a friend who had 'just been released from detention'. She also met former US attorney-general, Ramsey Clark, who'd spoken out so boldly against the judgment at the time of her father's appeal. But, observed Peter, in the wake of Zia's December 1982 official visit to Washington, which had given Pakistan 'full allied status', notwithstanding concerns over the country's nuclear weapons programme, 'she only got a low level meeting with the Reagan administration'.[†7]

It was a cold crisp spring morning when Benazir arrived in New York. I could hardly believe it as I opened the door of my apartment on Manhattan's West Side to welcome her and Yasmin. We hugged and then sat down to enjoy her favourite hamburger lunch before we had to head out. On this first day Benazir had meetings organised at the UN Plaza Hotel and while those were going on in one room, Yasmin and I sat in another and reminisced. There was a large Pakistani diaspora in New York, many of whom now wanted

---

* Mark Siegel (b.1946). Public Strategies Washington Inc. was established in 1991; in 2007 Siegel joined Locke Lord Strategies.

† Ronald Reagan (1911–2004) was the 40th US president 1981–89.

to see Benazir. One of them was Nighat Shafi, who had helped with the rejoinder, and in the evening we went to dinner at her house. She was now married with a baby, the five-year period from 1979 to 1984 when we hadn't met now seeming like an aberration.

The next day more old friends came to our apartment for brunch: Vikram Mehta who was at Oxford with us and whose sister, Vijay, was one of Benazir's friends when she was at Harvard and Vijay was at Smith College. Their father, Jagat Mehta, was an Indian diplomat who had become India's foreign secretary when we were at Oxford.* Another Harvard friend, Seth Paprin, was also at the brunch. He was, as Peter Galbraith recalled, one of the 'gang' who – like Benazir – used to visit the Galbraith family home in Vermont, and was now a successful New York real-estate lawyer.[8] Once again I was struck by how easily Benazir slipped back into old friendships, despite the painful years in between. Benazir and Yasmin then went to a lunch meeting with the senior editors of *Time* magazine, initiated by another Harvard friend and Rhodes scholar, Walter Isaacson, who was an editor at *Time*.† Since our apartment was near by I walked with them to the Time-Life building on the Avenue of the Americas. In the evening Benazir was speaking at a school in Queen's. 'Lovely to see Benazir in a political forum again after all these years,' I recorded in my diary. That evening an old colleague of her father's, Yusuf Buch, who had served as Bhutto's special assistant for five years and later as ambassador to Switzerland, came for dinner and we sat and talked.‡ And talked. Uppermost in Benazir's mind was returning to Pakistan to continue her political struggle against

---

* Jagat Mehta (1922–2014) was Indian foreign secretary 1976–79.
† Walter Isaacson (b.1952), Professor of History at Tulane University, New Orleans, later rose to become managing editor and then CEO of CNN.
‡ Yusuf Buch (1922–2019).

General Zia, mindful that the Soviet presence in Afghanistan was continuing to give him more legitimacy than his military dictatorship warranted. After Yusuf Buch left, and Benazir and Yasmin had gone to bed, when Stephen and I were alone, he looked at me and said: 'Now I understand.'[9]

While in London Benazir stayed in a flat in the Barbican Estate, where Dr Niazi and Yasmin were living (the rest of the family remaining in Pakistan). Built as a series of residential tower blocks in the 1960s and 1970s on land in the City of London devastated by bombs in World War II, its architectural style was 'brutalist'. But although there was nothing attractive about its concrete exterior, living in the Barbican suited Benazir. A caretaker oversaw all entrants and she felt secure in her tenth-floor flat in Lauderdale Tower.

Within no time her new home became the hub of the revived PPP, the Pakistani diaspora gathering to meet her. 'It is an irony of life that when I was in Pakistan I could not communicate with a single individual in the party; but from the distant shores of London, I am able to keep in touch with the people of Pakistan and the Pakistan Peoples Party. Of course I long to go back to my country, and, at the appropriate time, when it is going to be of political dividend, then I shall return.'[10]

As her political activity gained momentum, she assembled a team of helpers around her. One of them was Naheed Khan, a student activist in exile, while Bashir Riaz handled her interviews with the press. Yasmin, who had become engaged to Benazir's cousin – Aunty Manna's son Tariq – was ever present, doing 'anything and everything to help'.[11] In view of her loyal support for Benazir since they'd first met in 1978, it was wonderful that she would now become a member of the family. Given her busy lifestyle,

Benazir was also appreciating the beginnings of the revolution in communications, which included new telephone equipment. 'How is your answering service and cordless telephone?' I was enquiring from New York in early June. 'I am really building up to buying one or other or both!'[12]

I was back in London for three weeks in the summer for the launch of my book on the North-West Frontier. Its title, *Every Rock, Every Hill*, was a quotation adapted from Winston Churchill's account of his service with the Malakand Field Force in 1897 – 'Every rock, every hill has its story' – in order to illustrate that the book was as much about the people and the land as the politics. It seemed apt, since, the first time I had heard of Churchill's presence in the Frontier was when Benazir pointed out Churchill's picket to me on our Frontier tour in 1978. The subtitle: *The Plain Tale of the North-West Frontier and Afghanistan* satisfied Toby Buchan that the narrative was in the style of Charles Allen's acclaimed *Plain Tales from the Raj*.[13]

Happily my visit to London coincided with Benazir's thirty-first birthday party on 21 June, held in her flat; yet again I saw how she had adapted to her new circumstances, looking after herself as she had in her student days. I couldn't help thinking how much had changed since her thirtieth birthday, spent under house arrest. Surrounded by Oxford friends, it was wonderful to see her among so many familiar faces – those whose news I'd tried to share during the solitary visits I'd made to her five years previously: Alan [Duncan] and Daniel [Moylan], both of whom had gone on to become president of the Union after us, as had Damian Green who was soon to marry his girlfriend Alicia Collinson, who'd also been involved in the Union with us, and others, including Claire and Freya. As we sat together, laughing and chatting, it was almost as though none of what she had endured had happened.

Towards the end of the evening Aunty Behjat produced a cake, with one candle, and we sat around watching as Benazir delightedly opened all her presents. Mine was a copy of my book – which began another tradition: whenever I wrote a book, I gave her a copy. The next night we celebrated Yasmin and Tariq's engagement, the party again held in Benazir's flat.* Since it was now the mango season in Pakistan, in addition to wonderful Pakistani cuisine we feasted on mangoes for dessert. 'Ended up staying the night,' I wrote in my diary, 'since it got so late and we chatted taking our make-up off and discussing aerobics.'[14] In early July I returned to New York; Benazir was not yet going back to Pakistan and I knew we would meet up again on my next visit.

One of those Benazir met regularly in London was Peter Tapsell, MP, who'd known her father and who, on Benazir's request, had obtained audiences with King Khalid of Saudi Arabia and Sheikh Zayed bin Sultan Al Nahyan, the ruler of Abu Dhabi and president of the United Arab Emirates,† urging them to persuade Zia not to execute Zulfikar Ali Bhutto.[15] 'I took her out to lunch at the White Tower [a Greek restaurant in Fitzrovia], on a number of occasions,' he recalled. Sir Peter also had a special affinity with the Oxford Union dating from his time at the University in the 1950s when he served as librarian.‡

Three months later, on 31 October, we all awoke to the news of Indira Gandhi's assassination in New Delhi. 'The attention of the media here has been fully directed on India,' I wrote to Benazir

---

* Yasmin and Tariq married on 14 August 1984.
† King Khalid bin Abdulaziz Al Saud of Saudi Arabia (1913–82) was king of Saudi Arabia 1975–82; Sheikh Zayed bin Sultan Al Nahyan (1918–2004) was ruler of Abu Dhabi 1966–2004 and the UAE's first president 1971–2004.
‡ Sir Peter Tapsell, MP (1930-2018). Later it was thanks to him that the Oxford Union's finances were put in better shape than when we were undergraduates. By helping to set up the Mitsubishi Trust Oxford Foundation in 1988 a £1 million loan from the Japanese corporation was arranged.

from New York soon afterwards, mindful that Indira Gandhi was one of the people I had written to requesting her to use her 'best offices' in support of our campaign for Benazir's release. 'I was remembering how, when I went to see Mrs Gandhi in Delhi in 1981, she had asked kindly after you and Begum Sahiba, and later she made some strong statements in support of the various campaigns we were trying to organise for your release. It is strange, too, that both she and your father were assassinated. I wonder what Zia was really thinking when he sent his condolences.'[16]

I didn't see Benazir when I went home in November to see my father, who died soon after my arrival in England. But we met again when Stephen and I came home for Christmas and Benazir wrote a lovely letter of condolence to my mother. She had only met my father a few times, mostly at the Oxford Union but also when she came to our home and he described his experiences as a young naval officer in Karachi, when he went duck shooting on the jheels in Sindh. With her generous spirit, after listening to his recollection, despite his advancing age, she'd encouraged him to plan a return visit to Karachi.[17]

In Pakistan, to our dismay, General Zia was working to legiti-mise his rule. In December 1984 he held a national referendum to ask the people whether they endorsed the process he had initiated 'for bringing the laws of Pakistan in conformity with the injunctions of Islam as laid down in the Holy Qur'an and Sunna of the Holy Prophet (Peace Be Upon Him) and for the preservation of the ideology of Pakistan...' Voting 'yes' meant the people would endorse Zia's authority for a term of five more years. Most people, however, saw through the ruse. *The Times* of London described the referendum as 'a blatant fraud and a brilliant stroke of genius... behind the front of Islam the General is in fact sneaking himself past the population... Had General Zia frankly and courageously put himself to the test, without the cover of "religion", he would, in all probability, have lost.' Having received 98% of votes cast, according to the widely disputed official tally, Zia thanked the nation, announcing that elections would be held the following year on a non-party basis.[18] All political parties remained banned.

When general elections were held in February – the first since 1977 – voter turnout was recorded at nearly 53 per cent. Pakistan's new prime minister – picked by Zia – was Mohammed Khan Junejo, a Sindhi landowner who had served in Ayub Khan's administration in the 1960s. For the position of chief minister of Pakistan's most populous province, the Punjab, Zia selected a businessman whose political aspirations he had promoted by making him finance minister in 1981: Mian Muhammad Nawaz Sharif.* But, despite the induction of elected civilians into the administration, Zia and the army remained in control.[19]

Benazir was back in New York in April 1985. This time she was staying out of Manhattan. I had since moved to an apartment on the 27th floor of a building on the West Side. She knew that I was expecting a baby in May and so she arrived to see me with three baby outfits and a porcelain dish. 'Our conversation ranged around Zia, the elections – Reagan, etc.' I noted. I also told her that I'd been asked by an American magazine, Ms, founded in the early 1970s by the feminist activists Gloria Steinem and Dorothy Pitman Hughes, to write a profile on her and so she agreed to give me a fresh 'on the record' interview. A few days later we sat together in my apartment, with its wonderful view over the Hudson river, to record it.[20]

---

* Mian Muhammad Nawaz Sharif (b.1949) was prime minister of Pakistan 1990–93, 1997–99 and 2013–17; Mohammed Khan Junejo (1932–93) was prime minister of Pakistan 1985–88.

It was moving to listen to her describe her early days of political activism, which I had witnessed, how she'd become involved in politics because of the political vacuum while her father was in jail 'and the people needed someone to come to for information'. She went on to describe the solitude of her house arrest in Al Murtaza as 'living and yet one was not living', a quotation I was to use frequently in the years to come in my own interviews and other articles on her. Despite the continuing immense void of her father's loss, the pain she'd described in her BBC interview with David Lomax in 1979 seemed to have become less acute. Finally we talked about her political future and her motivation. 'Ultimately, you see, there is the conscience of a human being and I think it is not possible for people born with a conscience to put up with injustice when they see it occurring around them.'[21]

After completing my profile, I submitted it to *Ms* but – such are the vagaries of journalism, and perhaps they did not realise how politically prominent Benazir would become – they decided not to publish it. When I told Benazir, she responded sympathetically; her concern wasn't the loss of publicity but the effort I'd taken to write the article. 'I'm sorry the article in *Ms* was dropped, only because it takes time to do and write up an article.'[22]

As on her previous visit, while Benazir was in the United States, uppermost in her mind was what could be done to keep up the momentum and interest in Pakistan when, despite having a civilian prime minister, martial law was still in force. On this occasion, one of those she met was Michael Posner, the founding executive director of the Lawyers Committee for International Rights (now Human Rights First).* A lunch was also held in her honour by the Council on Foreign Relations; true to form,

---

* Michael Posner (b.1950) was assistant secretary of state for Democracy, Human Rights and Labor 2009–13.

the topic she addressed was 'Implications of military rule for Pakistan'.

Since I was living in New York I saw less of Benazir than I might have done if we'd both been in London, but we were often in touch. When my daughter, Alexandra Rose, was born in May, Benazir telephoned me excitedly to congratulate me as well as giving me the news that Yasmin had had a son, Khurram. I was happy to know that she was busy in London as well as travelling abroad, getting to know the Pakistani communities in Europe's different capital cities in addition to those in Britain. Sunny and her husband Nasir were living in a flat in Queen's Gate, South Kensington, with their baby daughter, Azadeh, born on her grandfather's (Zulfikar Ali Bhutto's) birthday, 5 January 1985. Whereas, after leaving Afghanistan in 1982, Murtaza had gone to live in Syria, Shahnawaz eventually chose to settle in the south of France; Aunty Behjat and her husband, Karim, had a home in Cannes and in the summer of 1984 they had all spent the month of July together. The following year the family was once more reunited. Six years had now passed since their father's execution and, even though she and Murtaza still disagreed about their 'differing approaches to unseating Zia', I liked to think that Benazir and her siblings had found some emotional peace and stability.[23]

Then came 18 July and the tragic news that Shahnawaz had been found dead in his home in Cannes. He was only twenty-six. I wrote immediately to Benazir to offer my condolences. Soon afterwards I received a black-edged notification with a tribute which was sent to all those who had sent messages of condolence: 'Shahnawaz was a revolutionary and a warrior. He was a dreamer with plans of the future for his people. He was filled with honour and courage. He had a sharp intelligence and a warm and loving heart. He was fearless and identified himself with the cause of oppressed people everywhere.'

Shahnawaz's death was heart-breaking, as was the realisation that he had never managed to fulfil his potential as he might have done had his life taken a normal path. The photographs I saw of Benazir, accompanied by Sunny, returning to Pakistan with their brother's body were terribly sad. 'The pain of the people of Pakistan is my pain,' Benazir said to a crowd of thousands after the burial. 'Shahnawaz's death is not just my personal loss, it has saddened the whole nation. Everyone knows how many difficulties we have faced. We will continue the mission of Shaheed Bhutto. We will continue our war against injustice and poverty which has been inflicted on the people. I am your sister and will be with you at every step. My feelings are the same as yours and our goal will remain the same too.'[24] When I heard the news that, on returning to Karachi after the burial, she had again been put under house arrest, with 70, Clifton declared a sub-jail, I had a dreadful sense of foreboding. Thankfully in November she was released, so that she could return to France to attend the court hearing relating to Shahnawaz's death.[25]

'We were convinced as a family that Shah had been killed and filed charges of murder against unknown persons,' Benazir later wrote. Not only were there suspicions that General Zia's agents had sent an assassin who had poisoned him but also that his wife Rehana was complicit, because she had failed to assist 'a person in danger'. While Rehana was held by the French authorities in Nice Central Jail, Sassi was taken to live with her Afghan grandparents in California. Eventually, after nearly three years, with no trial having taken place, the French authorities permitted Rehana to leave France to join Sassi and her family in California. 'To our disappointment the court also ruled that there was insufficient evidence to uphold our charge of murder against unknown persons,' continued Benazir.[26] The effect of Shahnawaz's death and the allegations against Rehana resulted in the break-up of Murtaza's marriage to Rehana's sister, Fauzia, and she too went to the United States, while Murtaza took Fatima back to Damascus. For Benazir, Shahnawaz's death marked another turning point in terms of her determination to return to Pakistan to continue the struggle against Zia. 'There have been too many sacrifices,' she said.[27]

By the end of 1985 change was in the air for Pakistan. In August – soon after Benazir's arrival in Pakistan for Shahnawaz's burial – Prime Minister Junejo had promised that martial law would be lifted. On 31 December, while addressing a joint session of the Senate and National Assembly General Zia announced that 'martial law stands lifted here and now'. But he cautioned against expecting any radical changes and warned of 'terrible conse- quences' if people tried to disrupt the transition to 'democratic rule'. As Steven Weisman observed in the *New York Times*: 'Few people in Pakistan doubt that General Zia will also continue to stop his foes from mounting an effective opposition. Under civilian rule, he will have, for example, ample police powers to ban demonstrations and strikes and to outlaw certain political parties.'[28]

In March 1986 I received a letter from Benazir containing some important news: 'I am going back to Pakistan in early April as I feel the time is right to press for snap elections. I wish you could get a magazine to sponsor you to cover my return but I know it's difficult because of Alexandra.' Later when we talked about her return she said that the love and affection shown by the people when she went back with Shahnawaz's body had also made her feel she must return.

As usual our correspondence mixed the mundane with the important. In a previous letter I'd told her that I had acquired a personal computer. 'Now that I've got the hang of its various functions, I am finding it very useful and definitely makes life easier than the tippy-type of my manual machine,' to which she now responded: 'Mine has been shipped back to Pakistan and I really miss it. Not that I know how to use it beyond word processing.' She also told me that the British journalist Ian Jack was writing an article for *Vanity Fair* which was to be illustrated by photographs taken by Princess Margaret's ex-husband, Lord Snowdon, of whom she wrote. 'He seemed a quiet person with a quiet air about him – and shy.'* And since I was living in the States and less in touch with our Oxford friends, just as I used to give her news, she now told me what everyone was up to. 'Tricia [Yates] and Steve are engaged and I'm simply delighted for Trish. Tony [Fry] and his wife [Anne] came over for dinner. She is an extremely nice person. Victor [van Amerongen]'s wife Amanda is expecting their second child. Everyone seems happy and doing well.' Then came some political commentary. 'The fall of Marcos was a sight to watch. All the Pakistani exiles in particular felt a close identification. The sheer joy of the Filipinos was one we knew we'd share when Zia is finished and a new order comes to Pakistan.'[29]

Benazir's return to Pakistan on 10 April 1986 created a sensation. To make the greatest impact, she had decided to arrive in Lahore, the heart of the Punjab. 'The sight of Lahore the night before Benazir's arrival was like that of a giant carnival or festival,' recalled Amna. 'Camps were set up all over the city with food and drink. There were food stalls as well along the road to the airport. The whole city was in the hands of the people.' I wished I could have been present, but contented myself with watching Benazir's progress from the airport to the city on television. She was standing at the front of a large truck; there were people waving at her as far

---

* Ian Jack (b.1945); the Rt Hon. the Earl of Snowdon, GCVO, FRSA, RDI (1930–2017).

as the eye could see and she was waving back. The crowds were unprecedented, some reports saying that three million people had come to greet her. 'Zia out. Zia must go,' they shouted. She seemed so strong yet so fragile, injecting new energy into the Movement for the Restoration of Democracy.[30]

On arrival at the Minar-i Pakistan, the national monument built on the site where the All India Muslim League's 1940 Lahore Resolution was announced, Benazir addressed a huge crowd in Iqbal Park, the people roaring in appreciation. 'Main baghi hoon' ['I am a rebel'], she shouted, quoting from a poem written at the time of her father's execution in 1979 by a dedicated PPP supporter, Khalid Javaid Jan:*

> I am a rebel
> Against those who burden us with rules,
> And choke our lives like fields of thorns,
> Those offspring from an evil mother born,
> Who work our land to bloodied pools.
> I am a rebel, I am a rebel
> Bring on all the pain you have for me.[31]

'When I clapped my hands over my head as my father had done, the crowds clapped back, their upraised arms undulating like ripples on a vast field of wheat.' So responsive were the people that, as Benazir later wrote, 'with just a word' the regime could have been brought down there and then.[32]

After Lahore Benazir progressed onwards throughout the

---

* Dr Khalid Javaid Jan, 'Main baghi hoon (I am a rebel)' (1979), verse 1 of 6, tr. Jim Carruth; Khalid and his wife Shaista were both present in Iqbal Park. According to Shaista, Benazir began with the last verse: 'I wave the flag of justice always in my hand though on unlawful gallows I will hang.' In subsequent speeches Benazir often quoted Main baghi hoon.

Punjab until she reached Rawalpindi; from there she went to Peshawar before returning to the Punjab, Balochistan and eventually home to Larkana, having addressed thousands of people in nineteen cities. 'It seems unbelievable that you have now been back in Pakistan for two months,' I wrote from New York in June. 'All the news reports (and there have been a few) talk about the incredible crowds which come to meet you and their support must be very heart-warming. Yesterday's report said that you had returned to Larkana... to be met by thousands who broke through police barriers.'[33]

There was a change in Benazir's appearance, since she was now wearing her *dupatta* on her head. Henceforward this was how she would appear in public. While some people criticised her for adhering to the increasing trend towards conservatism throughout the Islamic world, covering her head seemed to be an accommodation she was prepared to make. In time, the white *dupatta* – which frequently slipped off and which she would quickly reposition – became a familiar symbol of her official persona.

8

The People's Wedding: 1987

You must agree that Benazir will serve the nation.
That's all right with me, for I will serve the
nation by serving my wife.[1]

'How time does pass. It is lovely being back in Pakistan – and free (although one never knows how long that will last),' Benazir wrote from Karachi in June 1987. Her comment was not without meaning since, following a rally in Karachi on Pakistan's independence day the previous year, she had again been arrested and kept for nearly a month in jail. 'It is soon going to be ten years of Zia's rule – the mind shudders to think of all that has happened and how any individual could be so cruel, and continue to be cruel. The PPP workers are still being persecuted, picked up on false civil charges, kept without question for 15 days, beaten up and degraded.'[2]

After three years of living in the United States I was now living in London again, and in the summer Benazir came for a visit. As now became a tradition, we arranged to meet up with old Oxford friends – the difference between her existence and ours in the period when we had not met evaporating. Two years since Shahnawaz's death I felt that she seemed 'to hurt less'.[3]

On one warm evening in late July a group of us was having dinner at Maggie Jones's in Kensington, after which Stephen and I gave Benazir a lift back home to her sister's flat. She was sitting in the back of the car slightly leaning forward so the three of us could talk.

'I have something I want you to know before it gets in the papers,' she said. 'I have agreed to get married.'

My head spun round in excitement. 'Oh that's absolutely wonderful!' I exclaimed, looking at her smiling face.

'Don't be surprised,' she continued, 'but it is an arranged marriage.'

I wasn't surprised. She could hardly be said to have had the same opportunities that we all had had to find a life partner, having spent most of her late twenties and early thirties either in jail, under house arrest or immersed in leading a political movement against a military dictatorship. Besides, arranged marriages in Pakistan were the norm even among educated liberal families.

For Benazir especially, marriage was an important political decision since it would give her the status of a married woman in a traditional Islamic society, where most of her political colleagues were men. As she later explained: 'I got married because I wanted a house of my own and single women in Pakistan with good reputations don't live in homes of their own so, in a way, you could say I got married because the realities of the Eastern culture descended on me and I realised that if I did not marry I would not be able to pursue my political life.' Because her brother was married, if and when he returned to Pakistan he would have seniority in the household 'and that meant that in my own home I would have to go and ask "can I invite guests to dinner?", "can I use the room to have a committee meeting of the Pakistan Peoples Party?" I couldn't do that.'[4] It was also emotionally time for her to settle down and start a family. Although General Zia was coming under increasing pressure internationally to 'democratise' his administration, there was still no indication that he was intending to step aside. If he lasted another decade, she would be in her mid-forties.

The man Benazir had agreed to marry was thirty-two-year-old Asif Ali Zardari. Although the Zardari tribe was originally from Balochistan, the family had settled in Nawabshah district in Sindh*. Asif's father, Hakim Ali Zardari, the head of the Zardari tribe, was a local landowner and politician, who had been elected to the National Assembly in 1970 on a PPP ticket. He also had business interests and owned several cinemas in Sindh. Although Hakim Ali did not remain with the party, in terms of essential credentials the Zardaris had not had any direct association with Zia. Asif's mother, Bilquis Sultana, was the granddaughter of Hassan Ali Effendi, credited with establishing the first educational institute in Karachi, which the founder of Pakistan, Jinnah, had attended. Hakim Ali's second wife – Asif's stepmother – was Cambridge-educated Zarine Ara (Timmy) Bukhari, whose father had been the first director-general of Radio Pakistan.† After attending Cadet College in Jamshoro district,‡ Asif had wanted to join the army but his eyesight was not good enough. So, as the only son, he'd gone into the family construction business. Although he hadn't received the same elite education as Benazir, he had studied business administration in London and hence, like her, had an understanding of 'the West'. As he later related, his first recollection of his future wife was when he saw her at the preview of the 1968 film, *Mayerling*, with Omar Sharif and Catherine Deneuve, at one

---

* Nawabshah district was renamed Shaheed Benazirabad district after Benazir's assassination.

† Hassan Ali Effendi (1830–95).

‡ Hakim Ali Zardari (1930–2011) married first Bilquis Sultana and secondly Zarine Ara Bukhari.

of his father's cinemas in Karachi. 'He gives her a ring and inside the ring, he writes: "Until death do us part". I had those words engraved on the engagement ring I gave Benazir.'[5]

By her own admission Benazir did not love Asif: 'My mother tells me that love will come.'[6] Soon after she told me of her impending engagement, the announcement appeared in the papers. In early August her future in-laws held an 'engagement' party in London at the Bombay Taj restaurant, in Victoria. It was the first time I met Asif, although I had met his stepmother, Timmy, at the English Speaking Union some years earlier. Initially, Asif seemed rather overawed at the prospect of his new life, and the words that he would utter two decades later, under tragically different circumstances, perhaps best described his feelings: 'How difficult my marriage was going to be, nobody knew. Obviously I didn't know how deep the waters were I was diving into.'[7]

The wedding was to take place in Karachi in December. As with most traditional Pakistani weddings it would extend over several days, starting with the Mehndi ceremony on Thursday 17 December, when the bride and close family friends would have their hands decoratively painted with red-orange henna paste, associated with good luck (the decorations of the bride's hands being the most elaborate). This was followed by the more solemn Nikah – the exchange of vows – the following day. On Sunday 20 December the Valima, or marriage banquet, would be hosted by Benazir's future in-laws. The invitations were unlike any others I have ever received.

First there was a printed letter from Begum Bhutto: 'We hope you are able to come and share our happiness with us... as the post for overseas may be delayed or uncertain particularly at that time of year, we will retain your cards for when you arrive.' The invitation cards were in two colours: for the Mehndi ('for ladies only' – although male family members and close friends were welcomed), the card was bordered in red with embossed gold lettering, while for the Nikah the following day it was bordered in green, also with embossed gold lettering. A third invitation for the Valima was from Mr and Mrs Hakim Ali Zardari 'for a reception and dinner to celebrate the wedding of their son Asif Ali with Benazir'.[8]

Numerous Oxford friends were invited as well as her close friends from Harvard. The world's press was also in attendance, because Benazir's wedding wasn't just going to be for family and friends. It was to be an *Awami* (people's) wedding with a huge reception in the poorer district of Lyari, one of the PPP's political strongholds. I desperately wanted to accept my invitation, but I had the minor impediment of having to get permission to enter the country after my deportation in 1981. My first representation to the Pakistan Embassy in London was turned down, as was my second; then, following what I heard were reports in the local press about 'Benazir's friend being refused permission to come to her wedding', almost at the last minute, I received a telephone call from the Embassy informing me that a visa would be granted. I was overjoyed and, having presented myself at the Embassy in Lowndes Square on 14 December, I returned home with a precious stamp in my passport which stated informatively: 'Type of visa: entry'; 'Purpose of visit: visit'. I spent the rest of the day rushing around doing last-minute Christmas shopping and writing cards because I knew that it would be too late by the time I got home. My impending absence also required some domestic reorganisation: only Benazir's wedding would make me leave my two small children, Alexandra, aged two-and-a-half, and Anthony, who was six months. Stephen kindly agreed to remain at home to look after them.

Because of the uncertainty surrounding my departure, I was only able to get a flight that arrived just before the wedding celebrations began. For the first time I flew Emirates, a relative newcomer to the skies, which meant changing planes in Dubai. As the coastline of Pakistan came in sight, I realised that I would soon be stepping onto Pakistani soil eight years after I had left, and six years after my abortive attempt to land in Karachi in 1981. Several other Oxford friends had already arrived: David Soskin and Keith Gregory, both of whom had visited Pakistan in the summer of 1976, Colin Clifford, Ross McInnes, Keith Hutchence, his wife Julie (who came with a large hat, fashionable for a British wedding but which, in any crowded environment, was highly vulnerable!) and Freya. Claire wanted to come, but she was now a teacher and couldn't get the time off. A generous and well-known Sindhi landowner, Rafi Kachelo, had offered to pay the hotel bills of all Benazir's Oxford friends and so we all stayed happily together in the Sheraton Hotel.*

When I arrived, Anne Fadiman, Benazir's friend from Harvard, greeted me warmly; although we'd never met, she knew that I had lived in Pakistan during Bhutto's appeal and we formed an instant bond – something which happened frequently in the years to come: many of Benazir's friends became friends of each other because we shared Benazir in common. The writer Linda Francke was also among the foreign guests: for several months before the wedding she had been 'joined at the hip' with Benazir because she was under contract to help write Benazir's autobiography;† her previous assignments included the autobiographies of Jehan Sadat, widow of Egyptian president Anwar Sadat, and Geraldine Ferraro,

---

* Muhammad Rafi Kachelo (1943–99); the Kachelo family was famous for its mangoes grown in Sindh.

† Anne Fadiman (b.1953) essayist and writer; Linda Francke (b.1939).

vice-presidential candidate for the Democrats in the 1984 US presidential election.[9]

Among the large contingent of journalists was John Elliott, *The Financial Times*'s correspondent in Delhi, and Donna Foote, *Newsweek*'s Asia correspondent, our shared experience at the wedding creating yet more friendships. Another guest was twenty-two-year-old Christina Lamb, who'd been at Oxford a decade after us.* Having had the opportunity to interview Benazir in the summer, which led to the publication of 'her first big article' in a national newspaper, she too had received an invitation to Benazir's wedding and had decided on impulse to come to Karachi. As she later wrote, the decision altered the direction of her journalistic career. Instead of continuing to work as a trainee at Central Television, making 'death knock' calls about drink-driving accidents between the M1 and M6, the following year she returned to Pakistan, taking up the position held by my old friends, Simon Henderson and Chris Sherwell, stringing for *The Financial Times*, and sensibly basing herself in Peshawar to be able to report on the continuing war in Afghanistan.[10]

Part of the 'press pack' given to all foreigners for Benazir's wedding was a special folder which included details relating to the three days of events and – for the benefit of us Westerners – an explanation of the significance of an arranged marriage. The Mehndi ceremony, held in the grounds of 70, Clifton, was a kaleidoscope of colour. During my previous time in Pakistan the dominant image had been of lawyers in black suits, and on those sad occasions when I visited Benazir under detention we were hardly concerned with what we were wearing. Now I was observing the

---

* Christina Lamb, OBE (b.1965). Her reports on Pakistan and Afghanistan 1988–89 won her the title of Young Journalist of the Year in the British Press Awards 1989.

opulence of women dressed in vibrant clothes, their smiling faces showing the happiness they felt that, after the emotionally tough decade she had endured, Benazir was getting married. It was said that there wasn't a single embroiderer left in Karachi who hadn't been overworked.

Soon after greeting everyone I was taken to where the henna decorating was taking place to have my hands painted. Throughout the evening there was music as the women danced in celebration. People were also dancing in the streets and thousands of presents were left at the gates of 70, Clifton. Benazir looked stunning, dressed in red, and during the early part of the evening her face was covered by a red veil. Her sister, Sunny, with her daughter Azadeh, who was nearly three, and their mother, Begum Bhutto, were in constant attendance. Benazir was also surrounded and supported by her cousins and her close friends: Yasmin, a cousin by marriage, Samiya and Salma Waheed and Amna Piracha, all in their brightly coloured *shalwar kameez*. We Westerners felt dull in comparison – or, as Anne Fadiman said, 'like drab little caterpillars surrounded by butterflies'.[11] Some of our male Oxford friends had tried to look the part by wearing *shalwar kameez*, even getting up to dance.

The Nikah the following day was equally colourful. A special 'wedding dais' with a canopy decorated with red and white flowers was prepared in the garden, with hundreds of fairy lights embellishing the surrounding trees and walls. Benazir was dressed in green, with gold and pink embroidery and a deep pink veil which covered her face. While the mullah read the marriage vows to Asif, where the men were assembled, as Muslim tradition dictated Benazir gave her responses to a male cousin. 'Before I realised it, I had said the customary "yes" three times to the male witness, and was a married woman.' Finally Asif took his place beside her, but, according to tradition, they did not look at each other.

Instead, having exchanged vows, the first time he saw her face was in a mirror. Her mother and aunts then 'ground sugar cones over our heads so our lives together would be sweet, then knocked our heads together to signify our union'.[12]

Suddenly all the invited guests were on the move again, first to the reception at the nearby Clifton Gardens, where dinner was served for the several hundred guests – huge dishes piled high with chicken, lamb kebabs, vegetables, roti and rice; then we were off to Kakri Ground in Lyari where Benazir – now dressed in white with gold embroidery and an armful of bracelets – and Asif took their places on stage for the *Awami* reception, attended by Benazir's supporters in their thousands.

Prophetic among the programme of entertainment were the words of a song in Urdu, sung (or as Benazir said 'warbled') by her friends and relatives, a line of declaration on the part of Benazir followed by a line of response on behalf of Asif.

'Benazir will serve the nation.'
'That's all right, because I will also serve the nation by serving
her.'
'Benazir will continue with her politics.'
'I don't mind that, I'll get votes for her as well.'
'You will not do any politics.'
'It doesn't matter, I will do my own work.'

Other verses stipulated that Asif must look after the children while Benazir was out campaigning and not prevent her from going to jail.[13]

As the evening drew to a close there was a wonderful display of fireworks and in their excitement people fired guns in the air. Unfortunately, one person was killed by a ricocheting bullet and several others were injured. A few of us then returned to 70,

Clifton. When the time came for Benazir to leave her home for that of her husband, she had invited Anne and me to witness her departure. We were the only two of her Western friends to be given this special privilege.

The Valima at the Zardaris' home on the third day of celebrations was equally spectacular. Benazir was dressed in fuchsia pink and her mother in pale green; yet again large quantities of food were prepared for the several hundred guests, served from long tables buffet-style. Once the festivities were over, we went our separate ways home for Christmas. I was so happy to have seen Benazir in such a different environment from our previous encounters in Pakistan. My most difficult challenge had been what to bring her as a wedding present. In the end I had chosen to give her a silver key ring, because I thought that at last she had the key to a future in which she would not be alone.

The next time we met was in April 1988. While Benazir and Asif were in London I invited them to dinner, along with some Oxford friends, many of whom had not been able to come to her wedding. Again there was an important piece of news Benazir wanted to impart: she was pregnant, the baby due to be born sometime in the early autumn. We were all overjoyed with the news and several friends, myself included, were only too happy to offer advice on having one's first baby (get plenty of rest, go out in the weeks preceding the birth, don't worry if breast-feeding is too difficult). We knew, of course, that having a baby in Pakistan with an extended family and servants would be very different from how it was for most of us in Britain, but it was fun to share in the excitement and feel that, in some way, her life was mirroring ours. No one could realise just how different the circumstances of the birth of her first child would be.

Benazir was still working on her autobiography with Linda Francke. As she later acknowledged, it was a 'cathartic experience', enabling her to put the past behind her.[14] My task over the previous year had been helping to fill in some of the gaps about our time in Oxford, which meant going through the records of the debates at the Union and contacting friends for any recollections. I also sent Linda information about Zulfikar Ali Bhutto's trial and appeal for her to incorporate in the draft, which Benazir then checked and sometimes sent to me for an opinion. 'I am sending you the finalised Trial chapter to have a look,' Benazir wrote soon after our dinner in London.[15]

Meanwhile the political scene in Pakistan seemed to be functioning like a medieval court, in which favourites rose meteorically only to fall and be replaced with similar speed. Having supported Mohammed Khan Junejo as prime minister since 1985, on 29 May 1988 Zia unexpectedly sacked him, which 'stunned and surprised many Pakistanis, including Mr Junejo himself', noted Steve Weisman in the New York Times. 'Among those most surprised and upset about General Zia's action were representatives of the United States, Pakistan's most powerful ally. Mr Junejo visited Washington two years ago for meetings with President Reagan that were part of a broad American effort to assert that the Junejo Government was a sign of a Pakistani move toward democracy. In ousting Mr Junejo and dissolving the National Assembly, General Zia asserted that the Government was indecisive, corrupt and soft on crime and drugs. He said it also failed in its promise to make Pakistan conform with Islamic law.' 'I'm wondering what Zia is up to,' I wrote to Benazir on 14 June. 'He still hasn't set an election date and it doesn't seem that he will do so until he thinks the timing is to his maximum advantage.'[16]

On the afternoon of 17 August I came home after taking my children to the park. I put on the radio and caught the tail end of the news on Radio 4, which seemed scarcely believable. '... Zia has been killed in a plane crash.' Momentarily I wondered if the Zia they were talking about was the widow of the Bangladeshi president, Zia Ur Rahman, who had been assassinated in 1981. Had she too been assassinated? Or could it possibly be *General* Zia? I immediately put on the television. The newsreader confirmed what I thought – but could not believe – I had just heard: General Mohammed Zia-ul-Haq, president of Pakistan, had been killed while travelling in a C-130 plane shortly after taking off from Bahawalpur in the Punjab. Several senior generals and the American ambassador, Arnold Raphel, were with him.* There were no survivors. I was incredulous. I tried to telephone Benazir but could not get through, so I phoned Yasmin, who had just returned to live in Pakistan.

'Yes, yes,' she was saying. 'We can't believe it, but, yes, Zia is dead.'[17]

---

* Arnold Raphel (1943–88) was US ambassador to Pakistan 1987–88.

9

Dear Prime Minister: 1988–90

There are moments in life so stunning, so unexpected,
that they are difficult to absorb.[1]

General Zia-ul-Haq's death changed everything. For over eleven years he had dominated the political and military scene in Pakistan; he had covertly directed the war against the Soviets in Afghanistan, aiding those mujahideen who espoused more traditional Islamic views; he had also sown the seeds of a more belligerent policy towards India in relation to the disputed state of Jammu and Kashmir; finally he had dismantled the political apparatus of Pakistan's parliamentary system and led a programme of Islamisation aimed at radically changing the character of society. When I had first gone to Pakistan in 1978, there was little evidence of Islamic radicalism: women did not feel obliged to wear the veil in public and there was a more liberal and progressive mind set among many middle-class Pakistanis. During his dictatorship all this had begun to change, the fall-out from the Afghan war affecting Pakistani culture with the spread of conservative *madrassas* – religious schools funded by Saudi Arabia – which followed a strict Islamic curriculum.

Benazir's reaction to General Zia's death was measured: 'I would have preferred to defeat Zia at the polls. But life and death are in God's hands,' she later wrote. 'The national sense of celebration was unseemly... many others died on the plane and, for their families, the sense of jubilation was not right.'[2] In the immediate aftershock, there was concern that the elections scheduled for November might be cancelled and that another general would step into General Zia's shoes. But to everyone's relief, his successor as acting president, Ghulam Ishaq Khan, former chairman of the Senate, announced that, as scheduled, elections would be held on 16 November 1988.*

For Benazir, there was the added complication of her pregnancy. Since it was known that she was expecting, there was speculation that the election date was deliberately chosen to coincide with the baby's birth (which might prevent her from actively campaigning). As a precaution, misleading information had been leaked to the press about her due date, which was earlier than suggested. Benazir gave birth to a boy on 21 September, giving her time to recover from the birth and go on the campaign trail. Even so, as she admitted, her pregnancy and the accompanying worry about the baby's condition due to the stress she was under, had 'cast a strain over what was already a tense period'. The name she chose for her son was Bilawal, derived from the name Bil Awal, which, as she recorded, means 'one without equal'.† There was also a Sindhi saint called Makhdoom Bilawal 'who fought against oppression in his time'.[3]

'What momentous days these are for you at present – rewriting the face of history after the Zia era which went on for far too

---

* Ghulam Ishaq Khan (1915–2006) was president of Pakistan 1989–93. He became acting president after Zia's death, and president after the election.

† One of Asif's ancestors was called Bilawal. Benazir's name is often recorded as meaning 'one without equal' but she gave the meaning as 'without comparison'.

long,' I wrote on 4 November. 'I really feel that all your hard work and dedication will come to fruition. It will be a tremendous step forward if civilian rule can once more be restored to Pakistan.' 'It is hard to recapture in words the excitement of those days,' recorded her Harvard friend, Peter Galbraith, who was in Pakistan with Benazir for the last days of the campaign. 'In Benazir's Larkana constituency, even the cows were decorated with the PPP arrow [the party's symbol]. And, outside the Bhutto compound, journalists from all over the world – including the BBC, Deutsche Welle, and the three American networks, waited.'[4]

Benazir's political opponents were equally determined to win the election. The Pakistan Muslim League had now split, as Nawaz Sharif competed for control of the party against the former prime minister Junejo, whose government had been dismissed by Zia three months before his death. To oppose the PPP in the elections, a new alliance of nine conservative parties backed by the army was formed, the Islami Jamhoori Ittehad (IJI). Although officially under the leadership of Ghulam Mustafa Jatoi, a former member of the PPP and former chief minister of Sindh, the IJI's key player was Nawaz Sharif.* There were also numerous independent candidates standing for the National Assembly and the Senate. When, following the 16 November election, the results were announced, the PPP emerged as the largest single party with 94 out of 207 seats in the National Assembly. This meant that, although Benazir was ten seats short of an outright majority, she had the right of first refusal to form a government. But the old regime did not part instantly with power. Instead she had to wait while the military decided on the conditions on which she would be allowed to govern, one of which was insisting that she support Ishaq Khan's election as president as

---

* Ghulam Mustafa Jatoi (1931–2009) was prime minister in the interim government for three months in 1990.

well as retaining Sahabzada Yaqub Khan as foreign minister.* In order to gain a majority, she was also obliged to form an alliance with the regional Muhajir Qaumi Movement (MQM), whose supporters had won seats in Karachi and Hyderabad. Formed in 1984 by Altaf Hussain, its power base was in urban Sindh, its members coming from among the 'muhajir' (immigrant) Muslims, whose families had come from India after 1947.† 'Her initial reaction was an emphatic "no" and the ideological members of her party also felt that conceding to the military's demands would be suicidal and it would be better to sit in opposition,' recalled Amna Piracha, who had remained close to the family. 'Finally she was prevailed upon to accede on the basis of the argument that thousands of PPP workers who were languishing in jail, some under long sentences, would continue to rot in jail and this would impact negatively on the morale of the party.' Observing events from London, I wrote an article for *The Independent*, describing how Benazir now stood at the centre of Pakistan's political stage; the headline was: 'The making of the daughter of Pakistan'.[5]

On 4 December Benazir Bhutto was sworn in as prime minister of Pakistan. Watching her inauguration on television was very moving, knowing what she had endured. She looked so solemn dressed in a green *shalwar kameez*, created by the Pakistani fashion designer Maheen Khan, with her white *dupatta*, the colours of the Pakistani flag. Her own words best describe the occasion: 'I walked down the red carpet in the Presidential Palace underneath the bright chandeliers. This was not my moment, but the moment of all who had made sacrifices for democracy.'[6]

---

* Benazir later said agreeing to appoint Ishaq Khan was a mistake but it was an attempt at 'reconciliation'.
† Altaf Hussain (b.1953). He created the MQM from a student organisation founded in 1978, the All Party Muhajir Student Organisation (APMSO).

In the early weeks of Benazir's tenure as prime minister, a glorious euphoria prevailed, as she embarked on fulfilling the pledge she had made in her inauguration speech 'to heal the wounds and undo the damage' of General Zia's eleven-year dictatorship. 'During the dictatorship there was a brutalisation of society,' she said in her first press conference. 'So we intend to promote the ideas of peace, tolerance, brotherhood and harmony.' One of her first actions was to release hundreds of political prisoners and lift restrictions on the press. Recognising that Pakistan was part of the 'golden crescent' supplying drugs to Europe and the United States, she pledged a crackdown on the spread of narcotics. She also committed to continuing Pakistan's Afghan policy in support of the mujahideen fighting the Soviets and reducing tensions with India.[7]

From a distance it was hard to imagine quite how demanding Benazir's life had suddenly become, having to navigate her way between her political opponents and the Pakistan army who, until so comparatively recently, had supported the military dictator who hanged her father. But, although the army still remained influential, Pakistan was once more under civilian leadership, which was a huge boost to collective morale. In an attempt at retaining continuity with her father's administration and in recognition of their loyalty, some former ministers were reappointed while Yahya Bakhtiar once more became attorney-general. There were some ghosts, however, which she did not wish to confront: instead of returning to the prime minister's residence in Rawalpindi, where she had lived when her father was prime minister, she chose to stay in the state guest house before moving into Sindh House which became the prime minister's house.*

---

* Each province had a residence in the federal capital of Islamabad: Sindh House, Punjab House, NWFP House, Balochistan House. Being from Sindh, Benazir stayed in Sindh House.

'We planted the seeds of democracy,' she later wrote, 'we funded the electrification [of] villages in Pakistan... we also funded the building of roads and the availability of safe, potable water to our people... we introduced mobile phones... we set up a one-window investment operation to facilitate investment... we legalised private investment banks, full banks and insurance companies... what I am probably most proud of, though, is what we managed to accomplish in promoting the rights of women and girls.'[8]

One of her first official guests was Rajiv Gandhi, prime minister of India since his mother's assassination in 1984.* His arrival on 29 December to attend the fourth summit meeting of SAARC (South Asian Association for Regional Cooperation) was the first visit of an Indian premier in twenty-eight years (the last being that of his grandfather, Jawaharlal Nehru, in 1960). A stunning photograph of the two prime ministers smiling at a press conference seemed a portent for change. 'I am sure each of us will give our best and I hope the time would come when historians would point to your time in India and my time in Pakistan for heralding the dawn of a new era,' Benazir proclaimed. Albeit the youngest, most recently elected prime minister and the only woman, throughout the conference, as she later wrote, 'I wasn't shy and asserted my views.' I wasn't the only one to think what a great opportunity there was for these two political figures – as Benazir said, 'both young and children of the post-Partition subcontinent' – to set in motion the beginnings of a new relationship which would resolve India and Pakistan's longstanding enmity. It was one of those moments in time when you could dare to hope that things might be different.[9]

'Dearest Victoria,' Benazir wrote in her official prime minister's

---

* Rajiv Gandhi (1944–91) was prime minister of India 1984–89. He was assassinated in 1991.

'Greetings of the Season' card, 'What a year this has been – almost like a novel. So much has happened. Longing to see you. Whenever you come to Pakistan please stay as our guest. If there is anything I can do for you, don't hesitate to ask. I can never forget the difficult days you shared with my family and the people of Pakistan and your efforts when our human rights were violated. It seems such a sense of peace and satisfaction to know that my father, brother and all those that died – their lives did not go in vain.' I also received a letter from Begum Bhutto: 'I am naturally so happy for Benazir; she has worked hard and suffered tremendously so she deserves to be in this high post, but she is competent too, even though it is I, her mother, who says so.'[10]

It was extraordinary to think how much had happened since December the previous year: her marriage, Zia's death, the birth of her first child and now she was being applauded for being the first female prime minister of a Muslim country.* In the same year her autobiography was published. Although she was only thirty-five years old, by publishing 'the story so far', she seemed to be drawing a line under the past before beginning the next phase of her life. Published with the title *Daughter of the East* (and in the United States as *Daughter of Destiny*), the book instantly became a bestseller.†

'To write one's autobiography at the age of 35 bears witness to an exceptional life,' I wrote in my review for Lady Margaret Hall's alumni publication, the 'Brown Book'. 'Sometimes it is hard to realise that this is the same woman who debated in the Oxford

---

* Dr Fatema Mernissi (1940–2015), Moroccan feminist and sociologist, pointed out that she was not the first Muslim ruler since Islamic history is littered with Muslim queens and sultanas: 'Benazir is not the first', *Jeune Afrique*, undated [1988].

† *Daughter of the East* was published by Hamish Hamilton in 1988. For all quotations I have used the later edition published by Harper Perennial in 2008.

Union, loved Anna Belinda dresses and drove a yellow MGB sports car. Yet time and again throughout the book we see Benazir's strength in her ability to adapt to the circumstances in which she finds herself.'[11] And so she did, undertaking her role as prime minister with the same intensity of purpose she'd adopted when faced with house arrest and solitary confinement in jail.

One of the questions posed after Benazir became prime minister was what action she would take in relation to her father's trial and execution. Would she exact revenge? Would she embark on a 'witch hunt' against anyone involved? Would she call for a re-trial? Most importantly, how could she set the record straight without opening up old wounds and undermining the integrity of the judiciary? The course of action which she endorsed was to hold a seminar in Karachi on 2–3 April 1989, bringing together those who were present at the trial and appeal, as well as independent lawyers, journalists and academics.[12]

The organisation of the seminar was carried out by Dr Niazi, who had returned from his years in exile, Amna Piracha and Aitzaz Ahsan, a PPP member from Lahore, who was imprisoned under Zia and had become Benazir's interior minister.* Her cousin Tariq Islam, happily back in Pakistan with Yasmin, was on the coordinating committee, as well as Salima Agha, whose father, Dr Hayee Saeed, was Begum Bhutto's doctor at the time of her departure abroad for medical treatment in 1982.

Among the foreign guests who attended the seminar was the former US attorney-general Ramsey Clark. Other guests included

---

* Aitzaz Ahsan (b.1945) was minister for interior and narcotics, federal minister for parliamentary affairs, federal minister for education 1988–90 and briefly minister for law and justice 1988.

Dr David Owen, Britain's foreign secretary during the critical years 1977–79; the former Indian foreign minister, Sardar Swaran Singh, who had sparred with Bhutto at the UN over the war in East Pakistan and its secession to become independent Bangladesh; Leslie Wolf-Phillips, a senior lecturer at the London School of Economics, who was Bhutto's 'constitutional adviser' from 1975 to 1976; and Etienne Jaudel, general secretary of the International Federation for Human Rights, who had attended the appeal in its early stages. The historian Stanley Wolpert, author of a biography of Mohammed Ali Jinnah, who had recently been commissioned to write Bhutto's biography, had also come to Karachi. I too received an invitation to attend.*

The seminar's patron, Begum Bhutto, gave the welcome address at the inaugural session. One of the most heartfelt messages was sent by former French president Giscard d'Estaing: 'I wished to be with you, among you, at this moment of intense emotion when his glorious family and the reborn Pakistan have come together, at this special moment when the greatness of a man who made the supreme sacrifice is tracing out the destiny of his country, when the recent painful past is opening up on a present and future of democracy and peace.' He also quoted extracts of the letter Bhutto had written from jail; listening to his words, it was hard to believe that, over a decade ago, in the heat of a Karachi summer, I had sat typing the letter from Bhutto's handwriting when he was still alive.[13]

For two days we sat revisiting the legal proceedings. 'When looking at the relevant facts,' noted Ramsey Clark, 'the trial of Mr Bhutto is not a trial, but it is an assassination.' Yahya Bakhtiar

---

* The Rt Hon. the Lord Owen, CH, PC, FRCP (b.1938); Leslie Wolf-Phillips (1929–2009); Sardar Swaran Singh (1907–1994) was Indian minister of external affairs 1970–74; Stanley Wolpert (1927–2019), *Zulfi Bhutto of Pakistan: His Life and Times* (Oxford University Press, 1993).

again referred to the case as being 'patently false, fabricated and politically motivated'. David Owen described how, 'in desperation the British Government, through the Prime Minister, James Callaghan, reminded General Zia of the old soldiers' saying "The grass grows swiftly over a battlefield but never over a scaffold."' Pointing out that 'time is the great healer, respect the great reconciler', he paid tribute to the efforts of Dr Niazi to raise awareness about Mr Bhutto's conditions in jail. 'As foreign secretary I received hundreds of letters, but when I began to read Dr Niazi's letter, I realised that we had something in common. I was a doctor, he was a dentist and so I felt a natural affinity and perhaps that is what made me read his letter more intently than I might have otherwise.' Justice Dorab Patel gave the concluding remarks. As one of the three 'minority' judges who had upheld Bhutto's appeal against the death sentence, he had earned considerable respect from Bhutto supporters, especially when, in 1981, he had refused to take an oath of allegiance to General Zia and had resigned from the Supreme Court, forgoing the opportunity of eventually becoming chief justice. Throughout, Dr Niazi was 'his usual modest self, always looking after the well-being of the delegates and wondering if everything is going to be all right'.[14]

Each day our discussions were reported in the press. 'The Bhutto trial was seen even by detractors of the PPP regime as a travesty of justice and the manner that it was conducted threw doubts into the independent and autonomous character of the judiciary,' noted the journalist Mushahid Hussain in the *Frontier Post*, in an article captioned 'Legal controversies over Z. A. Bhutto's prosecution.'[15]

When the seminar concluded, all the foreign guests flew to Larkana. 'Very strange to be back at Larkana after more than ten years. So much has happened and yet all seems the same – the birds make the same sound they always used to, the servants –

older perhaps – look the same and the heat is the same,' I wrote in my diary. 'There is a tremendous sense of peace and tranquillity about Al Murtaza – an oasis in the middle of the desert. And I'm trying to imagine what it must have been like for Benazir when she was confined here month after month and it became a prison. Its beauty must have appeared somehow overwhelming when the world outside was so near and yet so far.'[16] Accompanied by General Naseerullah Babar, at dusk Benazir and I went for a walk in the gardens, where the abundant orange trees still hung over the now empty swimming pool. Although Benazir said that the best roses had died there were still rows upon rows of flowerbeds filled with the deep red roses – *jaibadi bijasani* – native to South Asia. The following morning, before leaving for the graveyard, I went to sit on the steps of the verandah, listening to the birds calling to each other. Benazir came to join me and we stayed there for a while, both lost in thought. It was exactly ten years to the day since the news broke of her father's execution.

'As we approached the grounds where the Mazar is, hundreds of buses and thousands of people had already assembled,' my diary continued, describing our arrival at Garhi Khuda Bakhsh, where Benazir was to give a speech at the family graveyard. 'The dust swirled around and made visibility impossible. The jeep Benazir was in virtually disappeared from sight. As we got out the crowds surged forward... when she got up to speak, the people roared and cheered. She suddenly seemed transported, on a different plane – regardless of headaches or fatigue – she exhorted the people to remember the ideals of her father. My mind went back to the young girl at the Oxford Union – how things have changed.'[17]

Later we sat together having tea and fruit: 'conversation focused around the proper mausoleum to be built for Shaheed [martyr] as her father is called'; which would mean that all the graves would be protected from the rain and sun. Later in the day I accompanied

David Owen on a walk around the gardens; his understanding of the opposition Benazir faced was prescient. 'He expressed his concern that the army was poised ready to take over; and that the president, Ghulam Ishaq Khan (whom he'd met in Islamabad) was not at all favourable to BB and was someone to be watched.'[18]

Soon after our return to Karachi, I was told that the prime minister was going to Balochistan, and my name was on the list of those accompanying her. Flying across this vast province's lunar landscape to Quetta, we travelled onwards by helicopter to Ziarat, just under 100 miles away from the provincial capital, where we would spend the night at the famous Quaid-i Azam residency, built in 1892, where Mohammed Ali Jinnah had spent the last weeks of his life. Renowned for its lush juniper trees and wonderfully cool weather in the heat of summer, Ziarat was rather colder than we might have liked and, before Benazir had to go out for her meetings, she, Asif and I sat in a room wrapped in blankets. As we chatted, we touched on the fact that some of the foreign journalists in Islamabad wanted to interview Asif, who had been thrust into the limelight by Benazir's fame. Not yet adjusted to his new role as the husband of the prime minister, however, Asif was reluctant to engage with the media.

'But you could give an interview to Victoria?' Benazir suggested encouragingly.

And so while she was out visiting the local political leaders, I remained in the residency with Asif and he gave his first interview to the 'international press'. I began where I had to begin, by asking him what it was like being married to the prime minister of Pakistan: 'Difficult,' was his immediate response. 'In one word, it's just difficult – the fact that everybody else is looking at you and looking for your faults, looking at you as a man, as an individual. And you're married to a woman who is very high profile... If I were a male prime minister and my wife was around, they wouldn't question her being around at all. But the fact that I am a man, she happens to be the prime minister and she's my wife, the first question that comes to everybody's mind is: what is he doing here, why is he here?'

Given that the Urdu press was already beginning to write critical articles about him, his tone was defensive: 'I'm the best punching bag going. Her graph has gone up so high, internationally and otherwise; she's so popular that even if her opponents criticise her, people are not willing to listen. But they can talk about the husband of the prime minister... It isn't that I am so important, it is just a form of getting at her. So anybody who is trying to disfigure me even now, it's just basically that they are trying to hit at her, and I'm the soft spot.' As Asif recognised, the scrutiny had begun the moment he had become engaged to Benazir:

There was this grand plan by the opposition and the intelligence services to bring her popularity down, so they started criticising me, the individual she's marrying – 'He's got a big moustache, he wears the wrong kind of clothes, he sits wrong, he talks wrong.' They had different reasons: some people thought I wasn't good enough; others thought she shouldn't have got married at all; while some of the poorer people had given her the status of a goddess over and above the reach of humankind. Some people were politically jealous – they thought that a man might tell her things that otherwise she wouldn't have found out.

Having admitted that no one had expected her to attain such political prestige so soon after their marriage, Asif's response to my next question: 'Where would you like to go on holiday?' was telling: 'Anywhere in the world where nobody would be around, preferably in the mountains... People feel that all this popularity is nice and good and that they want it, but ask the people who have it, they'd rather be unknown.'

Still wrapped in blankets because of the cold, Asif also told me about his early life, and how he had wanted to join the army but his poor eyesight meant that he was not accepted; and so, as the only son, he chose to look after the family construction business, as well as being involved in local politics in his home in Nawabshah, although he 'never thought of politics on a larger scale than district politics'. Finally, I asked how he thought he could be most supportive to Benazir: 'As far as I'm concerned, just the fact that I'm there, I feel makes a lot of difference. For somebody who was alone…' His voice trailed off as though he was back thinking about her earlier life and so I stopped the tape. We'd talked long enough. After I returned to London, *The Independent* published the article, entitled: 'A political punching bag'.[19]

Ramadan had begun a week earlier and that evening, once Benazir returned, we broke the fast at sunset, sharing the traditional evening meal – *iftar* – with the Baloch tribal chiefs. As we threaded our way down the steps from the residency to a large *shamiana*, set up in the gardens below, the scene was exceptionally beautiful, with fairy lights twinkling, the crisp night air devoid of any urban pollution and the indigo blue sky studded with stars. At dinner I was placed at a table next to General Babar, while Benazir sat with Nawab Akbar Khan Bugti, chief of the influential Bugti tribe, who had recently been appointed chief minister of Balochistan (having been provincial governor under her father). Although I understood more about Pakistani politics than I had on my arrival a decade previously, I was less familiar with the internal dynamics of Balochistan, whose relationship with the federal government was periodically explosive.* When her father was prime

---

* Nawab Akbar Khan Bugti (1927–2006) was provincial governor 1973–74,

minister, the elected government of the province was dismissed and the leaders were arrested on charges of 'anti-state activities'; this was followed by a controversial five-year military operation against Balochi separatists and tribesmen, resulting in thousands of deaths. When Zia took power, after the institution of martial law an amnesty was offered and development programmes promised, which had reduced, but not eliminated, tensions. Noticing that all the tribal chiefs had their weapons carefully resting by their tables and chairs, I asked General Babar about our security. He shook his head, marvelling at my naivety. 'We are receiving Balochi hospitality; they would never harm us in their own home.'[20]

By describing himself as a 'political punching bag', Asif was partially correct. Internationally Benazir remained very popular but within the country complaints about how little she had achieved were already beginning to circulate. She had only been in office for four months, but it seemed everyone believed she could work miracles, much as many Americans expected miracles from Barack Obama after his election in 2008.*

After our return to Islamabad I was dismayed to see an article headlined 'Bhutto in Blunderland', written by the Lahore-based journalist, Ahmed Rashid, describing 'Pakistan's faltering administration'. 'Part of the problem,' Ahmed wrote, 'is her own charismatic personality and corresponding inability to de-centralise government. Everyone from top industrialists to poor widows

---

chief minister 1989–90. The federal government's relationship with Balochistan remains precarious; the Balochistan Liberation Army continues to call for the province's secession, while other groups (including Bugti before his death) are demanding greater autonomy and a fairer share of Balochistan's natural resources.

* Barack Obama (b.1961) was the 44th US president 2009–17.

feels that only by meeting her can their problems be solved... In her ornate, oak-panelled office, Ms Bhutto puts in a 16-hour day. At times she has files beside her stacked to the ceiling, and she has just enlarged her Cabinet to an unprecedented forty-one ministers in the hope that they will take more responsibilities. But until now her young government has proved embarrassingly incompetent.' However, as we all knew, and Ahmed himself admitted, constraints were imposed on her by the army. 'She had to accept the army's choice for president and foreign minister and the military's continued control of Afghan and defence policies... Most people still want her to succeed, for the future of democracy in Pakistan hangs on it.'[21]

It was also assumed that she would have the same efficient bureaucratic support that a prime minister would have in the West. 'I entered an empty office both literally and figuratively,' she would say when questioned on her progress. I too saw the quantities of files she had to go through, responding to questions and writing letters which I thought should have been dealt with by someone other than the prime minister. And although the PPP had won the national elections, Nawaz Sharif's IJI party was dominant in Pakistan's most populous province, the Punjab, of which he was still chief minister. 'A great deal has to be done to rebuild Pakistan after the decade of military dictatorship,' she told Sir Peter Tapsell, 'but there is satisfaction in every achievement.'[22]

More damaging were stories of 'corruption' involving her husband, which were circulating in the local press in Pakistan. When I told her that they were themselves becoming a 'news story' which would soon be reported in the Western press, Benazir was horrified. 'You mean people are believing what is written?' she asked. We then had a long discussion about how damaging these perceptions were because, if they weren't contradicted, people could think they were reality.

During my visit, one of my assignments for BBC World Service was to make a radio feature on 'Women in Pakistan' in an attempt to understand the difference Benazir's position as prime minister was making to women in other professions. For the opening sequence I chose a statement Benazir had made in the BBC's *It's Your World* telephone-in programme, recorded after her first 100 days in government: 'I certainly do consider myself as a role model. I think that the course of my career and my life have proved that a woman is like a man, a person in her own right and that she can set her targets and achieve her goals, she can have a home, a child and a career.'[23]

Among other contributors was the fearless human rights lawyer, Asma Jahangir, whom I met for the first time, our friendship continuing until her death in 2018.* 'There is a feeling amongst women in professions that they can now come to a position of power,' observed Asma. 'Previously it was not possible for a woman to think that she would be at the decision-making point in any field that she was in; today the feeling is there, that if I do well I can make it to the top.' But as Asma and several others emphasised, Benazir's position as a female prime minister in a traditional male-dominated Islamic society was fragile.[†] 'I think it is very difficult for somebody in the West to understand, but when a government takes over after eleven years of dictatorship, it is not only political will that matters, it is also how far they can take public opinion with them. And that has to take time.'[24]

'We are trying to achieve pure Islamic values,' observed the Shia cleric, Agha Murtaza Pooya, information secretary for Sharif's IJI,

---

* Asma Jahangir (1952–2018) co-founded and chaired the Human Rights Commission of Pakistan.

† Other contributors were Maleeha Lodhi, editor of the *Muslim*; Salima Agha, businesswoman; Rehana Sarwar, minister, women's division; Ameena Sayyid, general manager of OUP, Karachi.

and formerly editor-in-chief of the *Muslim* newspaper, who provided an alternative viewpoint. 'Under pure Islamic values a woman's position is relegated more to managing the house, rather than participating in the open politics of the country and it's only when it is absolutely necessary for them to work and perform certain functions that they work and perform those functions.' In his opinion, education was 'the strongest vehicle for change. If education is conducted on proper lines, on Islamic lines, and the underlying themes are Islamic, I think we can hope to achieve our aims far quicker. At the moment we have the shadow of other civilisations being cast on us, just as we cast shadows on other civilisations, so there is an interaction going on. As soon as the Islamic forces pick up strength, and education is used as a vehicle, I think we can see the restructuring of society closer to being an Islamic model and paradigm.'[25]

Looking back I don't think we in the West fully comprehended Benazir's achievement as a woman in a Muslim society. The general feeling was: 'We've got Margaret Thatcher, Pakistan's got Benazir Bhutto'; but, as I was witnessing first hand, the prejudice was entrenched, certain men refusing to shake her hand because she was a woman, and mullahs in the mosques preaching that it was un-Islamic to have a woman as a prime minister.

Some years later, when asked to describe the problems her gender had caused in the political arena, Benazir responded with candour:

I have not had much difficulty in dealing with my supporters in government and in opposition. However, I have been taken aback by the venom of those political opponents who believe a woman's place is behind four walls. Their attacks have been violent and unforgiving. I have also found it difficult to establish political relations with leaders who believe in tradition and tribalism... The elite institutions of the country have found it difficult to accept me as prime minister because they believe I usurped a man's place in an Islamic country. Their lack of support and, at times, covert opposition caused difficulties to me in terms of governing smoothly. However, my male colleagues and supporters have given me tremendous respect and support.[26]

*

Having said goodbye to Benazir in mid-April, I met her again in July when she came on an official visit to Britain. Weeks before her arrival, the Pakistani ambassador, His Excellency Shahryar Khan, had contacted me as 'a friend of the prime minister' to help with the unofficial aspects of her visit. A career diplomat descended from the royal family of the former princely state of Bhopal, he combined aristocratic dignity with practical informality.*

The previous month Benazir had taken Washington by storm, when she was hosted by the recently elected President George Bush and his wife, Barbara, and attended a state banquet at the White House.† How emotional it must have been for her, mindful of her father's official visits to Washington as prime minister in 1973 and again in 1975. When she addressed a joint session of Congress, she received a standing ovation. She also visited her alma mater, Harvard, where memories of the past now merged with the present.

Benazir's arrival in London was scheduled for Wednesday 5 July. By the time I reached the Ritz hotel in the late afternoon, shortly before she and her entourage arrived, a crowd of supporters had

---

* Shahryar Mohammad Khan (b.1934) was ambassador/high commissioner to London 1987–90; foreign secretary of Pakistan 1990–94.
† George H. W. Bush (1924–2018) was the 41st US president 1989–93.

assembled and were chanting the familiar slogan '*Jeeay* Bhutto'. I've no idea what the Ritz's clientele of mainly American guests thought of this show of political enthusiasm, but there was no stopping the slogan-raising, the noise amplifying as her car drew up.

The next week passed in a round of lunches, dinners and other official engagements. A highlight was an audience with Her Majesty the Queen. Benazir amused us all by relating the correct protocol she was told to observe, including when she should curtsey and when she would know that her audience was over. She also went to Chequers, the prime minister's country house, to have lunch with Mrs Thatcher. Then there was 'Breakfast with the editors' – of all the top national newspapers – and an 'ambassadors reception' at Claridge's in her honour. Benazir's schedule even included a visit to Wimbledon, as Shahryar Khan, himself a keen sportsman, thought it would be good for the image of the prime minister of Pakistan to be seen in the royal box at what is one of the highlights of the social calendar. Another dinner, hosted by the foreign secretary, Sir Geoffrey Howe, was held at Lancaster House. Both Stephen and I were on the guest list and I found myself sitting next to the BBC's eminent world affairs editor, John Simpson.* As we were about to sit down, he picked up my place setting to see my name.

'Ah, didn't you write that rather good book on Afghanistan?', by which he meant *Every Rock, Every Hill.* I was hugely flattered!

In addition to Benazir's official functions, a 'quiet dinner' was fitted into her schedule for her Oxford friends. The venue was my home in Westbourne Park Road. At about 5 p.m. on the day of the dinner (8 July) there was a ring on the doorbell, which heralded the arrival of security officers coming to 'sweep' my house. In

---

* John Simpson, CBE (b.1944), BBC News foreign affairs correspondent and world affairs editor.

addition to Tariq and Yasmin, who'd accompanied Benazir from Pakistan, about thirty Oxford friends came to dinner. Once more our different lives, and now her status, seemed irrelevant, as she relaxed into an evening of catching up. As a record of all those who came, I asked everyone to sign a 'dinner party book': Benazir signed first and then Asif. In the space where Benazir had put 'Prime Minister's House, Islamabad', he wrote 'a nobody'. It was an unexpected comment, no doubt meant as a joke, but it left me wondering whether being married to Benazir was, as he'd said in our interview, more difficult than he outwardly showed. 'BB was marvellous & everyone was delighted to see her,' I wrote in my diary that evening, recording how Patricia Yates 'thought she was very prime ministerial!' 'BB looked so very well despite all the stresses and strains,' David Soskin wrote to me afterwards. 'I am sure she really appreciated the chance to get away from the official programme and into such cordial and welcoming surroundings.' Freya made an observation we all shared: 'It was so lovely to see her so relaxed and "normal" – I don't know why one thinks that someone stops being normal just because they become public property but somehow one does!'[27]

Another highlight was Benazir's return to Oxford, which included a visit to the Oxford Union. The newly elected president of the Union was another woman, Diana Gerald, which delighted Benazir, as the number of female presidents was still only in single figures (Diana was the eighth). Yet again I had a feeling of the wheel turning. It was twelve years since we'd been undergraduates, and yet so much had happened in between. A quick visit to St Catz was followed by lunch at our old college, Lady Margaret Hall, hosted by the principal, Duncan Stewart.* Having set aside her prepared speech, Benazir spoke *ex tempore*, injecting humour

---

* Duncan Stewart (1930–96) was principal of LMH 1979–95.

and serious content into her remarks, which extolled the value of education. She was delighted when both Lady Margaret Hall and St Catherine's made her an honorary fellow.

Benazir's last official function in London was lunch at the Mansion House hosted by the Lord Mayor. Her next destination was Paris to attend the celebrations for the 200th anniversary of the French Revolution. Before leaving Britain, she wanted to go for a walk around the Serpentine in Hyde Park, and so we set off together with Yasmin, the security men following on behind. By the end of her stay I had attended more official functions than my normal social calendar would warrant in a year. At the request of Shahryar Khan, I spent the next few days drafting 'thank you' letters on Benazir's behalf, one of which required me to find out the correct protocol to follow when writing to the Queen.[28]

One of Benazir's initiatives, which became known as 'mango diplomacy', involved the despatch of boxes of mangoes to certain individuals – to which end I was asked to compile a list of Oxford friends and others including journalists and members of Parliament. There was, however, an early mishap. 'During her first Premiership I received a large cardboard box without any stamps on it at the House of Commons,' recorded Sir Peter Tapsell. 'The security people rang up and said that there was a very suspicious unmarked box addressed to me and would I give them permission to blow it up. I agreed to this and it turned out that the box was full of mangoes from Benazir, which spattered all the police over a considerable distance!' It seemed strange that the unmistakable smell of the mangoes had not alerted the police to the contents but perhaps they were thinking back to General Zia's assassination, with stories circulating that the bomb was carried onto the plane in a crate of mangoes, the story later fictionalised by Mohammed Hanif in his novel *A Case of Exploding Mangoes*.[29]

As time passed, the list of recipients of Benazir's 'mango diplomacy' grew longer. Even when she was not in office, she continued to send the mangoes. After her death, Asif sent them in her memory. It remained a wonderful tradition to which everyone looked forward, including, we understood, the Queen – when a box of mangoes from 'Bilawal House' (as their home in Karachi had been called since Bilawal's birth) was observed being loaded into the back of a Land Rover one summer, destined for Balmoral.

Once Benazir's July visit to London was over, I returned to my routine of working for the BBC World Service in Bush House preparing short feature programmes. Since it was the year of France's revolutionary bicentennial, I was working on a series of programmes on 'Women of the French Revolution'. While I was at work one day, one of my colleagues said that there was a Pakistani who wanted to talk to me urgently on the phone. It was Ashraf Kazi, editor of the London edition of the Karachi-based Urdu newspaper, *Daily Jang*. His voice was deadly serious.

'I've been phoned by someone who says that there's going to be an assassination attempt on Benazir. He wanted to speak to someone "close to the family". You were the person I thought to call. I've given him your number.'

I was dumbfounded. Surely not? But as soon as I reached home I received a phone call from Ashraf Kazi's informant, Barry Edwards, who outlined the threat in very convincing terms. Since David Owen had said that I should contact him if ever there were a problem in relation to Benazir, I duly did so. I explained the essence of the phone call and he said that someone from the FCO (Foreign and Commonwealth Office) or Scotland Yard would be in touch. Within the hour I received a phone call from a member of the FCO who said he would be my liaison person while the 'threat' was investigated. After several more phone calls from Edwards, each more worrying than the last, it turned out that the threat was fabricated. Barry Edwards was a well-known conman, who had numerous other aliases including Barry Gray. But there was an important outcome: if I needed to talk to someone urgently about Benazir's security, I knew who to get in touch with. Later I wrote to Benazir to tell her about the hoax, in case she heard of it through another source, or in case Edwards/Gray tried the same thing with someone else close to the family. She was shocked that someone would indulge in a hoax about such a serious matter. In 1995 Gray was caught and jailed for two years for deception. As time went on, genuine threats to Benazir's life were to become a regular occurrence, with ultimately a tragic conclusion.[30]

In the same letter in which I told her about the hoax, I had a message to transmit. Benazir's hairdresser in London was Richard Dalton, who had started his hair-styling career in Fenwick of Bond Street's in-store salon. In 1981 – the year Lady Diana Spencer married Prince Charles – Richard had become Diana's official hairdresser. Once Benazir and Princess Diana realised they shared the same hairdresser, an unofficial method of passing messages was adopted, which sometimes involved transmitting communications between prime minister and princess along the following lines: 'Message from my friend to your boss'. After the London visit, Richard had phoned me to pass on a message that the Princess was 'simply longing' to visit Pakistan and it would cut out about 'ten months of red tape' if she were to receive an official invitation.[31] Not long afterwards, an official invitation was duly dispatched.*

---

* HRH the Princess of Wales (1961–97) visited Pakistan in September 1991, by which time Benazir was no longer prime minister. She divorced Prince Charles in 1996 becoming Diana, Princess of Wales. Prince William later followed in his mother's footsteps, visiting Pakistan in October 2019.

In mid-July Benazir welcomed Rajiv Gandhi on a state visit to Islamabad. It was his second visit to Pakistan in six months, their meeting once more engendering hopes for securing peace in the region. Picking up on the discussions Benazir and Rajiv had held during their December meeting, an important issue for Pakistan and India was reaching agreement on the military confrontation between their respective armies on the Siachen glacier. Stretching for 47 miles (76 km) beyond the agreed terminus (at point NJ 9842) of the ceasefire line established in 1949 after their first war over Jammu and Kashmir, it was assumed that the area was too remote and the altitude too high for anyone, except mountaineers, to want to venture. But in April 1984, in what was described as a 'pre-emptive strike', the Indian government had airlifted troops onto the Saltoro ridge, giving them a strategic advantage and compelling Pakistani troops to take up a defensive position to the west. Since then sporadic fighting had taken place, as both sides attempted to improve their positions. The conditions were gruelling, more men dying of frostbite than gunfire in the world's highest battleground. Both Benazir and Rajiv saw the advantage of withdrawing troops from the glacier 'without prejudice' to their differing viewpoints.

But, despite the personal goodwill between the two leaders, no agreement was reached. In the months to come, it did not take long before political compulsions in both countries pulled them apart. The 'dawn of a new era' Benazir had hoped for remained a dream. After being defeated in India's general elections later in the same year, Rajiv Gandhi was assassinated by a member of the militant Liberation Tigers of Tamil Eelam (LTTE) – Sri Lanka's Tamil Tigers – in May 1991, by which time Benazir was no longer prime minister. 'I sometimes think that South Asia and possibly the entire world would have been a much different place if Rajiv had lived and I was allowed to finish my term,' Benazir observed in hindsight.[32]

*

One afternoon in late September 1989 I was at home when the telephone rang. It was the Pakistani ambassador, Shahryar Khan.

'Are you sitting down?' he asked.

'Yes,' I replied, as I hurriedly sat on a chair.

'The Prime Minister would like you to join the Pakistan delegation at the 11th Commonwealth Heads of Government Meeting in Kuala Lumpur, scheduled for 18 to 24 October. Will you be available?'

'Of course,' I replied, without knowing whether I was, but thinking that I would just have to work out the logistics of husband and children. More importantly, since Pakistan was rejoining the Commonwealth after an absence of eighteen years, Benazir would be making a speech. Would I, the ambassador (soon to become high commissioner) asked me, 'set down some points which she could include in the speech, for example, relating to the history of the Commonwealth and Pakistan's membership?'[33]

Pakistan's official re-entry into the Commonwealth took place on 1 October, the United Kingdom's current ambassador to Pakistan, Nicholas Barrington, becoming high commissioner.* When he came to change the plaque at the entrance to the embassy in Islamabad, he found that, on the reverse side, was already engraved 'High Commission', dating from the building's earlier status as a high commission, and so he merely reversed the plaque again! What was significant in terms of what it demonstrated about Benazir, was that in 1972 her father had taken Pakistan out of the Commonwealth in response to other member countries' recognition of the newly independent Bangladesh.

---

* Sir Nicholas Barrington, KCMG, CVO (b.1934) was UK ambassador to Pakistan 1987–89 and high commissioner 1989–94.

Now, mindful of the benefits of being a member of this diverse multinational and multicultural body, she was bringing Pakistan back in. 'Britain's support of Pakistan during the Afghan war and of the restoration of democracy made my party take this decision,' she explained.[34]

On 16 October I flew from London to Kuala Lumpur. Benazir arrived from Pakistan with her delegation soon afterwards. Samiya and another friend, Najda Rashidullah Khan – always known as Putchy – were accompanying her. Asif had come too as well as the nanny with one-year-old Bilawal. What was clear now – which hadn't been in June – was that Benazir was pregnant again. If her first pregnancy was difficult because of the timing of the elections, the second pregnancy was equally so because, as prime minister, she could expect no sympathy from conservative elements in Pakistani society who still thought a woman's place was in the home.

The Commonwealth Heads of Government Meeting, or CHOGM as it's known, was a spectacular occasion, the city of Kuala Lumpur *en fête* with the flags of the forty-six attending member states in evidence at the Putra World Trade Center, where the opening session was to take place. The night before, I sat with Benazir and her foreign minister, Sahabzada Yaqub Khan, going through her speech. When, the following day, she took her place on the stage with the other heads of government, from my seat in the audience I could hear a murmur of approval as she got up to speak. Together with Her Majesty the Queen, who was presiding as head of the Commonwealth, and the British prime minister Margaret Thatcher, Benazir was the only other woman on the stage.

The next day, the heads of government left for their traditional 'retreat' to be held on Langkawi, an archipelago of nearly 100 islands on the west coast of Malaysia. While Benazir was on the retreat, she had arranged for Samiya, Putchy and me to go to

Singapore to stay with the Pakistani high commissioner and his wife; the highlight of our stay was watching a magical display of musical fountains on Sentosa island with beautiful views of the city.[35]

The major achievement of the 1989 CHOGM was the Langkawi Declaration, which embodied a significant recognition by the Commonwealth of the growing environmental threats to the future of the world and a call for new approaches to development, balanced by a recognition that less developed countries needed to tackle poverty and increase prosperity for their own populations. 'Past neglect in managing the natural environment and resources' was cited as the cause of current problems including the greenhouse effect, damage to the ozone layer, acid rain, marine pollution, land degradation and species extinction.[36]

Once the Commonwealth Summit was over, Benazir prepared to return to Pakistan and had invited me to travel back with her. When we landed in Islamabad, her arrival was overshadowed by reports that in her absence her political opponents, spearheaded by Nawaz Sharif and the IJI, had united to call for a no-confidence vote in her government. The vote was scheduled for 1 November. As I understood it, 119 votes were needed for the no-confidence motion to pass. Since the PPP had 92 votes, Benazir needed another 27 votes to survive. With only 54 votes, the IJI needed to gain the support of 65 members of the National Assembly to ensure Benazir's dismissal. 'With both parties in need of additional votes, a battle to woo parliamentarians to their respective sides began in earnest,' observed writer Shaikh Aziz. It was a tough fight. As later revealed by the former director general of the Intelligence Bureau, Masood Khan Khattak, 'non-political forces were behind the vote'.* According to Khattak, there had been a misappropriation of

---

* The case was heard in the Supreme Court of Pakistan in 2013.

funds from the Intelligence Bureau, President Ishaq Khan and the army chief, General Mirza Aslam Beg, being the 'two individuals who wanted to dislodge the Benazir government in the shortest possible span of time'.[37]

But their attempts failed. When the result was announced the PPP had won by just twelve votes. Benazir was relieved. To have been ousted after less than a year as prime minister would have been very disappointing. 'I think it is time for reflection,' she said in a press interview. 'Reflection by my government and by the moderate opposition. The no-confidence motion should have given everyone food for thought.' It was a tough lesson in how determined was her opposition and how challenging would be the years ahead. 'Dearest Vicks,' she wrote on a signed photograph of herself, which she gave me as a memento. 'So glad you were with us on the day we won the vote—!' A few days later I returned to London.

One of the long list of foreign journalists who wanted to interview Benazir was Margaret Thatcher's daughter Carol, who was working for the *Sunday Express*. The first time she'd interviewed Benazir was a year previously 'in the nerve-wracking days between her election victory and appointment as Prime Minister, which, until it happened, was by no means guaranteed'. They had met again in the summer when Benazir had lunch with Mrs Thatcher at Chequers. There was some similarity in their lives: Carol was almost the same age as Benazir and both had experienced being the daughter of a prime minister, albeit in very different political climates. In late November Carol returned to Pakistan to record another interview. 'Have you found it lonely at the top?' she asked. Benazir's answer revealed both the woman I'd known since Oxford, who enjoyed the simple things in life, and the resilient woman she'd become, who knew what her priorities were. 'You don't have time to yourself, in the sense that you can never go out. I love window shopping and browsing in bookshops or choosing material for my clothes, but those are things I can't do. So I'm a little cut off, but I'm not lonely because I have my husband and son.'[38]

Meanwhile Benazir's balancing act continued. One of the resident journalists observing events was Christina Lamb, who had been so inspired by Pakistan when she came to Benazir's wedding in 1987. In late October she was the only journalist chosen to accompany Benazir when she visited the Siachen glacier – the first Pakistani prime minister to do so. 'And it was a splendid site,' [sic] Benazir later wrote. 'All around us was the whiteness of the icy glaciers which melted seamlessly into the blueness of the skies.'[39] Unfortunately, despite the friendship which had developed between the two women, like others before and after her, Christina upset the military and intelligence services when she wrote a story about a potential coup (or, as the publicity for the book she later wrote put it, 'military machinations' against a civilian government). It was left to Aitzaz Ahsan, Benazir's interior minister, to inform Christina that she had to leave the country. British newspapers imaginatively described her deportation as 'Lamb to the slaughter'.[40] In terms of her analysis of Benazir's precarious position, however, Christina was right.*

Such was Benazir's global stature that she now merited a waxwork. '"You" are being unveiled at Madame Tussauds on 27 November,' I informed her. 'Shahryar has asked me to be present.'[41] Dressed in the same green *shalwar kameez* which she'd worn at her swearing-in ceremony, the impression was so realistic that,

---

* Christina Lamb returned to Pakistan in September 1990 and was handed a file headed 'Activities of Christina Lamb' dating from January 1989.

seeing the photograph of her sister Sunny standing next door to her waxwork, 'Benazir' almost seemed real.*

Following the no-confidence motion, I'd been approached by a correspondent of the *Atlanta Journal-Constitution* newspaper. I wasn't sure how interested the people of the American state of Georgia were in Pakistan but, whenever I was asked to write an article, I was happy to describe some of the challenges Benazir faced so that people could better understand the environment in which she was operating. Perhaps the most meaningful sentences of this article were at the end: 'While the opposition continue to chip away at her support Ms Bhutto walks a political tightrope. She cannot even announce when her next child is due, lest her opponents seize on the date as a suitable occasion for another assault on her government.'[42]

Benazir's second child was born on 25 January 1990. Called Bakhtawar, she acquired the nickname 'Itty' because she was an 'itty little thing'. 'It is tremendous to have a boy and a girl,' I wrote enthusiastically. 'I hope you've made a good recovery from the birth and have managed to rest a bit.' Taking rest was not something Benazir could easily do and I realised that she would hardly have had more time off than it took her to have her baby, mindful that she was the first serving prime minister to give birth. 'Well what a lot has happened since we met,' I continued. 'The situation in Eastern Europe and the Soviet Union is quite unbelievable. For all our lives we have grown up with the "cold war" mentality/two superpowers pitted against each other etc. and all of a sudden the whole power structure has collapsed. Who knows what will replace it.' As usual I kept her in touch with our friends. 'Claire is having a

---

* Judy Craig, head of Madame Tussauds' portrait studio, and Mark Richards worked on her sculpture; see http://www.markrichards.eu/waxworks (accessed 11 May 2020).

baby in the summer... Colin [Clifford] has been offered a job with the BBC in the newsroom... Helen and David are moving to West Kensington – David is still writing, Helen working in TV. Everyone seems fine, getting on with their lives, jobs and children.'[43]

We all knew that Benazir's life bore no comparison to ours in London. Although she'd survived the no-confidence motion the previous October, her political opponents were as vocal as ever. Even in her home province of Sindh, the city of Karachi was turbulent: the alliance which the PPP had made with the MQM was falling apart amid allegations that their 'accord' had not been honoured. The wider region remained volatile. The withdrawal of Soviet troops from Afghanistan in February 1989 may have been greeted with jubilation in the West as a victory of one 'super-power' leading to the virtual demise of the other, but the situation in Afghanistan was far from stable. President Najibullah, who had replaced Babrak Karmal in 1986, was still being opposed by an alliance of mujahideen groups, whose power bases were mainly in the north and east of the country. Having successfully thwarted a coup in 1989, the following year Najibullah embarked on a programme of national reconciliation. He introduced a multi-party system, made Islam the state religion and renamed the communist-led People's Democratic Party of Afghanistan (PDPA) the Hezb-i Watan (Homeland Party). But these initiatives were not successful and it was only a matter of time before his government was again tested, the former mujahideen refusing to share power with their erstwhile communist enemies.

On Pakistan's eastern border, with the longstanding dispute over Jammu and Kashmir still unresolved, an insurgency had begun in the valley of Kashmir. As one of the three regions of the former princely state under Indian administration (the other two being Jammu and Ladakh), disaffection had been rising following allegations of rigged elections to the state legislative assembly in

1987. Inspired by the success of the Afghan jihad, groups of political activists had taken up arms in what they described as a 'freedom struggle' against Indian rule. In so doing they were referring back to the events of 1947–48 and the fact that a plebiscite – confirming or rejecting the state's accession to India, with the option of joining Pakistan – had never been held.

Although Pakistan's official position was that it was only giving the insurgents 'moral and diplomatic' support, it was clear, given Pakistan's own claim to the former princely state of Jammu and Kashmir, that military and financial help were being provided. It was no secret that 'training camps' were established in what the Pakistanis called *Azad* (free) Jammu and Kashmir (AJK) – the narrow strip of land gained during India and Pakistan's first war after independence.* While Kashmiris from the valley crossed over the line of control to train, their numbers were bolstered by others from the Pakistani side returning to fight with them. As prime minister of Pakistan, Benazir was in the unenviable position of dealing with the entrenched viewpoints of both her own country's establishment, notably the military, and that of India. As she had already experienced with the failure of the talks over Siachen, political will was difficult to assert, when powerful vested interests were at stake.

'I am thinking of you again today and feeling that you must have once more returned to Al Murtaza,' I wrote to Benazir on 4 April 1990. 'A year ago we sat together on the steps at Larkana – do you remember? I wonder if the mausoleum has been built.'[44]

---

* Referred to by the Indians as Pakistan-occupied Kashmir (POK) while the Pakistanis refer to the area under Indian administration as Indian-held Kashmir (IHK).

I also wanted to tell Benazir that I would be coming to Pakistan in May to launch a new edition of *Bhutto: Trial and Execution*. Some months previously I'd been contacted by Amir Hussain Agha of Classic Publishers, Lahore, who wanted to republish the book in English with an Urdu translation. For this new edition, I had written a 'Postscript: For the record', filling in the events of the past decade, culminating with Benazir's election as prime minister. Under the heading: 'Trial and Execution, in hindsight', I included a number of fresh observations. In addition to my conversations with Justice Safdar Shah, I had also met Dorab Patel who, following his resignation from the Supreme Court, was devoting himself to human rights issues and had just been elected to the International Commission of Jurists, headquartered in Geneva.

One point which had surprised us at the time, and which Patel clarified when we met in London, was why the three minority judges had voted with the four majority judges to dismiss the review petition. As he now related, during these critical last days, one of the judges (Patel did not say who) had come to him and read out observations 'which suggested that General Zia should exercise clemency in the matter of the sentence against Mr Bhutto'. Patel had gained the impression

> that the majority judges would incorporate these observations, or observations suggested by us in their order, if we decided not to review their judgment. I re-read the observations brought by the judge and suggested alterations to make it clear to the President that he should exercise his prerogative of mercy in favour of Mr Bhutto. A few days later, the learned Judge read out to all of us, when we were having tea in Chambers, the observations about mercy as corrected by me. We suggested one or two minor changes which were immediately agreed to... [45]

This astonishing information, which I included in my 'post-script', served to endorse the conclusion I had reached ten years earlier: 'No one could honestly say that Zulfikar Ali Bhutto was sent to death for his alleged part in a murder. He was sent to death because in the political climate of Pakistan at the time, the people who had the power wanted him out of the way. Otherwise mercy could easily have been shown by the executive authorities.'[46]

To launch the book, Classic hosted a seminar at the Avari Hotel in Lahore. One of those who spoke was Bhutto's defence lawyer, D. M. Awan, who repeated the old arguments about *malafides* which I remembered so well from the proceedings. As was to be expected, there was considerable press coverage, but not all was favourable, the predictable establishment complaint being that bringing Pakistan's 'superior judiciary into disrepute will be no service to the country'.[47]

On this visit, instead of interviewing others for potential articles or radio programmes, I found the roles reversed when a Karachi journalist, Pervez Ali, wanted to interview me as 'the prime minister's friend' for a weekly fashion magazine, *MAG*. First he asked me about our days together as students at Oxford and the year I'd spent in Pakistan throughout Bhutto's appeal; his questions then focused on the present:

Q: And then your Oxford friend created history when her struggle succeeded; her party swept the polls in 1988 and Benazir became the first lady Prime Minister of the Muslim world. What were her emotions like? Did she ever describe them to you?

A: I think her description at that time was that she felt a tremendous sense of peace. One has to put it in the context of all that had gone before, that she had worked for, for so long.

I was about to say that it was a vindication, but Pervez Ali took the word out of my mouth.

Q: Vindication of…
A: Vindication of her struggle… She had got all that without compromising. She had got what she had intended… what her father had wanted.

Other questions were more complex:

Q: What do you think about the political shrewdness of Benazir as the Prime Minister?
A: Well, how do you define shrewdness…?
Q: Let's say her competence if you are to appraise her performance.

I remember pausing as I thought carefully about my answer. Whereas others might like to criticise her, it was certainly not something I wanted nor felt necessary to do. The answer I gave was, I thought, fair.

A: I think one of the problems is that the people began to judge her from the day when she took office. If a chief executive takes over a company that's [been] fairly ransacked, which has to be turned around, then they normally give him [or her] a period, say, a two-year period and then people criticise, but, in her case, from the very beginning, her every action has been observed, monitored, criticised.[48]

Once the launch was over, I was free to go to Islamabad to spend a few days with Benazir. 'Lovely to see BB and chatted freely,' I wrote in my diary on 5 June. 'She is nowhere near as isolated from events as people make out and very much in touch, reading newspapers etc.'[49] Having left my own children at home, I enjoyed playing with her children, Bilawal, aged nearly two, and Itty, who was just a few months old. Sometimes Benazir and I would go down to the riding arena in the precincts of the prime minister's house and sit together in the cool of the evening and watch Asif and his friends exercising his polo horses. Bilawal was already being acclimatised to sitting on a horse with a special circular safety harness, protected by a groom keeping watch.

While in Islamabad, as was habitual, I visited my home from home, Niazi house. The passage of time was evident from the trees in their garden, which had grown tall, and their twins, Mona and Sultan, whom I had known as nine-year-olds and who were nearly twenty-one. All the journalists I had known before had moved on. The current BBC correspondent in Islamabad was Lyse Doucet, a Canadian who had previously worked in west Africa and whose name and unusual accent signified that she was of Acadian origin.* She seemed instantly to understand the dilemma I often faced of safeguarding the confidentiality of my friendship with Benazir, while wanting to take account of all news and views to maintain the professional credibility of my own commentary, and we instantly became friends. With the situation in Karachi deteriorating, my diary entry for 10 June was as follows: 'Lunch at Lyse's. Cathy Evans of the *Guardian* also there, quite emphatic that the Sindh situation is out of the government's hand and now in control of the military, who will dictate their terms.'[50] As in the old days, whatever I learnt of interest in the welter of conflicting reports and rumours, I transmitted back to Benazir. 'Oh really,' she would sometimes say. 'Is

---

* Lyse Doucet, OBE, CM (b.1958), was BBC correspondent in Pakistan 1989–93. She is now the BBC's chief international correspondent.

that what people think?' or 'Yes, I know, the situation is serious.' When I bade her farewell on 11 June 1990, I did not envisage that, within two months, she would no longer be prime minister.

10

Leader of the Opposition: 1990–93

The politics of personal destruction was a potent weapon for the hardliners to use.[1]

'Unbelievable news,' I wrote in my diary on Monday 6 August 1990. 'Benazir has been dismissed from office.'[2] But her dismissal was not the lead story in Britain. Our media was preoccupied with Iraq's invasion of Kuwait four days previously.

The day after her dismissal, I managed to speak to Benazir on the telephone; her overthrow, she said, was with the cooperation of the military and there had been 'a systematic attempt' to undermine her government. She also suggested that her actions against the drug barons had made her unpopular with the establishment.[3] Unfortunately, once she was no longer in office, her critics became more vociferous, maintaining that her achievements were negligible and alleging corruption and maladministration. Both she and Asif were forbidden from leaving the country.

In early October Asif was arrested on charges of 'kidnapping and extortion', the allegation being that he had arranged for the kidnapping of a wealthy businessman and that a large ransom was paid for his release. The worrying question was would Benazir also be arrested on other charges? The answer was fortunately 'no' and she remained at liberty to campaign for the national elections – the seventh in Pakistan's forty-three-year history – scheduled to take place on 24 October.

The winner was Benazir's political rival, Nawaz Sharif, the leader of the opposition alliance, the Islamic Jamhoori Ittehad (IJI), which increased its representation by gaining fifty-six seats while the PPP lost fifty. What was interesting was that the IJI had secured 37.4 per cent of the vote, while the PPP – which had run in a coalition with three political parties as the Peoples' Democratic Alliance (PDA) – obtained 36.8 per cent. I didn't think this was the 'comprehensive defeat' for the PPP which, in a BBC radio interview, I was asked to endorse – the IJI having won by a margin of just over 100,000 votes. In Benazir's opinion the elections were a 'farce'. During the campaign 'hundreds' of PPP workers were arrested without charge.[4] As had happened when she was prime minister, Benazir believed – as was subsequently confirmed – that the president and the army were working against her behind the scenes, on this occasion to influence the result against her.*

Benazir's new political role was as the leader of the opposition, her constituency still her home town of Larkana. For the first time Asif had contested a seat and was elected from jail to the National Assembly for the constituency of his home town, Nawabshah. When the inaugural session took place, she staged a walk-out by the PPP members in protest against her husband's continuing imprisonment.

The next phase of Benazir's life was testing. After hurriedly

---

* On 19 October 2012 the Supreme Court of Pakistan ruled on a petition relating to allegations that the 1990 elections had been rigged; its findings were that General Aslam Beg and General Asad Durrani, then head of the Inter-Services Intelligence (ISI) agency, together with President Ghulam Ishaq Khan, had provided financial assistance to certain parties, the objective being to weaken the PPP's mandate.

moving out of the prime minister's house, her main operational base was her home in Karachi, Bilawal House. With Asif under arrest, her two small children had to adjust from seeing their father in 'PM house' to visiting him in prison. I remember seeing one photograph of Benazir emerging from the jail holding Bilawal by the hand and carrying Itty, which was illustrative of the family's changed circumstances. 'Needless to say, you have been constantly in my thoughts these past weeks,' I wrote on 1 November. 'I have tried telephoning you on several occasions at Bilawal House but it has not been possible to get through – number always seems busy. We heard you on radio and television of course.'[5]

On 16 January 1991 Benazir arrived in London. 'She is quite her old self, very much enjoying her anonymity and saying how happy she felt in London,' I recorded. One of the first things she did was to congratulate me in person on the birth of my baby daughter, Olivia, born at the end of November 1990. That evening we had dinner in Kensington with two other Oxford friends. 'Relaxed evening,' I continued, 'strangely – as the Gulf War began.' With the passing of the 15 January deadline for Iraq's withdrawal from Kuwait, as we were sitting quietly enjoying dinner and catch-up conversation, a massive aerial bombardment of Iraq had begun, destroying military and civilian installations, which signified the beginning of Operation Desert Storm, instigated by US President George Bush. Even at this early stage, Benazir's concern was that Islam would be invoked to justify resistance against the huge army of coalition forces mobilised against Saddam Hussein. In her opinion the best way forward was for a ceasefire and resumption of diplomatic negotiations.[6]

The following evening, together with Sunny and their aunt, Behjat Hariri, we went to the launch of the third edition of the Islamic scholar Dr Charis Waddy's acclaimed book, *The Muslim Mind*, first published in 1976. Now in her eighties, her friendship with Benazir had begun while Benazir was living in London in the 1980s. In terms of her understanding of Islam, what Benazir appreciated was that, being Australian-born, Charis had approached the study of Islam from 'a southern angle' without any of the traditional stereotypes prevalent in the 'West'. That she had attended our college, Lady Margaret Hall, being the first woman to study Oriental Languages (Arabic and Hebrew), also created a special bond. When Benazir became prime minister she had ensured that, in recognition of her contribution to the understanding of Islam, Charis was awarded the *Sitara-i-Imtiaz* (Star of Excellence), Pakistan's third highest honour and civilian award.* In time, I came to share in this friendship, because if Charis wanted to get in touch with Benazir she often sent letters through me.[7]

Benazir's visits to London also meant that she could spend time with Sunny, who remained permanently settled in London, and their children could play together. Murtaza was still living in Damascus. Having divorced Fauzia, in 1989 he had married Ghinwa Itoui, his daughter Fatima's Lebanese ballet teacher, who had fled Lebanon during the continuing civil war.† Their son, Zulfikar Ali Bhutto, named after his grandfather, was born the following year. Shahnawaz's widow Rehana was still living with her daughter Sassi in California. 'I always pray,' Benazir said to me one day, 'that when she grows up she will want to know about her father's family and will come to visit Pakistan.' Despite her brave face, Benazir worried constantly about Asif. On one shopping expedition she wanted to buy him a small portable TV, so that he

---

* Dr Charis Waddy (1909–2004), https://www.independent.co.uk/news/obituaries/charis-waddy-550475.html (accessed 11 May). In addition to her writing, Dr Charis Waddy had dedicated her life to the spiritual movement Moral Rearmament (founded in 1938 as a successor to the Oxford Group), which was renamed Initiatives of Change in 2001.

† The Lebanese civil war lasted from 1975 to 1990.

could watch television in jail 'as he is in solitary; it all seems very unreal', I noted in my diary. When we were in the car I asked her if she wanted to give up politics. 'No,' she replied. 'I have a mission to complete and so many people depend on me.'[8]

Once she'd returned to Pakistan I resumed my letter writing. 'I am really quite frightened for the future because, as we discussed, Saddam has managed to make this appear as a war of the West against Islam,' I was writing in late February, 'and the Americans are not helping by their jingoistic attitude.'[9] On this occasion our fears of a full-scale Middle Eastern war were not realised. On 27 February Saddam Hussein withdrew his forces from Kuwait, its 'liberation' widely celebrated. But, as we now know, the sequel over a decade later was to turn out less well.

While in political opposition in Pakistan, Benazir began a routine of travel which lasted for over fifteen years. With the help of Mark Siegel, whom she had met in Washington DC in 1984 through Peter Galbraith, and who had become her lobbyist, she began a series of 'lecture tours' in the United States, Europe and Asia. In time she travelled the length and breadth of the USA, speaking to universities, think-tanks, congressmen and senators. Although the lecture tours were hard work and meant living out of a suitcase for several weeks, they not only gave her a valuable source of income, but they provided an important platform. 'It was a chance for me to talk to opinion-formers about the state of democracy in Pakistan, to meet with the print and electronic press and with elected officials.' She was also constantly reminding her listeners of the dangers of military dictatorship and extremism.[10]

In April 1991 Benazir returned to London, having come directly from Saudi Arabia where she had performed *Umrah*, the traditional pilgrimage to Mecca, the holiest city for Muslims. She had first done so in 1986 before returning to Pakistan, a pledge she had made to her father before his death.[11] Soon after her arrival she went to see Margaret Thatcher, whose own political career had been terminated abruptly when she was obliged to resign as prime minister the previous November. While the two former prime ministers spent time together, I sat and waited. Benazir emerged from her meeting at Thatcher's home in Eaton Square quite excited.* 'I do like Mrs T,' she said. 'She told me that she never reads the newspapers and advised me to do likewise.'[12]

An important focus of her London visits remained interacting with media and opinion makers. Bashir Riaz, who had been her press spokesman when she was prime minister, kept her appointments diary. Sometimes she would write a note on the long list of those who wanted to see her, saying 'regret, next visit', others she would accept, such as Ian Jack, who had interviewed her for *Vanity Fair* in the 1980s and was now writing for *The Independent on Sunday*. David Frost, one of the 'famous five' who had launched the ITV programme TV-AM in 1983, became a regular interviewer.† In late April we went to the TV-AM studios in Camden Lock for one such recording. 'It all went v. well,' I noted in my diary, 'Bilawal sat on my knee and watched.'[13]

As I listened to Benazir during her many interviews, it was fascinating to hear her expound her political vision. Like her father, she would have a thought and then develop it. While being interviewed by Raymond Whitaker, a senior journalist for *The Independent*, she embarked on the subject of nuclear proliferation. In terms of revealing the stage of development of Pakistan's nuclear programme, it would be better for Pakistan to act 'coy because you can get your cake and eat it too'; once Pakistan had

---

* Benazir's visit to Mrs Thatcher took place in London, 26 April 1991. Margaret Thatcher's successor was her former chancellor of the exchequer and briefly foreign secretary John Major (later the Rt Hon. Sir John Major, KG, CH) (b.1943), who was prime minister of the UK 1990–97.

† Sir David Frost, OBE (1939–2013). *Breakfast with Frost* ran from 1993 to 2005.

demonstrated its nuclear capability, she said, the country would be isolated from the benefits of regional cooperation, both environmental and economic. She then moved to outlining the importance of filling the political vacuum left by the Soviet Union's demise.

> One of the exciting areas where I feel Pakistan has missed out is the idea of the association of democratic nations… you see the world doesn't live in a vacuum, people are always attracted to one polarity or another polarity; in the past that was communism, but with the decline of communism people are going to look at the other polarity or identity which is going to be race, religion or nationalism, which – in the pre-communist world – were the powerful forces across the globe. What the association would do is to give a platform to countries from Europe, Asia, Africa, Latin America to allow differing cultures, geography, races and religions to gather around a common ideology and that would be an association of democratic countries.[14]

Not for the first time I thought what an important role she could play internationally if only she could rise above what Whitaker, in his questioning, described as the political 'Punch and Judy show' prevailing in Pakistan.[15]

As well as meeting members of the press, Benazir took advantage of her time in London to write several letters to organisations she hoped might be influential in Pakistan. 'I am concerned by the infringement of the human rights of those political opponents of the current regime,' she told Dr David Tonkin, the secretary-general of the Commonwealth Parliamentary Association (CPA) and a former premier of South Australia.* 'Many of our party

---

* Hon. Dr David Tonkin, AO (1929–2000), 38th premier of South Australia 1979–82.

supporters are now facing trumped up criminal and civil charges. Scores of people have been arrested and tortured, including women activists belonging to the Pakistan Peoples Party... Unless an independent election commission is set up free from Presidential and governmental influence, elections will become a farce.' Her letter received a polite response saying that 'sadly, Pakistan has not yet submitted its application for membership to the CPA. We are looking forward very much to receiving it.' But the secretary-general did give Benazir the opportunity to put forward her own views by submitting a 2,000-word article to the association's journal, *The Parliamentarian*, which she duly did.[16]

She also wrote to the general secretary of the Inter-Parliamentary Union (IPU), David Ramsay, requesting a delegation from the IPU to visit Pakistan. Ramsay's response was also negative: 'Regrettably I cannot accept an invitation to send a delegation of our members to a country unless the invitation is endorsed by that country's mission in London... I am sure that if such an invitation is received then my Officers will give it favourable consideration; however I must advise you that our programme for the next twelve months is already very full.'[17]

As on previous visits there were lunches and dinners with friends. To thank me for one dinner I'd organised, Benazir arrived with a small box. As she handed it to me, her expression was one of amusement and disappointment. Inside the box was a pair of pearl earrings. 'Well,' she said, staring at the almost identical pearl earrings I was wearing. 'You have two daughters and now you have two pairs of pearl earrings!'

A quality that Benazir never lost was her desire to match-make, mainly because she loved seeing other people happy. At another dinner, this time at San Lorenzo's in Knightsbridge, the two people she wanted to introduce were Carol Thatcher and one of our Oxford friends, Jonathan Marks – the future Lord Marks – who had recently divorced. She had also invited Alan Duncan, by now the Conservative candidate for Rutland and Melton, plus Stephen and myself. When I telephoned Jonathan to invite him, he immediately asked if he could bring his new girlfriend.* Having relayed this to Benazir, she said that was not the point of the evening at all, and I was duly requested to tell him that, while he was welcome, his girlfriend wasn't or words to that effect.

'Hello, er… well the thing is Benazir wanted to keep the party small,' I faltered.

'Oh… does that mean she doesn't want me to come?'

'Well, no, yes, I mean, not with your girlfriend.'

'Oh, OK, well thanks anyway,' and he hung up.

About an hour later he phoned back.

'Well actually I would like to come after all,' he said apologetically, his girlfriend having been told I've no idea what. Although the idea of match-making him with Carol Thatcher was obviously a non-starter, we had an interesting evening; as I recall, Carol spent most of the time talking to Alan, their conversation duly noted in the diary page of the *Evening Standard*: 'Carol Thatcher seems to be assuming a little of her mother's stridency. Last night she was dining at San Lorenzo with her old friend Benazir Bhutto. Between this exquisite pair sat Alan Duncan…'[18]

One of Benazir's last appointments on this visit was a courtesy call on prime minister John Major; the meeting was facilitated by David Owen, who, during a lunchtime meeting in February, had reminded her that, regardless of what the future held, her status was now as a former prime minister. He therefore believed that she should be meeting people on a level that her stature merited.

---

* The Lord Marks of Henley-on-Thames, QC (b.1952). Jonathan Marks later married Medina Cafopoulos, (not the girlfriend in question!), the mother of five of his seven children.

On the appointed day I accompanied Benazir to 10 Downing Street. While she met the prime minister, I sat in another room drinking coffee from a china cup served on a silver tray. When she emerged from her meeting, she was evidently pleased by the welcome she'd received; their discussions had ranged from the situation of the Kurds living in Iraq, which had become critical in the Gulf War, to the Afghan refugees, millions of whom remained in Pakistan despite the withdrawal of the Soviets, to the importance of revitalising the United Nations, as well as the elections in Pakistan. They'd even had time to discuss their respective children.[19]

Benazir's return to Pakistan on this occasion was tearful. With Asif in jail, she'd decided to leave Bilawal, nearly three years old, with Sunny and return home with Itty. 'I shall never forget as long as I live the sight of Bilawal,' she recalled. 'He was staring at me silently and stoically with the saddest brown eyes in the world as I took Bakhtawar with me and left him behind.'[20] Even my five-year-old daughter, Alexandra, who came with me to say goodbye, realised how upsetting it was that they were not all leaving together. 'I had an overwhelming feeling of sadness and of how brave and courageous she is,' I wrote in my diary, 'going on against such odds.'[21]

She was, however, taking back some unusual souvenirs. A feature of England in springtime that Benazir loved was cherry blossom. After a day's outing in the country, she said she would love to take some saplings back to Pakistan to see if they would grow and so we'd stopped at a garden centre to buy four small trees, which I kept in my garden until her departure. The day before she was ready to leave, I packed them up, removing the soil and dampening the roots, hoping they would survive the journey. Alas, they did not, but the idea that she'd wanted to take home flowering cherry trees to remind her of England showed a side of Benazir rarely revealed.

*

One successful outcome of Benazir's letter writing was the agreement of the International Federation for Human Rights to send a two-man delegation to Pakistan, one of whom was the human rights lawyer, Etienne Jaudel, who had come to Pakistan for the April 1989 seminar as well as attending the appeal in Rawalpindi in 1978; the other was Judge Alain Girardet.

The delegation arrived in late May; after visits to Islamabad, Karachi and Lahore, they produced a report indicating 'that even though a number of activists and leaders of the PPP, who were arrested at the beginning of the elections of October 1990, have since been freed, several hundred still remain under detention, especially in Sindh... The representatives of the IFHR heard numerous accounts concerning the torture of most of those arrested, notably in specialised centres of the police and the Army.' Their report concluded by protesting against the use of lashing 'which continues to be used, sometimes even in public'. They also condemned chains being used on prisoners, even in court, 'which is cruel, inhuman and degrading'. Finally they made it clear that, despite having asked to meet members of the government and the federal judicial authorities, their request was denied. From Benazir's point of view, the delegation proved its worth by documenting what Jaudel and Girardet described as the 'unacceptable excesses' against members of the PPP.[22]

Back in London in September, David Owen had invited her to dinner at his home in East London and she asked me to go with her. We were already on our way when she said we must stop to get a present. The only obvious place available at this stage on our journey was a petrol station, so I stopped the car and she got out to buy some flowers. I often wondered what the petrol attendant would have thought if he'd known who was buying the flowers or for whom they were destined. On arrival, David and his wife Debbie greeted us warmly. Since it was still summer we sat outside on the patio looking out at the River Thames as darkness fell and the surrounding buildings began to glow. Our conversation focused on politics and her political future; Benazir also wanted to know whether David Owen regretted his decision to leave the Labour Party – the implication being that, had he not done so, he might have become prime minister.

'No,' he replied. He then went on to explain that both the Conservative Party and the Labour Party were now espousing the 'social democratic' principles which he, as a member of the Gang of Four (together with Roy Jenkins, Bill Rodgers and Shirley Williams), had sought to establish by founding the Social Democratic Party in 1981. As we left he gave us both a signed copy of his 800-page autobiography, *Time to Declare*,* which had just been published.[23]

Another longstanding member of parliament with whom Benazir had remained in touch was Sir Peter Tapsell. While having tea one day on the terrace of the House of Commons, enjoying cucumber sandwiches, he had turned to Benazir and said, in a fatherly tone of voice: 'You know, Pakistan is ungovernable, you really ought to leave.' She smiled, saying that she knew his advice was meant with her best interests at heart, but that relinquishing her political role was not something she felt she could do. Sir Peter likewise conceded that he knew what he was suggesting was difficult and that he respected her commitment. The topic of conversation moved on.

It was also to Sir Peter that Benazir turned for advice when she was contemplating taking legal action in relation to Christina Lamb's recently published book, *Waiting for Allah: Pakistan's*

---

* David Owen, *Time to Declare* (Michael Joseph, 1991).

*Struggle for Democracy.** Benazir, who was still sensitive about her dismissal, interpreted certain statements in the book as defamatory, especially in relation to the description of the corruption allegations against her. Sir Peter immediately introduced her to Lord Goodman. In his late seventies, he had the physical presence to match his towering reputation. When Benazir and I went to see him in his offices my mind went back to a more benign time when, as Master of University College, Oxford, he had invited the great violinist Yehudi Menuhin to play in front of a select group of students, of which I was one. Now we were in the real world discussing defamation and libel.

After Lord Goodman took the matter up with Christina's publishers, the offending passages were amended in the paperback edition and the matter forgotten. But, having learnt that there were occasions when she could take a stand, once her grievances were addressed, Benazir did not harbour a grudge. She restored her friendship with Christina, who continued her distinguished career as foreign correspondent for the *Sunday Telegraph* (and then as chief foreign correspondent for the *Sunday Times*), their paths often crossing in the decades to come. Goodman died in 1995 but when Benazir needed legal advice thereafter she turned to his firm, Goodman Derrick & Sons.†

In early October I went into hospital for a minor operation. Rather to my surprise, Benazir, accompanied by her stepmother-in-law, Timmy Zardari, arrived during visiting hours, carrying a very large box which definitely did not look like chocolates. She was looking particularly pleased. When I opened it, I saw that it was a fax machine, a device which over the previous decade had

---

* Christina Lamb, *Waiting for Allah: Pakistan's Struggle for Democracy* (Hamish Hamilton, 1991).

† Lord Goodman, CH (1913–95). Now Goodman Derrick LLP.

become an essential method of international communication. 'So we won't only have to rely on letters,' she said.[24] 'Fax to Bilawal House', I was writing on 25 November after Benazir (happily, with both children) had returned to Pakistan:

> Please pass on to BB... Urgent... from Victoria. Re. Aung San Suu Kyi. I've been contacted by Burmese section of BBC who would like, in conjunction with *Sunday Times*, to run a 'statement' by you on Aung San Suu Kyi relating to the recent book edited by her husband and her role as winner of Nobel Peace Prize fighting for democracy in a violent country – circa 500 words... deadline circa 10 days... would you like me to fax you a draft by Friday, or would you prefer to do it all from your end?[25]

Meanwhile, as the old communist 'Union of Soviet Socialist Republics' ceased to exist, new relationships were developing. On 8 December 1991 the three republics of Russia, Byelorussia and Ukraine formed the Commonwealth of Independent States (CIS). Two weeks later eight more republics joined the CIS and on 25 December 1991 Mikhail Gorbachev resigned as president of the Soviet Union.* 'Free elections have become a reality,' he announced. 'Free press, freedom of worship, representative legislatures and a multi-party system have all become a reality.' We all heaved a sigh of relief, thinking that perhaps this signalled a brave new era. How wrong we were!

*

---

* Georgia joined two years later; the only three which did not join were Latvia, Estonia and Lithuania.

Throughout 1992 Benazir and I continued to correspond by letters and fax. 'Helen and David have had a baby girl, which is great as they desperately wanted a girl. I'm going to see her later this week,' I was writing in March. 'All well with our children... Colin Moynihan got married... he'll be on his honeymoon when the general election takes place (anticipated for 9 April). It looks as though it is going to be a tough fight between Labour and Conservative. Everyone recognises that we are in a world recession and can't blame the Conservatives, but there are also problems with the National Health, Education etc which don't look good.'[26]

When the UK general election took place on 9 April 1992, the results took everyone by surprise, the Conservative Party winning for the fourth consecutive time and John Major remaining as prime minister. So unexpected was the Conservative victory that commentators immediately compared it with the surprise win of the Labour Party in 1945 when Clement Attlee defeated Winston Churchill. Among our Oxford friends, Alan Duncan won the Conservative seat for Rutland and Melton; and Barbara Roche and Peter Mandelson both won seats for the Labour Party. Colin Moynihan, one of our first contemporaries to enter the House of Commons in 1983, lost his Lewisham East seat to Labour, later succeeding to a baronetcy. Another contemporary, Tony Blair, was rising fast in the ranks of the Labour Party. He too had become an MP in 1983, but, since he wasn't involved in the Oxford Union, we barely knew him.*

Ever since Benazir's dismissal, Asif had remained in prison in Karachi. In May 1992 after over eighteen months, he was moved to stay in one of the parliament lodges (allocated to members of the National Assembly) and then briefly to house arrest. This at least meant that Benazir had the opportunity for more regular visits.

---

* Tony Blair (b.1953) was prime minister of the UK 1997–2007.

But the respite was short-lived. His release on bail was blocked by a special government ordinance, which had withdrawn the court's authority to release him. From London I couldn't understand the rationale. I was expecting to see Benazir in London in July but at short notice she cancelled her visit.[27]

After two years in government, Nawaz Sharif's popularity was declining. 'Fiscal irresponsibility had played havoc with the lives of ordinary citizens,' observed Benazir. 'Power shutdowns that had been eliminated by the PPP government reappeared. Corruption scandals hit the newspaper headlines.' In November she organised a 'long march' to force the government's resignation. Starting by train from Karachi, Benazir progressed through the Pakistani heartland to Lahore and onwards to be greeted by crowds in their thousands, once more chanting the familiar slogan: *Jeeay* Bhutto! *Jeeay* Benazir!' 'From the four corners of Pakistan, caravans were getting ready to move to Rawalpindi in a display of people's power.' To prevent the protest movement gaining momentum, Nawaz Sharif banned Benazir from entering Rawalpindi. Undaunted, she managed to break through the barbed wire and road blocks and reach Liaquat Bagh, where her rally was due to take place on 18 November. But the police came after her. 'Our single jeep was tear-gassed from all sides. Police sirens were blaring away. There was pandemonium. The car chase was like something from a James Bond movie – or perhaps more like a Bollywood movie.' After the police had surrounded the car, Benazir and her companions were taken into custody and then released later in the day. In Benazir's opinion 'the day's events had weakened the regime'.[28]

Perhaps, as a hangover from the Zia years, I still preferred to send letters through a friend or another member of the family rather than relying on the ordinary post. 'At last the opportunity to write you a proper letter!! I have been waiting for a courier for ages,' I wrote in late November. As usual, political commentary was interspersed with social. Samiya was getting married in early December.* 'Do please give her best best love. I shall be thinking of her and of course remembering your wedding five years ago. What a lot has happened in those five years. As you have so often said, fact is stranger than fiction.' When possible I included small presents for the children, my letter ending with a postscript: 'I hope Bilawal enjoys *The Minpins*. Ours love the stories of Roald Dahl – and I am sending a little doll for Bakhtawar.'[29]

In January 1993 Benazir arrived in London. This time her stay was to be for longer. She had had problems with her gall bladder which needed to be removed; but there was an added complication since she was again pregnant (which made it all the more remarkable that she'd undertaken the 'long march' the previous November). Before having the gall bladder operation, she first had to give birth. On 3 February she was admitted to the Portland hospital in London's West End. I remember again thinking how courageous she was, still combining her political life with motherhood. 'In the evening went to see B. & her new baby,' I recorded in my diary, 'a sweet tiny little girl.'[30] She was called Aseefa – after her father – her name meaning 'gentle'.

A few days later came news of Asif's release, bail finally having been granted.[31] 'Benazir's gentle gift from God' the *Sunday Express* proclaimed, stating that 'Baby makes Bhuttos a family again after the years of turmoil in troubled Pakistan.'[32] Begum Bhutto was in constant attendance in the hospital as well as Sunny. Flowers and congratulations flooded in from around the world including from Princess Diana (whose separation from Prince Charles had been announced the previous year), Margaret Thatcher, Sonia Gandhi and countless others, including the Canadian prime minister,

---

* Samiya Waheed married Jan Ali Junejo on 9 December 1992.

Brian Mulroney. I bought some notepaper and, taking my manual typewriter to the Portland, typed her thank-you letters which she then signed. *Hello!* magazine wanted photographs, and so did *Paris Match* and *OK!* My mother sent a baby outfit etched in pink and was thrilled to see, when the photographs appeared in one of the magazines, that Aseefa was wearing the outfit she'd sent; it was another of Benazir's thoughtful gestures which she knew would give my mother pleasure.

Shortly after giving birth, Benazir had surgery for her gall bladder. Once she had recovered from that operation, she resumed her busy schedule, which, on this visit, included giving a briefing to the Foreign Press Association on 18 March 1993 and numerous other meetings. By the time she was ready to return to Pakistan, the political wheel was clearly turning. 'It's been lovely being here & now it's time to go home,' she wrote to me shortly before leaving.[33]

On 18 April Nawaz Sharif was dismissed on charges of corruption and maladministration by President Ghulam Ishaq Khan, who promised to hold fresh elections within ninety days. 'Dear Benazir,' Sir Peter Tapsell wrote in May,

Gabrielle and I have been following the political developments in Pakistan with the greatest of interest since your return to your country. I hope all goes well in your forthcoming elections. You know that I have always worried about your physical security, so I hope you will not take any avoidable risks and will make sure that you have really professional body-guards, preferably trained by our SAS or some comparable organisation... [You are] looking as radiant as ever despite the incredible stresses of the life you lead. I hope that your baby daughter is thriving and that you are steadily recovering from your operation. You should not push yourself back into full activity until you are compelled to do so.[34]

Sharif, however, was not prepared to give up the premiership without a fight; having accused the president of 'hatching conspiracies', he challenged his dismissal in the Supreme Court of Pakistan. When, in May, the ruling went in his favour, he was reinstated.[35] Over the next few weeks the power struggle between president and prime minister continued until, under pressure from the Pakistan army, both agreed to resign and, in July, a caretaker government was established. Indicative of the manner in which political fortunes could fall and rise, one of the eighteen cabinet ministers was Asif Zardari.

Elections were scheduled for October 1993. Once Nawaz Sharif was no longer prime minister, the Islamic Jamhoori Ittehad (IJI) party dissolved and he resumed leadership of the Pakistan Muslim League – the (N) Nawaz faction as opposed to the Junejo (J) faction led by former prime minister Mohammed Khan Junejo. Yet again Benazir went on the campaign trail, addressing rallies and presenting the PPP as the party of progress and liberalism. Her description of the difficulties she faced were a warning of what was to come:

During the election campaign that began with Nawaz's ouster, my earlier confrontations with the military hardliners in the security apparatus came back to life. In 1993, they had more direct plans to keep me from office. The ISI (Inter Services Intelligence) was no longer satisfied with trying to keep me out of power by funding the opposition [as she believed they had done previously]. This time they wanted me permanently out of the picture, removed as an obstacle to their dream of caliphate once and for all. Thus in the fall of 1993 my assassination was ordered, and the chosen assassin was a Pakistani with ties to the ISI during the Afghan jihad.[36]

Fortunately the attempt failed. The intended assassin, Ramzi Yousef, later gained notoriety for having taken part in the first attack on the World Trade Center in February 1993, as well as the bombing of a Philippines Airlines flight in December 1994.* Yousef was extradited to the United States in 1995.[37]

A newcomer to the political scene was Benazir's brother, Murtaza, who, although still living in Damascus, had decided to contest the elections. It had been over fifteen years since he had lived in Pakistan before their father's execution. Since he was still wanted in connection with the 1981 PIA hijacking, he sent his wife, Ghinwa, to Karachi to campaign on his behalf. As the wife of the elder (and now only) son of Zulfikar Ali Bhutto, she took up residence in the family home at 70, Clifton. Instead of contesting elections on behalf of the PPP, Murtaza set up a new party, the Shaheed Bhutto (Bhutto the Martyr) PPP. Begum Bhutto offered her support, which upset Benazir because she feared the PPP would be weakened in the constituencies Murtaza was contesting. To sour relations still further, Murtaza openly criticised the PPP, alleging that it had been taken over by 'opportunists and big businessmen' instead of following Zulfikar Ali Bhutto's socialist manifesto. Although we didn't realise it at the time, Benazir was on the threshold of one of the most difficult periods of her personal and political life.

---

* Ramzi Yousef (b.1968) received two life sentences and 240 years; his uncle was Khalid Sheikh Mohammed, leader of Al Qaeda, implicated in the killing of Daniel Pearl.

11

Prime Minister Again: 1993–96

Destiny's hand moves on,
Writing its own tale,
Of triumphs and tragedies,
Of wars and peace... [1]

When the results of the October 1993 elections were announced, the Pakistan Peoples Party had won eighty-six seats while Nawaz Sharif's Pakistan Muslim League (N) had won seventy-three. As in 1988, Benazir did not have an outright majority, and so, in order to form a government, she had once more to make alliances with independents and smaller parties. On 19 October she took the oath of office as prime minister of Pakistan. 'Given the extraordinary opportunity of serving as prime minister for the second time,' she later wrote, 'I was determined to use every day to improve the daily lives of the working families of Pakistan and to help stabilise the dangerous international environment... Again I tried to work as quickly and effectively as possible to bring Pakistan into a modern era.' Perhaps because it was second time around, the occasion did not receive the same worldwide publicity as in 1988 but it was still a remarkable achievement for Benazir to have once again become prime minister of a Muslim country while only forty years old.[2]

'Wonderful to be back writing to you again as prime minister,' I wrote in early November, 'although I fear you will have less time to read my letters, but still I shall keep writing, so that you know I am thinking of you!!' Among other news was that I had just unveiled her portrait in the Oxford Union debating chamber. It had been painted by the British artist, Diccon Swan, whose portfolio included other political leaders, notably Margaret Thatcher. In recognition of her achievement as a former president of the Union, our mutual friend Alan Duncan had both chosen the artist and organised for the painting to be done.* 'So now you are up there,' I continued. 'It rather stunned me to look at all the undergraduates and realise they were all just born as we went up to Oxford and that they were looking so grown up and confident. Still much water has passed under the bridge since then especially for you with all that you have accomplished.'[3]

The country of which Benazir was again prime minister was, however, in crisis. Rising ethnic violence, a bankrupt exchequer, instability in neighbouring Afghanistan and allegations that Pakistan was 'exporting' terrorism across the border to India by supporting the insurgency in Jammu and Kashmir, all contrived to make her second term of office even more difficult than the first. As before, she had to accommodate the expectations of her political supporters in a superficially democratic environment, while still restricted by the system of patronage and preferment which had remained the hallmark of Pakistani politics since inception. The

---

* Diccon Swan (b.1947). When President Musharraf came to speak at the Oxford Union on 29 September 2006 the painting was removed for 'cleaning'. Traditionally ex-presidents who have also become prime minister are recognised with a sculptured bust.

political alliances she had to make all came with a price tag, as ministries were allocated and positions traded. Added to this was the need to keep the Pakistan army on board, without whose support she would not be able to govern.

Benazir also had the challenge of her fractured relationship with her brother, which was to cast a long shadow over her second administration. Having stayed in Damascus, *in absentia* Murtaza had won a seat in Sindh's provincial assembly for a constituency in Larkana district; with the PPP remaining dominant in rural Sindh, it was the only seat his Shaheed Bhutto party won. Despite their strained relations, Benazir supported her brother's return to Pakistan. 'Whatever political life he wants to follow, whether to join the PPP or to oppose it, is quite a separate matter. On a personal level I would be very happy any day he chose to return. Why shouldn't he come back? It's his home, it's his country.'[4]

On 3 November 1993 Murtaza landed in Karachi, but, since charges were still pending because of the 1981 PIA hijacking, as soon as the plane touched down he was arrested. Benazir's point of view was that if she took steps to have the charges against her brother dropped, it would indicate that she was showing favouritism to a family member and so she believed that 'the law' had to take its course. Already, she said, she had been criticised for providing him with a passport and granting amnesty so that he could return. Murtaza viewed the situation differently. When his trial started, he believed that, on Benazir's instructions, the prosecutor was using delaying tactics to keep him confined for as long as possible.

I was saddened that brother and sister had become so estranged. I recalled how both, in their own ways, had worked tirelessly to save their father's life. But although Murtaza conceded that Benazir's role during those days was 'heroic', he said the politics of their respective positions prevented a reconciliation. Benazir put his opposition to her in the context of the political landscape throughout Pakistan. 'There are two forces in this country, one is the PPP and the other is the anti-PPP. Every step he has taken has been in support of the anti-PPP forces.'[5]

Begum Bhutto's political backing for Murtaza also created a rift. On 3 December Benazir took the controversial decision to dismiss her mother as co-chairman of the PPP, a position she had held since Zulfikar Ali Bhutto's death. The public family quarrel was, alas, meat and drink for the newspapers. 'The Battle of all Mothers' was the headline given to Michael Fathers' article in *The Independent*: an obvious play on Saddam Hussein's earlier threat that the coalition forces could expect the 'mother of all battles' when they initiated Operation Desert Storm to regain Kuwait in 1991. 'Murtaza has openly admitted that he is seeking to rally the disaffected Bhuttoists,' wrote Fathers. 'Benazir, he argues, has sold out to their father's enemies, who are intent on destroying the party. There are no holds barred in this dynastic conflict. Expect the fight for the PPP to be fierce and bloody.'[6]

Yet despite the difficulties Sir Peter Tapsell had recognised of governing 'the ungovernable', ostensibly Benazir's position seemed stronger. Not only was she more experienced but, instead of a hostile president, she now had the support of the new incumbent, Farooq Leghari, former foreign minister, and minister for water and power in her first government. Having joined the PPP in 1973 Farooq had stood by Benazir throughout her father's trial and execution and I had vivid memories of him coming to Flashman's Hotel during Bhutto's appeal. So concerned was he that the military authorities might have bugged all the rooms that, whenever he wanted to talk confidentially, he insisted on travelling around Rawalpindi in a car.*

---

* Sardar Farooq Ahmed Khan Leghari (1940–2010) was president of Pakistan 1993–97. He was at St Catherine's College, Oxford, but left before Benazir arrived there.

'You know Farooq is now the president,' Benazir said to me in delight when I arrived in Islamabad in March 1994. 'I'll make arrangements so that you can see him.' And so she did, my visit to the luxurious presidential palace overlooking Islamabad being fixed soon afterwards.

Since my last visit to Pakistan in 1990, I had given thought to a comment Benazir had made when I went to say goodbye to her shortly before her dismissal that August. 'Come back soon,' she had said. 'Come back and write some articles on Kashmir.' But instead of writing articles, I'd decided to write a book. As I already realised, having briefly raised the issue when I met Indira Gandhi in 1981, there were different 'truths' depending on whether one accepted the Indian belief that the state of Jammu and Kashmir was part of India because the ruling maharaja, Hari Singh, had, with some qualifications, chosen to join India in 1947, or the Pakistani viewpoint, that his accession was not valid because the inhabitants of the state had not been consulted. After some preliminary research, and armed with a synopsis, I had gone to see a well-known literary agent, Murray Pollinger.

'Kashmir?' he said rather doubtfully. 'Why do you want to write on such a difficult topic, which will never be resolved?'

'Oh,' I said naively, still thinking that difficult political issues could be resolved. 'It's a really important subject.'

There was a pause. I continued: 'All the books written on the issue are about the land as a piece of real estate, from an Indian or Pakistani perspective. I want to write about the people.' Murray could see that my mind was made up and, after going through my synopsis, he agreed to submit my proposal to I. B. Tauris, an independent publishing house, founded in 1983 by an Austro-

Iranian, Iradj Bagherzade.* His list included Middle Eastern and South Asian topics, into which Murray thought my Kashmir book might fit. When I told Benazir I was going to write on Kashmir, she was delighted. 'It'll mean more visits to our part of the world,' she enthused.

So here I was in Islamabad, ready to start recording interviews. I also wanted to visit Muzaffarabad, the capital of what Pakistan called 'free' Jammu and Kashmir. Then I planned to fly to Gilgit, renowned for being the place where the three great mountain ranges of the Hindu Kush, Karakoram and Himalayas meet and which, as 'the Northern Areas', formed part of the disputed state, north of which lay the Siachen glacier. Then, 'God willing' – as the Pakistanis always say – I intended to go to India, and back to the valley of Kashmir where the insurgency against the Indian government was at its height, with certain areas regarded as 'no-go' because of the presence of militants. The troubled situation had led the Indian government to bring in a substantial military presence, with 'crackdowns' and cordon and search operations becoming part of daily life, resulting in tremendous hardship for the local people.

As was all too obvious, those historic occasions in 1988 and 1989 when Benazir and Rajiv were looked upon as children of the post-partition generation who might resolve the two countries' differences had long since gone. Instead, a more combative rela-tionship was emerging between Benazir and her Indian counter-part, Congress leader and prime minister P. V. Narasimha Rao.† In February she'd made a persuasive speech at the fiftieth session of the UN Commission on Human Rights in Geneva: 'The situation in Kashmir is intolerable; as is the world's conscience. We ask that

---

* Iradj Bagherzade (b.1942) was born in Austria of Iranian parents.
† P. V. Narasimha Rao (1921–2004) was prime minister of India 1991–96.

the representatives of the Kashmiri people be allowed to come before you to inform the Commission of the oppression to which they are being subjected. We urge this Commission to investigate these violations of human rights.'[7]

Although, due to lack of support, Pakistan had to withdraw its motion calling on the UN to send a fact-finding mission to the Kashmir valley, what Benazir said had made an impact. When some weeks later I met the former chief minister of Jammu and Kashmir, Dr Farooq Abdullah, who had been a member of India's high-level delegation to Geneva, he recalled how the prime minister of Pakistan took centre stage with her charismatic delivery, even though he was bound not to support her viewpoint.[8]

On 23 March 1994, as usual, Pakistanis celebrated Pakistan Day, in commemoration of the passing of the Lahore Resolution in 1940. Instead of being held at Rawalpindi race course, where I had witnessed the spectacle in 1979, it now took place on the streets of Islamabad under the gaze of the Margalla Hills. 'In resplendent sunshine, the President of Pakistan, Farooq Ahmed Khan Leghari, and the Prime Minister, Mohtarma Benazir Bhutto, stood to attention on a raised dais, as a long parade of soldiers, massed bands, tanks and armoured vehicles rumbled by; they were complemented by a noisy fly past of Pakistan fighter planes with a lone F-16 spiralling high into the sky,' I recorded.[9]

A special foreign guest was Margaret Brown, who had come to receive the *Sitara-i-Imitiaz*, awarded posthumously to her husband, Major William Brown, MBE. His role, as commandant of the Gilgit Scouts, in ensuring that Gilgit became part of Pakistan in 1947 was legendary among Pakistanis although, for obvious reasons, condemned by India. After his early death, his widow had found his journal, in which he had recounted his exploits and which she had privately published as *The Gilgit Rebellion*.* As my research on Kashmir progressed, I came to realise how strategically significant this territory was for Pakistan, providing land access to China along the Karakoram Highway to the Khunjerab pass, the first stretch of which was opened in 1978 under General Zia.

Although Benazir was as busy as ever, while I was in Islamabad we managed to spend some time together. Invariably she was going through mounds of files but there was occasional free time when we could talk, generally late at night. Her new 'home' was a newly constructed Prime Minister's House in Islamabad. Every morning Bilawal, now six, and Itty, nearly four, both neatly dressed, went off to school. Asif was of course around; but the person who had signed himself 'A nobody' in my Visitors' Book four years earlier was now anything but, since, after his spell as a minister in the caretaker government, Benazir had appointed him federal minister for investments. It was a decision she subsequently defended on the grounds that John F. Kennedy appointed his brother, Robert, attorney-general.[10]

In early April we went again to Larkana to commemorate the fifteenth anniversary of her father's death on 4 April. This time we did not stay at Al Murtaza, which was now occupied by Murtaza and Ghinwa, but at the house at Naudero where her stepmother, her father's first wife Shireen Ameer Begum, lived. Like Al Murtaza, the interior was typical of Sindhi craftsmanship, the walls covered in variegated blue tiles and exuding a feeling of antiquity. At Garhi Khuda Bakhsh, wearing a traditional Sindhi *ajrak*, I witnessed Benazir once more address the throng of supporters who had gathered at the graveyard, the customary '*Jeeay* Bhutto' slogans resounding. As she paid her respects to her

---

* Margaret Brown (b.1933); Major William Brown (1922–84), *The Gilgit Rebellion 1947* (Ibex, 1998).

ancestors, she stood by the graves of her father and brother – both considered to be 'martyrs' to the cause of democracy – their graves piled high with rose petals and covered in velvet cloth. Soon, she hoped, the mausoleum would be completed. Once again I saw how traditional life somehow defied progress, the men and women working in the fields as they had done for centuries. Remembering my first visit over fifteen years earlier, there was still the same sensation of being in the interior of a great landmass where water determined the prosperity of the region, the name 'Sindh', as I now knew, meaning river.

Accompanying us on this visit was television reporter Etienne Duval, who was at Oxford with us and was now working for a number of French-speaking television channels. He had come to Pakistan to make a documentary on Benazir and was following her around with a film crew. Back in Islamabad he recorded a long interview while I sat listening to her go back over her life, describing her 'pampered' childhood, her 'carefree' youth including her time at Harvard and Oxford, which were 'the best days' of her life, her father's death, including the tragic last meeting and why she entered politics. In response to how 'Eastern' or 'Western' she felt, she said: 'I am very Eastern in that I was born here. I have a strong attachment to the soil, my family earned its living through agriculture and so I am very rooted in my own culture.' But, she continued, because she had the opportunity of seeing Western culture, she understood the West. Given that there was good and bad in both East and West, with extremism in both societies, she declared her objective to be more universal. 'What we have to do is to evolve a global society where forces of moderation can prevail.'[11] It was an aspiration to which she would return time and again.

On the eve of my departure to India, I went to Benazir's room in PM House to say goodbye. 'Oh no,' she said in a disappointed tone. 'Do you have to go to India?'

I knew she was half-joking and so was I when I responded: 'I can hardly write a book on Kashmir and not go to the valley.'

'I know,' she continued. 'Well, take good care of yourself.'

On arrival in Srinagar, I saw how both militancy and military occupation had taken their toll; there were many burnt-out buildings and tourism was at a standstill. Compared with my first visit in 1981, military bunkers had mushroomed on street corners, soldiers were standing with rifles at the ready and there was an abundance of barbed wire. My visit was to be one of many – my interest in Kashmir emerging from my friendship with Benazir, yet gaining a momentum of its own.

'HAPPY BIRTHDAY!!' I began in a letter which I hoped would reach Benazir on 21 June. 'I hope you have a lovely day and that you manage to spend some time with the children. Amazing to think it is now twenty years since your 21st, which you celebrated in the summer of 1974 at the end of your first year at Oxford – just before we met. I shall be thinking of you and with you in spirit.'[12]

We met again in early July 1994 when Benazir came on a brief unofficial visit to London. Among her engagements was a dinner in honour of Carol Thatcher to which she'd invited me and several other friends. But during this visit I owed her an apology. An interview which she had given in Islamabad before leaving had not gone well and I was instrumental in persuading her to give it. Some weeks previously I'd received a telephone call from the *Sunday Times*, asking if I would meet the journalist Barbara Amiel – wife of the newspaper magnate Conrad Black – who was going to Pakistan to write a colour supplement special. 'If you could give her some background information, that would be helpful,' my *Sunday Times* interlocutor asked. It was lovely weather when

Barbara came to my house and so we sat in the garden, talking about Benazir and how difficult her life was.

I heard nothing more, and then a friend, Nasreen Rehman, asked if I would meet a young journalist, William Dalrymple, who was living in India and had written two acclaimed books, *In Xanadu* and *City of Djinns*. Instead of Barbara Amiel, he was now going to be writing the colour supplement article on Benazir for the *Sunday Times*. William had a problem with his Indian photographer's visa to Pakistan. 'Would I,' Nasreen asked, 'be able to help?' I agreed to meet William and his wife, Olivia, for lunch in Nasreen's flat off Moscow Road near my home in Bayswater. But when I mentioned the impending interview to Benazir, she appeared less keen. By now the newspapers were full of the rift with her mother and her difficult relationship with her brother, who, on being released on 5 June, verbally attacked both Benazir and Asif, describing his brother-in-law as 'Asif Baba and [the] forty thieves'.[13]

'William Dalrymple,' I tried to reassure her, 'you remember his brother, Hew, who was at Oxford with us. He read History with me. I am sure he'll write a balanced piece.'* Critically, this assurance of familiarity – the brother of an Oxford contemporary – meant that Benazir reluctantly agreed. But the interview was not a success. It may be that she was having a bad day or that William Dalrymple simply took a dislike to her, but her charisma, which so many people admired, did not shine through. Comparing her manner to 'a Roman empress in *Caligula* or *I, Claudius*', the tone of his article had a sharp edge which, although emphasising her strong qualities, was hostile. When Benazir saw the article, she was upset:

---

* William Dalrymple FRAS, FRSL, FRGS, FRSE (b.1965); Sir Hew Hamilton-Dalrymple (b.1955).

'I only agreed to the interview because of what you said,' she said despondently.

All I could do was say how sorry I was. Having expressed her distress, Benazir put the episode behind us. 'Never mind,' she continued. 'What's done is done.'[14]

Some years later I met William Dalrymple when he was launching another book, *White Mughals*.

'I owe you an apology,' he said.

Agreeably surprised that he'd remembered the awkward position he had put me in, I thanked him for that appreciation. But I'd already learnt my lesson. Whenever anyone asked me to 'put a word in' on their behalf regarding an interview with Benazir, I declined. My response, which may have sounded unhelpful but was for their own good, was: 'If I help you get an interview, you might feel obliged to write more favourably than you would do otherwise. It is better that you go through the established channels,' to which I would happily direct the aspiring interviewer. What I also meant, but did not say, was that it was too distressing for Benazir (and me) to have someone I might have recommended write harshly about her.

In early November 1994 Benazir was in Paris on a three-day official visit. With the French capital now only a two-and-a-half-hour train journey from London thanks to Eurostar, she'd invited me to come and visit her. In addition to talks with President Mitterrand, Prime Minister Edouard Balladur, the defence minister François Leotard, politicians and business leaders, her official functions included lunch at the Hôtel de Ville, hosted by the mayor of Paris, Jacques Chirac, and dinner at the Quai d'Orsay, hosted by the minister of foreign affairs, Alain Juppé.

Benazir also had a meeting with Giscard d'Estaing, former

president of France, who was so supportive of her father; she then addressed the Foreign Relations Committee of the Assemblée Nationale, the lower house of France's bicameral parliament, of which d'Estaing was chairman. Since whatever she said officially about the Kashmir issue was relevant for my book, I sat assiduously taking notes. 'Let us resolve the core issue,' she proclaimed, asking if people in Palestine, South Africa, Algeria, could demand their self-determination then 'why not the people of Jammu and Kashmir?' She also cited the example of Haiti, where in September, after a series of military coups, the United States had intervened militarily in order to negotiate the departure of Haiti's military leaders as part of Operation Uphold Democracy, leading to the return of the democratically elected president, Jean-Bertrand Aristide.* 'Human and political rights cannot be selectively applied,' she continued, urging the députés to use their 'moral authority' on India to accept UN mediation. 'Universal rights must be applied universally.' But her remarks were seen in France as controversial and, in its coverage of her visit, *Le Monde* highlighted the fact that 'she was being criticised by her opponents for bringing the Kashmir issue to international fora too often'.[15]

Another issue which was being hotly debated in France was the wearing of headscarves by French Muslim girls in schools. Known as *l'affaire du voile* or *foulard* – the affair of the veil or scarf – the French government was proposing to adopt a memorandum put forward by François Bayrou, minister of national education, which outlined the difference between 'discreet' religious symbols and more 'ostentatious' ones which were to be forbidden in public places.† Benazir's comment, quoted in *Le Figaro*, seemed crafted

---

* When elections in Haiti were held in 1995, Aristide was defeated.

† François Bayrou (b.1951) was president of the Democratic Movement and minister of national education 1993–97; between 1993 and 2004 about 100

to appeal to both sides of the argument: people, she said, should remember that the Holy Prophet (PBUH) said the true veil of a Muslim woman is her eyes.[16]

Having returned to Islamabad, at the end of November Benazir was back in London on another week-long official visit. As before, her programme was full and included another audience with the Queen. Having called on prime minister John Major at 10 Downing Street when she was leader of the opposition, she met him again for formal talks as prime minister. She also had a meeting with our Oxford contemporary Tony Blair, who had recently become leader of the Labour party following the sudden death of John Smith.* In addition, the former prime minister Margaret Thatcher, now the Rt Hon. Baroness Thatcher of Kesteven, called on Benazir at the Dorchester where she and her delegation were staying. As on her previous visit, Stephen and I were among those she included in some of the official functions. I was even telephoned at the last minute by a member of her staff to attend a formal lunch at Admiralty House hosted by the home secretary, Michael Howard, because Asif was unable to attend and they didn't want an empty seat around the table.† Once again during her free time, family and friends came to the hotel to see her, my children overwhelmed at being invited to 'tea at the Dorchester'.[17]

Since the focus of the visit was promoting Pakistan, one of the main events, in addition to an exhibition of Pakistani folk art, a music festival and a day-visit to Bradford to meet the local Pakistani and Kashmiri community, was giving the inaugural address to

---

girls were expelled from French schools for wearing the headscarf. In half of the cases, the suspension was annulled in court. See Nicky Jones, 'Beneath the veil: Muslim girls and Islamic headscarves in secular France', *Macquarie Law Journal*, 2009.

* John Smith, QC (1938–94) was leader of the Labour Party 1992–94.
† The Rt Hon. Lord Howard of Lympne, CH, PC, QC (b.1941).

the Confederation of British Industry at their headquarters in Centre Point, Tottenham Court Road. The theme of her keynote address was 'Pakistan Today – Prospects for British business'. As President of the Board of Trade, Michael Heseltine spoke before her;* mindful that both he and Benazir were ex-presidents of the Oxford Union – although decades apart (she in 1977, he in 1954) – he described the room as being 'packed to the rafters' which was more what one would expect at 'freshman debates at the Oxford Union than at the headquarters of the CBI', Heseltine's point being to emphasise the exceptionally high level of interest in the investment potential in Pakistan.[18]

One of the several media interviews Benazir agreed to record was with Sir David Frost, who in January 1993 had set up his own Sunday morning show, *Breakfast with Frost*, and in the same year received a knighthood. Again I sat listening as the interview took place. After asking the usual questions about what she hoped to achieve in her second government and the problems she faced, there was a pause. Frost then looked at Benazir and launched himself into his next question:

'Am I to understand that you are to be congratulated?'

Benazir looked temporarily taken aback. Suddenly I saw that she had grasped his meaning. Because she had not managed to regain her figure after Aseefa's birth the previous year, David Frost thought that she might again be pregnant (rumours were circulating to that effect in the press). Her reply was classic Benazir. With a huge smile she spoke slowly.

'Why is it that when a man puts on weight, no one makes a comment, but when a woman puts on weight, people think there must be another reason?!'

---

* The Rt Hon. the Lord Heseltine of Thenford, CH, PC (b.1933) was secretary of state for Trade and Industry and president of the Board of Trade 1992–95.

Having already realised that he had made a blunder, Frost looked doubly apologetic at having drawn attention to her weight. When I asked the producer whether they were going to run that section, he replied: 'Of course', which I understood to mean that Frost would have a media scoop by being the first to disprove the rumours.[19]

Looking back, 1994 was hard work for Benazir. She had made a record number of foreign visits trying to enhance Pakistan's international image. 'We attracted a record-breaking $20 billion in foreign investment, more in one year than had been attracted to Pakistan in the previous forty years,' she recorded proudly. She had also continued to focus on policy initiatives which favoured women, including setting up women police stations and women's banks. 'We began training an army of women, 100,000 strong, to educate women in both population planning and in taking better care of their children,' she continued. 'As a result population growth came down and infant mortality was reduced.'

Another campaign that was close to her heart was the eradication of polio. 'When my doctor advised me to give my daughter, Aseefa, polio drops, I asked what the polio rate in Pakistan was. Shocked to learn that one in five children... with polio were from Pakistan, my government began a massive volunteer-based programme to provide polio drops to all the children of Pakistan.'[20] Benazir personally led the campaign by publicly administering polio drops to Aseefa.*

Throughout 1994 Benazir's administration had also had to deal with unprecedented unrest in her home town of Karachi, where the MQM – the Muhajir Qaumi Movement – had established a virtual monopoly of political control. Having emerged in the

---

* After her mother's assassination, Aseefa took on the role of ambassador for polio eradication.

late 1980s as the political mouthpiece of the Urdu-speaking Muhajir community, following the elections in 1988 and 1990 it had formed alliances with the government, first with Benazir's PPP and then with Nawaz Sharif's IJI. But it had soon developed differences with both, complaining of ethnic discrimination and inadequate political representation relative to their numbers. By the early 1990s, MQM factions in Karachi had turned to violence, using terror and torture tactics against their political opponents, whether rival factions, media critics or Sindhi nationalists, as well as the growing community of Pashtuns, who resented muhajir domination; they also clashed regularly with the Sindh police who tried to intervene. During Nawaz Sharif's administration, he had endorsed the launch by the police and the Pakistan army of Operation Clean Up in order to tackle 'anti-social' elements and crackdown on the MQM. In 1992, the MQM leader, Altaf Hussain, fled to London, where he was granted political asylum, but his control over the MQM remained unchallenged.*

When Benazir became prime minister she endorsed the 'clean up' operation, renamed Operation Blue Fox, and carried out under the instructions of Major General Naseerullah Babar, whom she had appointed interior minister. Babar adopted a 'search and destroy' policy, once again bringing in army units to assist the Sindh police in restoring order. But the fighting and killings on the streets of Karachi were some of the bloodiest on record, with thousands killed or recorded as missing – the government counter-insurgency tactics effective but brutal.

One aspect of Benazir's government which had disappointed human rights groups was its inaction over the controversial

---

* In 1997 the party renamed itself Muttahida (United) Qaumi Movement. The party is currently split between the London-based and Karachi-based factions.

Hudood ordinances; passed by General Zia in 1979 as part of his Islamisation process, the ordinances stipulated severe penalties for adultery and fornication. Yet, as her party members were at pains to point out, both in her first administration and in her second, the government did not have the necessary support in the National Assembly to repeal them, the opposition to change reflecting the prevailing religious conservatism across the political spectrum. But this did not mean her administration was not concerned about human rights, later passing the 1996 Abolition of Whipping Act, forbidding sentences or punishments of whipping and reducing the instances of corporal punishment. In time there was also to be a sequel to the reform of the Hudood ordinances.*

Benazir began her second year in government with her customary optimism, speaking expansively about what the PPP could do for Pakistan. 'It was a whirlwind of activity on the domestic front and a simultaneous programme to re-establish our credentials in the world community.'[21] But the problems she faced both domestically and regionally were still immense. In neighbouring Afghanistan, the government of Burhanuddin Rabbani, president of the Islamic State of Afghanistan, which had taken power after Najibullah's government collapsed in 1992, had failed to establish a cohesive administration and, despite claims of impartiality, Pakistan was being drawn into the attempt to bring stability.† Lawlessness in Afghanistan meant that the refugees in camps throughout the North-West Frontier had not returned home and the area remained awash with weapons left over from the Afghans' jihad against the Soviets; in Karachi the situation remained unpredictable and fighting on the streets again broke out in May.

---

* See Chapter 13 Exile.
† President Burhanuddin Rabbani (1940–2011) was president of the Islamic State of Afghanistan 1992–96.

Preoccupied as Benazir was, our correspondence had become less frequent; but, sharing news and views was so much part of our tradition, that, when possible, I would send a letter. 'It was lovely to talk to you on the phone before Christmas,' I wrote in early January 1995. 'The Macmillan Appeal [to raise money for the Oxford Union] were extremely grateful for the scarf you sent... thank you so much for taking the trouble to do this. They were most appreciative.' Once again I wanted to let her know that I was coming back to Pakistan and India for more research on Kashmir. 'I feel I must try and return to Srinagar especially if elections are to be held.' Her replies, although more formal in style, on thick embossed writing paper headed 'Prime Minister', invariably ended with her sending her love to my children.[22]

My arrival in Islamabad coincided with that of the American First Lady, Hillary Clinton, who was on the first stop of a ten-day tour to five South Asian countries (including India, Nepal, Bangladesh and Sri Lanka). Accompanied by her fifteen-year-old daughter, Chelsea, it was her first 'solo' visit without her husband.* Since I was in Pakistan, Benazir invited me to attend several functions, including a lunch in Islamabad and a display of Khattak dancing, originating in the North-West Frontier, traditionally performed with swords and handkerchiefs.

After being formally introduced to the First Lady, I also managed to have a brief conversation with Robin Raphel, assistant secretary of state for South and Central Asian affairs (and the ex-wife of the former US ambassador, Arnold Raphel, killed when Zia's plane crashed in 1988).† When I told her I was working on the insurgency in the valley of Kashmir, she gave me a useful insight

---

* Hillary Rodham Clinton (b.1947); Chelsea Clinton Mezvinsky (b.1980).
† Robin Raphel (b.1947) was first assistant secretary of state for South and Central Asian Affairs 1993–97.

into the US administration's thinking. 'Ah yes,' she remarked: 'we felt it was time to get out our Kashmir file, dust it off and see what could be done.'[23]

The finale to the visit involved flying down for the evening to Lahore for a spectacular dinner under the stars in the precincts of the Lahore Fort, noted for its many fine monuments dating from the time of the sixteenth-century Mughal emperor, Akbar. The 'gem', built by his grandson, Shah Jehan, was the Sheesh Mahal – the palace of mirrors – its walls decorated with a vast mosaic of reflective glass tiles. Once the VVIP guests had visited the Sheesh Mahal, others were allowed in to marvel at its beauty. After the dinner was over we went straight to the airport to wave off the First Lady and her entourage, the idea being that once the American plane left, we would return to Islamabad. This took more time than one might have expected because of the security checks. While we waited, Benazir stood patiently on the tarmac, chatting with her own staff. But as soon as the Americans had gone, the pilot of her plane approached, politely asking to have a word with her.

'Madam,' he said. 'The weather has closed in at Islamabad and it would now be too dangerous to fly back tonight.' Benazir was surprised because the weather seemed fine in Lahore. 'I would not be doing my professional duty if I did not alert you, Madam, that it is not safe to fly.'

Apart from the fact that she had appointments in the early morning which needed rescheduling, neither she nor anyone in her immediate entourage had brought a change of clothes. But she necessarily accepted the pilot's advice and accommodation was swiftly provided for us in the Governor's splendid residence in Lahore. A shortage of some necessary cosmetics meant that I found myself going out late at night to the market with a member of her staff to find a pharmacy. The following morning we returned to Islamabad.

In mid-April, having recorded additional interviews and undertaken more research on Kashmir, I left for India to go back to the valley of Kashmir. I then returned to London.

'I have set aside [writing about] militants, elections, human rights abuses to write to you!' I began a letter to Benazir at the end of April. In order to share some of the insights I'd gained during my travels, I then proceeded to outline the viewpoints of the various Kashmiri political leaders I'd interviewed, the biggest change in their rhetoric now being the additional demand for *azadi* or independence, which had not been an option in 1947. 'I know Pakistan has not conceded the "third option" but whether or not it has, ironically the Kashmiris would probably oppose holding the plebiscite unless the "third option" were included,' I continued, giving Benazir a verbatim quotation from the Jammu and Kashmir Liberation Front leader, Yasin Malik, who had told me that 'until they put the third option into the UN resolution, it will be unacceptable to the people of Jammu and Kashmir'. 'I think it is an unbelievably difficult problem to solve, now that it has gone on for so long,' I concluded. 'And emotions are so high on all sides.'[24]

Given the sensitivity of the Kashmir issue, Benazir was obviously conscious of Pakistan's official position, but whenever I learnt something relevant I wanted to tell her just in case it proved useful in her analysis. By the same token I was grateful to her because, throughout my research, she never attempted to influence what I might write. As usual in my letters, I gave her news of our mutual friends. In July I was telling her that Victor van Amerongen and his wife, Amanda, had just had a little girl, having previously lost their eight-year-old son to a rare illness: 'wonderful that they had the courage to start again with another child, having lost one'. I did not know it then, but my next comment had an awful prescience: 'I always remember you saying how, once one is a mother, one feels rather different about life – wondering who would look after the little defenceless children if, for whatever reason, one wasn't around. It somehow makes life all the more vital.'[25]

By the beginning of 1996 instability in the region meant that there was no respite for the PPP government. Afghanistan was in chaos. And, with the insurgency in the valley of Kashmir still smouldering, relations between India and Pakistan remained strained, albeit, as Benazir said, not confrontational.[26] In the federal capital of Islamabad, Benazir was encountering opposition not only from Nawaz Sharif, her main political opponent and rival, but from the smaller parties as well. On 20 July 1996, the leader of the conservative Jamaat-i Islami party, Qazi Hussain Ahmed, announced a series of protests, including his intention to undertake a 'long march' in September.*

In the midst of this 'spiralling political uncertainty' as she described events at the time, personal tragedy struck again. Over the summer, helped by Bashir Riaz, who was close to both Benazir and Murtaza, there was an attempt at reconciliation. In July brother and sister met for the first time since his return to Pakistan. 'It was a good meeting,' related Bash. 'And they agreed to meet again.' For Murtaza's forty-second birthday on 18 September Benazir sent her brother a cake and flowers.[27] Three days later I was at home in London when the telephone rang. It was Charis Waddy, her elderly voice revealing extreme distress.

'Have you heard the terrible news from Pakistan?' she asked. It was early morning and I hadn't yet listened to the radio.

---

* H. D. Deve Gowda (b.1933), prime minister of India 1996–97, was succeeded by I. K. Gujral (1919–2012), prime minister of India 1997–98; Qazi Hussain Ahmed (1938–2013), emir of the Jamaat-i Islami 1987–2009.

'No,' I responded.

Before I had time to let my imagination run wild, she continued. 'It is Murtaza. He was shot last night in the streets of Karachi. I just hope and pray that the family can recover from another tragedy.'[28]

As the circumstances of Murtaza's death became clear, the concern Charis had shown became more comprehensible. He had died in a shoot-out with the police outside the Bhutto home at 70, Clifton. When Benazir heard the news, her grief was uncontrollable: footage of her rushing through the hospital, barefoot and in tears, was broadcast internationally. But the fact that she was prime minister and the police force was under the control of the Sindh government caused the final family rupture. As Murtaza's fourteen-year-old daughter, Fatima, grew to adulthood, she believed her aunt and Asif were responsible for her father's death.[29]

From London I tried to understand what had happened. Only later did a fuller, but still incomplete, picture emerge. 'The chain of events pointed to a more prosaic explanation of the tragedy,' recalled Irfan Husain, a senior journalist at *Dawn*, based in Karachi. The conspiracy theories that Asif had Murtaza killed 'for publicly running him down – that Benazir ordered the hit on her brother to prevent him taking over the PPP – ring hollow, because Murtaza was no political threat to Benazir, and there is no way the police would have followed Zardari's orders to kill the prime minister's brother'.[30]

'The lead up to the shooting had happened a few days previously,' explained the superintendent of police for investigations, who arrived at the scene soon afterwards. 'The police had arrested one of Murtaza's key aides, Mohammed Ali Sunara, wanted on charges of terrorism relating to Al Zulfikar's operations. In an attempt to locate him, Murtaza and his supporters stormed into two CIA (crime investigation agency) centres, where they believed Sunara might be held; Murtaza and his men abused and slapped the police officers in charge, appropriated some weapons and ammunition, and then left.' After this 'high-handed' behaviour and with Ali Sunara threatening from jail that the 'whole of Sindh will rise up for me' (or words to that effect), the police were put on high alert. Two bomb blasts, one near the secretariat and the other near the PIA office narrowly missing a number of girls on their way to school, heightened tensions. 'The authority of the state was being belittled by the prime minister's brother. That was the key issue. Despite having tamed the tiger – the MQM – the police were under pressure from the press and other law-enforcing agencies for letting Murtaza Bhutto and his armed body guards roam the streets of Karachi unchallenged.'[31]

On 20 September Murtaza left his house to attend a political rally. On his way back, just after dusk, his cavalcade was stopped by Haq Nawaz Sayyal, the station house officer in charge of the local Clifton police station. According to the superintendent, 'his orders were not to touch Murtaza but to disarm his bodyguards on the understanding they were carrying illegal weapons'.[32] A tense standoff followed, during which Shahid Hayat Khan, assistant superintendent of the neighbouring Saddar division, was called in to assist Rai Tahir, the ASP (assistant superintendent of police) in charge of the Clifton sub-division. As soon as he arrived he went to talk to Murtaza. Suddenly shots were fired, causing a fusillade from both sides, killing a number of Murtaza's supporters and a taxi driver and injuring others. In the first round of firing, Murtaza was hit several times, one bullet penetrating his neck; Hayat was hit in the leg; Haq Nawaz received a minor wound in his ankle.

Instead of making the twenty-minute journey to the Jinnah or the Aga Khan hospitals on the other side of the city, Rai Tahir took Murtaza to the Mideast hospital in Clifton, which was only a few minutes' drive away. By this stage Murtaza was still conscious and able to sit on the stretcher himself. 'The Mideast had the reputation of being one of the best hospitals,' continued the superintendent. 'But the staff on duty that night did not understand the difference between an arterial and a jugular wound. Instead of clipping the jugular bleed while waiting for the surgeons, it was packed with towels resulting in more bleeding. What was a non-fatal wound became fatal.' So Murtaza literally bled to death on the operating table. 'This, too, has provided ammunition to the conspiracy theorists,' Irfan Husain told me.[33]

The police account was not what Murtaza's family and supporters believed. 'The Mideast was not a properly equipped and functional hospital. It was instead a building consisting of a number of private consultancy rooms with some very basic peripheral services. Mir had no chance of surviving in a place like that,' observed his cousin, Tariq Islam. 'Yes, he was breathing when his body was virtually dumped there and in fact breathed his last while I stood by his side along with Fatima and Ghinwa.' Benazir arrived later. 'She went into an uncontrolled frenzy and fell to the ground weeping and screaming.'[34]

In the disastrous aftermath, numerous questions remained, one of which was an unaccountable washing down of the streets, destroying vital evidence, and most importantly who had fired the first shots.* Before any investigation could take place, and with allegations of a 'fake encounter' being staged, the belief that Asif, and by association Benazir, were responsible gained credence. Even Begum Bhutto, by then suffering from Alzheimer's, blamed her daughter and son-in-law. When Benazir attempted to attend the funeral, her car was stoned by the angry crowd.[35]

---

* Eighteen police officers were charged with Murtaza's death, including the deputy inspector-general, Shoaib Suddle. In 2009 they were acquitted by the District and Sessions Judge. Shahid Hayat Khan (1966–2019) died of cancer; Haq Nawaz Sayyal committed suicide/was murdered a few days after the shooting.

'Things fall apart, the centre cannot hold,' I wrote in my diary on 28 September, recalling that the South African writer and anti-apartheid activist, Alan Paton, had introduced me to W. B. Yeats's poem in 1976.* At the time I was on a 'study tour' in South Africa with some of our Oxford contemporaries and the country was in turmoil after the suppression of riots in the Soweto township. Twenty years later Yeats's words had come to mind again.[36] A few days previously I'd gone to Rotherham, South Yorkshire to speak at a launch event for my book *Kashmir in the Crossfire*, my host a Labour councillor, Nazir Ahmed, whom I'd met one evening at the Pakistani High Commission.† But any enthusiasm I might have felt over my book's publication was overshadowed by Murtaza's death and Benazir's increasingly vulnerable position.

Still in mourning, Benazir had to travel to the United States to address the UN General Assembly in New York. On 29 September she arrived in London in transit. I immediately went to see her at Claridge's Hotel, where she was staying. As a present, I'd brought her some crystal prayer beads which I'd found in a shop in Queensway, and which the shopkeeper said were from Palestine. When I arrived, Sunny was with her. Others came and went to condole: their cousin, Laila Crawford, and their friend, Farida Ataullah. Later we were joined by the Pakistani high commissioner in London, Wajid Shamsul Hasan, a former journalist and longstanding supporter.‡ When the others went home, Wajid and I stayed on. We sat late into the night going over the events of Murtaza's death, the allegations of Benazir's involvement too painful to contemplate. 'That was one of the most difficult times in

---

* Alan Paton (1903–88); W. B. Yeats, 'The Second Coming', 1919.

† Victoria Schofield, *Kashmir in the Crossfire* (I. B. Tauris, 1996); Lord Ahmed of Rotherham (b.1957).

‡ Wajid Shamsul Hasan (b.1941) was high commissioner for Pakistan to the UK 1994–96 and 2008–14.

my life,' she later said. 'When Murtaza was killed the propaganda was so insidious, some of the people I expected to turn to us, who were childhood friends, didn't. I thought there would be unconditional support.'[37]

The next day Benazir had agreed to give some television interviews – which I sat in on – to CNN, Sky, and BBC *Newsnight* with Peter Snow, the topics ranging from Afghanistan (where, on 27 September, Kabul had fallen to the Taliban, a group of Afghans, who had been fighting against Rabbani's Islamic State government), Murtaza's death, and corruption. That afternoon she gave a lecture to a London research institute, the International Institute for Strategic Studies (IISS), held in the New Connaught Rooms, Holborn. But the mood both at the press conference and among the IISS audience was hostile, someone asking when she was going to quit. Still emotionally distraught from Murtaza's death, Benazir's tone was defensive. 'I am not going to quit because if I quit who will get to the bottom of Mir's murder?' she asked, using the name by which his family still called him. 'It's an eerie feeling knowing there are people out there who could kill your brother – and I'm the prime minister.'* When corruption was again mentioned, she said roundly that she was 'fed up' with the allegations which amounted to political assassination.[38]

Travelling onwards to New York, Benazir gave one of her best speeches encompassing world issues in the 'twilight' of the twentieth century. 'Today the UN stands at the crossroads, not just of the calendar, but of the direction of the community of nations,' she proclaimed, describing the proliferation of conflicts, the spread

---

* Benazir arranged for a team of retired Scotland Yard officers to visit Pakistan to conduct an investigation into Murtaza's death. They arrived in October but because of her dismissal in November they were unable to complete their investigations.

of poverty and a growing sense of alienation. 'The manner in which we address these problems will determine the quality of life that we bequeath our children.' As in other fora she took the opportunity of pointing out that Jammu and Kashmir was the 'core issue' that divides India and Pakistan. Dressed in a brilliant blue *shalwar kameez*, she also emphasised that 'there is no place in Islam for acts of terrorism'.[39] As I watched the news coverage, I marvelled at her presence of mind to speak so eloquently at such a time of personal sadness. It was the last time she spoke as prime minister on the world's stage.

On her way back to Pakistan Benazir stopped again in London. On the night before her departure, I said I would come early in the morning to say goodbye. She looked at me as if to say: 'Really, it's not necessary'; but something in her expression made me determine to return. She was sitting on her own when I arrived with my children, en route to taking my son Anthony to Sunday morning choir practice. In that moment I sensed the loneliness of her position. 'She kissed the children graciously and asked them how school was and who their best friend was,' I recorded in my diary. 'She also thanked me for spending so much time with her – which of course I was so pleased to be able to do.'[40] I felt depressed when I had to leave, perhaps realising what lay ahead.

On 4 November Benazir's government was dismissed by President Leghari on charges of corruption, maladministration and extra-judicial killings in Karachi. Asif was again put in jail; more charges were to follow, including his being complicit in Murtaza's death. Benazir's second tenure as prime minister had lasted just three years. *The Times* asked me if I would write an article on her dismissal, aptly headlined 'The end of a dream'.[41] Now began Benazir's long fight to restore her name and the fortunes of the PPP, while fighting court cases at home, against the backdrop of rising turbulence in the region and international terrorism.

12

Déjà Vu: 1996–99

There is nothing new under the sun.[1]

'How are you feeling?' I asked Benazir on the telephone the day after her dismissal.

'Well you know, third time round there is a sense of *déjà vu*,' she replied.

By saying 'third', I realised that she was including her father's dismissal in 1977. As previously, she was steadfast in her defence. 'Allegations of corruption have been used by every dictator to get rid of democracy.' Compared with her first dismissal, this second one was even harder, coming so soon after the tragedy of Murtaza's death. She was also upset that she had been dismissed by Farooq Leghari, her own appointee as president. Once more a caretaker government was established pending fresh elections. Although, like Nawaz Sharif, she challenged her dismissal in the Supreme Court of Pakistan, the judges did not find in her favour. Press coverage was brutal. 'It's been a long four months for Benazir,' wrote Seumas Milne in an article titled 'The Crumbling House of Bhutto'. 'Her brother has been killed, her husband has been jailed, her relatives have talked of fratricide, and she has been sacked as prime minister for the second time.'[2]

When the elections were held in February 1997, voter turnout was low and the PPP's popular vote was recorded as being only half that of the PML(N). Nawaz Sharif gained what was hailed as a landslide victory, winning 137 seats, while the PPP won only 18 seats, a dramatic turnaround from nearly a decade previously. But like Benazir's, Sharif's second administration was to have its highs and lows, ending with his premature removal from power three years later; also like Benazir, he had to deal with two traditionally problematic neighbours.

To the west in Afghanistan, the situation was fast approaching a watershed. Following the fall of Kabul the previous September, on 24 May the Taliban captured the northern city of Mazar-i-Sharif, which meant that they could now claim to hold all the main cities of Afghanistan. The following day Pakistan recognised the regime as the legitimate government, known officially as the Islamic Emirate of Afghanistan, as did Saudi Arabia and the United Arab Emirates (although the UAE later withdrew its recognition).

Although the PPP was no longer in the government, as the Taliban continued to assert their authority over Afghanistan, closing girls' schools, breaking television sets and instituting strict Sharia law with summary punishments, the role of Benazir's administration in fostering their rise came under international scrutiny, Benazir gaining the sobriquet 'the mother of the Taliban'. But, as with all aspects of South Asian regional relationships, the situation was more complex.

'Afghanistan was in a state of virtual disintegration just before the Taliban emerged at the end of 1994,' noted journalist Ahmed Rashid, whose bestselling *Taliban* later catapulted him to international fame as a commentator on South and Central Asia. 'The country was divided into warlord fiefdoms and all the warlords had fought, switched sides and fought again in a bewildering array of alliances, betrayals and bloodshed.' It was from this chaos that the Taliban had emerged, from groups of Pashtun students either in full or part-time attendance at the *madrassas*. Despairing of the prevailing situation, Rashid explained, they had come together to work out an agenda to 'restore peace, disarm the population, enforce Sharia law and defend the integrity and Islamic character of Afghanistan'. Instead of adopting the name of a political party, they had kept the name Taliban to differentiate themselves from the mujahideen. 'They saw themselves as cleansers and purifiers of a guerrilla war gone astray, a social system gone wrong and an Islamic way of life that had been compromised by corruption and excess,' continued Rashid. Initially their agenda was welcomed by the local Afghans.[3]

From Pakistan's viewpoint, supporting the Taliban had been logical and strategic. Not only did they appear to have increasingly widespread support in Afghanistan, but, given their natural affinity as Pashtuns with those living in the NWFP, General Babar – himself a Pashtun and Benazir's interior minister – believed they would be well disposed towards Pakistan, unlike the Tajiks and Uzbeks who had dominated Rabbani's Islamic State government; moreover many of them, including their leader, Mullah Omar, had grown up in the refugee camps in Pakistan.[*] Finally, because of the uneasy relationship with India in the east – as outlined to me in 1989 by the director-general of the ISI, General Hamid Gul – Pakistan was anxious to foster 'strategic depth' in the west (which also explained Zia's interest in backing proxies at the height of the Afghan jihad). Afghanistan, they believed, was Pakistan's 'backyard'.[4]

---

[*] Mullah Mohammed Omar (1960–2013) assumed the title of Amir-al Mu'minin (Commander of the Faithful or Supreme Leader of the Muslims).

With this mindset, and with the chaos left behind by the Mujahideen government, the hope was that the Taliban's Islamic Emirate would restore some order. Only when they finally took control of Afghanistan did the true nature of their religious conservatism and repressive measures become evident. As Benazir later explained, 'the [Afghan] people were living in such pitiable circumstances. We wanted there to be peace. We thought the Taliban would bring it. But we were wrong.'[5]

Once the policy was in place, however, Pakistan's support of the Taliban continued, which meant that, with a more 'stable' and 'friendly' western frontier, Nawaz Sharif could turn his attention towards India. One of Sharif's first actions as prime minister was to send a message to India's prime minister, I. K. Gujral, whose own 'doctrine' envisaged adopting a friendlier approach towards India's neighbours. In May 1997 the two prime ministers met at the South Asian Association for Regional Cooperation (SAARC) conference in the Maldives. It was the first such meeting at prime ministerial level since Rajiv Gandhi's state visit to Pakistan in 1989 when Benazir was prime minister.

The spirit of rapprochement between the two countries coincided with preparations for their respective celebrations of fifty years of independence in August 1997. A highlight of the festivities was a visit to Pakistan and India by the Queen in October in her capacity as head of the Commonwealth, her first visit to either country since 1961. Over the years I had met many of the British high commissioners to Pakistan as well as members of the UK Foreign and Commonwealth Office who knew of my work, especially in relation to Jammu and Kashmir. As preparations for the royal visit proceeded, I was requested to write the text of a brochure on the British–Pakistan relationship, which could be distributed to all those involved in the visit. The production of the brochure meant making a rapid visit to

Pakistan at the end of April 1997 to interview various officials connected with our joint relationship in business, education and sport.

'Will you see your friend Benazir?' my FCO liaison officer asked me tentatively, as we made the programme for my itinerary.

'Well,' I responded, somewhat guardedly. 'As you know she is a friend and so I might well see her if we are in the same city at the same time.'

As it happened my schedule was so rushed that when I was in Karachi she was in Islamabad and vice versa and so we didn't meet. But I noted the cautionary approach which the FCO was taking towards Benazir now that she was no longer in office. Needless to say, when I told her I was writing the brochure on behalf of the UK government, she was delighted. 'Anything I can do to help, please let me know,' she enthused.

Soon after my return from Pakistan we met up in London during her summer visit. 'Lunch with B. Biked over to the flat & we took a taxi to Jo's Café in Sloane St. She seemed relaxed and so pleased to be in London,' I recorded on 3 July, mindful that it was now almost twenty years to the day since Zia overthrew her father in the military coup and she had become actively involved in politics.[6] Outings included visits to the Harbour Club in Chelsea which she'd recently joined – maintaining fitness always being one of her concerns – and lunch in Harry's Bar with Alan Duncan, who was still an MP, having managed to retain his safe seat of Rutland and Melton for the Conservatives despite Labour's land-slide victory on 1 May 1997. Yet despite the enthusiasm she showed for our excursions, her dismissal still rankled. Talking about Murtaza's death was extremely painful.

The Queen's visit to Pakistan in October passed off well, but the atmosphere on her arrival in India was soured because while in Pakistan the foreign secretary, Robin Cook, had assured Sharif of Britain's 'good offices' over the 'Jammu-Kashmir' issue.* When the remark was reported in the Indian press it was interpreted as an offer of mediation ('Cook spoils the broth, wants finger in the Kashmir pie'), which the Indians roundly rejected, while Cook denied that British mediation had ever been offered.[7] Of course I wished that Benazir had been prime minister of Pakistan for the anniversary celebrations, but we both recognised that the wheel of fortune had turned.

The year 1998 began badly. In January a huge exposé 'tracing the Bhutto Millions', written by John Burns, appeared in the *New York Times*. Then in April came another article in the *Sunday Times*: 'The hunt for Benazir's booty'. The articles repeated the widespread allegation – which had gained Asif the nickname of Mr Ten Percent – that part of his wealth came from taking a cut on government contracts while his wife was prime minister.[8] Although distressed by the articles, Benazir maintained that she was not guilty of any wrongdoing and that all the enquiries into their financial affairs were being made in order to discredit her politically and exhaust her psychologically.

I too was upset on her behalf; having witnessed her political struggle and the sacrifices she'd made for so long to rebuild democratic government in her country, I knew how damaging the allegations could be for her reputation internationally. I'd also grown to understand how the system in Pakistan worked, how easy it was to use 'corruption' to malign political opponents, and for the military to exercise leverage over a succession of political leaders, a fact people in the West might not fully appreciate. Once governments changed it was inevitable that a process of 'accounta-bility' would be instituted and, for that reason, allegations were

---

* Rt Hon. Robin Cook (1946–2005) was secretary of state for Foreign and Commonwealth Affairs 1997–2001.

rarely taken at face value in Pakistan. In the same way General Zia's regime had produced the White Papers to discredit her father during his appeal against the death sentence. My response, as her friend, was to continue to support her emotionally as much as I could, as I had always done.

Meanwhile the India–Pakistan relationship was once more about to hit the international headlines. In India I. K. Gujral's government had fallen the previous December. Following general elections in February 1998 the Hindu nationalist BJP (Bharatiya Janata Party) took power as the largest party in a coalition government. India's new prime minister was Atal Bihari Vajpayee, the seventy-three-year old politician from Gwalior south of Delhi.* Included in the BJP's manifesto was a commitment 'to re-evaluate the country's nuclear policy and exercise the option to induct nuclear weapons'. While stating that it was committed to a 'nuclear free world' it could not agree to the Comprehensive Test Ban Treaty (CTBT), the Fissile Material Control Regime (FMCR) and the Missile Technology Control Regime (MTCR), which would be accepting 'a world of nuclear apartheid'.⁹ Between 11 and 13 May 1998 India carried out five nuclear tests in the Rajasthan desert.

The groundswell of public opinion in Pakistan following these tests meant that it was only a matter of time before Pakistan demonstrated its nuclear capability. Benazir's suggestion (made to journalist Raymond Whitaker in 1991) of acting 'coy' was simply not an option. On 28 May an announcement came that five nuclear tests had been carried out in Balochistan, a sixth taking place two days later. Sanctions by the United States and other Western countries were immediately imposed against both countries. Pakistan's demonstration of its nuclear capability was public proof of the

---

* Atal Bihari Vajpayee (1924–2018) was prime minister of India in 1996 (but was unable to form a government), and again in 1998–99.

success of the programme, which Benazir knew her father had put in motion over two decades earlier. His determination was illustrated when, following India's first test in 1974, he had boldly suggested that Pakistanis 'will *eat grass*, even go hungry, but we will get one [i.e. a nuclear bomb] of our own... We have no other choice!'[10]

While the two countries weathered the sanctions, which were eventually relaxed when both India and Pakistan agreed to a moratorium on nuclear testing and made a commitment (which neither country observed) to sign the Comprehensive Test Ban Treaty,[11] Pakistan's military was still smarting under the strategic advantage which India had gained in northern Jammu and Kashmir, when they had airlifted troops to occupy the Siachen glacier in 1984. Since then – and with the failure of talks on Siachen initiated by Benazir and Rajiv Gandhi in 1988 and 1989 – successive Pakistan army officials had been trying to determine how they could redress the balance, which would inevitably entail some form of infiltration across the Line of Control.

Benazir related how, during her first administration, Pakistan's chief of army staff, General Aslam Beg,* had offered her 'one hundred thousand battle-hardened Mujahideen' to take Srinagar (with the objective of then re-taking the Siachen glacier). But she refused. 'I was not prepared to fall for flattering stories of glory which I felt would bring ignominy to my country and was careful to ensure that the military understood that the government did not favour war with India.'[12] During her second administration she had again been approached, this time by the director of military operations, Major General Pervez Musharraf.† 'It seemed like déjà

---

* General Mirza Aslam Beg LOM, NI, HI, SBt, TeJ (b.1931) was chief of army staff 1988–91.

† General Pervez Musharraf (b.1943) was chief of army staff 1998–2007, chief executive 1999–2002 and president of Pakistan 2001–08.

17. Benazir's portrait by Diccon Swan, 1993, which hangs in the Oxford Union debating chamber. *In recognition of her achievement as a former president of the Union and now prime minister, our mutual friend, Alan Duncan, MP, had arranged for the painting to be done.*

▲ 18. Benazir with her children, Bilawal (right) and Bakhtawar, Islamabad, June 1990.

▼ 19. Pakistan Day: the Investiture Ceremony, 23 March 1994. Prime Minister Benazir Bhutto, President Farooq Leghari with Mrs William Brown. *A special foreign guest was Margaret Brown, who had come to receive the Sitara-i-Imtiaz, awarded posthumously to her husband, Major William Brown, MBE.*

*To Victoria,
with love,
Benazir.*

20. Prime Minister Benazir Bhutto welcoming guests to the lunch in honour of First Lady, Hillary Clinton, at the Prime Minister's House, Islamabad, 26 March 1995.

21. Benazir introducing me to First Lady, Hillary Clinton. *Since I was in Pakistan, Benazir invited me to attend several functions, including a lunch in Islamabad.*

22. Bilawal's 11th birthday tea party, London 1999. Benazir with her three children, Bilawal, Bakhtawar, Aseefa, and me with two of mine, Alexandra and Olivia. *Benazir liked organising outings for her children; she believed that what children remembered about being with their parents was days out rather than days spent at home.*

23. A picnic in Kensington Gardens, London 2000. Benazir with Bilawal and Aseefa; me with Anthony, Victoria (my goddaughter) and Olivia. Taken by Bakhtawar.

24. Benazir, Bilawal, me, Christ Church, 2 October 2007. *Before returning to Pakistan, Benazir's most pressing family commitment was settling Bilawal into Oxford.*

25. Bilawal and me, Christ Church, 28 July 2012. *As we stood proudly side by side, this time with Sunny taking the photograph, Bilawal's sisters and friends standing nearby, we were all painfully aware of Benazir's absence.*

opposite

26. Benazir on her homecoming truck, surrounded by her supporters (and me at back centre left), 18 October 2007. *'I kept looking around me in amazement,' Benazir later wrote, 'remembering other rallies and other campaigns. I also remembered past tragedies as well as past triumphs.'*

overleaf

27. Benazir addressing the people at Liaquat Bagh, Rawalpindi, 27 December 2007. *'I will save Pakistan, you will save Pakistan, we will save PAKISTAN,' Benazir roared.*

28. The Bhutto family mausoleum, Garhi Khuda Bakhsh, Sindh. *Finally, from the helicopter, for the first time I saw the white domed mausoleum, looking like a modern Taj Mahal.*

29. (inset) Benazir's grave which I first visited on 22 March 2010. *Passing under an archway, I found myself looking at a gigantic portrait of Benazir.*

30. Benazir's grave (with her father's grave behind), both with ornate canopies, 2018.

vu as I once again heard how Pakistan would take Srinagar if only I gave the orders to do so.' Benazir's response was: 'And what next?' In other words, she had refused to get drawn into sanctioning a plan that risked spiralling dangerously out of control and would most likely lead to 'humiliation and isolation'.[13]

In late 1998, regardless of the consequences, and the fact that Nawaz Sharif had just embarked on initiating a dialogue with his Indian counterpart, Prime Minister Vajpayee, the Pakistani military set in motion a plan for an incursion, not across the line of control towards Srinagar, but further north, in the mountainous region of the Kargil heights, bordering Ladakh. Undertaken in complete secrecy, the operation initially involved only four generals: General Pervez Musharraf, now chief of army staff, General Mohammed Aziz Khan, chief of the general staff, Lieutenant General Mahmud Ahmed, X Corps, and Major General Javed Hassan, Force Commander Northern Areas.* According to Pakistani journalist Nasim Zehra, 'they believed such a covert operation, combined with the global anxiety of Kashmir becoming a possible "nuclear flashpoint", would force India to resolve the Kashmir issue, or at least pull back from its 1984 occupation of Siachen'.[14] As members of Pakistan's Northern Light infantry moved forward, although conditions in the mountainous region of the Himalayas were harsh, to their surprise they found they were able to advance further across the Line of Control than they had originally anticipated. And so mission creep set in.

---

* General Mohammed Aziz Khan (b.1947); Lt General Mahmud Ahmed (b.c.1944), who became director-general of the ISI in October 1999. Both Ahmed and Aziz Khan assisted Musharraf in October 1999 with his military takeover: Aziz Khan by ordering X Corps to take over the prime minister's secretariat in Islamabad; Ahmed by taking over Jinnah International airport so that Musharraf's plane could land.

While the Pakistani military was drawn deeper across the Line of Control, Nawaz Sharif was continuing his political rapprochement with India. The culmination of discussions between the corresponding ministries was Vajpayee's visit to Lahore to mark the inaugural run of the Delhi–Lahore bus service on 20 February 1999. In a symbolic gesture, Prime Minister Vajpayee visited the Minar-e-Pakistan. His relaxed presence, reciting poetry, signified what many Pakistanis now hoped was a new beginning to the Indo-Pakistani relationship. During his visit an eight-point memorandum of understanding was signed, pledging to 'engage in bilateral consultations on security concepts and nuclear doctrines'. Known as the Lahore Declaration, it committed both prime ministers to intensify their efforts to resolve all issues, 'including the issue of Jammu and Kashmir'. Looking back, it was staggering that the Pakistan military had embarked on its occupation of the Kargil heights, jeopardising what was perhaps the most promising attempt at reconciliation between the two countries since the Benazir–Rajiv talks a decade earlier.

When, in late May, as the snows melted, the Indians discovered that their posts had been taken over and news broke of an incursion across the Line of Control, the Pakistani government immediately denied any involvement, instead insisting that those occupying the Indian posts on the Kargil heights were 'Kashmiri mujahideen', intent on 'liberating' Kashmir. Since the 'Kargil war' was part of the larger Kashmir issue, my publishers had asked me to revise my book, *Kashmir in the Crossfire*, to take account of recent developments. It was both frustrating and disappointing that the Pakistani government seriously thought the Western media would accept that Kashmiri militants could have passed through this difficult terrain without the knowledge or assistance of the Pakistan army. 'You cannot venture up there in shorts and a singlet,' observed Brian Cloughley, one of my army friends who had served as deputy head of the UN Military Observer Group in India and Pakistan (UNMOGIP) in the early 1980s.[15]

In support of their allegations of official Pakistani involvement, the Indians released the transcript of a recorded conversation between Musharraf and General Aziz, chief of the general staff, revealing that the Pakistanis intended to use the operation as a publicity exercise to alert the international community to the danger of escalation between two nuclear neighbours. As far as they were concerned, it seemed that the more publicity they got, the better: 'Today for the last two hours the BBC has been continuously reporting on the air strikes by India. Keep using this – let them keep using this – let them keep dropping bombs. As far as internationalisation is concerned, this is the fastest this has happened,' Aziz was reported as having told Musharraf.[16]

Initially, Nawaz Sharif had only been given 'deceptive' briefings designed to make him think that 'small-scale operations could complement his political and diplomatic efforts to move forward on detente and peace with India'. On 17 May the prime minister was given a fuller briefing, without, however, being informed that Pakistani soldiers had crossed the Line of Control. Instead, even at this stage, he was told that 'Kashmiri militants' had occupied the heights and all the army was doing was providing logistical support. Only after additional briefings, and when he visited Skardu's Combined Military Hospital in Baltistan where he saw injured Pakistani soldiers, did the truth dawn.[17]

Relations between India and Pakistan understandably nose-dived, as Vajpayee accused Pakistan of 'betraying India's friendship' after the warmth of the meeting in Lahore. As Benazir had predicted when she had refused to sanction the plan to take Srinagar, few were convinced by Pakistan's denials of involvement, and the incursion was not bringing Pakistan any political dividends. Instead the international response was far more supportive of India's demands for a withdrawal than of Pakistan's request for discussions to solve the 'core' issue of Jammu and Kashmir. At the end of May the UN secretary-general, Kofi Annan, offered to send an envoy to New Delhi and Islamabad to defuse tension, but Vajpayee rejected the offer. President Clinton likewise urged restraint and the resumption of talks between the two leaders.* In early July Sharif requested an urgent meeting with President Bill Clinton in Washington, following which they issued a joint statement, affirming Pakistan's commitment to take 'concrete steps' for the restoration of the Line of Control in accordance with the 1972 Simla Agreement between Indira Gandhi and Zulfikar Ali Bhutto. Clinton also gave an assurance that he would take 'a personal interest in encouraging an expeditious resumption and intensification' of Indo-Pakistani bilateral efforts, once 'the sanctity' of the Line of Control was fully restored.[18]

On 12 July Sharif broadcast to the nation, explaining his reasons for ordering the troops to withdraw. 'My dear Countrymen, we have decided to give diplomacy another chance. This decision is neither hasty nor has it been taken under pressure or out of nervousness. It has been said that it takes more courage to extricate oneself from war than to start one.'[19] Two days later Vajpayee described the Indian Operation Vijay to push back the Pakistani troops as a success. By the end of July all Pakistani troops had been withdrawn. The loss of life was considerable, with at least one thousand casualties, dead and wounded, on each side.† The extent

---

* Kofi Annan (1938–2018) was 7th UN secretary-general 1997–2006; Bill Clinton (b.1946) was the 42nd US president 1993–2001.

† Statistics for loss of life vary. Official Indian figures: 527 dead while General Musharraf claimed there were 1,600 Indian dead; figures for Pakistani dead: between 300 and 400, although Nawaz Sharif claimed up to 4,000 were killed on the Pakistani side. See, e.g., B. Muralidhar Reddy, 'Over 4,000 soldiers killed in Kargil: Sharif,' the *Hindu*, 17 August 2003.

of the Pakistani advance – and the amount of time required to force their forces to withdraw – created pressure on Indian supply lines to the Siachen glacier. This led Indian sources to believe that Pakistan's objective from the outset was to dislodge their forces from the glacier.[20] Most significantly, the Kargil War, as it became known, had once more jeopardised any prospect of improving relations between India and Pakistan.

Having opposed the military interventions proposed to her as prime minister, Benazir described the incursion into Kargil as the 'biggest blunder' in Pakistan's history, 'which has cost Pakistan dearly. Those who were killed were sent back quietly because the Pakistani government did not have the courage to own them.'[21]

13

Exile: 1999–2007

Seasons change, realities change, the rest is a test,
better a life of test, than a wasted life of rest.[1]

While Indian and Pakistani troops were fighting in the Kargil heights, Benazir and her party members were being subjected to the process of 'accountability' instituted by the Nawaz Sharif government. Much to her dismay, in April 1999, the Lahore High Court convicted her *in absentia* for corruption,* giving her and Asif a five-year prison sentence and imposing a fine of $8.6 million.[2] When the verdict was announced, she was in the United States on a lecture tour. With Asif already in jail and fearful that she would be arrested on her return to Pakistan, she decided to base herself in London, beginning what she called a period of 'self-imposed' exile. When she left her home in Karachi, I don't think she ever imagined how long she would be away nor how brief would be her return.

In Pakistan, relations between Sharif and Musharraf were reaching breaking point. The denouement came with Sharif's

---

* In 2001 the Supreme Court of Pakistan set aside the conviction and ordered a re-trial (see later in this chapter).

attempt to dismiss Musharraf as chief of army staff and his refusal to let Musharraf's inbound plane land in Karachi (even though remaining airborne could mean running out of fuel). To avert a potential disaster, members of the Pakistan army took over the airport and Musharraf duly landed, ousting Sharif in a bloodless military coup. On 14 October 1999 he declared a state of emergency, suspending the constitution. Instead of calling himself the chief martial law administrator, Musharraf preferred to describe himself as the chief executive. A key component of his seven-point agenda was to revive the economy and restore 'investor confidence'.* Subsequently Nawaz Sharif was charged with kidnapping, attempted murder, hijacking, terrorism and corruption. Although sentenced to life imprisonment, following pressure from the international community, he was allowed to go into exile in Saudi Arabia. Despite Musharraf's 'softer' approach, his tenure signified the reassertion of military rule in Pakistan, while continuing the process of accountability through the National Accountability Bureau, set up in November 1999.

Meanwhile Benazir was busy establishing herself in London. Unlike her first period of exile, fifteen years earlier, when she was on her own, she now had her three children to worry about. Although she had 'Nanny' (who, by this stage, was Theresita from the Philippines, always known as Sita, or Ceta, as Benazir wrote her name), decisions had to be taken regarding their education. She was also running the PPP *in absentia* and keeping up her contacts with the Pakistani diaspora both in Britain and in Europe, which meant a busy travel schedule.

---

* Musharraf's 'seven point agenda' was as follows: i. Rebuild National Confidence and Morale; ii. Strengthen federation... iii. Revive economy and restore investor confidence... iv. Ensure law and order and dispense speedy justice... v. Depoliticise State institutions... vi. Devolution of power to the grass roots level... vii. Ensuring swift and across the board accountability.

In the autumn of 1999 she went to Oslo to meet the Norwegian branch of the PPP; many of its members were from *Azad* Jammu and Kashmir, who formed the largest ethnic community in the capital. Like many in Britain, they had left their homes to seek a more prosperous life in a European country while retaining their links with their homeland. One of them, Ali Shahnawaz Khan, had established the Kashmiri Scandinavian Council. In the course of his lobbying he made contact with several members of the Norwegian parliament. One of them was Lars Rise, a former television journalist, who had been elected in 1997 to represent the Christian Democratic Party in a predominantly Muslim constituency in Oslo * While Benazir was in Norway, Ali invited Lars, who had recently returned from a visit to *Azad* Jammu and Kashmir, to dinner to meet her. This was followed by a breakfast meeting the following day. 'We mainly spoke about faith and values and God and the teachings of Jesus. Benazir gave statements about her faith in God, and her faith in prayer.'[3] During the conversation, Lars said it seemed only natural to ask Benazir if she would like to attend the National Prayer Breakfast in Washington DC.

'National Prayer Breakfast? What is that?' responded Benazir.

Lars went on to explain that it was an event traditionally held at the beginning of February, the main function of which was a Thursday breakfast attended by the president of the United States. He assured her that it was focused more on the teachings of the historic person of Jesus, than on one specific religion and that leaders of all faiths were included. With its origins in the 1940s when a Norwegian Methodist clergyman, Abraham Vereide, had inspired members of Congress – both Democrats and Republicans –

---

* Lars Rise (b.1955) set up the All Party Parliamentary Group for Kashmir in the Norwegian parliament.

to pray together in small groups on a weekly basis, the first National Prayer Breakfast, attended by President Dwight Eisenhower, was held in 1953. Since then all US presidents, as well as many foreign leaders, have attended the prayer breakfast every year. Vereide's work was organised through a foundation called The Fellowship, and his successor, a charismatic American named Douglas Coe, had considerable influence behind the scenes, for example, during the 1978 Camp David accords.*

Benazir agreed to go the following year on condition Lars Rise accompanied her. She instantly felt comfortable, away from the harsh, judgmental atmosphere of the international media. Henceforward the National Prayer Breakfast became an important fixture in Benazir's calendar (although it invariably meant missing Aseefa's birthday on 3 February). In the early years she took her cousin Laila Crawford with her. Later, when Asif was released, he accompanied her. Among the many senators and congressmen and others she met were Hillary Clinton and Ted Kennedy. As the years passed, I saw how Benazir drew emotional strength from attending the National Prayer Breakfast and her friendship with Doug Coe, who became a mentor to her.

When, after her assassination, Asif asked me if I would attend the National Prayer Breakfast to represent the family, I was deeply moved. At the closing dinner I agreed with Doug to play a recording of an interview with Benazir in which she described the impact the National Prayer Breakfast had had on her and her faith, embodied by a remark she made to me: 'I am not a fanatic but I am devout and I believe God tests the ones he loves.'[4]

*

---

* Abraham Vereide (1886–1969); Douglas E. Coe (1928–2017) was named one of the 25 most influential evangelicals in the United States by *Time* magazine.

In January 2000 the revised edition of my book on Kashmir was published in paperback with a new title: *Kashmir in Conflict*.* Nazir Ahmed again offered to organise a launch. Since the first launch in 1996 in Rotherham Town Hall, when Ahmed was a Labour councillor, he had been raised to the peerage as Lord Ahmed of Rotherham. On this occasion the launch took place on 20 January in a committee room in the House of Commons, hosted by Denis MacShane, Labour MP for Rotherham.[5] Both Benazir and Sunny came to support me. After my presentation there was a question and answer session; when someone from the audience remarked that the former prime minister of Pakistan was in the audience and it would be interesting to hear her viewpoint, Benazir politely declined, saying that she was present to support the author and not to take political advantage to project her own views. I wouldn't have minded if she had spoken, but I did wonder which other former prime minister, presented with such an opportunity, would have indicated so selflessly that they did not wish to take centre stage.

In early February I returned to Pakistan to attend a conference on Kashmir to mark 'Solidarity' day, held annually on 5 February, which was instituted as a national holiday in support and recognition of the Kashmiris who had died since the insurgency began. With Benazir in exile it seemed strange to be going to her country in her absence. As usual, she wished me well, offering me hospitality if I needed it. Before the conference General Musharraf gave a briefing on the Kashmir issue to the foreign guests, affirming Pakistan's official position that there should be a plebiscite as outlined by the UN resolutions of 1948 and 1949. Later I had a private interview with him and I pressed him on the issue of when he would return Pakistan to civilian government. 'Three years,' he

---

* There were also subsequent revised editions, published in 2003 and 2010.

said emphatically. 'I do not expect to remain as chief executive for more than three years.'[6]

Benazir had also been thinking about a topic in which she took serious interest throughout her life – whether or not Islam was compatible with parliamentary democratic government. In late February 2000 she was invited by the president of the Oxford Union – Lucy Aitken – to oppose the motion: 'This House believes that Islam is incompatible with the West.' Also opposing the motion was Dr Zaki Badawi, principal of the Muslim College of London, while those proposing it were Jay Smith, a tutor at the London Bible College (now the London School of Theology), an expert on Muslim–Christian relations, and Janine di Giovanni, author and foreign correspondent for *The Times*.

I would have loved to hear Benazir speak at the Oxford Union for the first time in twenty-three years, but I was going on holiday with my family for the school half-term. 'It seemed like the debating chamber was packed with every Muslim student in Oxford and so it was clear we were going to lose,' recalled Janine di Giovanni, who, for the sake of the debate had agreed to speak in favour of a motion she did not personally believe in. Having worked as a journalist in Pakistan, di Giovanni was not among Benazir's political fans, but she remembered being surprised by how charming the former prime minister was when they sat together at dinner and how impressive she was during the debate: 'She shredded every argument we had.'[7]

Since Benazir was no longer in government, she had resumed her lecture tours, organised by Mark Siegel. In May 2000 she was scheduled to lecture on 'The politics of democracy' to the Women's Foundation of Colorado in Denver. Some weeks beforehand I'd received a note from Dr Jack Gravlee, who, with his wife Rhonda, had hosted me in Fort Collins on the 1977 English Speaking Union debate tour. Knowing of my friendship with

Benazir, he had enclosed a page from the *Denver Post*, advertising her lecture and encouraging its readers to 'come meet this true world leader and visionary'. 'Why don't you come with her and we will show you beautiful Estes Park?' Jack wrote encouragingly. Although I couldn't make it, I liked to think of Benazir travelling the length and breadth of the United States, exhausting though it was, getting her message across. It was reassuring that, every so often, she would be heard by people I knew.[8]

Benazir had not, however, found the logistics of living in London easy. Although Sunny was near by, an added complication was the declining health of their mother, who now required twenty-four-hour care. After a year in London, Benazir moved to Dubai, taking her mother and children with her and setting up home in the gated community of Emirates Hills – home to wealthy expatriates and named after Beverly Hills in Los Angeles. The president of the United Arab Emirates, Sheikh Zayed bin Sultan Al Nahyan, was a longstanding friend who had supported her family since her father's days and she felt comfortable in a more secluded environment. Dubai had the further advantage of its relative proximity to Pakistan; party members could visit in under two hours. The disadvantage was that, much as she was welcomed by the government, political activity was restricted. So she made a compromise: in the summer, when the children were on school holidays, she would come to London, where she could be more politically active, and the weather was pleasantly cooler.

On 20 June 2001 General Musharraf contradicted all his statements about the temporary nature of his assumption of power by making himself president. In this new position, he began his own attempted 'peace process' with India, following UN secretary-general Kofi Annan's request to both governments to maintain the spirit of the 1999 Lahore Declaration.[9] In early July he made a high-profile visit to Agra to meet the Indian prime minister,

Atal Bihari Vajpayee. Included in the agenda for the two-day Agra summit was Kashmir, as well as nuclear risk reduction and establishing commercial ties. Unfortunately, Pakistan's continuing support for the insurgency in the valley of Kashmir, which the Indians insisted on calling 'cross-border terrorism', proved to be a sticking-point. Despite the warm welcome Musharraf received, no agreement was reached.

Before leaving Dubai to spend the summer in London, Benazir had some good news. In April the Supreme Court of Pakistan had found that the High Court judge who had convicted her and Asif of corruption in April 1999 had taken 'a personal interest in the case' and used his 'influence' over a junior member of the trial bench to secure a guilty verdict* and the conviction was over-turned.[10] This did not mean that she was free from allegations of corruption since, almost immediately, more cases were filed against her. But, following the Supreme Court's judgment, she began seriously to think about returning to Pakistan.

In addition to her political meetings and press interviews, while in London Benazir liked organising outings for her children; she believed that what children remembered about being with their parents was days out rather than days spent at home. Among my memories of the time we spent together were picnics in the park; the children playing in the Princess Diana Memorial Garden in Kensington Gardens; my son Anthony throwing a cricket ball to Bilawal, a year his junior; Aseefa playing on the swing in

---

* The judge was Malik Mohammad Qayuum (b. 1944) who resigned 'for the dignity of the judiciary'. His father was Malik Mohammad Akram, one of the four judges who rejected Zulfikar Ali Bhutto's appeal against the death sentence.

our back garden; Itty sharing an early interest in music with my children; Alexandra and Bilawal playing chess in our home. On one occasion Benazir and I had gone to a shop in the Whiteleys shopping mall in Queensway, which sold T-shirts personalised with a name or pattern. Among our respective children, only Alexandra was with us. While Benazir was choosing designs for her children, she noticed Alexandra's excited young face staring at the brightly coloured T-shirts, with their interesting potential. 'Come on, you choose something for yourself too,' said Benazir. 'And also for your brother and sister as well.'

Through another Oxford friend, Nick Rayne, I'd met Akash Paul – the son of steel magnate Lord Paul – whose wife, Nisha, was on the global advisory board of an Indian 'luxury lifestyle' magazine, *Verve*. Would I, Nisha asked one day when we were having lunch at Mark's Club, consider writing a profile of Benazir for the magazine? I hesitated, wary of writing on Benazir for an Indian audience. Nisha continued: 'Indians are absolutely fascinated by Benazir. There is huge admiration for her.' I said I would ask Benazir, and, if she was happy, I would go ahead.

During her summer visit Benazir agreed to give me a recorded interview, as we had done previously, so that whatever she said would be 'on the record' instead of being culled from our private conversations. Once more I sat down with my tape-recorder. Her response to one question resonated with her earlier life: 'Each day I cope by trying to stop thinking. I keep myself so busy that I prevent myself trying to think of the odds that I have to overcome. So, in a sense, I work on autopilot. It is the times when I want to do something with the children and we are together and I have a little more time to think that I realise the enormity of the challenge. But most days I cope by keeping too busy, going for press interviews, appointments and having very little time to reflect.'

Over a decade since she'd entered the limelight as prime minister, she admitted that she now had a different attitude towards criticism, which in the past had offended her. 'I've come to accept that every person needs to have critics because that is the plurality of the system.' She also recognised how, compared with her early years of political activism, the ways in which she could communicate had been revolutionised.

I have two days in my life: one is when I am stationary; the other when I am on tour. When I am stationary, I work through virtual reality. There are PPP supporters in Pakistan and overseas and so we remain connected through the information highway. Of course two decades ago, we had a different momentum going for us which was the sheer fervour of the people, who had been radicalised by the martyrdom of my father. But when my government introduced the internet technology back in 1995 we hardly understood then how important this would be to our own struggle for the restoration of the democratic process. Certainly our main engine to push the movement is the internet.[11]

Finally she paid tribute to friendship. 'I often find the friends one makes at school or college are the friends that last. Even though we get married, grow up and become very different because we have different experiences, nonetheless we share a common bond at a time of youth that sustains the friendship.' How true, I felt, as I reflected on why she so cherished meeting Oxford and Harvard friends, in addition to her Pakistani school friends like Samiya and Salma. She also displayed her extraordinary ability to put her own life in perspective: 'Just recently, I picked up a book on Mary Queen of Scots and I said, "my goodness, what this woman had to endure!"'

When my feature article was published, the headline was 'Survivor!'[12]

On 11 September 2001 – 9/11 – terrorist attacks, orchestrated by Osama bin Laden and the Al Qaeda network, were carried out against the World Trade Center in New York and the Pentagon in Washington. The fall-out for both Afghanistan and Pakistan was devastating. Both countries were once more centre stage: Afghanistan because of bin Laden's presence and the Taliban's refusal to hand him over, Pakistan because its logistical assistance was necessary as a frontline state in what President George W. Bush called the 'war on terror'. Just as the Soviet invasion of Afghanistan in 1979 gave General Zia a lifeline, so 9/11 gave Musharraf a new international lease of life.

'I was stunned and heartbroken,' related Benazir after 9/11. 'Watching the Twin Towers burn in New York, realising that thousands were dying the most dreadful kind of death, could not have been more painful to me. Educated at Harvard and later at Oxford University, I considered the United States and Britain to be my second homes.' She felt the same when, four years later, on 7 July 2005 – '7/7' – London's transport system was targeted. She was especially upset that the acts of terror were carried out in the name of Islam and often linked with Pakistan. Mistakes, she wrote in her updated autobiography, were made on all sides. 'The disquieting pattern of the link between terrorist plots and attacks against the West and Pakistan is not coincidental. To me the pattern is sadly relevant, an often overlooked consequence of the West allowing Pakistani military regimes to suppress the democratic aspirations of the people of Pakistan as long as their dictators ostensibly support the political goals of the West.'[13]

The terrorist attacks were also proof that the jihadi movement, which first emerged to combat the Soviet presence in Afghanistan in the 1980s, and which spawned the chaotic governments of the Mujahideen and the Taliban in the 1990s, had spiralled out of control, creating lawlessness throughout the region. On 13 December – just two weeks after Benazir had returned to Dubai from a private visit to New Delhi – there was an attack on the Lok Sabha.* The government of India immediately blamed two terrorist organisations based in Pakistan – Lashkar-e Taiba and Jaish-e Mohammed – which again sent Indo-Pakistani relations into a nose-dive. In an attempt to counter the prevailing belief that the Pakistan establishment, notably the ISI (Inter-Services Intelligence), was behind the attack, in January 2002 Musharraf appeared on national television to announce a ban on four radical Islamic groups, which included Jaish-e-Mohammad and Lashkar-e Taiba. But the cycle of violence on the streets of Pakistan continued, with frequent bomb blasts and kidnappings. In February a video was released of the beheading of an American journalist, Daniel Pearl, in Karachi, which shocked the world.†

In the wake of 9/11 it was also increasingly clear that the narrative over Jammu and Kashmir was changing: the separatists fighting in the valley of Kashmir could no longer expect to be classified as 'freedom fighters' comparable to the mujahideen in Afghanistan. Instead the Indian government's position that they were 'terrorists' was gaining wider currency. Yet again I needed

---

* During her visit she met prime minister Vajpayee, home minister L. K. Advani and Sonia Gandhi, leader of the opposition in the Lok Sabha, as well as members of the All Parties Hurriyat Conference (APHC).

† Daniel Pearl (1963–2002); Khalid Sheikh Mohammad (b.?1964/65) was arrested in March 2003 in Rawalpindi, and in March 2007 he claimed responsibility for the killing under military interrogation at Guantanamo Bay internment camp. His trial was scheduled for 2021, but was postponed. See Asra Q. Nomani. 'This is Danny Pearl's final story', *Washingtonian*, 2012.

to revise my book on Kashmir and in March 2002 I travelled to
Pakistan with the intention of going on to India and the valley
of Kashmir. While in Islamabad I had 'an exchange of views'
with President Musharraf. After some general pleasantries and a
reaffirmation of Pakistan's position that the Kashmiris should be
allowed their 'right of self-determination', Musharraf asked me
to turn off my tape-recorder. I duly obliged, while his director-
general of Inter-Services Public Relations (ISPR), Major General
Rashid Qureshi, left the room. Musharraf's presidential posture
softened slightly as he turned to me:

'You're a friend of Benazir Bhutto, aren't you?'

'Yes, Mr President,' I replied. 'That fact is well known. I have
never concealed it from anyone.'

'Well, then,' he continued. 'You know we are holding elections
this year. Could you ask her not to return?'

There was an awkward pause. 'President Musharraf,' I began.
'It is also well known that I do not interfere in Pakistan's politics
and, although I am a friend, I am in no position to ask her to do
anything in relation to the political decisions she makes.'

He looked a little crestfallen but then regained his composure.
From what he said, I realised that his dislike of Benazir was deep-
rooted and extended to her father. I was amazed that he had made
such a request, surely knowing that he'd be rebuffed. We talked a
little more about his prospects in the forthcoming referendum which
was being held to confirm his assumption of the presidency the
previous June. 'Insha'Allah I will win,' he said, as I got up to leave.[14]

As I already knew, it was not an auspicious time to travel
from Pakistan to India. Because of the Delhi attack the previous December, relations between India and Pakistan were once
more tense, their two armies facing each other 'eyeball to eyeball'
along the international border; all flights to and from Delhi
were suspended as well as the bus service inaugurated by prime

ministers Sharif and Vajpayee in 1999. But there was one loop-hole. Although the border at Wagah – the only crossing point along the 3,000 km border, equidistant between Lahore and Amritsar – was officially closed, it remained open to nationals on 'official' business and foreigners crossing on foot and so that was the form of transport I proposed to take. As I had explained in an email to Benazir: 'I cannot claim to be a "Kashmir expert" without visiting.'

'Good luck on your visit to Pakistan and to India,' she responded. 'It is brave of you to go through Wagah to Kashmir. The Kashmiris are lucky to have you take an interest in them, especially in these difficult days for them. If you see Mirwaiz [Umar Farooq], or [Syed Ali Shah] Geelani, Yasin [Malik], [Abdul Gani] Lone and the main leaders, do convey my good wishes to them. Take care and lots of love to the children and to you.'[15]

My experience at Wagah was surreal. Since I appeared to be the only foreigner and there were no nationals on 'official' busi-ness wanting to cross, I felt as though I had landed on a stage set, constructed for a play, where the stage hands waited expectantly for actors who seldom appeared. 'A white line painted across the road marks the boundary, half of which is in Pakistan, the other half in India,' I recorded. 'On one side the Pakistani flag flutters proudly, on the other the Indian. At sunrise and sunset both flags are ceremoniously raised and lowered, as their respective soldiers goose step and salute before the gates are slammed shut.'[16] Away from the actual crossing, barbed wire and searchlights at regular intervals made it clear that no one crossed at random. As I looked north and south, I noticed a dusty track, which the Pakistani colonel in charge assured me was swept every night so that, in the morning, they could see if there were any tell-tale footprints showing signs of illegal crossings.

Having filled in the necessary forms for my departure from

Pakistan, I approached the border. In anticipation of my imminent arrival, porters hovered eagerly on the other side, ready to receive my two suitcases from the Pakistani porters who had carried them thus far, as though they were passing on batons in a slow-moving relay. And so, as my luggage disappeared on the heads of the Indian porters, I turned my back on Pakistan, stepped across the white line and walked into India.[17]

When I arrived in the Kashmir valley, because of the strained relations between India and Pakistan following the December 2001 attack on the Lok Sabha and the continuing insurgency, it was in lockdown. The computer booths, which had recently been installed in various shops, were empty. Curfew was in full force. I had wanted to stay in my traditional 'home' – Butt's Claremont Houseboats on Upper Dal lake – but I needed to be near a landline telephone to arrange meetings for the following day. And so, having made my way to my various interviews, I cautiously returned to Ahdoos Hotel before dark. In the evenings I sat in my hotel room, wrapped in blankets because it was cold, writing by candlelight, since the electricity kept failing. Overall, my visit to the Kashmir valley was sad. Buildings which had been damaged in the fighting were still unrepaired, while the military's bunkers looked more like permanent fixtures. I heard stories of the 'disappeared' and of women who were consequently 'half widows' – they could not remarry because they had no confirmation of their husbands' deaths – all adding to the trauma of people living in conflict. I was left with huge admiration for the Kashmiri people and an overriding feeling that the 'Jammu-Kashmir issue' was hostage to India and Pakistan's failure to sit together and work determinedly to find a resolution. It was nearly twelve years since the failed Rajiv–Benazir talks and no progress had been made.[18]

Predictably Musharraf won the referendum, confirming his

presidency for five years. But the election process was widely criticised for having been rigged. 'It was more Politburo than democracy, but the international community, transfixed by the growing threat of Islamic terrorism, cast a blind eye,' observed Benazir.[19] Although she had seriously thought of returning to Pakistan, in the end she decided not to go back to contest the October 2002 general election held under Musharraf's watchful eye. The restrictions he had imposed on all political parties meant that the PPP had to fight the election as the Pakistan Peoples Party Parliamentarians (PPPP).

With Nawaz Sharif still in exile in Saudi Arabia and his party much weakened by defections, a new faction of the Pakistan Muslim League had been created, the Pakistan Muslim League (Q) Quaid-i-Azam, whose members supported Musharraf, earning it the nickname 'the King's Party'. Despite Benazir's absence, the PPPP – led by the party's deputy, Makhdoom Ameen Faheem – won the highest percentage of the vote, but only 81 seats, whereas the PML(Q) won 126 seats.* Nawaz's party – the Pakistan Muslim League (N) – secured just 19 seats, only two more than the regional Muttahida Qaumi Movement (MQM). As an illustration of the emerging polarisation in Pakistan's society, the recently formed MMA – the Muttahida Majlis-i-Amal (MMA) – a combination of six religious parties which opposed Musharraf's support of the international intervention in Afghanistan – won 63 seats.†

*

---

* Makhdoom Ameen Faheem (1939–2015) was senior vice-chairman of the PPP.
† The US-led invasion of Iraq in 2003 added more fuel to the fire and gave the Islamic parties a reason for unity and a chance to increase their influence and leverage.

Meanwhile Benazir continued to travel between her two homes in Dubai and London. Throughout the years of exile, Naheed Khan worked as her political secretary *in absentia* in Islamabad. On visits to London, Bashir Riaz was also willing to assist with her interviews, as was Wajid Shamsul Hasan, who, as a former high commissioner still living in London, always accompanied her to political meetings.

Another young British Pakistani who began helping Benazir was Rehman (Ray) Chishti whose family had come from Muzaffarabad in *Azad* Jammu and Kashmir after Bhutto's execution. Brought up in Kent, he had trained as a barrister but was also interested in politics. Over the next few years, along with pursuing his political career, Ray became, as Benazir said, her 'most brilliant assistant'. Later, when speaking at a dinner in support of Ray's campaign to become Conservative MP for Gillingham and Rainham, she described how having Ray as their parliamentary candidate would be her loss and their gain.* This was typical of Benazir, her enthusiasm for other people's success being one of her most endearing qualities.[20]

When in London her 'office' was the entrance hall of her flat in Queensgate, a few buildings from Sunny's. Whenever I arrived, my first sight would be of her bent over her computer, hard at work. She also revelled in the new technology of the Blackberry smartphones, which effectively gave her a mobile office, allowing her to keep in touch with her political colleagues and a wide range of journalists, many of whom became friends. Her base for political meetings was the house of her former additional director

---

* Rehman Chishti, MP for Gillingham and Rainham (b.1978). In 2005 he stood as a Labour Party candidate for Horsham but lost; having joined the Conservative Party he won the marginal seat of Gillingham and Rainham in the 2010 general election.

of the Federal Investigating Agency, Rehman Malik, in Norfolk Crescent, Paddington. Like many others, once Benazir was no longer in power he had moved to Britain, becoming politically active on behalf of the Pakistani diaspora.

While Benazir was focusing on maintaining her political position, world events were shifting away from South Asia and Afghanistan back to the Middle East. The Taliban had been ousted during the military operations against Afghanistan in late 2001 and technically the country was on the road to democracy, or so the international community hoped. President George W. Bush was now focused on a new adversary:* Saddam Hussein in Iraq, who was alleged to be developing weapons of mass destruction.

By late 2002 plans for a multinational invasion of Iraq had been set in motion. The following year, early in the morning Baghdad time on 20 March, after a huge aerial bombardment, United States forces, followed by British and other coalition forces, crossed the frontier from Kuwait into Iraq. Unlike the outcome of the Gulf War in 1991, and despite Saddam Hussein's brutality and unpopularity within Iraq, his summary removal was controversial, both within the countries of the Western world and in the Muslim world. Not only was the allegation that Iraq was producing weapons of mass destruction proved to be false, but the coalition plan for reconstruction was badly formulated, leading to immense suffering. As the subsequent history of the region revealed, the destabilisation of Iraq led to a prolonged and devastating civil war, which spilled over to neighbouring Syria. Most importantly, an emotional fissure developed between segments of society in the Muslim world and Western countries.

*

---

* George W. Bush (b.1946) was the 43rd US president 2001–09.

On 21 June 2003 Benazir celebrated her fiftieth birthday in Dubai, holding a party for fifty people. Although Asif was still under arrest, he had arranged to send her a huge basket containing fifty bunches of red roses. 'Fifty bunches,' she said to me enthusiastically when we met up later in the summer in London. 'Asif sent me fifty bunches to celebrate my fiftieth!' In recognition of her half-century, she'd written a long narrative poem, the theme of which was her life in exile and when she might return to Pakistan. She called it 'The story of Benazir, from Marvi of Malir and Shah Latif', drawing inspiration from the poetry of Shah Abdul Latif.*

> From dust to dust
> loved ones return
> to what they were
> When will I walk home from Arab lands
> To my own sweet Motherland....
> Strands of white my hair now shows
> My face is gaunt with sadness
> I to my people want to go.[21]

In early August Benazir and I had a day out in Oxford. She still loved returning to her British alma mater with its familiar associations. It was poignant to recollect how fiercely we had clung to those old memories when I used to visit her during her desperate days of house arrest in 1978 and 1979. First we went to see Dr Charis Waddy, now in her nineties, in a nursing home in Boar's Hill, just to the southwest of Oxford. Knowing how busy Benazir always was, Charis was thrilled to see her, greeting our arrival with her familiar broad smile and a twinkle in her eye. To me our visit also

---

* Marvi was a young woman who lived in the village of Malir in the Thar desert; the story of her life is a famous Sindhi love story.

showed the regard Benazir had for this elderly lady who had helped her emotionally during her early years of exile.

Next on our agenda was lunch with Dr Frances Lannon, Lady Margaret Hall's principal since 2002, and Gillian Peele. As Benazir's former politics tutor, Gillian had been the 'go to' person for anyone wanting to find out what sort of student Benazir was at Oxford. Over the years they had met intermittently. On one occasion, when Gillian was short of time and heading off to a hospital appointment, Benazir agreed that we would accompany her in a taxi to the hospital so that we could chat on the way! Another old friend, Dr Jeremy Catto, the senior librarian at the Oxford Union when we were at university, was also at the lunch.* 'B. [was] marvelled [at by] all,' I commented in my diary, 'by talking high politics about Iraq and meetings with Gorbachev and having warned John Major ages ago about the growing extremist menace in the mosques.'[22]

On our way home, we called in at the Oxford Centre for Islamic Studies to meet Dr David Browning, the founder registrar, whose experiences working with Muslims from different backgrounds had inspired him and others to work towards establishing the centre 'as a catalyst for positive change'. Given Benazir's interest in presenting an alternative image of Islam from the stereotypical extremist one, she had wanted to understand the centre's influence, as Browning was later to write, 'in a world where human affairs are so often sullied by fears of inter-civilisational conflict'.[23]

Two days after our happy day out in Oxford, a Swiss judge, Daniel Devaud, convicted Benazir and Asif of money laundering, pronouncing a suspended sentence of six months in jail and a fine of $50,000 each, as well as requiring them to return over

---

* Dame Frances Lannon, DBE, FRHistS (b.1945); Gillian Peele, MA, MPhil FRHistS (b.1949); Dr Jeremy Catto (1939–2018).

$2 million to Pakistan. Benazir was shocked and upset by the verdict and immediately filed an appeal against the conviction. In this instance she took assurance from her own lawyer, who described Devaud's decision to sentence them as 'rubbish'.[24]

Meanwhile, as a result of the continuing fall-out from 9/11 and the military intervention in Afghanistan, lawlessness in Pakistan had increased. In December Musharraf was the victim of two assassination attempts in the space of a fortnight. Although he was unhurt, in the second attack fourteen people, including two suicide bombers, were killed, and nearly fifty injured. 'These blasts have given new strength to my resolve to eliminate terrorists and extremists from the country and, God willing, this mission will be accomplished,' a visibly shaken Musharraf stated on national television.[25] But what the attacks revealed was that neither the Pakistani political establishment nor the military was in control of the extremist sentiment which, nurtured during the Zia years, had taken hold among certain sections in society. Militant Muslims were now mobilising not only against the United States, categorised as the 'Great Satan', and its intervention in the Middle East, but also against the Pakistani establishment itself.

Benazir returned to London in the summer of 2004. My mother had died in April and she had phoned from Dubai to say how sorry she was, remembering how, for her farewell debate at the Oxford Union in 1977, my mother had given her a bouquet of white flowers with green and white ribbons, representing the colours in the Pakistani flag. She again condoled with me when we met.

One of Benazir's first engagements was as a keynote speaker at an 'International Kashmir Conference' held at the old Commonwealth Institute (now the Design Museum) in Kensington and organised by one of the many members of the Kashmiri diaspora,

Dr Syed Nazir Gilani, president of the London-based Jammu and Kashmir Council for Human Rights (JKCHR). I too was invited.

'The aim of the International Kashmir Conference is to ensure that the common man is empowered,' said Gilani in his opening remarks. 'The loss of a generation has to be accounted for.'[26] The first speaker was Sajad Ghani Lone, the son of Abdul Ghani Lone, whom I'd interviewed in Srinagar in 1995, and who had been assassinated in 2002.* Addressing his remarks to the audience but also to Benazir, mindful that Zulfikar Ali Bhutto had spoken out on Kashmir, Sajad began: 'The people of Kashmir have always had a very warm spot for you and your family.' He described himself as coming into politics, like Benazir, 'by tragedy'. But, he said, there was a difference: 'You could cry, you could accuse. I don't have that luxury – if I did, there would be another coffin.' But, he said, 'the agony of the past should not become tied to the future'. The main focus of his presentation reflected a depressing reality: 'conflict creates pockets of vested interest who prosper at the cost of keeping the issue unresolved'. He also pointed out the danger of continuing militarisation of the contested region: 'a manageable level of violence suits both India and Pakistan. As long as guns are there, there is very little the politicians can do.'[27]

Speaking after Sajad, Benazir described how moved she was when she heard the news of Abdul Ghani Lone's assassination. She also recognised how difficult it must have been that Sajad was unable to speak out and accuse those whom he held responsible, lest he be targeted. As in other fora she'd addressed, she

---

* Abdul Ghani Lone (1932–2002). As a veteran of the freedom movement, he had been moving towards initiating dialogue with the Indian government, and his assassination in May 2002 dismayed those who believed he was killed by hard-line separatists who were not prepared to make any accommodation with India.

emphasised the importance of intra-Kashmiri dialogue and of open borders. Knowing that Musharraf was embarking on renewed dialogue with India, Benazir made it clear that, despite their political differences, she wanted to see the peace process succeed. But, she said, it would only be effective if the inhabitants of the state were involved. 'The PPP and I consider Kashmiris as key to a solution. It is important for us to listen to all voices. We need to talk to each other rather than at each other.'* Finally she pointed out that since 9/11 the world had changed: 'there is zero tolerance for violence'.[28]

When it was his turn to speak, Farooq Abdullah, Jammu and Kashmir's former chief minister, whom I'd met several times both in London and in Srinagar, illustrated the futility of the continued dispute because, although India and Pakistan had fought several wars, 'the line [of control] is still where it is'.[29] Their arguments were by now familiar to me, but I remember it as an exceptional conference with Benazir, Farooq, Sajad and others expressing their respective viewpoints without being shouted down. It was also good to see Benazir in her element in a political environment. It was over a decade since her second administration began and she'd been in the spotlight.

For relaxation we continued with our traditional dinner parties at my home. Invariably, when we were drawing up the guest list, Benazir would suggest seeing someone we hadn't met in years and I would find myself asking friends of friends if they were in touch. For this particular dinner party in 2004 that person was one of her Labour Club friends, Simon Mares from University College.

---

* In 2003 she had said, 'Without prejudice to Pakistan's position [i.e. the demand for a plebiscite to be held to determine the future allegiance of the state]', she would work for open borders to let families unite. 'We have to move on.' My notes of Benazir's press conference, Rehman Malik's house, London, 2003.

Benazir was delighted when I tracked him down and found that he had a successful career working for ITV. There was also a regular group, including Freya and her husband, John Newman, as well as Colin Clifford (whom she had tried to match-make with several friends, her last attempt failing because Colin was vehemently opposed to smokers and the woman in question was a heavy smoker!). Other regulars were David Soskin and his wife Alexandra, Keith and Lynne Gregory, Victor and Amanda van Amerongen, and Daniel Moylan, all of whom remained bound in friendship from our Oxford Union days despite our different career paths.

'Dearest Victoria,' Benazir wrote after she'd returned to Dubai at the end of July. 'It was lovely being with you in the summer. Thank you for organising the summer party. It was wonderful seeing Oxford friends again. Dubai is so hot. I feel I am melting even inside with the air conditioning.' I had at last managed to send her back some furniture and personal possessions which had been in store ever since her extended stay in London when she gave birth to Aseefa. 'The furniture and stuff from 1993 arrived. It brought back so many memories. Including how thin I was. I can hardly believe the changes, personal, political and governmental that have taken place since 1993. It seems a century ago.'[30]

One of Benazir's enduring sadnesses was the separation from her brothers' children. While Fatima, Murtaza's daughter, continued to believe that Asif – and, by association, Benazir – was responsible for her father's death, contact with Shahnawaz's daughter, Sassi, who had grown up in California, was sporadic. Now it seemed that Sassi wanted to visit. 'The news is wonderful,' Benazir continued. Describing how she had been 'burning up the telephone lines' to organise Sassi's passport, she felt the important thing was 'that she wants to visit which moves me tremendously... I want her to see my Mother and of course the children too. I know the passport will finally come through and if not this year, then surely by next.' Happily Sassi got her passport and was able to see her cousins in Dubai. But it was not until 2008 that, accompanied by Fatima, she visited her father Shahnawaz's grave in Garhi Khuda Bakhsh for the first time.[31]

In November 2004, after eight years in prison, Asif was released on bail. The children whom he had last known as pre-teenagers were now verging on adulthood, since regular visits to him in jail had been precluded by Benazir's exile abroad. He did not initially return to live in Dubai but instead went to New York for medical treatment. This led to speculation that he and Benazir were leading separate lives and were about to divorce,* which Benazir denied, later writing: 'I found joy and fulfilment in marriage despite difficult circumstances.'[32]

As usual Benazir returned to London in the summer of 2005; during this visit she had agreed to attend a Speaker's meeting at the Oxford Union organised by the librarian and future president of the Union, Sapana Agrawal. By this time my daughter Alexandra was studying at Oxford at our old college, Lady Margaret Hall, and so she too came to listen. As the students were lined up to meet the celebrated guest speaker, Benazir shook their hands formally, saying a few words as she progressed along the line. She did the same with Alexandra and then suddenly she stopped, all formality vanishing as she said delightedly, 'Oh, Alexandra, hello. I didn't immediately recognise you.'

Once more her theme was the importance of a working democratic system to combat extremism and the dangers of endorsing

---

* This was not the first time rumours circulated about the state of their marriage; see Christina Lamb, 'Bhutto leaves husband in quest for comeback', *Sunday Times*, 7 September 1997.

military dictatorship. 'I know it is my obligation to be part of this battle no matter what the personal price to restore democracy to Pakistan... The fight for freedom is the fight for values that can build a pluralistic world... the stakes are high and the implications are great.' It so happened that Benazir was speaking on the day of the British general election which enabled her to make reference to the merits of a free and fair election.* 'What is happening in Britain tonight in a general election is that people who are representing the public make themselves accountable to the court of the people and accept the verdict of the people; the people are the ones who are really the masters of the state.' It was the first (and last) time I heard Benazir speak in the debating chamber since we were undergraduates.[33]

The next day we went together to attend Dr Charis Waddy's memorial service, following her death, aged ninety-four, the previous August. When Benazir got up to speak I sensed surprise among the audience that the former prime minister of Pakistan had maintained such a close association with this remarkable woman, not perhaps knowing of their long friendship, nor their shared alma mater, Lady Margaret Hall. In addition to praising Charis's contribution to Islamic scholarship, Benazir reminded the audience that she was one of the few women to have received the *Sitara-i-Imtiaz*, awarded in Benazir's first administration in 1990.[34]

One of Benazir's cherished ambitions was to initiate a system whereby Oxford undergraduates would go to Pakistan for a few weeks to teach at SZABIST, the Shaheed Zulfikar Ali Bhutto Institute of Science and Technology, branches of which were set up in her father's memory in Karachi, Islamabad, Larkana and Dubai.

---

* Britain's Labour Party won the general election, Tony Blair remaining prime minister.

The first person to do so was a friend's daughter, Pandora Crawley. By chance, the previous summer I had arranged for Ruzwana Bashir, who in March 2004 had become the first Muslim woman since Benazir to be elected president of the Oxford Union, to meet Benazir in Dubai and Pandora (who was a friend of Ruzwana's) had accompanied her. While they were chatting, Benazir had spoken enthusiastically about working for SZABIST and Pandora had agreed to go, spending several weeks teaching at SZABIST in Islamabad. She later gave Benazir a detailed account of her activities, which had included travelling to the Northern Areas (Gilgit-Baltistan):

The students were keener and a lot brighter than I had anticipated. It was interesting to sense their attitudes towards me as a 'Westerner' and what they thought about politics, women, and religion. I am sure they all thought I was a bit of an enigma. Nevertheless they displayed a strong keenness to learn and find out about me. I was particularly impressed by the girls, who, I know, comprise nearly a third of the university, since they were often the ones who asked the questions and did best academically... The experience has also meant that my opinions back here in England about Pakistan are grounded in real knowledge. Not many people have that knowledge as a twenty-two year old British undergraduate. It is invaluable. I hope that I benefited SZABIST and the younger adults I met and taught there. It was great to exchange opinions on the same level, being their age, and talking to them about England and Western culture and society.

Pandora concluded her account by saying that she hoped she had paved the way 'for this kind of relationship and mutual exchange of knowledge to happen again'.

Benazir was delighted. 'Dear Pandora,' she wrote in her own lengthy response.

I read with pleasure of your exposure to the Pakistani academic world and interaction with the University students. I am glad you had the first hand experience of learning how the Pakistani youth, particularly the girls, view politics, women and religion. Pakistan has a rich culture which your travel to the cities of Lahore, Gilgit, Hunza, Chitral, Naga and Peshawar would have demonstrated. Other areas of Pakistan, in the south, including Sindh, Punjab and Baluchistan [*sic*], offer their own unique culture. In particular, the remains of the 5,000 year old Indus Civilization tell you a lot about how people of the region lived in peace with each other. My ancestors come from this area. The people of Pakistan are peaceful, hard working, and friendly. We strongly believe in co-existence and good relations. I am sure you must have experienced the same in your travels. It is unfortunate, however, that in recent years, others have exploited religion for their own vested interest. With my good wishes, Benazir Bhutto.[35]

Pandora had indeed paved the way because the following summer of 2006 Alexandra went to teach at SZABIST. Benazir was again thrilled. 'Dearest Vicks, please keep me posted about Alexandra. I am most excited about her contributing towards SZABIST's goals.'[36] Sadly the tradition did not continue. When a friend of Alexandra's wanted to go the following year, her parents became anxious about the security situation and so she cancelled her visit.

Just because Benazir was no longer in Pakistan didn't mean that the PPP wasn't actively pursuing a political agenda. Over the previous four years an attempt was being made to reform the Hudood ordinances, which Benazir's previous administrations had been unable to tackle. As Sherry Rehman* explained:

> When I moved the amendment to reform the Hudood ordinances in 2002 Benazir remained supportive and engaged with the whole process; finally General Musharraf was forced to constitute a committee to accept the crucial Zina [adultery, rape] amendment. Because of this reform no women rot in jail anymore for simply reporting rape, as the ordinance conflated rape with adultery unless it was witnessed and testified to by four male witnesses, which is of course absurd. It was therefore ultimately the PPP, through my bill, that led to the 2006 Women's Protection Bill during Musharraf's tenure, in response to our initiatives.[37]

In 2006 Benazir was also thinking about Bilawal's university career. Her first choice was that he should study at Christ Church, Oxford, where her father and brother had gone and so, during her London visit that summer, we went together with Bilawal to look at the colleges. We also went to see Lady Margaret Hall, where Frances Lannon welcomed us warmly. While Alexandra showed Bilawal around, we had coffee together. As we were chatting in the comfortable surroundings of the Senior Common Room, Benazir remarked how nice it must be to be principal of an Oxford college. Later, when Frances was out of earshot, she turned to me: 'Vicks, wouldn't it be wonderful if one day we could both be

---

* Sherry Rehman (b.1960) is currently a member of the Senate and is chairman of the Senate Committee on China Pak Economic Corridor (CPEC). After a career in journalism, encouraged by Benazir, Sherry Rehman entered politics in 2002, and was elected a PPP member of the National Assembly.

principals of an Oxford College?!' Her remark was a reminder that, like everyone else, Benazir liked to think that one day she might pursue different career options. But, as we know, her destiny was otherwise. When, having taken his A-levels, Bilawal was accepted at Christ Church, Benazir was overjoyed.

By 2007 Benazir had set in motion her plans to return to Pakistan after eight years in exile. Since Asif was now free and able to spend time with their children, the timing seemed right and a tentative date was fixed for the autumn so she could campaign for the next general election. If the PPP won a majority it would mean that she would become prime minister of Pakistan for a third time, an eventuality which Musharraf had assiduously tried to prevent. But Musharraf was running against the political tide. Like Zia over two decades previously, he had initially benefited from the knowledge that he had the backing of the United States, but that support was now weakening.

Musharraf's decline was also of his own making. In May he came into confrontation with Pakistan's judiciary by arbitrarily dismissing the chief justice of the Supreme Court, setting in motion what became known as 'the lawyers' movement' whose supporters campaigned on the streets of Pakistan for the chief justice's restoration. The fall-out was both domestic and international, especially in relation to the 'peace process' which Musharraf was continuing to pursue with the Indian prime minister, Manmohan Singh. The initiative, which had brought the two countries closer to resolving the Jammu-Kashmir issue than they had been for at least a decade, fell apart once the Indians saw that he no longer commanded full authority.[38]

By contrast Benazir's political star was again rising. The previous year she had come to an agreement with her political adversary,

Nawaz Sharif, still in exile in Saudi Arabia. In May 2006 they had signed the Charter for Democracy, a document which set out a plan to restore democratic civilian rule. But, as she knew too well, the country to which she planned to return had become a hotbed of militancy. Musharraf's regime 'cohabits with extremists who plot against innocent women, children and men on planes, trains and buses all across Europe, America and Pakistan', she observed. 'Musharraf doles out ostensible support in the war on terror, one spoonful as needed, to keep him in the good graces of Washington and London, but his policies also empower the enemies of the West.'[39]

Once again Benazir was being courted by the world's press for interviews, including by old favourites, like Sir David Frost. Another interview which she gave in Dubai was with *The Times'* feature writer Ginny Dougary, who was meeting Benazir for the first time.* 'The four hours spent in her home in Dubai are a roller-coaster of copious laughter and floods of tears,' wrote Dougary. '... noncommittal cautiousness and breath taking openness, plain-speaking to the point of impertinence and insinuating charm, high-handed loftiness and affectionate intimacy. Bhutto is the most extraordinary woman who says the most extraordinary things, veering wildly between self-aggrandisement and a knowing, sometimes humorous, recognition of how she can come across.'[40]

When Benazir told me about the interview, ever keen to make connections, one of the highlights she described was discovering that Ginny's mother and mine were close friends in the Women's Royal Naval Service – the WRNS – during the war!

As always, whenever Benazir spoke, it was interesting to hear her expound her views, invariably centred on the progressive

---

* Ginny Dougary (b.1956).

nature of Islam. 'Consultation and consensus are at the heart of Islam,' she said when addressing the students at the London School of Economics in April. And so democracy, women's rights 'are at the heart of Islam too.' As with other talks I'd heard her give, she wanted to highlight the achievements of both PPP administrations in taking on the fundamentalists, introducing the information age and starting the process of deregulation. Pursuing another familiar theme she described how 'the West' supported dictators for short-term gains but 'the fanatics came back to haunt them'. She also explained the reasons for living in exile, describing how the Prophet Mohammed (PBUH) went to Medina when the situation became difficult for him in Mecca. Pointing out that she had small children to raise, she said she had never given up the struggle, confirming that she intended to go back to Pakistan by the end of the year.[41]

But the country to which she was planning to return remained extremely unstable. In addition to regular bomb blasts, since 2006 a mosque in Islamabad, known as the Lal Masjid (Red Mosque), together with the adjacent madrassa, the Jamia Hafsa, had been occupied by Islamic militants. In addition to demanding the imposition of Sharia law and calling for the overthrow of the government, they had provoked violence on the streets as well as carrying out acts of arson. On 23 June 2007 the situation came to a head, when some Chinese women working in a massage parlour were taken hostage, their captors alleging that the parlour was a brothel. The Chinese government immediately showed its displeasure at the 'terrorist' attacks on Chinese citizens.[42]

On 3 July, following an attack on the Ministry of Environment, Musharraf ordered the complex of buildings to be surrounded while negotiations began for the militants' departure. But no agreement could be reached and a week later Musharraf gave the order for the buildings to be stormed. While the residents of Islamabad were relieved to have an end to the occupation, the military forces went in with such a heavy hand that more than 150 people were killed (some reports even citing 300–400 dead). In response the pro-Taliban militants along the Afghan border reneged on the peace accord they'd agreed with the government in September 2006, setting in train a series of suicide attacks on Pakistani armed forces leading to an upsurge of violence. Despite their political differences, Benazir supported Musharraf's action on the grounds that the government could not tolerate a group of armed individuals occupying a mosque in the heart of Islamabad.[43]

Throughout the summer in London dozens of visitors came and went. One of them was the American 1995 Pulitzer prize-winning author and former *Wall Street Journal* journalist Ron Suskind, who was writing a book on how the United States had 'lost its way'. Published the following year under the title *The Way of the World: A Story of Truth and Hope in an Age of Extremism*, one passage described a tea party to which Benazir had invited him.* Sunny was there as well as several friends, including Alan Duncan, Patricia Yates, my husband Stephen and myself. Fourteen-year-old Aseefa was wandering about in the background.

Benazir had also invited Ginny Dougary, whose interview, captioned 'Destiny's Daughter', was published in *The Times* in April. 'She looked younger and lighter, and freer, than when we last met,' related Ginny, 'her hair flowing freely, wearing hardly any make-up and dressed in an almost hippyish kameez, lime-green and flame-orange in colour. She was, as I remember it, walking barefoot.' 'Festiveness warms the room,' observed Ron Suskind. But while describing our mutual enjoyment of tea and

---

* Ron Suskind (b.1959). The tea took place on 11 July 2007.

scones, and our discussion of terrorism and jihad interspersed with light-hearted chat, Ron's closing comments were ominous, if somewhat opaque. In response to Alan's comment that Benazir could be a bridge between communities in Britain and Pakistan, he wrote: 'Certainly one can hope, sitting high above London – [Benazir's flat was on the fifth floor of a mansion block in Queensgate] – compacts may be made, under duress, between governments. Power-sharing arrangements struck. Deals cut. But all of those gathered here in the clouds for high tea suspect something, a hard disquieting thing that they'd rather not discuss: to have true clout in the modern world, you have to walk through the valley and survive it. And you can't get there from here.'[44]

On 20 July Benazir spoke at the IISS (International Institute of Strategic Studies), whose offices were in Arundel House overlooking the Thames. The room was packed. Her theme was all too familiar: 'As we meet, Pakistan is in crisis,' she began. 'It is a crisis that began almost fifty years ago when the first military ruler of Pakistan – General Ayub Khan – seized control in 1958.' As before her argument focused on the need to strengthen democratic institutions lest extremist elements in society take hold. 'As we gather together, much to the dismay of the people of Pakistan, Islamabad is the primary training and staging area for Al Qaeda.' Referring to the takeover of the Red Mosque, she again affirmed the PPP's support of Musharraf when he decided to storm the mosque. 'But we believe this crisis should have been dealt with six months ago.' Her conclusion mirrored beliefs she had held all her life. 'Restoring democracy through free, fair, transparent and internationally supervised elections in 2007 is a giant step towards regional peace and stability.'[45]

Among the audience, whom Benazir was pleased to meet as she mingled afterwards, was Gordon Corera, the BBC's security correspondent, author of *Shopping for Bombs: Nuclear Proliferation,*

Global Insecurity and the Rise and Fall of the A. Q. Khan Network. Having already read the book herself, Benazir had bought me a copy as a 'memento' of a visit we'd made to Oxford. 'It's a page turner,' she'd said. 'I couldn't put it down.' And, when I read it, nor could I, his narrative emphasising that Khan's admission of nuclear proliferation in 2004 was only part of Pakistan's still untold story.[46]

During these last weeks before her return Benazir was constantly on the move. On 15 August she spoke at the Council on Foreign Relations in New York, once more assuring her listeners of the need to restore democracy and free Pakistan 'from the yoke of military dictatorship'. In late September she was in Washington DC. It was evident, however, that Musharraf was only reluctantly accepting her return, in the expectation that it would be after the elections scheduled for January 2008. But Benazir was adamant that she needed to go back before that date in order to campaign. In an op-ed written in the *Washington Post*, she announced the date – 18 October.[47]

While in Washington, at the invitation of the president of the Middle East Institute, Ambassador Wendy Chamberlin, Benazir spoke in the historic Caucus room in the Senate Building on Capitol Hill. In the question-and-answer session which followed, her answer to how she could 'remain her own woman' in a coalition with Musharraf showed a new resolve. Describing how she was 'very much' her own person in her first term of office, but then had 'decided to be co-opted' in her second term in order to return to power, she continued: 'but I think on the third time around, being over fifty now, I would like to be my own person, even if it means not lasting very long. Because even when you try to last long by making compromises – compromises that you think will help you stay in power – you still don't stay long anyway.'[48] 'Thank you,' Wendy Chamberlin responded, impressed by 'Benazir's courage to return and stand up for what she believed in despite many warnings of increased threats'.*[49]

Two days later Benazir travelled west to give a last lecture at the Aspen Institute in Colorado.[†] 'It's a pity,' she had said to me before leaving for the United States, mindful that she'd been on the lecture circuit for over fifteen years since her first administration was dismissed, 'but when I am back in Pakistan, I won't have time.'

In this year of intense activity, Benazir had been asked to write a book, which was to have the title *Reconciliation, Islam, Democracy and the West*; the theme was the compatibility of Islam and democracy. Given her time constraints, she'd asked Mark Siegel to write a draft for her to review, which he painstakingly worked on, so that it would be ready for publication before the elections.[‡] In the summer I'd been approached by one of Dr Charis Waddy's 'Initiatives of Change' colleagues, Michael Henderson, to ask if Benazir would contribute a 'perspective' entitled 'The great forgiver' for a book he was editing called *No Enemy to Conquer*. It carried a foreword by the Dalai Lama entitled 'No peace without forgiveness', and other contributors included

---

* Ambassador Wendy Chamberlin was president of the Middle East Institute 2007–18. In relation to Benazir's security concerns, Ron Suskind (*Way of the World*, p. 268) describes Benazir receiving a telephone call from Musharraf while she was in Washington when she quoted him as saying: 'Your security is based on the state of *our* relationship.' Mark Siegel was also present when she described receiving the telephone call.

† Benazir travelled in a private plane with Zalmay Khalilzad (b.1951), who was ambassador to the UN 2007–9, having been ambassador to Iraq 2005–7.

‡ Benazir Bhutto, *Reconciliation: Islam, Democracy and the West* (Harper-Collins, published posthumously 2008) was translated into fifteen languages including Chinese and Romanian; Husain Haqqani (b.1956), former spokesman in Benazir's second administration, was consulted regarding the chapter on Islam.

Desmond Tutu and Rajmohan Gandhi, the Mahatma's grandson and a US academic. She had agreed but, since she was so busy, she asked me to provide a draft which she would look at when she came back through London. Once again I thought myself into her style of writing, focusing on one of the greatest challenges she had had in life: forgiveness.[50]

As Benazir went from one meeting to the next, seemingly gone were those awful days when all anybody would talk about was corruption. After eight years in exile, she would have the opportunity she had been waiting for to restore her reputation. The headline of Andrew Buncombe's article in *The Independent* was 'Benazir Bhutto: Pakistan's former prime minister has risen again'.[51]

14

Return to Pakistan: 2007

Whatever happens to you, you will ultimately
return here. Your place is here. The dust and
heat of Larkana are in your bones.[1]

Before returning to Pakistan, Benazir's most pressing family commitment was settling Bilawal into Oxford. On 2 October we drove to our old alma mater together, accompanied by Asif whom I had not seen since his arrest in 1996. I thought he looked older than his fifty-two years, the effects of his years of imprisonment showing on his face, his greying moustache and thinning hair. The former Pakistani high commissioner, Wajid Shamsul Hasan, who had been like a godfather to the children, came with us. Before going to Christ Church, we went to the Oxford Union. As soon as Bilawal began filling out the forms, it became apparent that he was missing some piece of identification.

'Well I am not sure that you can join without that,' Lindsey Warne, the bursar, was saying. She was obviously a little weary from overseeing new members' applications in rapid succession, and I don't think she had looked properly either at the name or who was standing in front of her. With a wry smile, and no hint of annoyance, and with me standing next to her, Benazir politely said:

'I think two former presidents of the Oxford Union are enough to vouch for him!' The bursar looked up and, slightly shocked that she hadn't instantly recognised Benazir, duly approved Bilawal's application as a life member of the Oxford Union. Our next stop was lunch at the Randolph Hotel, where we were joined by Gillian Peele. As we sat together in the dining room, the hotel's décor, with its starched white tablecloths, seemed unchanged since we were undergraduates.

At last we headed to Christ Church. Benazir could barely conceal her excitement that her son was following in her father's footsteps as well as Murtaza's. Once his suitcase was unpacked and his room set up to create good *feng shui* (which entailed moving the desk so he wouldn't be sitting with his back to the door), the time had come to say goodbye. Like any ordinary family, his parents stood proudly by the fountain in Christ Church quad to take photographs; we didn't know about 'selfies' and so we took it in turns. One photograph, which Asif took, was of Bilawal standing flanked by his mother on one side and me on the other. Several years later, when he took his degree, we returned to the fountain. As we stood proudly side by side, this time with Sunny taking the photograph, his sisters and friends standing near by, we were all painfully aware of Benazir's absence. 'How proud she would have been,' I murmured. But that was in the future; on this October day, as we bid Bilawal farewell, Benazir was so happy, tears forming in her eyes as she held the Holy Qur'an over his head and recited some verses.

The following day she had lunch scheduled with representatives from our Foreign and Commonwealth Office. Since I was in regular touch with whoever was on our FCO Pakistan desk, she had asked me to come with her. As was common knowledge, both the UK and the United States were supportive of her return to Pakistan, which was to be facilitated by the grant of immunity from any charges levelled against her and her political colleagues, embodied in the NRO (National Reconciliation Order). Amnesty was to be granted to over thirty politicians, bureaucrats, political workers and armed forces personnel, totalling over eight thousand people, accused of 'embezzlement, money laundering, murder' between 1 January 1986 and 12 October 1999, the understanding being that many of the allegations within this time-frame had been made for political reasons by political adversaries.* Nawaz Sharif would also be allowed to return to Pakistan from Saudi Arabia in order to contest the elections. Although Musharraf would step down as chief of army staff he would remain as a civilian president for five years. From the United Kingdom's and the United States' point of view, an elected civilian government working together with Musharraf, who still had the support of the military, appeared to be the best option.

Two weeks before Benazir's scheduled return the 'deal' was still being fine-tuned and, having arrived early at the Gore Hotel in South Kensington, where we were to have the FCO lunch, she sat in the car clarifying certain aspects on the phone. We then made our way to lunch, which was held in a private dining room so we could talk freely. As we discussed her return there was excitement in Benazir's voice but also apprehension. Although she joked about not knowing whether she would be arrested on arrival (even suggesting that she might give me her handbag before disembarking 'just in case'), she was hoping for a re-run of her arrival in Lahore in 1986, when she was greeted, in *New York Times* journalist Steve Weisman's words, by 'hundreds of thousands'.[2] Such a show of popular support would, she believed, demonstrate to General Musharraf (as it had to General Zia) that

---

* The NRO was issued on 5 October 2007. It was declared unconstitutional on 16 December 2009.

she and the PPP, rather than an unelected military general, had the support of the people.

'You know,' she said during our lunch, 'I recently met Sonia Gandhi in the VIP lounge at JFK in New York.' Their meeting, she assured us, was totally unexpected. Since they both had to wait for their onward flights, they had sat together talking. A focal point of their discussion was resolving the Kashmir issue as well as Benazir's concerns about the influence of Pakistan's ISI. Looking back, the vignette which she gave of herself and Rajiv Gandhi's widow, just seven years her senior, chatting like old friends was another tantalising picture of what might have happened if these two women could have overcome the prejudices and obstacles to peace in their two countries – if only, that is, Benazir had survived.*

That evening she was the guest of honour at a dinner held by the Defence and Security Forum and hosted by our mutual friend and former Conservative MP, Lady Olga Maitland. It was held at the RAF Club in Piccadilly and people were literally falling over themselves to get tickets. Her speech was Benazir at her best, explaining the challenges in a country caught in a seemingly perpetual vortex of violence and terrorism. She also described what she hoped to achieve, once more outlining her progressive liberal view of Pakistan which, she emphasised, was entirely compatible with its status as an Islamic republic. But, even as Benazir was excitedly anticipating her departure to Pakistan, she was receiving 'friendly' warnings that her life was in danger. I too was scared for her.

---

* When Benazir met Sonia Gandhi (b.1946), president of the Indian National Congress Party, during her private visit to Delhi in November 2001, 'The two leaders agreed that the Simla Agreement was the bedrock of relations between India and Pakistan': Rasheed Kidwai, '10 years on, mango memories linger', *Daily Telegraph*, 26 November 2001.

'You will take care, won't you?' I had said in the summer, when we were meeting in my home.

She looked at me intently. 'I will,' she replied, and then there was a pause. 'But life and death are in God's hands.' It was a sentiment I heard her express frequently in the weeks to come.

Benazir then left to spend the remaining time with the children in Dubai before her return to Pakistan. I had already decided that I too would travel from London to be among those accompanying her. Having been present at many of the important events in her life, I wanted to see her back home again. My daughter Alexandra said that her return was part of my life story, too. When I arrived at Heathrow on the afternoon of 17 October to take the plane to Dubai, even before heading to the departure gate, it was obvious where to go because all the familiar faces of the journalists who covered the region were there. First I saw the BBC's diplomatic editor of *Newsnight*, Mark Urban,* then Christina Lamb, who was covering her return for the *Sunday Times*. There was also Willem Marx, a friend's son, who had recently interviewed Benazir for CNBC news. Before my departure I'd been in touch with the *Sunday Telegraph*. Much as the *Spectator* had done nearly thirty years previously, the foreign editor, David Wastell, had said to get in touch in the event that Benazir's return became 'newsworthy'. Several family members came from London, including her sister Sunny, their cousin Laila, and two other cousins, Jason and Alex, the adult sons of her cousin Poncho – Prince Sidi Mohammed Muzzafar Khan as he was formally known, having descended on his father's side from the Nawab of Sachin, a former princely state in Surat district in western India.† After supporting Benazir

---

* Mark Urban (b.1961), journalist, historian and broadcaster.
† Prince Muzzafar Khan's mother was Zulfikar Ali Bhutto's elder sister, Mumtaz.

emotionally during her years in exile, they all wanted to witness her momentous return.

The journey was raucous, the plane full of Pakistani supporters and well-wishers, constantly raising the familiar slogan 'Jeeay Bhutto! Jeaay Benazir!' With many not bothering to keep their seat belts fastened, one person would stand up in order to start shouting a slogan and numerous others would follow in noisy competition, until there were more people standing than sitting. As soon as the plane had gone quiet, another 'Jeeay Bhutto' would be uttered followed by the usual refrain 'Jeeay Benazir', and so the process of sitting and standing began all over again. As we flew through the night, it became clear that many Pakistanis were not used to unlimited free alcohol, with detrimental effects in the aisles. Alexandra had given me Jodi Picoult's novel, Mercy, to read. It was an anguished story and perhaps not the best distraction from the surrounding mayhem. Now, whenever I see Picoult's books, I think of that journey and Benazir's return.

It was early morning when we reached Dubai and I immediately sent Benazir a message to tell her I'd arrived. As soon as she reached the airport she replied telling me to come to a particular lounge, where members of the press were already gathering to await her press conference.

'Oh hi Vicks! You look nice,' she said, as soon as she saw me, the compliment being for the shalwar kameez I'd changed into.

Asif, Itty and Aseefa were with her. The children were both saying that they wanted to go with her to Karachi but Benazir said firmly, 'No, you've got school.' In the press conference, she explained once again why she was going back and what she hoped to achieve. 'My return heralds for the people of Pakistan the turn in the wheel, from dictatorship to democracy, from exploitation to empowerment, from violence to peace.' It was, she said, not just a personal journey but the beginning of a journey for the people of Pakistan. She also said how grateful she was to the Pakistani expatriate community and thanked them for all the warmth they had shown her.[3]

Finally we boarded the Emirates flight to Karachi. Once more, the stewardesses had a challenging time because, instead of taking their allocated seats, many people just sat where they wanted in order to be as close as possible to Benazir. Although she was separated from them in first class, they thought that, when she got off the plane they could exit as soon as possible after her to take up their places in her retinue of supporters. But having so many people in the front of the plane affected the weight distribution. The stewardesses had the unpopular task of going through the plane to check every passenger's boarding pass and then redirecting those who had moved to the front to their allocated seats so the plane could take off.

Once we were airborne, Benazir walked through the aisles to greet her supporters, accompanied by more slogan raising. As soon as we touched down, but before we got to the gate, almost everyone who was on the plane again rushed forward. Yet again they had to be directed back to their seats, Benazir herself speaking through the loudspeaker to request everyone to respect what the stewardesses were asking so that the plane could reach the gate. Given the emotional significance of setting foot on Pakistani soil once more, instead of leaving the plane via a modern gangway that would take her directly into the airport, she insisted that old-fashioned steps be brought to the side of the plane so that her feet could actually touch the ground as she emerged. Having already exited by means of the gangway, Sunny and I were standing watching as Benazir at last appeared. Dressed in a green *shalwar kameez*, the signature white veil worn loosely on her head and holding a copy of the Qur'an, there were tears in her eyes as she knelt down and kissed the ground. She had finally come home.

As with her return in 1986, thousands – some said millions – had come to the Jinnah International Airport. A special open-top truck had been organised for her to progress along the road leading from the airport before turning right on the Shahrah-e-Faisal road towards the Mazar-e-Quaid – the large white domed mausoleum where Mohammed Ali Jinnah, the founder of Pakistan, was buried – from where she intended to make a home-coming speech. Among those on the top of the truck were her party colleagues, most of whom I knew well: Naheed Khan, her political secretary; the PPP senior vice-chairman, Makhdoom Ameen Faheem; former defence minister Aftab Shaban Mirani; former interior minister Aitzaz Ahsan; PPP information secretary Sherry Rehman; and Abida Hussain, who had been a Nawaz supporter but had recently joined the PPP. Then there were family members: her cousin, Tariq, Aunty Manna's son, as well as Laila, Jason and Alex, plus some Dubai friends and Timmy Zardari, her stepmother-in-law. Sunny went straight to Bilawal House (kindly taking with her my hand luggage, which included my laptop).

Part of our entourage was a contingent of police. There was also a cordon of young party workers in white T-shirts, the *jaan nisaar Benazir* (those willing to give their lives for Benazir), who followed on foot beside the truck with their arms linked, putting themselves in the firing line should the worst come to pass. I took up a position on the top of the truck on the right and for a long time I stood watching the joyful crowds in the sunlight. Some had climbed up the trees along the roadside to get a better view. Green, white and red PPP flags fluttered from every lamp post. For the early part of the journey, Benazir stood in the front of the truck, her white *dupatta* on her head. She looked elated as she waved continuously to the crowds cheering her on her way. 'I kept looking around me in amazement,' she later wrote, 'remembering other rallies and other campaigns. I also remembered past tragedies as well as past triumphs.'[4] If Benazir needed to sit down she could go to the lower deck of the truck by means of a moving platform in an enclosed shaft at the back to a special rest area which had been prepared for her.

A local 'press' bus and literally hundreds of cars were following behind. During our slow progress as we left the precincts of the airport, various members of the foreign press climbed onto the top of the truck in the hope of doing a brief interview with Benazir: one was Carlotta Gall working for the *New York Times*;[5] another was Christina Lamb. By this time, Benazir had left the front of the truck and was sitting chatting to her supporters and to other members of the press, who came and went, her place at the front temporarily taken by Fahmida Mirza, a PPP member of the National Assembly, whose husband, Zulfikar Mirza, home minister for Sindh, had been responsible for organising the logistics of the journey. As we continued onwards, while Benazir rested her feet, Fahmida, also wearing a white *dupatta*, waved on her behalf.

As we reached Star Gate, at the junction of Shahrah-e-Faisal road, darkness had already fallen and hundreds of doves were released, fluttering up into the night sky. One dove came to rest on Benazir's shoulder and stayed there for a while. We were given slices of hot pizza which we consumed hungrily. I passed the time talking to Tariq, discussing the significance of her return. We both agreed with the generally held view that she had picked the perfect time to come back to Pakistan, both in terms of her own increasing popularity and Musharraf's waning authority. Around 11 p.m. Benazir left the top of the truck to go down below and work on the speech she was going to give when we reached the Mazar-e-Quaid. Naheed accompanied her. Having come directly from London, with hardly any sleep, I settled down on one of the few available chairs and was beginning to doze off.

We'd already been advancing slowly for six hours, Tariq having reliably informed me that, at the pace we were going, it would take another five hours before we reached our destination, just over ten miles away, which, in normal circumstances, would take about half an hour by car. A half moon was shining and my dozing was intermittently interrupted as the crowd continued to roar in excitement. Suddenly, without warning, there was a loud explosion, the impact of which literally blew me out of my chair. When I opened my eyes I found myself crouching on the floor of the top deck.

At first, disbelief and confusion made me wonder whether the explosion might have been caused by a particularly big firework. But then Tariq, who was beside me, said 'no, that was a bomb blast'. Christina Lamb, who had remained on the truck and had been talking to Aitzaz Ahsan, was shouting 'we're a target, we have to get off'. But we found ourselves staring into a black abyss; whatever street lighting there was had been extinguished. The only way off was to descend the narrow vertical ladder on the back of the truck by which we had originally climbed aboard. But this seemed far too exposed. Another possible exit would be to jump from the top deck but again that had its dangers. While we deliberated what to do, another voice was heard, saying: 'No, we must stay where we are, there could be another explosion.' I remember lying down and thinking that I must do what I was told and I would be all right.

As we lay huddled together, the truck was shaken by another more deafening blast. Its impact was on the left, and those who were on that side were splattered with blood as well as pieces of flesh, which showered us all. A shard of glass hit Faheem's forehead. In the pandemonium of the moment, I was desperately worried about Benazir. Was she all right? What had been the impact of the explosion on the lower deck, where a fire was already raging? After the second blast Christina was again saying that we had to get off. Still hesitant about either jumping off the top of the truck (as some people later did) or going down the vertical ladder into the darkness, I thought the best way down was by means of the enclosed shaft which had been Benazir's means of getting to the lower deck. Although, without power, the platform was no longer able to go up and down mechanically, the fact of being enclosed at least provided some protection from whatever might assail us from outside. With a PPP party worker holding her hand, Christina made her way down, followed by someone else, and then it was my turn to be guided down into the darkness below. I called out to Christina, but she had already been picked up by someone in one of the cars which had been following the truck.

The first sight to confront me was the body of a dead police-man lying in the street. The pavement was strewn with mangled metal and shards of glass as well as quantities of shoes, their owners now prostrate around us.

'Where is Benazir, is she safe?' I asked a group of people standing around.

'Yes, she got away,' said Aftab Mirani, who'd also made it down from the top deck.

A voice from the crowd said: 'It was a suicide attack – I've just seen a head.' Fearing the truck might explode, I began to run.

'Where do you want to go,' I heard someone calling from a passing car.

'To Bilawal House,' I responded.

'OK then, I'll take you.'

As we drove through the darkened streets of Karachi, my mind was racing. If an attack could be made on Benazir at the moment of her return, what could happen next?

By the time I reached Bilawal House, crowds had begun to gather outside. The festive lights which had been put up to greet Benazir's arrival seemed grimly inappropriate after the bloodshed we'd witnessed. I went inside to find her sitting with members of her family and her political colleagues. The television was on and pictures of the fire and the wrecked truck, as well as bodies being carried on stretchers to the hospital, were flashing across the screen. I had been with Benazir during some of her darkest days, when she was fighting for her father's life in the late 1970s; now, in the aftermath of the bomb attack on the truck, she showed me the same affection that she always had: 'Come sit,' she said. 'I am just so relieved that you are safe.'

Combined with the shock and trauma of what we had just experienced were feelings of tremendous disappointment that a day, which had begun so gloriously in the sunshine, had ended so disastrously.

'A day of triumph has turned into tragedy,' said Benazir. There was no bitterness in her voice, but perhaps an awful realisation that her situation was as dangerous as certain 'friendly' governments – later revealed to be the UAE and Saudi Arabia – had been warning.*

As we talked and sipped tea, more and more people arrived including many who had been on the truck, like her cousins, Jason, Alex and Laila and also Timmy. Absent from the gathering was Abida Hussain, who had hurt herself by jumping from the top of the truck, and had had to go to hospital. With each new arrival, Benazir stood up and greeted them warmly, expressing her relief that they were unharmed. Our conversation then turned to her security arrangements. What had gone wrong? How had a suicide bomber apparently forced his way through the crowd? Had the bomb been placed in a car that had been left unattended? Most importantly, how many of the brave young *jaan nisaar* had perished in an attempt to protect her?

---

* Afghanistan and the USA had also sent warnings.

'It was the boys walking by the side of the truck as a human shield who protected us,' she continued. 'That, and the fact that the truck was armour-plated; otherwise we might all have died.'

Reviewing our slow progress, our attention focused on the ominous dimming of the street lights, which had bothered Benazir and had led her to ask Sherry to raise her concerns with the authorities. As darkness fell, with only intermittent search-lights illuminating the crowd, it was impossible to see from where danger might come. Rooftops crammed full of people could have provided easy cover for snipers; while a well-directed grenade thrown from a bridge could have eliminated us all. But somehow the carnival atmosphere had allayed our fears. Benazir also described her escape. Having moved from the front of the lower deck to the back, she was still working on her speech when the first explosion hit.

'I ducked because my husband had always told me if anything happens to duck.'

It wasn't until after the second explosion that she escaped from the truck to the safety of a back-up security car. We talked late into the night, the television screen flickering with pictures of the scene, the damaged truck still surrounded by police and ambulances. More shocking and distressing were the rising numbers of dead, which had already reached well over one hundred, with over four hundred wounded.

It was almost morning by the time we got to bed. I was sleeping in Bilawal's room. It was not the room of a nineteen-year-old but – given the family's eight-year absence – that of a child. A frieze of painted animals still danced across the walls. I opened one cupboard and found piles of clothes fit for a pre-teenager. By the time I woke, Benazir was up and dressed, making phone calls, thanking people for the messages which she'd received from across the country and the world. Even her political rivals, including

Nawaz Sharif and MQM leader, Altaf Hussain, had expressed relief that she was safe; so too had Musharraf. But she interpreted his warnings as designed to intimidate her and prevent her from campaigning.

'We can't let them force us to quit,' she said – 'them' being the shadowy figures behind the attack.

Cups of tea came and went. It must have been strange for her to be sitting in the living room of her home as though everything had been frozen in time, the photographs of her young children staring out at her, reminders of a life nearly a decade earlier.

With international interest in Benazir's presence heightened after the attack, she gave an impromptu press conference in the gardens of Bilawal House, where a large *shamiana* had been erected. A battery of cameras was assembled at the back, a reminder that the number of news media outlets, both foreign and domestic, had mushroomed since Benazir was last in Pakistan. Describing what had happened, Benazir maintained that it was an attack on democracy and on the empowerment of the people, a sinister warning that political leaders could not go out and campaign because if they did so they risked being bombed. 'The attack was not on me. The attack was on what I represent… We will not stop our struggle,' she concluded.[6]

One of the journalists present was Bruce Loudon, who'd been in Islamabad during Zulfikar Ali Bhutto's appeal against the death sentence. He was now working for the *Australian* and had come from Sydney. There were other familiar faces: Bronwen Maddox of *The Times* and Christina, who wrote a two-page spread in the *Sunday Times* describing the attack and our escape from the truck: 'It was what we feared, but hoped would never happen.' I'd also written a short article for the *Sunday Telegraph*, describing how I had been 'blown from my seat' when the bomb went off.[7] Much as Benazir was thankful that we had survived, the recorded number of dead had risen to more than 150 and she spent another afternoon meeting the bereaved families, embracing the grieving women. I sat near by, thinking of the woman I had known when Benazir had first embarked on her political journey. Then she had been young and bold, now she was still defiant but also maternal.

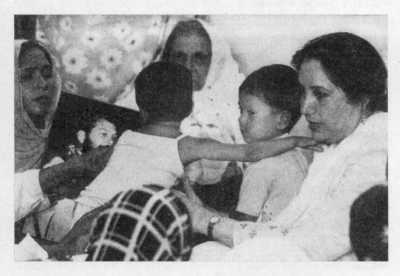

Benazir comforts the children of those killed in the suicide bomb attack October 2007. *'I sat nearby, thinking of the woman I had known when Benazir had first embarked on her political journey. Then she had been young and bold, now she was still defiant but also maternal.'*

Soon after arriving in Karachi, Benazir had intended to go to the family home at Naudero to visit the graveyard at Garhi Khuda Bakhsh. In her absence the large mausoleum she had been planning for nearly twenty years had almost been completed. But her safety remained a matter of deep concern and the visit was temporarily postponed. Under tight security she did, however, go to the Mazar-e-Quaid to give her speech. I didn't go with her but, as she later wrote, 'this was the speech – both in substance and in symbol – that would show the world that the people of Pakistan wanted, even demanded, a transition to democracy as soon as possible, and rejected the politics of dictatorship'.[8]

Among those who came to call on Benazir at Bilawal House was the American ambassador, Anne Patterson. She was accompanied by our old friend Elizabeth Colton, who had known Murtaza and Shahnawaz from her time working as a journalist in the Middle East in the 1980s; she'd also met and interviewed Benazir in Karachi soon after her return to Pakistan in 1986. Having joined the US foreign service in the State Department in 2000, she was now working as the ambassador's press attaché and spokesperson.* 'The Ambassador was very eager to show her support for Benazir,' explained Liz, 'which is why we came so quickly from Islamabad to see her.'[9]

My flight was booked to return to England on 24 October. It had been a long week and saying goodbye to Benazir was harder than ever. The night before we had dinner together. Timmy had brought fish cooked in a special way which Benazir liked. We all sat together in her wood-panelled study with our food on plates on our laps. Benazir looked tired and had a cold. She ate very little, before saying she must go to bed. I stood up to hug her goodbye. 'Catch you later,' she said, that same kindness in her smile. 'And thank you for coming.' Early the following morning, Sunny and I left together for London. We were both crying. I had a heart-wrenching feeling that I would never see Benazir again. And I never did. On 27 December she was assassinated after addressing an election rally at Liaquat Bagh in Rawalpindi.

---

* Anne W. Patterson (b.1949) was US ambassador to Pakistan 2007–10.

15

Assassination

A great and brave friend.[1]

After returning from Pakistan in late October I had sent several messages to Benazir to let her know that I was thinking of her. In early November President Musharraf announced a state of emergency on account of the 'visible ascendancy in the activities of the extremists and incidents of terrorist attacks'.[2] Yet again in Pakistan's turbulent history the constitution was suspended, elections postponed and political leaders, including Benazir, were briefly put under house arrest.* I immediately wrote again expressing my concern. Soon afterwards another announcement was made stating that elections would be held after all. As the days passed and our shops in London filled with Christmas paraphernalia, I began to relax. I hoped maybe the intense fear I had felt when I had said goodbye to Benazir was irrational, that she would get through the election campaign and all would be well.

Even so the events of 18 October kept replaying in my mind. What if the suicide bombers had been successful? What if we all

---

* The state of emergency lasted from 3 November to 15 December 2007.

had died? And so, in this limbo period, when the future was still uncertain, I decided to record the story of our friendship, if only so that our children would understand how it had all begun. In December I wrote again to Benazir to explain my motivation.

> What I have witnessed has been extraordinary and unique, inspired of course from the start by our friendship – from the time I first came to Pakistan, so comparatively young and naive, when the world ironically seemed to be a safer place in that there were no suicide bombings... That whole year I spent... I still think is critical in terms of understanding what is going on today: Zia promoting the religious parties, backed by the West because of Afghanistan, mercilessly executing your father...; and all that has happened since then, to which I have been an eye-witness, including my own trips into Kashmir during the insurgency in order to understand that complex and ongoing dispute.[3]

Benazir did not answer immediately. Understandably she was busy, campaigning for the elections, now scheduled for 8 January 2008. But when she had time to write, she responded, saying she was 'thrilled' and thanking me for suggesting she might want to read what I wrote. 'I appreciate it. You are a wonderful friend.' With all the sadness that was to come was the realisation, from the date of her email, that she had written to me the day before she died.[4]

As the enormity of Benazir's assassination began to sink in, I tried to picture how the last day of her life must have begun: the ritual of getting up and dressed, mentally focusing on the last speech she was to give at the conclusion of the election campaign. First she had agreed to meet the Afghan president, Hamid Karzai,* who was in Islamabad on a two-day visit;[5] then, in the afternoon, accompanied by Naheed Khan, the forty-five minute journey from her home to Rawalpindi, the sense of anticipation when her land cruiser became surrounded by an enthusiastic crowd as she neared Liaquat Bagh, entering the open space, crammed full of people eager to listen to her mesmeric delivery:

'I will save Pakistan, you will save Pakistan, we will save PAKISTAN,' she roared, as she openly challenged the militants who had tried to replace Pakistan's flag with their own in Swat. She was referring to the attempts of the recently formed radical group, the Tehrik-i Taliban (TTP), which aimed to take control of Swat district and impose Sharia law.† No one, she said, no one will be allowed to do that.[6] Then, once she'd finished her speech, there was the walk down the steps to get back into the land cruiser, the slogan-chanting and the decision to stand up to acknowledge her supporters as she departed.

'She was happy,' responded Makhdoom Ameen Faheem, who was also in the land cruiser, when I questioned him on her decision to stand up. 'Everything had gone well. She wanted to thank the people.'[7] And then the shot, the explosion, killing over twenty from among the crowd, followed by noise and confusion, Benazir falling back through the sunroof with Naheed sitting cradling her bleeding head in her lap. Since the tyres of the land cruiser had been blown, after some distance she had to be carefully transferred into Sherry Rehman's car to take her as quickly as possible

---

* Hamid Karzai (b.1957) was president of Afghanistan 2001–14.

† The Tehrik-i Taliban Pakistan (TTP) was founded in December 2007 when thirteen militant groups came together to fight against the Pakistani state. The battle for Swat continued for several years: in 2012 Malala Yusufzai (b.1997) was shot in the head while coming home from school, and two other girls were also targeted.

to Rawalpindi General Hospital. 'Her covering car had gone off,' explained Sherry, 'which is why my car opted to follow as a precautionary measure and she had to be shifted into it for her last journey.'[8] Finally there was the doctors' desperate attempt to revive her, only to realise that her life had already ebbed away.

To me Benazir's assassination was reminiscent of that of President John F. Kennedy, or even 9/11, events of such impact that long afterwards people could still remember where they were and what they were doing when they heard the news. Within that instant the hopes of the millions who supported her were irreversibly shattered. It seemed unbearably cruel that her three children could so suddenly have lost their mother, her sister her only surviving sibling, and her husband (who had spent over half of their twenty-year marriage in jail) his wife. Her extended family and friends were likewise abruptly bereft of the presence of an iconic woman, whose political journey they had followed, in my case, since those early days at Oxford in the 1970s. Tragically, the expectation that she could make a difference, which she so earnestly wanted to do, was now no more than that; we would never know what, as a woman in her political prime, she could have achieved for the people of Pakistan and on the world stage.

Following Muslim custom, her funeral had to take place as soon as possible before the second sunset. I watched the television in stunned disbelief as I saw her simple wooden coffin taken out of the hospital in Rawalpindi where she had been pronounced dead, a throng of people accompanying her journey to a waiting vehicle, which would take her to the airport to carry her back to Sindh. She was returning, as she knew she would, to be buried at Garhi Khuda Bakhsh. The photographs of Sunny and the children standing by her grave, piled high with rose petals, showed their faces overcome with grief.

Three days of mourning were called as Musharraf suddenly had to deal with the wrath of the people, who thought that he had been negligent in protecting her. That the scene of her assassination had been washed down so quickly, destroying vital evidence,* seemed to indicate collusion by the government.[9] When a spokesman from the interior ministry announced that, rather than being hit by an assassin's bullet (as was believed from camera footage showing a man pointing a gun at Benazir as she stood in the land cruiser), her death had been caused by her striking her head on the sunroof, her supporters were furious at what appeared to be an attempt to belittle her 'martyrdom'. In an eruption of anger and despair, thousands came out onto the streets, burning shops, buses and cars. So great was the unrest in Pakistan that the elections were postponed until February 2008.

In the days afterwards, I was in and out of BBC studios. Reports filled the newspapers and the internet, their dramatic headlines – 'Fears rise as Bhutto falls' – 'Turmoil after Bhutto killed' – 'Bhutto assassinated' – once more underlining the awful finality of her death.[10] Suddenly everyone was talking about Benazir, those who had been close to her sharing what they had found special about their friendship. I made my contribution to the coverage in an article headlined 'Benazir Bhutto: A great and brave friend'.[11] But having only just begun my memoir about our friendship, I set it aside. With her assassination, it was too soon, the last chapter of what I would write too raw.

Following the outcry over the cause of Benazir's death, Musharraf agreed that a team from Scotland Yard's Metropolitan Police Counter Terrorism Command (SO15) should go to Pakistan in

---

* The streets were also washed down after the October attack. See Musharraf's memoirs, *In the Line of Fire* (Free Press, 2006), pp.246, 249, in which he recognises how crucial small pieces of evidence were in determining the perpetrators of the assassination attempts on his life in 2003.

early January to establish 'the cause and circumstances'. After over two weeks of extensive enquiries, the team's report concluded that 'the only tenable cause for the rapidly fatal head injury in this case is that it occurred as the result of impact due to the effects of the bomb blast'. But Benazir's supporters refused to accept that she had not been killed by a bullet from an assassin rather than by the explosion. 'The plan,' observed Aitzaz Ahsan, Benazir's former minister for the interior in her first government, 'was to immobilise the vehicle by the explosion so that Benazir would have to exit and then snipers would target her. It was the same strategy as in Karachi but in October she had managed to escape into a back-up car. The issue of her standing up in the land cruiser was an unexpected "advantage" for the assassins.'[12]

PPP members were also disappointed at Scotland Yard's narrow focus which left 'the wider investigation to establish culpability' up to the Pakistani authorities. Although Baitullah Mehsud, the leader of the TTP whom Musharraf had blamed,* denied his involvement, in the shadowy aftermath, without forensic evidence and a full investigation, including autopsies on the other fatalities, how, people were asking, could they verify his denial? Most importantly, did the order emanate from within the TTP or from somewhere else?[13]

In 2009 a United Nations commission of enquiry was appointed by secretary-general Ban Ki-moon which also focused on the arrangements for Benazir's security:

A range of Government officials failed profoundly in their efforts first to protect Ms. Bhutto and second to investigate with vigour all those responsible for her murder, not only in the execution of the attack, but also in its conception, planning

---

* Baitullah Mehsud (c.1972–2009) was killed in an American drone attack.

and financing. Responsibility for Ms. Bhutto's security on the day of her assassination rested with the Federal Government, the Government of Punjab and the Rawalpindi District Police. None of these entities took necessary measures to respond to the extraordinary, fresh and urgent security risks that they knew she faced.[14]

The UN report went on to describe how the collection of twenty-three pieces of evidence 'was manifestly inadequate in a case that should have resulted in thousands... The one instance in which the authorities reviewed these actions, the Punjab (provincial) committee of inquiry into the hosing down of the crime scene, was a whitewash. Hosing down the crime scene so soon after the blast goes beyond mere incompetence; it is up to the relevant authorities to determine whether this amounts to criminal responsibility.'[15]

In 2014 the head of the three-man investigating team, the Chilean diplomat, Heraldo Muñoz, published his book, *Getting Away with Murder*. From the pages of his narrative emerged a dismal account of failure to assume responsibility and a lack of transparency, highlighting collusion and cover-up. 'We will probably never know with full certainty who killed Benazir, who was behind the planning of the assassination, or who organised and funded the execution of the murder,' concluded Muñoz. 'There are pieces of the murder puzzle but painfully few elements to put them all together.'[16]

And so the mystery remained and those responsible went unpunished. Both Christina Lamb and Owen Bennett-Jones, BBC correspondent in Islamabad during Benazir's second administration in the 1990s, also undertook considerable research, recording their findings in well-sourced articles.[17] But, although suspicions focused on the four men Benazir herself had warned the authorities might want to kill her, proving guilt was much harder.* In Benazir's long and tangled relationship with the Pakistan army there seemed little doubt that certain individuals felt threatened by her return to power. But would they order her death? In September 2007, when she was speaking at the Middle East Institute in Washington, Benazir had been asked whether she would allow the nuclear scientist, Dr A. Q. Khan, then under house arrest in Pakistan for sharing nuclear technology with Libya, North Korea and Iran, to be interviewed. Her response was 'no' to Western access but 'yes' to that of the International Atomic Energy Authority (IAEA).† By sanctioning a line of enquiry which would inevitably involve scrutinising the role of the Pakistan army, had she, Owen asked in his documentary *The Assassination*, provided a motive for her assassination?[18]

Immediately after her death, discussions within the PPP hierarchy focused on Benazir's successor as chairman of the PPP. Following her assassination, the family's loyal nanny, Ceta, had rushed from Dubai with an envelope which Benazir had left before she had returned to Pakistan in October. It contained her 'political will', dated 16 October, in which, to everyone's surprise, she had named Asif as her successor 'in the interim' as the person who could keep the party together. So amazed were her supporters that she should have handed over control of the PPP to her husband, that almost immediately people began to say that the 'will' was forged. Her handwriting looked authentic to me and,

---

* The four men were the intelligence bureau chief Ijaz Shah, who in 2019 became federal minister of the interior; the former chief minister of the Punjab Chaudhry Pervaiz Elahi (b.1945); the former chief minister of Sindh, Arbab Ghulam Rahim (b.1956); and the former ISI chief, Hamid Gul.
† Mark Siegel was present at the Middle East Institute when she made this response; Mark Siegel to me, email, 1 April 2020. Dr A. Q. Khan was released from house arrest in 2009 but not permitted to leave the country.

failing any other instruction to the contrary, her wishes were observed. To placate the party stalwarts who might object to Asif's influence, nineteen-year-old Bilawal was named co-chairman, the use of 'Bhutto' emphasised in his name. His little-known face immediately flashed up on television screens as, in taking up his mother's political mantle, he repeated her words: 'democracy is the best revenge'.[19]

In early 2008, just days after his mother's assassination, Bilawal arrived in England in order to return to Oxford. The world's press knew virtually nothing about him and pressure was mounting for him to be interviewed. Asif had remained in Pakistan and so it was left to the former high commissioner, Wajid Shamsul Hasan, Sunny – who'd come home after the funeral – and me to work out what was best. Our concern was that Bilawal should have some privacy while he was at Oxford, so that, despite his now high-profile status as a political leader, he could lead a normal student life. Instead of giving several interviews, we decided that he should give a press conference, which would burst the bubble of expectation and give the journalists the much-needed quotations and photographs for their articles. He would also make the plea for privacy, such as Prince William and Prince Harry had been granted after Princess Diana's death a decade previously.

When one of our Oxford friends, Simon Walker, telephoned me to ask if there was anything he could do, I immediately enlisted his help to chair the press conference. Simon had been commu-nications secretary to the Queen and would, I hoped, be able to field any awkward questions, especially in relation to the dynastic implications of Bilawal's position, and the ever-present issue of corruption. I also thought it would help Bilawal to have the pro-tective assistance of one of his mother's old friends.

Not surprisingly, all the senior journalists came on that cold January day to the basement of the Gore Hotel in South

Kensington, where we had booked a room. I saw familiar faces, among them Lyse Doucet and Jeremy Paxman, well known for his interrogative interviewing style, and many others.* 'What really stayed with me was how packed the room was,' recalled Lyse, 'and that sense of anticipation as Bilawal took this first step into this huge role. I was also taken by the pillars who supported him – the people who had walked with his mother. Their sense of duty was also so palpable.' Watching Bilawal, my heart went out to him as he stood reading his prepared speech. In addition to asking for privacy, he attempted to explain the reasons why he had become co-chairman of the PPP: 'The precedent was set when my grandfather was executed, my grandmother, Begum Nusrat Bhutto became chairman; as you know my mother then assumed this role. The important thing now is for the party to face the challenge of the forthcoming general election with a united front. And so I urge you to accept that, for the greater good of the party, the continuity of my family's involvement was considered best.' When it came to the Q and A, I thought he handled the questions brilliantly, difficult as some questions were, with Paxman challenging Bilawal on perpetuating a political dynasty and what he described as 'the sense of inherited right'.[20]

Within days Bilawal was back in Oxford, to be embraced by the group of friends he had made in his first term. Soon afterwards, on 17 January, the Oxford Union held 'the Benazir Bhutto memorial debate', in observance of the tradition that the house would adjourn for a minute's silence whenever an ex-president of the Union had died. Sunny was present with Bilawal. Our friend, Alan Duncan, MP, gave a tribute, as did I, both of us describing the charismatic woman we had been so lucky to have known.†

---

* Jeremy Paxman (b. 1950), presenter for BBC Two's *Newsnight* 1989–2014.
† On 15 May 2008 Dr Frances Lannon organised the Benazir Bhutto Memorial

Meanwhile Itty and Aseefa, soon to turn eighteen and fifteen respectively, had returned to Dubai, where they too had to pick up the routine of school but with an immense void in their lives. Begum Bhutto was still in Dubai but in the advanced stages of Alzheimer's. I'm not sure if she ever understood that her elder daughter had been assassinated – which meant that, before her own death in 2011, she had lost three of her four children.

In the aftermath of Benazir's assassination, relationships re-formed, friends who had known her clinging together because of her. For me the most important relationship was with her sister Sunny. I had always been Benazir's friend and so we were only inter-mittently in touch unless her 'sis', as she called her, was in town. Now, in her sister's absence, we began to forge a closer friendship.

Our next priority after Bilawal's press conference was to arrange a 'memorial reception' for all those in and near London who would want to pay their respects to Benazir. The date was fixed for 10 February 2008 and the location was the Intercontinental Hotel in the heart of London, close to where Benazir used to love to walk in Hyde Park. I invited all the Oxford friends I could think of who, over the years, had come to all those dinner parties, and many more besides. We also invited journalists and the members of parliament Benazir knew who had been consistently concerned about her well-being. Among them was Norman Lamont, who had remained in touch with Benazir throughout her time in exile and whom I asked to say a few words.* His tribute to Benazir included narrating an amusing episode when, not long after meeting her

Lecture at Lady Margaret Hall, with guest speaker Sir Mark Lyall Grant, former British high commissioner in Pakistan. On 15 November 2019 former prime minister Theresa May gave the inaugural Benazir Bhutto Memorial Lecture at the Oxford Union. There were numerous other tribute meetings.

* The Rt Hon. the Lord Lamont of Lerwick, PC (b.1942) was chancellor of the exchequer 1990–93.

for the first time, he had encountered her at Nice airport. 'I saw this woman walking around 50 yards away from me who looked just like Benazir, but I thought it couldn't possibly be her because she would have had a retinue of people with her. When she went into the Duty Free, I thought I would follow her to see if it really was her. She was in the queue and I went up behind her. Without turning around, I suddenly heard her familiar voice saying "Hello, Mr Lamont"'– her astute awareness taking the former chancellor of the exchequer by surprise.[21]

We then showed a short film, which the Pakistani TV journalist and documentary film maker Farah Durrani had offered to make, using clips from some of her interviews with Benazir, which charted the progress of Benazir's life and political career. There were few dry eyes when we turned the lights back on again. Wajid Shamsul Hasan spoke movingly about the woman he had loyally supported as high commissioner in London. Afterwards we had tea and cakes which, with Benazir's famously sweet tooth, we thought she would have enjoyed. It was touching to see groups of people gathered to reminisce and share their favourite stories about her. There was laughter too, as people remembered Benazir's good humour and sense of fun.

Elections in Pakistan had been rescheduled for 18 February. When the results were announced, the PPP had won 118 seats, the Pakistan Muslim League (N) 89 seats, while Musharraf's party, the Pakistan Muslim League (Q) won only 50 seats. Bilawal had been too young to contest, the minimum age being twenty-five. A party stalwart, Yusuf Raza Gilani, became prime minister, while Asif remained as co-chairman.* As I watched the television

---

* Yusuf Raza Gilani (b.1952) was prime minister of Pakistan 2008–12. The

coverage and the faces of those standing near by, I knew that there was no one among them who wasn't wishing that it were Benazir taking the oath of office. For the third time since the end of the Zia military dictatorship, the PPP was in power, briefly going into coalition with the PML (N) before old rivalries resurfaced.

Soon afterwards, Benazir's book, *Reconciliation: Islam, Democracy, and the West* was published posthumously. Her old friend from Harvard, Peter Galbraith, who had played such a tenacious role in securing her release from house arrest in 1984, wrote a fitting comment for the cover: 'Pakistan has become the critical battlefield in the so-called war on terror. *Reconciliation* is the story of a courageous woman and her struggle for democracy and moderation in Islam. Benazir Bhutto, not the extremists who killed her, represented the vast majority of Pakistani Muslims, and this book is a reminder of how much we have lost.'[22] In Benazir's absence, I was asked to take on the role of promoting the book at various London events, one of which was *Start the Week* with Andrew Marr.* Still coming to terms with her death myself, I felt like I was standing in for her because she was on a trip abroad, not because she was never coming back.

When I returned to Pakistan for the first time since her death in August 2008, the first thing to strike me was that the airport I had flown into so many times was now called 'Benazir Bhutto International Airport'. While in Islamabad I wanted to go to Liaquat Bagh in Rawalpindi where she had been assassinated. The sun was shining and the streets were clean, with just a few people strolling in the park. It was hard to believe that it had been the scene of such chaos and carnage nine months previously. A stall at

coalition with the PML(N) fell apart and the PPP went into coalition with smaller regional parties including the Awami National Party (ANP).

* *Start the Week*, BBC Radio 4, presented by Andrew Marr, 4 February 2008.

the entrance to the park had been set up, displaying photographs of Benazir on that last fateful day, with a red-and-white garland of flowers around her neck. Amjad Yusuf, a Kashmiri political activist I'd met through my work on Kashmir, who had corresponded with Benazir about Kashmir, had offered to accompany me. As a 'souvenir' he bought me a photograph of her from the stall. It now sits on my desk at home in London, her courageous face looking out at me as I write.

One evening during this 2008 visit I went to see Asif. I'd known him ever since the wedding but, without his wife, I now felt reticent – the Englishwoman, 'Benazir's friend', whom his children called Aunty.

'You know,' I said tentatively, 'you can always rely on me to help the children if there is something you need in England, especially while Bilawal is at Oxford.' There was a pause. I continued somewhat shakily. 'Of course I don't want to intrude but I just wanted you to know I am always there for them.'

Asif looked at me intently and then spoke slowly. 'Yes of course. You must stay in touch with them. You know they smell her on you.'[23]

Nearly two years later, when I was in Karachi, I determined to go to Garhi Khuda Bakhsh to visit Benazir's grave. With the PPP government in power, Asif had become president of Pakistan in succession to Musharraf.* Although I could have taken a commercial flight to Sukkur, he had put the chief minister of Sindh's plane at my disposal. But it developed a technical fault before take-off and so I made the 250 mile (400 km) journey from Karachi

---

* Asif Ali Zardari was president of Pakistan 2008–13. The PPP government was the first to finish its term of office and stand for re-election. On 8 April 2010 the 18th amendment to the Constitution was passed, removing the power of the president to dissolve parliament unilaterally. In June 2019 Zardari was arrested on charges of corruption; he remains on medical bail.

by helicopter. Passing at low altitude over the parched desert of Sindh, we approached the lands watered by the irrigation system of the Indus river as it snaked its way onwards, a patchwork of fields spread out beneath me. Finally, from the helicopter, for the first time I saw the white-domed mausoleum, looking like a modern Taj Mahal. As soon as the helicopter landed, I went directly to the mausoleum.

On entering, I took off my shoes, relishing the cool of the marble on my hot feet. Passing under an archway, I found myself looking at a gigantic portrait of Benazir. It was not a family birth or death anniversary, when thousands traditionally converge and so, with the exception of some villagers who had come in from the fields, and a few attendants, the mausoleum was empty. When I approached, one of the attendants came forward to offer me a basket of rose petals to scatter. Benazir's grave, covered in a red velvet cloth, was next to her father's, which now had an ornate marble canopy.[24] As I grasped a handful of rose petals, I thought again of my first visit to Garhi Khuda Bakhsh over thirty years ago, when Benazir and I had stood side by side in the open air by the graves of her ancestors, the triumphs and tragedies of the future as yet unknown. Now she lay with them.

The sorrowful smell of the mist
Lingering over the Indus,
Gentle waves of rice, dung and rind
This is the salt cry of Sindh
As I die let me feel
The fragrance of tears.[25]

Acknowledgements

It may seem strange to thank someone who is no longer alive, but my first thanks are to Benazir, to whom I owe so much since the day we first met at Oxford in 1974. In her absence, I remain grateful to her family, especially her sister, Sanam, her children, Bilawal, Bakhtawar, Aseefa, and her husband, Asif Ali Zardari. I am also grateful for the support I have received from Benazir's cousin, Tariq Islam and his wife, Yasmin; Benazir's school friends, Samiya Junejo and Salma Waheed; her press spokesman, Bashir Riaz; her Harvard and Oxford contemporary, Peter Galbraith, and her friend and lobbyist, Mark Siegel.

I should also like to thank all those who have understood how important my friendship with Benazir has been to me, and hence how challenging it has been to write my memoir: especially, David Page, who, since our first meeting in Rawalpindi in 1978, has given me generous advice throughout my writing career, and who has made innumerable valuable suggestions and comments on my manuscript; Amna Piracha, who agreed to re visit the harrowing experience we shared during Zulfikar Ali Bhutto's appeal in 1978-79; and my school friend, Catherine Tudhope, who kindly agreed to read the manuscript in its early stages.

Where possible I have checked my narrative with others present at certain times; among them, I am grateful to former senator Aitzaz Ahsan, Farkhanda and Maqsooma Bokhari, ambassador Wendy Chamberlin, Elizabeth Colton, Lyse Doucet, OBE, CM,

Linda Francke, Janine di Giovanni, former high commissioner Wajid Shamsul Hasan, Irfan Husain, Khalid and Shaista Jan, Christina Lamb, OBE, the Rt Hon the Lord Lamont of Lerwick, PC, the Rt Hon the Lord Owen, CH, PC, FRCP, Rita Payne, Bashan Rafique, senator Sherry Rehman, Lars Rise, Simon Walker, CBE, Claire Wilmer, Timmy Zardari. Sadly I was unable to discuss my memoir with Asma Jahangir but her lecture at Lady Margaret Hall in memory of Benazir ten years after her assassination – days before her own sudden death in February 2018 – was one event which inspired me to complete the draft I had already begun.

I am also grateful to all those whose photographs I have used including my friends, Freya Darvall and Peter Fudakowski, professional photographers, Roger Hutchings, John Moore, Billett Potter, as well as others, the provenance of whose photographs remains unknown. Thank you also to Asma Khan Lone for her perseverance in obtaining the wonderful photograph of Benazir with Rajiv Gandhi from India Content News Agency.

Finally I should like to thank my agent, Sara Menguc, for her dedicated support; my editor, Richard Milbank and everyone at Head of Zeus, including Clémence Jacquinet, Anna Nightingale, Christian Duck and Matt Bray, for their enthusiasm in publishing my memoir (during an exceptionally difficult year when the Covid-19 pandemic put unprecedented restrictions on all our lives); Janey Fisher, another Oxford contemporary, for her diligent copyediting and excellent index, Jamie Whyte for a superb map; and, most importantly, my family: my sister, Elizabeth, who briefly endured the pain of thinking we had all perished after the October 2007 bomb blast, my husband, Stephen Willis, and my children – all now adults – Alexandra, Anthony, Olivia – who grew up knowing 'Aunty Benazir' and who fully comprehended my grief on that fateful day in December 2007 when she was assassinated.

Image Credits

Abbreviations

AJK	*Azad* (Free) Jammu and Kashmir
BB	Benazir Bhutto
CPA	Commonwealth Parliamentary Association
KP	Khyber Pakhtunkhwa
IISS	International Institute for Strategic Studies
IJI	Islami Jamhoori Ittehad
IPU	Inter-Parliamentary Union
MQM	Mohajir (later Muttahida) Qaumi Movement
MRD	Movement for the Restoration of Democracy
NWFP	North-West Frontier Province (now Khyber Pakhtunkhwa (KP))
PIA	Pakistan International Airlines
PML(J)	Pakistan Muslim League (Junejo faction) supporting Mohammed Khan Junejo
PML(Q)	Pakistan Muslim League (Quaid's party) supporting Pervez Musharraf
PML(N)	Pakistan Muslim League (Nawaz faction)
PNA	Pakistan National Alliance
PPP	Pakistan Peoples Party
PPPP	Pakistan Peoples Party Parliamentarians
PTI	Pakistan Tehrik-i-Insaaf (Justice Party)
SZABIST	Shaheed Zulfikar Ali Bhutto Institute
TTP	Tehrik-i Taliban
ZAB	Zulfikar Ali Bhutto

Dramatis Personae (select)

Names as they appear in the narrative
*Bhutto and extended family
⁺Harvard/Oxford contemporaries

Dr A. Q. (Abdul Qadeer) Khan, NI, HI, FPAS – nuclear physicist, who worked on Pakistan's uranium enrichment programme; detained in 2004 for being responsible for nuclear proliferation, released in 2009; a national hero for his contribution to Pakistan's nuclear weapons programme.

Aitzaz Ahsan – lawyer and member of the PPP; interior minister during Benazir's first administration 1988–90; on Benazir's homecoming truck on 18 October 2007. He was a member of the National Assembly 1988–90, 1990–93, 2002–07 and of the Senate 1994–97, 2012–18.

⁺The Rt Hon. Sir Alan Duncan, MP – St John's, Oxford; president of the Union, Hilary 1979.

*Alex Khan – Benazir's cousin, Poncho's son; on Benazir's homecoming truck on 18 October 2007.

Alexandra Willis – my elder daughter; Lady Margaret Hall, Oxford 2004–07; worked for SZABIST in Islamabad in 2006.

Altaf Hussain – leader of the MQM, went into exile in the UK in 1992.

Amna Piracha – lawyer who assisted Z. A. Bhutto's legal defence team during his appeal against the death sentence; married Saleem Zulfiqar Khan in June 1980. Established Khan & Piracha law firm in Islamabad in 1985.

⁺**Anne Fadiman** – Benazir's friend from Harvard, who came to Benazir's wedding in December 1987, reporting for *Life* magazine.

Anthony Willis – my son, who composed 'Bhutto' a requiem, performed by Bristol University's Symphony Orchestra, summer gala concert June 2009.

Anwar ul Haq – chief justice of the Supreme Court of Pakistan, one of the four judges who dismissed Zulfikar Ali Bhutto's appeal against the death sentence.

*****Aseefa Bhutto Zardari** – Benazir's younger daughter; Oxford Brookes University 2011–14; University College London 2014–15; after her mother's assassination, she took on the role of ambassador for polio eradication.

*****Asif Ali Zardari** – married Benazir in December 1987; elected as a member of the National Assembly 1993; co-chairman of the PPP December 2007; president of Pakistan 2008–13.

Asma Jahangir – human rights lawyer and social activist, imprisoned in 1983 for participating in the MRD; co-founder of the Human Rights Commission of Pakistan; UN special rapporteur on Freedom of Religion 2004–10.

*Azadeh (Azy) Bhutto – Benazir's niece, Sunny's daughter.

Babar, General Naseerullah – governor of the North-West Frontier Province (NWFP) 1976–77; interior minister during Benazir's second administration 1993–96.

Badinter, Robert – French lawyer who attended Zulfikar Ali Bhutto's appeal against the death sentence in the Supreme Court in 1978 (accompanied by his wife, Elisabeth); France's minister of justice 1981–86.

*Bakhtawar (Itty) Bhutto Zardari – Benazir's elder daughter; University of Edinburgh 2008–12; after her mother's assassination she took on the administration of SZABIST.

Bakhtiar, Yahya – former attorney general, head of Z.A. Bhutto's defence team in the Supreme Court of Pakistan; attorney general during Benazir's first administration 1988–90.

Bashir (Bash) Riaz – journalist, Urdu writer on pro-PPP newspaper, *Musawaat*, worked as Benazir's press spokesman in her first administration 1988–90.

*Behjat Hariri – Nusrat Bhutto's sister, Benazir's aunt, married to Karim Hariri.

*Benazir Bhutto – Harvard University, Mass. 1969–73; Lady Margaret Hall, Oxford 1973–76; St Catherine's College, Oxford 1976–77; president of the Union, Hilary 1977; leader and chairman of the PPP; prime minister of Pakistan 1988–90, 1993–96; assassinated 27 December 2007.

*Bilawal Bhutto Zardari – Benazir's son; Christ Church, Oxford 2007–10; co-chairman of the PPP December 2007; elected a member of the National Assembly 2018.

Bruce Loudon – correspondent for *The Daily Telegraph* in Pakistan during Bhutto's appeal against the death sentence in the Supreme Court of Pakistan; he came to Karachi in October 2007 to report on Benazir's return.

Charis Waddy, Dr – Australian Islamic scholar, Lady Margaret Hall, Oxford 1927–30; joined the Oxford Group (later called Moral Rearmament, and then Initiatives of Change); awarded the Sitari-i-Imtiaz in 1990.

Chris Sherwell – journalist stringing for the BBC and the *Financial Times* 1978–79.

Christina Lamb, OBE – University College, Oxford; came to Benazir's wedding in December 1987, worked for the *Financial Times* in Pakistan 1988–89; and continued to report on Pakistan/Afghanistan; on Benazir's homecoming truck on 18 October 2007. She is currently chief foreign correspondent for *The Sunday Times*.

+Claire (Clara) Wilmer – Lady Margaret Hall, Oxford; stayed with Benazir in Pakistan in 1979–80.

+Colin Clifford – Merton College, Oxford; came to Benazir's wedding in December 1987.

+The Rt Hon. Damian Greer, MP – Balliol College, Oxford; president of the Union, Michaelmas 1977.

⁺**Daniel Moylan, Lord** – The Queen's College, Oxford; president of the Union, Michaelmas 1978.

David Owen, the Rt Hon. the Lord, CH, PC, FRCP – UK secretary of state for foreign and commonwealth affairs 1977–79. He attended the seminar on Z. A. Bhutto's trial and appeal in Karachi, April 1989.

⁺**David Profumo** – Magdalen College; married Helen Fraser in 1980.

⁺**David Soskin** – Magdalen College, Oxford; president of the Union, Michaelmas 1975; visited Benazir in Pakistan in 1976 and came to her wedding in December 1987; married Alexandra (Lexi) Hockenhull.

D. M. Awan – former advocate-general Punjab High Court; Z. A. Bhutto's senior counsel for the trial in the Lahore High Court and member of his defence team in the Supreme Court of Pakistan.

Dorab Patel – one of the nine judges of the Supreme Court of Pakistan hearing Z. A. Bhutto's appeal against the death sentence; one of the three judges who upheld his appeal.

⁺**Etienne Duval** – Brasenose College, Oxford; came to Pakistan in 1994 as TV journalist to interview Benazir.

Etienne Jaudel – French lawyer, general secretary of the International Federation for Human Rights; came to Pakistan to attend Z. A. Bhutto's appeal against the death sentence in 1978, the seminar on his trial and appeal in Karachi in April 1989, and returned to Pakistan in 1991 to report on the human rights situation on behalf of the International Federation for Human Rights.

*Fakhri Ahmed Khan – Nusrat Bhutto's niece, married to Gulzar Ahmed Khan.

Farooq Ahmed Khan Leghari – St Catherine's College, Oxford; member of the PPP since 1973; imprisoned under the Zia dictatorship; deputy leader of the PPP under Benazir; president of Pakistan 1993–97.

*Fatima Bhutto – Benazir's niece, Mir Murtaza's daughter.

*Fauzia Fasihuddin Bhutto – Mir Murtaza's first wife, Fatima's mother.

Dame Frances Lannon, DBE, FRHist – principal of Lady Margaret Hall, 2002–15.

⁺Freya Darvall – St Hilda's College, Oxford; met Benazir in New York before she came to Oxford & went to Benazir's wedding in December 1987, married John Newman in 1994.

*Ghinwa Itoui Bhutto – Mir Murtaza's second wife, mother of Zulfikar Ali Bhutto, Jr. Chairperson PPP (Shaheed Bhutto).

Ghulam Ishaq Khan – minister of finance 1977–85; Senate chairman 1985–88; president of Pakistan 1988–93.

Ghulam Murtaza Bhutto – Benazir's great grandfather, after whom the house in Larkana, Al Murtaza, is named.

Ghulam Mustafa Jatoi – chief minister of Sindh 1973–77; arrested under Zia in 1983 and 1985; acting prime minister of Pakistan 1990.

Gillian Peele, MA, MPhil, FRHistS – Benazir's tutor in politics, Lady Margaret Hall, Oxford.

*Hakim Ali Zardari – Asif's father, Benazir's father-in-law. He served as a member of the National Assembly in 1972–77, 1988–90, 1993–96.

Haleem, Justice – one of the nine judges of the Supreme Court of Pakistan hearing Z. A. Bhutto's appeal against the death sentence; one of the three judges who upheld his appeal.

*Helen Fraser – St Hilda's, Oxford; married David Profumo in 1980. We acted in *Salad Days*, Trinity 1975.

Hussain Haqqani, – Benazir's press spokesman during her second administration 1993–96; worked with Benazir on *Reconciliation*. He served as Pakistan's ambassador to the US 2008–2011.

⁺Imran Khan, HI, PP – Keble College, Oxford 1972–75; chairman of the PTI; became prime minister of Pakistan 2018.

*Jason (Jehan Zeb) Khan – Benazir's cousin, Poncho's son; on Benazir's homecoming truck on 18 October 2007.

Junejo, Mohammed Khan – minister of railways 1977–79; prime minister of Pakistan 1985–88.

Karan Thapar – Pembroke College, Cambridge; president of the Cambridge Union, Spring 1977, when Benazir was president of the Oxford Union; now a well-known Indian journalist and commentator.

⁺Keith Gregory – Oriel College, Oxford; visited Benazir in Pakistan in 1976 and came to her wedding in December 1987, married to Lynne.

*Laila Crawford – Benazir's cousin on her mother's side; she often accompanied Benazir to the National Prayer Breakfast in Washington DC; on Benazir's homecoming truck on 18 October 2007.

Linda Francke – journalist and former editor of *Newsweek*, who collaborated with Benazir on her autobiography, *Daughter of the East* (*Daughter of Destiny*).

Lyse Doucet, OBE, CM – BBC correspondent in Islamabad 1989–93, also reporting on Afghanistan and Iran. She is currently the BBC's chief international correspondent.

Makhdoom Ameen Faheem – senior vice chairman of the PPP, chairman of the PPPP; on Benazir's homecoming truck on 18 October 2007 and with her in the land cruiser when she was assassinated on 27 December 2007.

Mark Siegel – lobbyist and friend of Benazir's since 1984, organised her lectures tours in the US, worked with Benazir on *Reconciliation*.

Sir Mark Tully, KBE – BBC South Asia correspondent based in Delhi; came to Pakistan during Bhutto's appeal against the death sentence in the Supreme Court of Pakistan 1978 and 1979.

Maulvi Mushtaq Khan – chief justice of the Lahore High Court, who sentenced Z. A. Bhutto to death for conspiracy to murder in March 1978.

Memon, Ghulam Ali – former advocate-general Sindh High Court; Z. A. Bhutto's leading defence lawyer in the Supreme Court; he died suddenly on 9 March 1979.

*Mir Ghulam Murtaza Bhutto – Benazir's brother; Harvard University, Mass. 1972–76; Christ Church, Oxford 1976–78; founder of Al Zulfikar; founder of PPP (Shaheed Bhutto) political party; member of the Sindh provincial assembly 1993–96; killed in a police shoot out on 20 September 1996.

*Mumtaz Ali Bhutto** – Z. A. Bhutto's cousin. He was a founding member of the PPP, governor of Sindh 1971–72; chief minister of Sindh 1972–73. In 1989 he founded the Sindh National Front which merged with Imran Khan's PTI in 2017.

*Munnawar (Aunty Manna) Islam** – Benazir's aunt, Z. A. Bhutto's only surviving sister, mother of Tariq, married to Naseem Islam.

Musharraf, General Pervez – chief of army staff 1998–2007; chief executive of Pakistan 1999–2002; president of Pakistan 2001–08.

Naheed Khan – Benazir's political secretary; on Benazir's homecoming truck on 18 October 2007 and with her in the land cruiser when she was assassinated on 27 December 2007.

Nawaz Sharif – joined Pakistan Muslim League in 1976, leader of the IJI, and then of the PML(N); prime minister of Pakistan 1990–93, 1997–99, 2013–17.

Niazi, Dr Zafar – Z. A. Bhutto's dentist, married to Shaukat, father of Yasmin, Samiya, Samina, Mona, Sultan. After retiring as a dentist, he set up the Mianwali Education Trust, Tameer-e-Millat School.

*Nusrat (*née* Ispahani) Bhutto** married Zulfikar Ai Bhutto in 1951, mother of Benazir, Murtaza, Sanam, Shahnawaz. She became chairman of the PPP in 1979 after Z. A. Bhutto's death.

Olivia Willis – my younger daughter; Lady Margaret Hall, Oxford 2010–13.

⁺**Patricia (Tricia, Trish) Yates** – Somerville, Oxford; one of Benazir's earliest friends at Oxford; stayed with Benazir in Pakistan in 1976. She married Stephen Clues.

⁺**Peter Galbraith** – Harvard University, Mass. 1969–73; St Catherine's College, Oxford 1973–75; Georgetown University; Senate Foreign Relations Committee 1979–93; he worked to secure Benazir's release from prison/house arrest 1981–84. His mother, Catherine, came to see Benazir in Pakistan in September 1978.

Peter Niesewand – correspondent for *The Guardian* in Pakistan during Bhutto's appeal in the Supreme Court. He died of leukemia in 1983.

Sir Peter Tapsell, MP – friend of Benazir and of her father. He served as an MP from 1966–2015 and from 2010–15 was 'the father of the House of Commons'.

*****Poncho (Prince Muzzafar Mustafa) Khan** – Benazir's first cousin; his mother was Mumtaz, Z. A. Bhutto's sister who died in 1974.

Qaiser Khan – one of the nine judges of the Supreme Court of Pakistan hearing Z. A. Bhutto's appeal against the death sentence; he retired at the end of July 1978.

Ramsey Clark – US attorney general 1967–69; he came to Pakistan in 1978 to attend Z. A. Bhutto's appeal in the Supreme Court of Pakistan, attended the Convention of International Jurists in London in 1979 and returned to Pakistan to attend the seminar on Bhutto's trial and appeal in Karachi in April 1989.

*****Rehana Fasihuddin Bhutto** – Shahnawaz's wife, Sassi's mother, lives in California, USA.

Safdar Shah, Ghulam – one of the nine judges of the Supreme Court of Pakistan hearing Z. A. Bhutto's appeal against the death sentence; one of the three judges who upheld his appeal.

Sahabzada Yaqub Khan – foreign minister of Pakistan 1982–91, 1996–97. He served with the Indian Army in North Africa during the Second World War.

Saleem Zulfiqar Khan – one of the lawyers on Bhutto's defence team, became Benazir's lawyer, married Amna Piracha in June 1980. Established Khan & Piracha law firm in Islamabad in 1985.

Salma Waheed – Samiya's sister and school friend of Benazir; she served in Benazir's second administration as federal secretary in the ministry of women's development and youth affairs.

Samiya Waheed (Junejo) – Benazir's close friend since their schooldays at the convent of Jesus and Mary and Karachi Grammar School. Salma's sister.

*Sanam (Sunny) Bhutto – Benazir's sister; Harvard University, Mass. 1974–78, 1978–79; she married Nasir Hussain in 1981 (later divorced); mother of Azadeh and Shahmir; married Hasan Chandoo in December 2019.

Sandy Gall, CMG, CBE – ITN foreign correspondent who came to Pakistan in 1979 to report on Bhutto's appeal against the death sentence. He subsequently reported regularly on Afghanistan and set up the Sandy Gall Afghanistan Appeal (SGAA) 1983–2020. He received the Sitara-i-Pakistan in 1985.

*Sassi Bhutto – Shahnawaz's daughter, lives in California, USA.

*Shahnawaz Bhutto – Benazir's brother, died in mysterious circumstances in the south of France in 1985.

*Shah Nawaz Bhutto, Sir – Benazir's grandfather, prime minister of Junagadh 1947.

Shahryar Khan –Pakistani ambassador to the UK 1987–89 and high commissioner to the UK 1989–90; foreign secretary of Pakistan 1990–94.

Sherry Rehman – former journalist, Benazir's information secretary, elected as a member of the National Assembly in 2002; and member of the Senate in 2015; leader of the opposition in the Senate 2018.

Simon Henderson – journalist, stringing for the BBC and the *Financial Times* 1977–78.

+Simon Walker, CBE – Balliol College, Oxford, president of the Oxford Union, Hilary 1974; gave Benazir her maiden speech; chaired Bilawal's first press conference January 2008.

Stephen Willis – Magdalene College, Cambridge; we married in March 1982.

*Tariq Islam – Benazir's cousin, Aunty Manna's son, married Yasmin Niazi in August 1984; on Benazir's homecoming truck on 18 October 2007.

*Timmy (Zarine Ali) Zardari – Asif's stepmother, Benazir's step-mother-in-law; on Benazir's homecoming truck on 18 October 2007.

Trevor Wood – Reuters correspondent in Islamabad 1978–79.

+Victor van Amerongen – Magdalen College, Oxford, president of the Union, Trinity 1975; visited Benazir in Pakistan in 1976; married Amanda Alexander.

Waheeduddin Ahmed, Justice – one of the nine judges of the Supreme Court of Pakistan hearing Z. A. Bhutto's appeal against the death sentence; he fell ill in November and was not allowed to return to finish hearing the case.

Wajid Shamsul Hasan – journalist, high commissioner for Pakistan to the UK 1994–96 and 2008–14.

*****Yasmin Niazi (Islam), Dr Zafar and Shaukat Niazi's eldest daughter; close friend of Benazir's and married her first cousin, Tariq Islam, in London in August 1984.

Zia-ul-Haq, General Mohammed, chief of army staff 1976–88; president of Pakistan 1978–88; died in plane crash 17 August 1988.

*****Zulfikar Ali Bhutto** – president of Pakistan 1971–73; prime minister of Pakistan 1973–77; overthrown in military coup d'état 5 July 1977; put on trial for conspiracy to murder a political opponent; executed 4 April 1979.

Notes

Chapter 1: Our Salad Days

1 William Shakespeare, *Antony and Cleopatra*, I:5, *The Complete Works of William Shakespeare* (Abbey Library, 1974), p.954.

2 Benazir Bhutto, *Daughter of Destiny* (Harper Perennial, 2008), pp.70–1.

3 Benazir's notes for her autobiography, 1987.

4 See Peter Galbraith, 'Memories of another day', *Newsline*, August 2017, https://newslinemagazine.com/magazine/memories-another-day-2/ (accessed 11 May 2020); Freya Darvall to me, email, 27 March 2020.

5 Benazir Bhutto, *Daughter of Destiny*, p.71; interview with Etienne Duval, Islamabad, 5 April 1994.

6 Benazir's notes for her autobiography, 1987; Oxford Union Society, Rough Minute Book 1972–75.

7 Oxford Union Society, Rough Minute Book 1972–75.

8 Benazir Bhutto, interview with Etienne Duval, Islamabad, 5 April 1994.

9 Benazir's notes for her autobiography, 1987.

10 Benazir's notes for her autobiography, 1987.

11 Quotation from her speech, December 1976. See 'This house proposes a new image', *Oxford Mail*, 26 November 1976; Benazir's notes for her autobiography, 1987.

12 'Oxford Union election upheld', *The Times*, 3 December 1976; Benazir's notes for her autobiography, 1987.

13 My diary, 19 November 2011.

14 Benazir notes for her autobiography 1987.

15 'King Arthur Receiving His Sword, Excalibur', by John Hungerford Pollen; 'The Death of Arthur', by Arthur Hughes.

16 Helen Fraser to me, undated [1988]. I was there but Helen's recollection is better.

17 Peter McIntyre, 'Pro-hanging side loses its champions', *Oxford Mail*,

18 February 1977; Sally Duncan, 'Capitalism suffers a defeat', *Oxford Mail*, 21 January 1977.

18   Victoria Schofield, presidential debate speech, Oxford Union Society, 3 March 1977.

19   Dear Victoria... from an anonymous voter; Dear Blonde Bombshell... love B, undated [March 1977].

20   Victoria darling... much love, Benazir xxx, undated [June 1977].

21   Benazir Bhutto, *Daughter of Destiny*, p.89.

22   'No politics for the premier's daughter who became president', *Daily Mail*, 2 June 1977.

23   My dear Victoria... much love Benazir xx, 9 September 1976.

24   Dearest Victoria... much love, Benazir xxx, 31 July 1977.

Chapter 2: 'Bhutto to hang'

1   Dearest Victoria... love Benazir, xeroxed letter with handwritten page at the back, undated [1977].

2   Ibid.

3   Ibid.

4   Benazir Bhutto, *Daughter of Destiny*, p.119. Dearest Vicki... love B xx, December 1977.

5   Dearest Victoria... much love, Benazir, 3 January 1978 (dated 1977: a common error at the beginning of a new year).

6   My dearest Mir... God bless you very dearest, lovable son... your father, Zulfikar Ali, excerpts in the *Daily Express*, 8 February 1979, *Viewpoint Fortnightly*, 1:19, a special Bhutto supplement, 1979.

7   Dearest Benazir... my love, always, Victoria xxxx, 15 April 1978.

8   Dearest Vicky and Claire... much love B. xxx, 26 April 1978.

9   Alexander Chancellor, 'To whom it may concern...', 24 May 1978.

10   Letter home, 2 June 1978, from Rawalpindi.

11   My dearest Vicks... all love B.B., 2 June 1978; Dear Mr Home Secretary... with best wishes, Miss Benazir Bhutto, 2 June 1978.

12   Dear Mr Zulfikar Ali Bhutto... sincerely, Victoria, Rawalpindi, 3 June 1978. Dear Victoria... yours sincerely, Zulfikar Ali Bhutto, June 1978.

13   My dearest Vicks... all love, B.B., 2 June 1978.

14   'The wayward heart', *The Risalo of Shah Abdul Latif of Bhit*, I:xv, in H. T. Sorley, *Shah Abdul Latif of Bhit: His Poetry, Life and Times* (Oxford University Press, 1940), p.327.

15   Benazir Bhutto, *Foreign Policy in Perspective* (Lahore: Classic, 1978), pp.118, 109, 60, 105. Quotation is from ibid, Dedication.

16   Dear Mr Zulfikar Ali Bhutto... sincerely, Victoria; Dear Victoria... yours sincerely, Zulfikar Ali Bhutto, 12 June 1978.

17   Victoria Schofield, 'The Trial of Bhutto', *Spectator*, 15 July 1978.

18   Letter home, 18 June 1978.

19   'My dearest daughter: A letter from the death cell' by Zulfikar Ali Bhutto, 21 June 1978, published as a booklet by Shahnawaz Bhutto Trust, 71 Clifton, Foreword by Yahya Bakhtiar, pp.7, 52, 56.

20   Letter home, 28 June 1978, from Karachi.

21   Bhutto: *Rumour and Reality*, undated [1978].

22   Letter home, 25 June 1978.

23   Benazir Bhutto, *Daughter of Destiny*, p.143.

24   My dear Victoria... thanks for everything, yours sincerely, Zulfikar Ali Bhutto, 2 July 1977, Zulfikar Ali Bhutto note, undated, 1978,

25   Dear Victoria... yours, Peter, 4 September 1979; additional letters 1980–81.

26   See *Judicial Murder* (Bhutto Legacy Foundation, 2016), pp.50–1.

27   See Victoria Schofield, *Bhutto: Trial and Execution* (Cassell, 1979), pp.142–3.

28   See Salman Taseer, *Bhutto: A Political Biography* (Ithaca, 1979), pp.12–13 for introduction to the Bhutto family and Larkana. Stanley Wolpert, *Zulfi Bhutto of Pakistan* (OUP, 1993) gives a fuller account, pp.3–18.

29   Ibid, pp.18–20.

30   Ibid, p.22; Stanley Wolpert, *Zulfi Bhutto of Pakistan: His Life and Times* (Oxford University Press, 1993), p.15.

31   Letter home, 29 July 1978, 11 p.m. from Karachi.

32   Zulfikar Ali Bhutto to President Valéry Giscard d'Estaing from Rawalpindi Central Jail, 30 July 1978.

33   Bhutto, *If I Am Assassinated* (Vikas, 1979), pp.197, 110.

34   Zulfikar Ali Bhutto note, undated, 1978.

35   Martin Woollacott, 'The life that is hanging by eighty thousand words', *Guardian*, 2 November 1978.

36   David Housego, Asia correspondent, 'Pakistan close to full nuclear capability says Bhutto', *The Financial Times*, 1978.

37   Khuswant Singh, 'Pakistan, India and the Bomb', *New York Times*, 1 July 1979, https://www.nytimes.com/1979/07/01/archives/foreign-affairs-pakistan-india-and-the-bomb.html (accessed 11 May 2020).

38   Bhutto, *If I Am Assassinated*, p.150.

Chapter 3: 'Within four walls'

1   Letter home, 7 September 1978.
2   Ibid.
3   See Olaf Caroe, *The Pathans: AD 550–1957* (Macmillan & Co., 1958), one of the seminal works from a British perspective.
4   Letter home, 9 October 1978.
5   Ibid.
6   My diary, recorded in my letter home, 9 October 1978.
7   Peter Galbraith to me, email, 14 February 2020.
8   My diary, 16 September 1978.
9   Benazir Bhutto, *Daughter of Destiny*, p.150; letter home, 4 October 1978.
10 Letter home, 24 October 1978; Benazir to me, quoted in my letter home.
11 Letter home, 24 October 1978.
12 Letters home, 4 and 19 November 1978.
13 Letter home, 18 November 1978.
14 My diary, 26 November 1978.
15 Dearest Vicks... lots of love, B xxxx, 28 November 1978.
16 ... love B xxxxxxxxx, undated fragment; William Buckley, *Stained Glass* (Doubleday, 1978).
17 Dearest Vicks... lots of love, B xxxx, 28 November 1978.
18 Dearest Vicks... love B xxxxx, 4 December 1978.
19 Letter home, 1 December 1978.
20 Amna Piracha to me, email, 17 March 2020; Victoria Schofield, *Bhutto: Trial and Execution*, pp.80, 163–5.
21 Dearest Vicks... with lots of love B xxxxx, 16 December 1978.
22 Zulfikar Ali Bhutto, 18 December 1978, quoted in Victoria Schofield, *Bhutto: Trial and Execution*, p.170.
23 My diary, 18 December 1978.
24 Zulfikar Ali Bhutto, recorded in my diary, 20 December 1978, and in Victoria Schofield, *Bhutto: Trial and Execution*, pp.185–86.
25 Dearest Vicks... lots of love B xxxxx, 23 December 1978.
26 Dearest Vicks... love B xxxxx, 4 December 1978.
27 Dearest Vicks... lots of love B xxxxx, 23 December 1978.

Chapter 4: 'Martyrs do not die'

1   Benazir to me, 14 February 1979, and quoted in Peter Niesewand, 'Judge refuses Bhutto's lawyers full month to prepare petition', *Guardian*, 15 February 1979.

2   Dear Prime Minister... yours sincerely, Victoria Schofield, 2 January 1979; Dear Miss Schofield... yours sincerely Jenny Jeger, political assistant, 9 January 1979.

3   Dear Mrs Thatcher... yours sincerely, Victoria Schofield, 1 January 1979; Dear Ms Schofield... yours sincerely Matthew Parris, 17 January 1979.

4   Dearest Vicks... love as always, keep your chin up, no matter how bad the times we must pass it with courage and dignity... B xxxxxx, undated [1979].

5   See 'Pakistan: a clue to the bomb mystery', *Economist*, 14 July 1979, https://nuclearweaponarchive.org/Pakistan/AQKhan.html (accessed 11 May 2020); Chris Sherwell to me, email, 31 March 2020.

6   Peter Niesewand, *In Camera: Secret Injustice in Rhodesia* (Weidenfeld & Nicholson, 1973); Victoria Schofield, *Bhutto: Trial and Execution*, p.85.

7   Conversations with Louis and Nancy Dupree and others, Islamabad, February 1979; my diary, 30 March, 9 April 1979.

8   Letter home, 3 February 1979.

9   Letter home, 6 February 1979.

10   Victoria Schofield, *Bhutto: Trial and Execution*, p.214; Criminal appeal no.11 of 1978, Zulfikar Ali Bhutto, 'Appellant versus the State – Respondent. Headnotes and Text of the Judgment': Anwar ul Haq, p.389; G. Safdar Shah, p.707.

11   Dearest Vicks... love as always, to a very dear friend, keep heart... love, B, undated [February 1979].

12   Victoria Schofield, 'Bhutto: The divided judgement', *Spectator*, 10 February 1979, pp.7–8.

13   Dearest Vicks... with love as always, Benazir, 9–11 February 1979. Benazir dated the letter March but it must have been February since they moved to Sihala in February.

14   Dear Mr Home Secretary, Punjab... yours sincerely, Victoria Schofield, 10 February 1979.

15   Dearest Vicks... with love as always, Benazir, 9–11 February 1979.

16   Letter home, 17 February 1979.

17   Dearest Vicks... love B, undated [1979].

18   Benazir to me, 13 February 1979, quoted in Peter Niesewand, 'Judge refuses Bhutto's lawyers full month to prepare petition', *Guardian*, 15 February 1979.

19   Dearest Victoria... with lots of love as always... B xxxxxxx, 20 February 1979.

20   Dearest Vicks... with much love as always... B xxxxx, 4 March 1979.

21   My diary, 9 March 1979; letter home 11 March 1979.

22   Dearest Vicks... undated [March 1979].

23   Yahya Bakhtiar, quoted in Victoria Schofield, *Bhutto: Trial and Execution*, pp.229–30.

24   Altaf Gauhar (1923–2000), 'Before the President fell', *Guardian*, 21 February 1979.

25   Dear Mr Home Secretary, S. J. K. Mahmud... yours sincerely, Victoria Schofield, 15 March 1979.

26   Letter home, 21 March 1979.

27   Dearest Vicks... love, B, undated [March 1979].

28   Victoria Schofield, 'Bhutto prepares to die', *Spectator*, March 1979.

29   Dearest Vicks... love as always, B xx, undated [March 1979].

30   My diary, 29 March 1979; letter home 4 April 1979.

31   My diary, 1 April 1979.

32   My diary, 2 April 1979; Robert Trumbull, 'Last-minute petitions for Bhutto are filed against his objection', *New York Times*, 1 April 1979. Robert Trumbull, 'Relative asks for mercy for Bhutto, raising hopes of his supporters', *New York Times*, 2 April 1979.

33   Dear Victoria... love B, 2 April 1979.

34   'Bhutto: The final act', *Spectator*, 7 April 1979.

35   Ibid.

36   Ibid.

37   Ibid.

38   Yasmin Islam to me, 12 November 2019.

39   My diary, 6 April 1979; Samiya Waheed Junejo to me, Karachi, 26 February 2020.

40   Ramsey Clark, Convention of International Jurists, 6–7 April 1979, transcript notes, later published as *Judicial Murder* (Bhutto Legacy Foundation, 2016, for which I wrote the Foreword), pp.50–51; see Victoria Schofield, *Bhutto: Trial and Execution*, pp.80, 163–5. Claude Morris, editor of *The Voice*, a Middle Eastern newspaper, helped to organise the Convention.

41   John Matthew, QC, *Judicial Murder*, p.63; Stanley Newens, MP, *Judicial Murder*, p.36.

42   Letter home, 11 April 1979.

43   Ibid.

44   Dearest Vicks... love B x, 24 April 1979.

Chapter 5: Street Fighting Years

1   Victoria Schofield, review of Benazir Bhutto, *Daughter of the East* (Hamish Hamilton, 1988), Lady Margaret Hall Brown Book.

2   Benazir Bhutto, interview with David Lomax, BBC1, *Tonight*, broadcast 12 June 1979.

3   Dear Victoria... much love and do write, Samiya, 19 Jun–16 Jul 1979 (Samiya began the letter on one date and finished it on another); Benazir Bhutto, interview with David Lomax, BBC1, *Tonight*, broadcast 12 June 1979; Benazir Bhutto, *Daughter of Destiny*, Preface to the 2008 edition, p.xi.

4   Benazir Bhutto, interview with David Lomax, BBC1 Tonight, broadcast 12 June 1979.

5   Dear Victoria... much love and do write, Samiya, 19 Jun–16 Jul 1979.

6   'Mir Bhutto forms guerrilla army', *Voice*, 1979.

7   Dearest Victoria... always Mir, 21 August 1979.

8   Murtaza Bhutto, quoted in Michael Fathers, 'The Bhutto inheritance', *The Independent*, 17 October 1993.

9   Dearest Victoria... love & xes, Clara, 30 August 1979; Benazir Bhutto, interview with David Lay, *BBC Profile*, broadcast on 19 October 1979.

10   Bashir Riaz to me, 9 September 1979; my diary, 9 September 1979; telephone conversations with Benazir, 9 and 22 September 1979.

11   My interview with Benazir, New York, 22 April 1985; Benazir Bhutto, *Daughter of Destiny*, p.26; AP, 'Pakistan President calls off elections', *New York Times*, 17 October 1979, https://www.nytimes.com/1979/10/17/archives/pakistan-president-calls-off-elections-general-zia-bans-political.html.

12   Ann Callender, 'Troubled sub-continent', *Daily Telegraph*, 27 December 1979; Tariq Ali, 'Death warrant', *New Statesman*, 8 February 1980; Christopher Dobson, 'Bhutto's fatal mistake', *Now!*, 23 November 1979.

13   'Timeline: Soviet war in Afghanistan', http://news.bbc.co.uk/1/hi/world/south_asia/7883532.stm.

14   President Carter, State of the Union speech, 23 January 1980.

15   Dearest Benazir... love Victoria, 13 April 1980.

16   *Encyclopaedia Britannica: Book of the Year, Events of 1979*, 1980, pp.72, 104; Dear Miss Schofield… yours sincerely, J. E. Davis, London editor, *Britannica Book of the Year*, 3 December 1979.

17   My dear Victoria… much love, and xes, Clara, July 1980; my diary, 29 July 1980.

18   Peter Niesewand, 'Bhuttos urge the army to act', *Guardian*, 25 September 1980.

19   Dearest B… as always, Victoria xxxx, 9 October 1980.

20   Dear Victoria… yours affectionately Dr. M. Z. K. Niazi and all the family, 11 November 1980.

21   Benazir Bhutto, Karachi, Reuter, 11 December 1980.

22   Peter Niesewand, New Delhi, 'Bhutto judge says trial was unfair', *Guardian*, 24 November 1980.

23   Ghulam Safdar Shah, 'Why I fled Zia's justice', *Observer*, 21 December 1980; my diary, 24 and 27 November 1980.

24   Dearest B… Victoria xxx, 22 January 1981.

25   Dearest Victoria… love to you… B xxx, 5 February 1981.

26   Benazir Bhutto, BBC World Service, *Assignment: Pakistan's political problems*: presenter Keith Parsons; producer Alastair Lack, February 1981.

27   Ibid.

28   My diary, 28 February 1981.

29   Murtaza Bhutto interview with Dr Ihlau, 'No Other Way,' *India Today*, 16–31 July 1981. He gave the interview in June.

30   My diary, 2 March 1981.

31   My diary, 6 March 1981; UPA, 'British author deported', *Daily Telegraph*, 7 March 1981.

32   My diary, 6 March 1981.

33   My diary, 11 March 1981.

34   Ibid.

35   My diary, 23 March 1981.

36   Tariq Bashir, *Friday Times*, 31 October 2014.

37   Benazir Bhutto, *Daughter of Destiny*, p.171.

38   Benazir Bhutto, *Daughter of Destiny*, p.174.

39   Maqsooma Bokhari to me, email, 6 and 14 February 2020; Sean Toolan, Colin Smith and Harold Byatt, 'Hostages go free in runway drama', *Observer*, 15 March 1981; Farkhanda Bokhari's autobiography, *Yeh Bazi Ishq Ki Bazi hai* (Sangemeel Publications, Lahore, 2012).

40   Frank J. Prial, Special to the *New York Times*, 'Pakistan reaction to hijack-

ing shows Zia's strength', 8 April 1981, https://www.nytimes.com/by/frank-j-prial (accessed 11 May 2020).

Chapter 6: Living But Not Living

1   Benazir Bhutto, *Daughter of Destiny*, p.175.
2   Benazir Bhutto, *Daughter of Destiny*, p.172–3.
3   My interview with Benazir, New York, 22 April 1985.
4   Benazir Bhutto, *Daughter of Destiny*, p.200; Dearest B… with much love, as always, Victoria, London, 25 August 1981.
5   Benazir Bhutto, *Daughter of Destiny*, pp.212, 216.
6   Michael T. Kaufman, 'Mrs. Thatcher visits Afghans on the Frontier, *New York Times*, 9 October 1981.
7   My interview with Benazir, New York, 22 April 1985.
8   Elizabeth Colton to me, email and telephone conversation, 30 March 2020.
9   Bashan Rafique to me, email, 3 March 2020.
10   Peter Galbraith to me, email, 11 March 2020; Peter Galbraith, quoted in Benazir Bhutto, *Daughter of Destiny*, pp.214–15.
11   Peter Galbraith to me, email, 11 March 2020; See Benazir Bhutto, *Daughter of Destiny*, pp.214–15, 219; Bernard Weinraub, 'Zia tells Reagan he won't build atomic weapon', *New York Times*, 8 December 1982, https://www.nytimes.com/1982/12/08/world/zia-tells-reagan-he-won-t-build-atomic-weapon.html (accessed 11 May 2020).
12   Dr Zafar Niazi to me, London, 27 May 1982.
13   Ian Hoare, despatch from Karachi, 26 March 1983 (telephone call 11.50 a.m.); see Benazir Bhutto, *Daughter of Destiny*, pp.235–6.
14   Ian Hoare, newscopy from Karachi, 26 March 1983 (telephone call 2.25 p.m.).
15   Ian Hoare, despatch from Karachi, 26 March 1983 (telephone call 10.00 p.m.). See Benazir Bhutto, *Daughter of Destiny*, pp.235–6.
16   Dear Victoria… best wishes David Johnson, General Synod of the Church of England, Board for Mission and Unity, 20 June 1983.
17   Polly Toynbee, 'The glittering socialite was transformed into a formidable political operator', *Guardian*, 20 June 1983; my diary, 14 June 1983.
18   General Mohammed Zia-ul-Haq, interviewed by Jeff Cox, BBC World Service, *The World Today*, 15 August 1983.
19   Tom Heneghan, 'Government warns of stiff punishments as protest front widens', Reuter, 22 August 1983.

20 AFP, Islamabad, 12 September 1983; William K. Stevens, '17 are reported killed in protests in Pakistan', *New York Times*, 30 September 1983, https://www.nytimes.com/1983/09/30/world/17-are-reported-killed-in-protests-in-pakistan.html (accessed 11 May 2020).

21 My dear Yasmin... with love from Victoria, 3 November 1983.

22 Dearest Benazir... lots and lots and lots of love as always to you. Insh'allah the bad times will soon be over xx Vicks xx, 1 November 1983.

23 Begum Nusrat Bhutto, quoted in Elie Marcuse, AFP, Munich, 2 December 1983.

Chapter 7: Benazir's Out

1   Benazir Bhutto, *Daughter of Destiny*, p.252.

2   My diary, 14 January 1984; Benazir Bhutto, *Daughter of Destiny*, p.252.

3   Benazir Bhutto, *Daughter of Destiny*, p.253.

4   Dearest Benazir... lots of love, Vicks, 10 February 1984.

5   Benazir Bhutto, *Daughter of Destiny*, p.255.

6   Peter Galbraith to me, email, 11 March 2020.

7   Mark Siegel, quoted in *Bhutto: You Can't Murder a Legacy*, a Duane Baughman film, 2010; Peter Galbraith to me, email, 11 March 2020.

8   Peter Galbraith to me, email, 14 February 2020.

9   My diary, 24 and 25 March 1984.

10 My interview with Benazir, New York, 22 April 1985.

11 Benazir Bhutto, *Daughter of Destiny*, p.261.

12 Dearest Benazir... very much love, Victoria, New York, 7 June 1984.

13 Winston Churchill, *Young Winston's Wars* (Leo Cooper, 1972), p.7. The actual quotation is 'Every rock, every hill, every nullah had its story.'

14 My diary, 21 and 22 June 1984.

15 'Both Khalid and Zayed told me that they had already pleaded with the General, but would now send him a further message saying that if he had Zulfikar Ali Bhutto killed, they would cut off all aid to Pakistan', Dear Victoria... yours ever, Peter, 5 February 2008.

16 Dearest Benazir... with much love as always Victoria xxxx, New York, 3 November 1984; Dear Prime Minister... yours sincerely Victoria Schofield, 14 July 1983.

17 See my father's memoir, Vice Admiral B.B. Schofield (1895–1984), *With the Royal Navy in War and Peace: O'er the Dark Blue Sea*, ed. Victoria Schofield (Pen & Sword, 2018), pp.71–2; Dear Mrs Schofield... sincerely, Benazir, 19 December 1984.

18 'Story of Pakistan: a multi-media journey', https://storyofpakistan.com/
referendum-1984 (accessed 11 May 2020); *The Times*, 20 December 1984;
AP, 'Around the world: Pakistani leader gets 98% of referendum vote',
New York Times, 21 December 1984, https://www.nytimes.com/1984/12/
21/world/around-the-world-pakistani-leader-gets-98-of-referendum-
vote.html (accessed 11 May 2020).

19 Michael Hamlyn, 'Pakistan PM takes on burden without power base',
The Times, 26 March 1985.

20 My diary 18 and 22 April 1985.

21 My interview with Benazir, New York, 22 April 1985.

22 Dearest Victoria... love Benazir, 2 March 1986.

23 Benazir Bhutto, *Daughter of Destiny*, p.282.

24 Benazir Bhutto, quoted in Hira Mirza, 'The mysterious death of Shahnawaz Bhutto,' *Pakistan Today*, 18 July 2016.

25 See Michael Hamlyn, 'Why Zia keeps this woman barred from view',
The Times, 19 September 1985.

26 See Benazir's own account of Shahnawaz's death in *Daughter of Destiny*,
pp.290–307.

27 AP, 'Bhutto's daughter, a foe of Zia, under house arrest in Pakistan', *New
York Times*, 30 August 1985, https://www.nytimes.com/1985/08/30/world/
bhutto-s-daughter-a-foe-of-zia-under-house-arrest-in-pakistan.html
(accessed 11 May 2020).

28 Reuters, 'Pakistan's ruler ends martial law', https://www.nytimes.com/
1985/12/31/world/pakistan-s-ruler-ends-martial-law.html (accessed 11
May 2020); Steven R. Weisman, 'For Zia much of the power remains',
New York Times, 31 December 1985.

29 Dearest Benazir... love Vicks, February 1986; Dearest Victoria... love
Benazir, 2 March 1986.

30 Amna Piracha, quoted in Benazir Bhutto, *Daughter of Destiny*, pp.319–20;
Steven R. Weisman, 'A daughter returns to Pakistan to cry for victory',
New York Times, 11 April 1986, https://www.nytimes.com/1986/04/11/
world/a-daughter-returns-to-pakistan-to-cry-for-victory.html (accessed
11 May 2020).

31 See http://www.cssforum.com.pk/off-topic-section/poetry-literature/
urdu-poetry/29905-main-baghi-khoon-benazir-bhutto.html (accessed 11
May 2020).

32 Benazir Bhutto, *Daughter of Destiny*, pp.322–5.

33 Dearest Benazir... take great care, Victoria, 9 June 1986.

Chapter 8: The People's Wedding

1   Urdu song, sung by Benazir's friends at her wedding, December 1987.
2   Dearest Victoria... love Benazir, 70, Clifton, Karachi, 29 June 1987.
3   My diary, 25 July 1987.
4   Benazir Bhutto, BBC Radio documentary, February 1993. Other contributors included myself, Tariq Ali and Dr Gowhar Rizvi.
5   My interview with Asif Ali Zardari, Ziarat, 15 April 1989; 'A political punching bag', *The Independent*, 1 May 1989.
6   Quoted in Anne Fadiman, 'Behind the veil', *Life Magazine*, December 1987. She made a similar comment to me.
7   Asif Ali Zardari interview for *Bhutto: You Can't Murder a Legacy*, a Duane Baughman film, 2010.
8   My wedding album for Benazir Bhutto and Asif Ali Zardari.
9   Linda Francke to me, 17 December 1987.
10 Christina Lamb, 'My life with Benazir', *Sunday Times*, 30 December 2007.
11 Anne Fadiman, 'Behind the veil', *Life Magazine*, December 1987; my diary 16–20 December 1987.
12 Benazir Bhutto, *Daughter of Destiny*, pp.363–4.
13 See Benazir's description in Bhutto, *Daughter of Destiny*, pp.360–5.
14 Benazir Bhutto, interview with Etienne Duval, Islamabad, 5 April 1994.
15 Dearest Vicks... love, Benazir, 14 April 1988.
16 Steven R. Weisman, 'Doubts grow that Zia will call an election soon', *New York Times*, 14 June 1988, https://www.nytimes.com/1988/06/14/world/doubts-grow-that-zia-will-call-an-election-soon.html (accessed 11 May 2020); Dearest Benazir... with much love from us all, 14 June 1988.
17 Yasmin to me, telephone conversation, 17 August 1989.

Chapter 9: Dear Prime Minister

1   Benazir Bhutto, *Daughter of Destiny*, p.374.
2   Benazir Bhutto, *Daughter of Destiny*, p.376.
3   Benazir Bhutto, *Daughter of Destiny*, pp.381, 384.
4   Dearest Benazir... with much love from us all, Victoria, 4 November 1988; Peter Galbraith, 'Memories of another day,' *Newsline*, August 2017, https://newslinemagazine.com/magazine/memories-another-day-2/ (accessed 11 May 2020).

5   Amna Piracha to me, email, 6 April 2020; Victoria Schofield, 'The making of the daughter of Pakistan', *The Independent*, 21 November 1988.

6   Benazir Bhutto, *Daughter of Destiny*, p.392.

7   Denholm Barnetson, 'Benazir Bhutto to release political prisoners, expand rights', UPI, 3 December 1988, https://www.upi.com/Archives/1988/12/03/Bhutto-to-release-political-prisoners-expand-rights/2143597128400/ (accessed 11 May 2020).

8   Benazir Bhutto, *Daughter of Destiny*, pp.396-8.

9   Benazir Bhutto, *Daughter of Destiny*, p.394; Shaikh Aziz, 'The "dawn of a new era" that became a dream', 21 August 2016, https://www.dawn.com/news/1278747 (accessed 11 May 2020).

10   Dearest Victoria... lots of love, Asif and Benazir, prime minister of Pakistan, Greetings of the Season and best wishes for the New Year [1989]; Dear Victoria... with love Nusrat Bhutto, 2 January 1989.

11   Victoria Schofield, review of Benazir Bhutto, *Daughter of the East* (Hamish Hamilton, 1988), Lady Margaret Hall Brown Book, 1989.

12   'The legacy of Prime Minister Bhutto', International Seminar April 2-3, 1989, Karachi.

13   Address from Mr Valéry Giscard d'Estaing, former president of the French Republic, Karachi, 2 April 1989.

14   Ramsey Clark, Yahya Bakhtiar, Dr David Owen, excerpts from speeches; 'The legacy of Prime Minister Bhutto,' International Seminar April 2-3, 1989; my diary, 6 April 1989; Lord Owen to me, email, 8 January 2020.

15   Mushahid Hussain, 'Legal controversies over Z. A. Bhutto's prosecution', *Frontier Post*, 14 April 1989.

16   My diary, 3-4 April 1989.

17   Ibid.

18   Ibid.

19   My interview with Asif Zardari, Ziarat, 15 April 1989: 'A political punching bag', *The Independent*, 1 May 1989.

20   General Babar to me, 15 April 1989.

21   Ahmed Rashid (b.1948), 'Bhutto in Blunderland', *The Independent*, ?30 March 1989.

22   Dear Sir Peter... with warm regards, Benazir Bhutto, 10 April 1989.

23   Benazir Bhutto, *It's Your World*, BBC World Service, March 1989: presenter Nick Worrall.

24   *Women in Pakistan*, BBC World Service, 31 May and 1 June 1989: presenter Victoria Schofield, producer Alastair Lack; my interview with Asma Jahangir, Lahore, 14 April 1989.

25 My interview with Agha Murtaza Poya [Pooya] (b.1941), Islamabad, 9 April 1989.

26 Benazir Bhutto's responses to questions for the book by Mona Bauwens and Peter Thompson, *Feminine Power: Conversations with the World's Most Powerful Women in the Fields of Politics, Business and Entertainment* (Mainstream Publishing, 1998).

27 My diary, 8 July 1989; Dear Victoria... yours ever, David, 17 July 1989; Dearest Victoria... lots of love Freya, 20 July 1989.

28 My diary, 10–12 July 1989.

29 Dear Victoria... yours ever, Peter, 5 February 2008; Mohammed Hanif, *A Case of Exploding Mangoes* (Knopf/US, 2008).

30 My diary, 31 July and 3 August 1989; Dearest Benazir... 16 August 1989; Mary Braid, 'Gentleman swindler jailed after 40 year spree', *The Independent*, 20 June 1995.

31 Dearest Benazir... 16 August 1989.

32 Benazir Bhutto, *Daughter of Destiny*, p.395.

33 HE Shahryar Khan to me, telephone conversation, 25 September 1989.

34 Benazir Bhutto, *Daughter of Destiny*, p.395.

35 My diary, 20 October 1989.

36 The Langkawi Declaration on the Environment, 21 October 1989, https://thecommonwealth.org/langkawi-declaration-environment (accessed 11 May 2020).

37 Shaikh Aziz, 'A leaf from history: Benazir's angels', *Dawn*, 18 December 2016, https://www.dawn.com/news/1302495; Mark Fineman, 'Bhutto survives no-confidence motion', *Los Angeles Times*, 2 November 1989, https://www.latimes.com/archives/la-xpm-1989-11-02-mn-307-story.html (accessed 11 May 2020).

38 Carol Thatcher (b.1953), 'Star of the East', *Sunday Express*, 26 November 1989, pp.11, 13.

39 Benazir Bhutto, *Daughter of Destiny*, p.xiii.

40 Christina Lamb, *Waiting for Allah: Pakistan's Struggle for Democracy* (Hamish Hamilton, 1991), p.286; *The Financial Times*, October 1989.

41 Dearest Benazir, London, 15 November 1989.

42 Victoria Schofield, 'Bhutto represents best hope for Pakistan to overcome stagnant past', *Atlanta Journal-Constitution*, 3 December 1989.

43 Ms Benazir Bhutto, Prime Minister... much love Victoria, London, 2 March 1990.

44 Ms Benazir Bhutto, Prime Minister... much love Victoria, London, 4 April 1990.

45   Justice Dorab Patel to me, London, 7 December 1989.
46   Victoria Schofield, *Bhutto: Trial and Execution* (Classic, 1990), pp.261, xii.
47   See 'Bhutto cult to end with PM's term of office', *Nation*, 5 June 1990, p.4; Ayesha Haroon, 'Justice – or political expediency?'; Our reporter, 'Bhutto's case was realisation of Zia's *malafide* intentions', *Frontier Post*, 6 June 1990.
48   Pervez Ali, 'Victoria Schofield on Benazir Bhutto', *MAG*, June 1990.
49   My diary, 5 June 1990.
50   My diary, 10 June 1990.

Chapter 10: Leader of the Opposition

1   Benazir Bhutto, *Daughter of Destiny*, p.407.
2   My diary, 6 August 1990.
3   My diary, 7 and 16 August 1990
4   My diary, 25 October 1990; Bhutto, *Daughter of Destiny*, pp.408–9; see Salman Masood and Declan Walsh, 'Pakistan's High Court resurrects election tampering case', *New York Times*, 29 February 2012, https://www.nytimes.com/2012/03/01/world/asia/pakistan-court-resurrects-election-tampering-investigation.html (accessed 11 May 2020).
5   Dearest B... love Victoria, 1 November 1990.
6   Benazir statement on Gulf War, my diary, 21 January 1991.
7   Charis Waddy, *The Muslim Mind* (Grosvenor, 3rd edition, 1990), p.xvi.
8   My diary, 4 February 1991.
9   Dearest B... love Victoria, 24 February 1991.
10   Benazir Bhutto, *Daughter of Destiny*, p.410.
11   Benazir Bhutto, *Daughter of Destiny*, p.317.
12   My diary, 24 April 1991.
13   My diary, 28 April 1991.
14   Benazir Bhutto, interview with Raymond Whitaker, 25 April 1991.
15   Ibid.
16   Benazir Bhutto to Dr David Tonkin, ?May 1991; Dr David Tonkin to Benazir Bhutto, 5 June 1991. Benazir Bhutto, 'Parliamentary democracy and the role of Pakistan in the Commonwealth,' *The Parliamentarian*, October 1991, LXXII, No.4, pp.271–72.
17   Benazir Bhutto to David Ramsay, ?May 1991; David Ramsay to Benazir Bhutto, 24 May 1991.

18   *Evening Standard*, undated [April 1991].

19   My diary, 1 May 1991.

20   Benazir Bhutto, *Daughter of Destiny*, p.xvi.

21   My diary, 5 May 1991.

22   Report of the visit of Etienne Jaudel and Alain Girardet, representing the International Federation for Human Rights, Karachi, Islamabad, Lahore, 20–27 May 1991. (The report was in French and I translated it into English.)

23   My diary, 15 September 1991.

24   My diary, 5 October 1991.

25   Fax to Bilawal House, 25 November 1991.

26   Dearest B... love from Victoria, 7 March 1992.

27   AP, 'Bhutto's husband leaves prison', *New York Times*, 7 February 1993, https://www.nytimes.com/1993/02/07/world/bhutto-s-husband-leaves-prison.html (accessed 11 May 2020).

28   Benazir Bhutto, *Daughter of Destiny*, pp.xvii, xviii–xix.

29   Dearest Benazir... much love Vicks xx, 20 November 1992.

30   My diary, 3 February 1993.

31   AP, 'Bhutto's husband leaves prison', *New York Times*, 7 February 1993, https://www.nytimes.com/1993/02/07/world/bhutto-s-husband-leaves-prison.html (accessed 11 May 2020).

32   'Benazir's gentle gift from God', *Sunday Express*, 21 February 1993.

33   Dearest Vicks... love xx, 26 March 1993.

34   Dear Benazir... yours Peter, 18 May 1993, copy sent to me. Gabrielle was his wife.

35   See Anwar Iqbal, UPI, 18 April 1993, https://www.upi.com/Archives/1993/04/18/Pakistans-president-sacks-government/1526735105600/ (accessed 11 May 2020); Edward A. Gargan, 'Pakistan chief's dismissal is overturned', *New York Times*, 27 May 1993, https://www.nytimes.com/1993/05/27/world/pakistan-chief-s-dismissal-is-overturned.html (accessed 11 May 2020).

36   Benazir Bhutto, *Daughter of Destiny*, pp.411–12.

37   See Ginny Dougary, 'Destiny's daughter', *The Times*, 28 April 2007, http://www.ginnydougary.co.uk/destiny%e2%80%99s-daughter (accessed 11 May 2020).

Chapter 11: Prime Minister Again

1   Benazir Bhutto, 'The story of Benazir, from Marvi of Malir and Shah Latif', 21 June 2003. Benazir wrote this poem when she was in exile covering her life. This verse seems apt as she becomes prime minister for a second time, with the triumphs and tragedies to come.

2   Benazir Bhutto, *Daughter of Destiny*, p.413.

3   Dearest Benazir… take very great care, very much love Vicks xxx, 10 November 1993.

4   Benazir Bhutto, quoted in Michael Fathers, 'The battle of all mothers', *The Independent*, 14 December 1993.

5   Murtaza Bhutto, quoted in Idrees Bakhtiar and Hasan Iqbal Jafri, 'I am an older member of the party than Benazir: Murtaza', *Herald*, June 1994, https://herald.dawn.com/news/1398865 (accessed 11 May 2020); Benazir Bhutto, interview with Etienne Duval, Islamabad, 5 April 1994.

6   Michael Fathers, 'The battle of all mothers', *The Independent*, 14 December 1993.

7   Benazir Bhutto, 3 February 1994, UN Human Rights Commission, 50th session, Geneva; see Shekhar Gupta, 'India shows the world it means business on Kashmir issue at Geneva meet', *India Today*, 31 March 1994.

8   Farooq Abdullah to me, Srinagar, April 1994.

9   Victoria Schofield, draft article for the *Scotsman*, 1994. See 'Pakistan's top honour for soldier hero', *Scotsman*, 24 March 1994.

10 My diary, notes of press conference, 30 September 1996.

11 Benazir Bhutto, interview with Etienne Duval, Islamabad, 5 April 1994.

12 Dearest Benazir… very much love Vicks xxx, 15 June 1994.

13 Murtaza Bhutto quoted in Idrees Bakhtiar and Hasan Iqbal Jafri, 'I am an older member of the party than Benazir: Murtaza', *Herald*, June 1994, https://herald.dawn.com/news/1398865 (accessed 11 May 2020).

14 William Dalrymple, 'Speaking in tongues', *Sunday Times* magazine, 12 June 1994.

15 My notes of Benazir's address to the Foreign Relations committee, Assemblée Nationale, Paris, 2 November 1994; *Le Monde*, 'What the French media say', 4 November 1994.

16 Benazir Bhutto, quoted in *Le Figaro*, in 'What the French media say', 4 November 1994.

17 My notes of Benazir's visit, November 1994.

18 My notes of Michael Heseltine's remarks, CBI Headquarters, London, 30 November 1994.

19   My notes of television interview with Sir David Frost, broadcast 29 November 1994.

20   Benazir Bhutto, *Daughter of Destiny*, pp.414–15.

21   Benazir Bhutto, *Daughter of Destiny*, p.415.

22   Dearest Benazir... lots and lots of love to you as always, 18 January 1995.

23   Victoria Schofield, *Kashmir in the Crossfire* (I. B. Tauris, 1996), p.287 (*Kashmir in Conflict*, (2010), p.191).

24   Dearest Benazir... Love to the children, hope they are OK, lots of love Victoria, 28 April 1995. Yasin Malik, JKLF, to me, Srinagar, April 1995.

25   Dearest Benazir... lots of love to the children and of course to you, take great care, Vicks, 7 July 1995.

26   Benazir Bhutto, *Daughter of Destiny*, p.416.

27   Benazir Bhutto, *Daughter of Destiny*, p.421.

28   Dr Charis Waddy to me, telephone conversation, 21 September 1996.

29   Fatima Bhutto, *Songs of Blood and Sword*, p.402.

30   Irfan Husain to me, Karachi, October 2007, and email, 11 June 2019; AP, 'Bhutto's brother dies in shoot-out', *The Independent*, 21 September 1996, https://www.independent.co.uk/news/world/bhuttos-brother-dies-in-shoot-out-1364266.html (accessed 11 May 2020).

31   Superintendent of Police, Investigations 2007 to me, telephone conversation, 28 March 2020.

32   Ibid.

33   Ibid; Irfan Husain to me, Karachi, October 2007, and email, 11 June 2019.

34   Tariq Islam to me, email, 1 April 2020.

35   AP, 'Policeman linked to Bhutto's death reportedly slain', *Los Angeles Times*, 29 September 1996, https://www.latimes.com/archives/la-xpm-1996-09-29-mn-48751-story.html (accessed 11 May 2020). 'From first fake encounter to Sahiwal encounter', *News*, https://www.thenews.com.pk/print/422345-aig-rai-tahir-from-first-fake-encounter-to-sahiwal-encounter (accessed 11 May 2020).

36   My diary, 28 September 1996.

37   My interview with Benazir, London, 31 July 2001.

38   My diary, notes of press conference and IISS meeting, New Connaught Rooms, Holborn, 30 September 1996.

39   Benazir Bhutto, address to the UN General Assembly, 3 October 1996.

40   My diary, 6 October 1996.

41   Victoria Schofield, 'The end of a dream', *The Times*, 6 November 1996.

Chapter 12: *Déjà Vu*

1   Quoted by Benazir Bhutto, *Daughter of Destiny*, p.424.

2   Victoria Schofield, 'I thought I'd call Benazir', *Spectator*, 16 November 1996; Seumas Milne, 'The crumbling house of Bhutto', *Guardian Weekend*, 25 January 1997.

3   Ahmed Rashid, *Taliban: Islam, Oil and the New Great Game in Central Asia* (I. B. Tauris, 2000), p.21.

4   My interview with Lt General Hamid Gul (1936–2015), 17 April 1989.

5   My notes of Benazir's lecture, 'The Current Political Situation in Pakistan,' London School of Economics, 24 April 2007.

6   My diary, 3 July 1997.

7   *Indian Express*, 10 October 1997.

8   John Burns, 'House of graft', *New York Times*, 9 January 1998; Stephen Grey and Rajeev Syal, 'The hunt for Benazir's booty', *Sunday Times*, 12 April 1998.

9   BJP Manifesto, 1996, library.bjp.org/jspui/bitstream/123456789/261/1/ BJP ELECTION MANIFESTO 1996.pdf (accessed 11 May 2020); John Cherian, 'The BJP and the bomb', *Frontline*, 15:8, 24 April 1998, https:// frontline.thehindu.com/static/html/fl1508/15080040.htm (accessed 11 May 2020).

10   Zulfikar Ali Bhutto quoted in 'Pakistan, India and the bomb', *New York Times*, 1 July 1979, https://www.nytimes.com/1979/07/01/archives/foreign-affairs-pakistan-india-and-the-bomb.html (accessed 11 May 2020).

11   Thomas W. Lippman, 'US lifts sanctions on India, Pakistan', *Washington Post*, 7 November 1998, https://www.washingtonpost.com/archive/ politics/1998/11/07/us-lifts-sanctions-on-india-pakistan/3771637b-b980-40b2-b5eb-7fb8a053870d/ (accessed 11 May 2020).

12   See Benazir Bhutto, *Daughter of Destiny*, pp.406–7.

13   See Benazir Bhutto, *Daughter of Destiny*, pp.418–19.

14   Nasim Zehra, *From Kargil to the Coup* (Sang-e-Meel Publications, Lahore, 2018), p.113.

15   Col. Brian Cloughley, quoted in Victoria Schofield, *Kashmir in Conflict* (2010), p.209.

16   See Victoria Schofield, *Kashmir in Conflict* (2010), p.211, as quoted in *Asian Age*, 12 June 1999.

17   Nasim Zehra, *From Kargil to the Coup*, p.150; Ejaz Haider, 'The heights of folly: A critical look at the Kargil Operation', *Herald*, 28 August 2018, https://herald.dawn.com/news/1398650 (accessed 11 May 2020).

18 'PM rejects UN chief's mediation offer', 30 May 1999, https://m.rediff.
    com/news/1999/may/30kash10.htm (accessed 11 May 2020); 'Clinton
    urges restraint in Kashmir', BBC World: South Asia, 15 June 1999, http://
    news.bbc.co.uk/2/hi/south_asia/369320.stm (accessed 11 May 2020);
    'Clinton urges India–Pakistan talks,' BBC News: World, South Asia, 5 July
    1999, http://news.bbc.co.uk/1/hi/world/south_asia/385534.stm (accessed
    11 May 2020).
19 Pakistani prime minister's Address to the Nation during the Kargil
    Crisis, 12 July 1999, https:/www.satp.org/satporgtp/countries/pakistan/
    document/papers/pakistani_pm_nawaz.htm (accessed 11 May 2020).
20 See Sumit Walia, 'Pakistani Kargil planners: How could they be so naïve!!!',
    Indian Defence Review, 26 July 2019, http://www.indiandefencereview.
    com/news/pakistani-kargil-planners-were-they-so-naive/ (accessed 11
    May 2020).
21 Quoted in Victoria Schofield, Kashmir in Conflict (2010), p.217.

Chapter 13: Exile

1   Benazir Bhutto, 'The story of Benazir, From Marvi of Malir and Shah
    Latif', 21 June 2003.
2   Nick Hopkins, 'Benazir Bhutto given five-year jail term and £5m fine
    for corruption', Guardian, 16 April 1999, https://www.theguardian.com/
    world/1999/apr/16/benazirbhutto (accessed 11 May 2020).
3   Lars Rise to me, February 2008, email, 29 March 2020.
4   My interview with Benazir Bhutto, London, 31 July 2001.
5   My diary, 20 January 2000.
6   General Musharraf, briefing, 3 February 2000; interview, 7 February
    2000.
7   Benazir Bhutto, Oxford Union debate 'That Islam is incompatible with
    the West', 24 February 2000; Janine di Giovanni to me, telephone con-
    versation, 31 March 2020. The Oxford Union Society does not have a
    recording of this debate and the Rough Minute Book 1998–2002 has
    disappeared.
8   Dr Jack Gravlee, note on the Denver Post, 19 November 1999.
9   UN News, 'Annan welcomes moves by India and Pakistan towards pos-
    sible summit', 24 May 2001, https://news.un.org/en/story/2001/05/8712-
    annan-welcomes-moves-india-and-pakistan-towards-possible-summit
    (accessed 11 May 2020).

10   Ahmed Rashid, 'Pakistan court finds Bhutto trial rigged by judge', *Telegraph*, 20 April 2001, https://www.telegraph.co.uk/news/worldnews/1316783/Pakistan-court-finds-Bhutto-trial-was-rigged-by-judge.html (accessed 11 May 2020); Barry Bearak, 'Pakistani Supreme Court gives Benazir Bhutto major victory', *New York Times*, 7 April 2001, https://www.nytimes.com/2001/04/07/world/pakistani-supreme-court-gives-benazir-bhutto-major-victory.html (accessed 11 May 2020).

11   My interview with Benazir, London, 31 July 2001.

12   Ibid, quoted in Victoria Schofield, 'Survivor!', *Verve* (First Quarter 2002).

13   Benazir Bhutto, *Daughter of Destiny*, pp.427–8.

14   Notes of my meeting with Pres Musharraf, 1 April 2002. See Benazir Bhutto, *Daughter of Destiny*, p.425, where she says that she received several messages from Musharraf intermediaries not to contest the elections, one of whom was Christina Lamb; Christina to me, Lahore, 20 October 2019.

15   Dearest Benazir... lots of love Vicks xxxxx; Dearest Vicks... take care and lots of love to the children and to you, Benazir, email, 24 March 2002. I was accompanied from Lahore to Wagah by a British Pakistani friend, Mushtaq Lasharie, CBE. I had been staying at Aitchison College, of which Shamim Khan was principal, and he had lent me his car and driver to take me to the border.

16   Victoria Schofield, 'Wagah Border', *Nation*, 9 May 2002.

17   See Victoria Schofield, 'Wagah Border', *Nation*, 9 May 2002.

18   My diary, 3–8 April 2002.

19   Benazir Bhutto, *Daughter of Destiny*, p.425.

20   Benazir Bhutto quoted in Simon Walters, 'The Tory Boy plotting Benazir's revolution... from Gillingham', *Daily Mail*, 11 November 2007, https://www.dailymail.co.uk/news/article-492856/The-Tory-boy-plotting-Benazir-s-revolution---Gillingham.html.

21   Benazir Bhutto, 'The story of Benazir: From Marvi of Malir and Shah Latif', 21 June 2003.

22   My diary, 4 August 2003.

23   Dr David Browning, *Dreaming Minarets* (Smokehouse publications, 2015), p.3; my diary, 4 August 2003; Dr Browning to me, telephone conversation, January 2020.

24   'Swiss judge convicts Bhutto', *BBC News*, 5 August 2003, http://news.bbc.co.uk/1/hi/world/south_asia/3125277.stm (accessed 11 May 2020); Dominique Poncet, quoted in 'Bhutto sentenced by Swiss magistrate', 5

August 2003, https://www.swissinfo.ch/eng/bhutto-sentenced-by-swiss-magistrate/3445356 (accessed 11 May 2020).

25 Salman Masood, 'Pakistani leader escapes attempt at assassination', *New York Times*, 26 December 2003, https://www.nytimes.com/2003/12/26/world/pakistani-leader-escapes-attempt-at-assassination.html (accessed 11 May 2020).

26 Dr Syed Nazir Gilani, my notes from the Kashmir International Conference, London, 29 May 2004.

27 Sajad Lone, my notes from the Kashmir International Conference, London, 29 May 2004.

28 Benazir Bhutto, my notes from the Kashmir International Conference, London, 29 May 2004.

29 Farooq Abdullah, my notes from the Kashmir International Conference, London, 29 May 2004.

30 Dearest Victoria, email, 30 July 2004.

31 Ibid; see Fatima Bhutto, *Songs of Blood and Sword*, p.486.

32 Benazir Bhutto, *Daughter of Destiny*, p.xii.

33 Benazir Bhutto, Speaker meeting, 5 May 2005, excerpts from tape recording, Oxford Union Society.

34 See Peter Everington, 'Charis Waddy: Islamic scholar and worker for MRA', obituary, *The Independent*, 15 September 2004, https://www.independent.co.uk/news/obituaries/charis-waddy-550475.html (accessed 11 May 2020).

35 Dear Benazir... kind regards, Pandora Crawley, email, 15 February 2006; Dear Pandora... with my good wishes, Benazir Bhutto, email, 27 February 2006.

36 Dearest Vicks... love Benazir, email, 12 June 2006.

37 Sherry Rehman to me, email, 27 March 2020.

38 See Khurshid Mahmud Kasuri, *Neither a Hawk nor a Dove: An Insider's Account of Pakistan's Foreign Relations* (Oxford University Press, 2015).

39 Benazir Bhutto, *Daughter of Destiny*, p.430.

40 Ginny Dougary, 'Destiny's daughter', *The Times*, 28 April 2007, https://www.ginnydougary.co.uk/?s=benazir+bhutto (accessed 11 May 2020).

41 Benazir Bhutto, my notes of her lecture, London School of Economics, 24 April 2007.

42 B. Raman, 'How China forced Musharraf to move', *Outlook*, 4 July 2007.

43 Benazir Bhutto, my notes of her lecture, LSE, 24 April 2007; Benazir to me, London, July 2007.

44   Ginny Dougary, 'I asked her whether she felt immortal. No, she answered', *The Times*, 28 December 2007, http://www.ginnydougary.co.uk/i-asked-her-whether-she-felt-immortal-no-she-answered/ (accessed 11 May 2020); Ron Suskind, *The Way of the World: A Story of Truth and Hope in an Age of Extremism* (Harper, 2008), pp.210–11.

45   Benazir Bhutto, 'The future of democracy', 20 July 2007, IISS, Arundel House, London.

46   Gordon Corera, *Shopping for Bombs: Nuclear Proliferation, Global Insecurity, and the Rise and Fall of the A. Q. Khan Network* (C. Hurst & Co. Ltd, 2006); Dearest Victoria.. lots of love Benazir, 20 October 2006.

47   'A conversation with Benazir Bhutto', transcript, Council on Foreign Relations, New York, 15 August 2007, pp.2–3, quoted in Heraldo Muñoz, *Getting Away with Murder: Benazir Bhutto's Assassination and the Politics of Pakistan* (W. W. Norton, 2014), pp.24, 27; Benazir Bhutto, 'When I return to Pakistan,' *Washington Post*, 20 September 2007.

48   Benazir Bhutto, 25 September 2007, quoted by Ron Suskind, *The Way of the World*, p.261. Wendy Chamberlin to me, email, 1 April 2020.

49   Mark Siegel to me, email, 1 April 2020; see Heraldo Muñoz, *Getting Away With Murder*, p.26.

50   Michael Henderson, *No Enemy to Conquer, Forgiveness in an Unforgiving World* (Baylor University Press, 2009), pp.137–39.

51   Andrew Buncombe, 'Benazir Bhutto: Pakistan's former prime minister has risen again', *The Independent*, 1 September 2007, https://www.independent.co.uk/news/people/profiles/benazir-bhutto-pakistans-former-prime-minister-has-risen-again-401070.html (accessed 11 May 2020).

Chapter 14: Return to Pakistan

1   Zulfikar Ali Bhutto to Benazir; quoted in Victoria Schofield, 'Roses in the dust', *Traveller*, 41:1 (2011).

2   Steven R. Weisman, 'A daughter returns to Pakistan to cry for victory', *New York Times*, 11 April 1986, https://www.nytimes.com/1986/04/11/world/a-daughter-returns-to-pakistan-to-cry-for-victory.html (accessed 11 May 2020).

3   Benazir Bhutto, press conference, Dubai, 18 October 2007, https://www.dailymotion.com/video/x1gu37t; my notes at Dubai airport, 18 October 2007.

4   Benazir Bhutto, *Reconciliation: Islam, Democracy and the West* (Harper-

Collins, 2008), p.7.

5   Carlotta Gall and Salman Masood, 'Benazir returns to a rapturous welcome in Pakistan', *New York Times*, 18 October 2007, https://www.nytimes.com/2007/10/18/world/asia/18iht-pakistan.4.7948518.html (accessed 11 May 2020).

6   Benazir Bhutto, my notes of her press conference, 19 October 2007; see also Owen Bennett-Jones, 'The assassination', https://www.bbc.co.uk/sounds/play/p05v1k08 (accessed 11 May 2020).

7   Christina Lamb, 'It was what we feared, but hoped would never happen,' *Sunday Times*, 21 October 2007; Victoria Schofield, 'Blown from my seat on Bhutto's bus,' *Sunday Telegraph*, 21 October 2007.

8   Benazir Bhutto, *Reconciliation*, p.11.

9   Elizabeth Colton to me, telephone conversation and email, 30 March 2020.

Chapter 15: Assassination

1   Victoria Schofield, 'Benazir Bhutto: A great and brave friend', *Daily Telegraph*, 28 December 2007.

2   'Proclamation of state of emergency', *Dawn*, 4 November 2007, https://www.dawn.com/news/274270/proclamation-of-emergency (accessed 11 May 2020).

3   Dearest Benazir... love and keep safe, as always, Victoria, email, 3 December 2007.

4   Dearest Victoria... keep well and love to the children, Benazir, email, 26 December 2007.

5   See Heraldo Muñoz, *Getting Away with Murder*, p.178.

6   Senator Sherry Rehman to me, email, 28 March 2020.

7   Makhdoom Ameen Faheem to me, Asia House, London, 24 March 2009.

8   Senator Sherry Rehman to me, email, 27 March 2020.

9   Senator Aitzaz Ahsan to me, Islamabad, 26 March 2014.

10 *The Times, The Financial Times, Guardian* respectively, 28 December 2007.

11 Victoria Schofield, 'Benazir Bhutto: A great and brave friend', *Daily Telegraph*, 28 December 2007.

12 Senator Aitzaz Ahsan to me, Islamabad, 26 March 2014.

13 Home office pathologist Dr Nathaniel Cary, quoted in Declan Walsh, 'Bhutto killed by blast, not a bullet, Scotland yard concludes', 9 February 2008, https://www.theguardian.com/world/2008/feb/09/

pakistan.benazirbhutto (accessed 11 May 2020); CNN, 'Scotland Yard report into assassination of Benazir Bhutto released', 8 February 2008, http://edition.cnn.com/2008/WORLD/asiapcf/02/08/bhutto.report/ (accessed 11 May 2020).

14 UN report on Bhutto murder finds Pakistani officials 'failed profoundly', https://news.un.org/en/story/2010/04/335482-un-report-bhutto-murder-finds-pakistani-officials-failed-profoundly (accessed 11 May 2020).

15 Ibid.

16 Heraldo Muñoz, *Getting Away with Murder*, p.180; Victoria Schofield, book review, *The Round Table, Commonwealth Journal of International Affairs* (2014), pp.445–7.

17 Christina Lamb, 'Who murdered Benazir Bhutto?', *Sunday Times*, 2 May 2010; Owen Bennett-Jones, 'Questions concerning the murder of Benazir Bhutto', *London Review of Books*, 34: 23 (6 December 2012).

18 Benazir Bhutto to General Musharraf, 16 October 2007, in 'PPP demands probe based on Benazir's letter', *Dawn*, 30 December 2007, https://www.dawn.com/news/282349/ppp-demands-probe-based-on-benazir (accessed 11 May 2020); Owen Bennett-Jones, *The Assassination*, Episode 3: 'The call', https://www.bbc.co.uk/programmes/p05rgkod (accessed 11 May 2020); see Ron Suskind, *The Way of the World*, p.260, and Shakeel Anjum, *Who Assassinated Benazir Bhutto?* (Dost Publications, Pakistan, 2010).

19 Bilawal Bhutto Zardari, quoted in Declan Walsh, 'My mother said democracy is the best revenge – Bhutto son', *Guardian*, 31 December 2007, https://www.theguardian.com/world/2007/dec/31/pakistan.topstories35 (accessed 11 May 2020).

20 Bilawal Bhutto Zardari, press conference, the Gore Hotel, London, 8 January 2008; Lyse Doucet to me, email, 13 January 2020; Jeremy Paxman to me, email, 13 January 2020; see Stephen Bates, 'Bilawal Bhutto meets the media pack', *Guardian*, 9 January 2008, https://www.theguardian.com/uk/2008/jan/09/pakistan.world (accessed 11 May 2020).

21 Lord Lamont repeated the story to me, London, 8 January 2020.

22 Benazir Bhutto, *Reconciliation: Islam, Democracy, and the West*, cover endorsement by Peter Galbraith.

23 Asif Zardari to me, Islamabad; my diary, 22 August 2008.

24 My diary, 22 March 2010; Victoria Schofield, 'Roses in the dust', *Traveller*, 41:1 (2011).

25 Shah Abdul Latif, quoted in Salmaan Taseer, *Bhutto: A political biography*, p.11.

Index

Illustrations are indicated by *italic* type

About the Author

Victoria Schofield is a historian and commentator on international affairs. She was educated at Lady Margaret Hall, Oxford, and graduated with a degree in Modern History. While at Oxford she was president of the Union, in succession to Benazir Bhutto. In 1978 she travelled to Pakistan to attend the appeal of Benazir's father, former prime minister, Zulfikar Ali Bhutto, against the death sentence in the Supreme Court of Pakistan. Since then, she has contributed to numerous media outlets including *The Sunday Telegraph*, *The Times*, *The Independent*, the *Spectator* and, as a commentator, for the BBC and Al Jazeera. Her previous publications include *The Black Watch*, *Wavell: Soldier and Statesman*, *Kashmir in Conflict*, *Afghan Frontier* and *Bhutto: Trial and Execution*. Over a decade since Benazir's assassination in 2007 she determined to complete her personal memoir of their friendship which had so inspired her longstanding interest in and love of South Asia.